Revitalizing
State and Local
Public Service

Frank J. Thompson, Editor

Foreword by William F. Winter

*A publication of the National Commission
on the State and Local Public Service*

Revitalizing State and Local Public Service

STRENGTHENING
PERFORMANCE,
ACCOUNTABILITY,
AND
CITIZEN CONFIDENCE

Jossey-Bass Publishers · San Francisco

Substantial discounts on bulk quantities of Jossey-Bass books
are available to corporations, professional associations, and other
organizations. For details and discount information, contact the
special sales department at Jossey-Bass Inc., Publishers.
(415) 433-1740; Fax (415) 433-0499.

For sales outside the United States, contact Maxwell Macmillan
International Publishing Group, 866 Third Avenue, New York,
New York 10022.

Manufactured in the United States of America

The ink in this book is either soy- or vegetable-based and during the
printing process emits fewer than half the volatile organic compounds
(VOCs) emitted by petroleum-based ink.

Library of Congress Cataloging-in-Publication Data

Revitalizing state and local public service : strengthening
  performance, accountability, and citizen confidence / Frank J.
Thompson, editor.
     p.   cm. — (The Jossey-Bass public administration series)
  Includes bibliographical references and index.
  ISBN 1-55542-572-0
  1. State governments—United States. 2. Local government—United
States. I. Thompson, Frank J. II. Series.
JK2443.R48 1993
353.9—dc20   93–14559
                                                CIP

Credits are on p. 446.

FIRST EDITION
HB Printing   10 9 8 7 6 5 4 3 2 1   *Code 9371*

The
Jossey-Bass
Public Administration
Series

Consulting Editor
Public Management and Administration

James L. Perry
Indiana University

Contents

Foreword

Devising ways to make government work better is not a task for the fainthearted or the short-winded. Most of us who have been involved at the state and local levels know how much patience and persistence have been required in the past to enable even modest reforms to be made. Now, when more than ever before there are pressing demands on government at every level to perform more efficiently and responsively, it is obvious that an intensified effort must be made to revitalize the public service.

That is what *Revitalizing State and Local Public Service* is all about. It represents an effort by some of the most knowledgeable and informed students in the field of state and local government to bring to the table ideas that will create a climate for truly meaningful reform in the way state and local public service operates. It is not overstating the case to say that unless we move in a serious and systematic way to address the need for reform, our political system is going to lose the confidence of the people whom it is designed to serve.

The problems of governance have now become so complex, the issues so convoluted, and the expectations of the public so intense that even the smallest and least affluent political subdivisions are finding it hard to function in the traditional ways. We simply cannot expect government to perform adequately in this new environment without substantial changes in the way it operates.

Yet we all know how difficult it is to effect meaningful changes in the established ways of doing things. There are no more tenacious defenders of the status quo than those who feel threatened by change. An important purpose of this book is to allay these fears and create a better understanding of the choices that confront us. Only through a thoughtful and realistic appraisal of the needs of public service can we begin to achieve the kind of reforms that are required.

As the book points out, the process of revitalization must begin with executive leadership. Governors, mayors, city managers, and county executives have the responsibility to create an atmosphere that encourages constructive change. Unless the commitment exists at the top, it is unlikely that satisfactory results will be achieved down the line. What we are really talking about is the promotion of the idea that public service must enlist our best and most able men and women. For when all is said and done, it is their creativity, resourcefulness, and dedication that make the critical difference in how well government works. While it is obviously important to have public agencies organized in the proper way, it is the performance of individuals that ultimately determines the success of those agencies.

The impressive collection of chapters that follows details a strategy for encouraging a higher level of performance by those who work or aspire to work in the state and local public service. New standards and procedures are presented for the recruitment and retention of individuals who would like to regard public service as a fulfilling and rewarding career, not merely a stop-gap job until something better comes along. As the chapter authors point out, financial compensation is an important factor, but of more significance may be the opportunities for creativity and innovation. Eliminating the bureaucratic straitjackets that diminish individual initiative is essential to the revitalization of the public service.

Other considerations that must be taken into account are addressed as well. The growing diversity of the workforce, the incredible advances in technology, particularly in telecommunications, and new models for the delivery of services, some of them in the private sector, all require the application of improved measures of performance in the future.

It is my hope that the progressive ideas advanced in this book will form a central part of the strategies for revitalizing state and local governance.

July 1993

William F. Winter
Chairman
National Commission on the
State and Local Public Service
Albany, New York

Preface

The National Commission on the State and Local Public Service, which was created in 1991, aims to assess and improve the capacity and performance of state and local governments. It seeks to enhance citizen understanding of these levels of the federal system and, ultimately, foster confidence in them.

Chaired by former Mississippi governor William F. Winter, the commission consists of twenty-seven distinguished members, including former governors, legislators, high-level state and local executives, journalists, and academics. Private foundations have provided funding for the commission. Bill Moyers, who heads the Florence and John Schumann Foundation, was a leading backer from the start. While the Schumann Foundation supplied most of the commission's budget, the Ford, Carnegie, and Kaiser foundations also gave generous grants, with Kaiser earmarking funds for inquiry into state and local health agencies. The Rockefeller Institute of Government in Albany, New York, houses the commission's staff.

Background and Purpose

My involvement in this book began more than a year before the commission's birth. At that time, Richard Nathan, Enid Beaumont, and I drafted an exploratory proposal to help create a knowledge base for what we hoped would become a full-fledged commission. An initial grant from the Schumann Foundation subsidized work on seven of the chapters (greatly updated since then) found in this book. Once the commission came to life, I became its executive director and arranged for nearly twenty additional studies to assist the commission's work. From the outset, we envisioned that efforts to construct a knowledge base for the commission would yield a by-product: a book that would enhance teaching and research in university and related professional settings. *Revitalizing State and Local Public Service* seeks to fulfill that goal.

Scope

The chapters that follow draw not only on the research papers prepared for the commission, but on the hearings it conducted around the country during the winter and spring of 1992. Fifty-four officials and other experts on state and local government testified at meetings in Jackson and Vicksburg (Mississippi), Austin, Chicago, Philadelphia, Sacramento, and Tallahassee. In the introductory and concluding chapters, I integrate major themes from these hearings with the findings of the research papers. Complete lists of the research papers and participants at the hearings appear in the commission's main report (see the Appendix).

Composing the book was itself an exercise in hard choices. Space limitations meant that I could not include all the papers prepared for the commission; nor could I completely exhaust the treasure of insights contained in the hearings. However, the chapters do reflect the most extensively studied topics and the dominant propositions found in the hearings. They undergird our central thesis: that the revitalization of state and local public service requires us at a minimum to meet leadership, workforce, management, and health care challenges.

Audience

Revitalizing State and Local Public Service will appeal to professionals and academics interested in the current movement to reform or reinvent government. It will be a valuable resource to individuals, agencies, and libraries wanting access to the basic documents associated with the main report of the National Commission on the State and Local Public Service. It also will serve as a textbook in courses on public administration or public management, as well as courses on state and local administration and politics.

Overview of the Contents

In the introduction, I provide an overview of some critical features of the American political landscape—namely, structural fragmentation, cultural mistrust, and fiscal stress—that hamper efforts to move toward more vigorous and responsive governance. I also briefly assess the nature of the leadership, workforce, management, and health care challenges, to set the stage for the contributions that follow.

Part One focuses on the leadership challenge. The tough issues of state and local governance demand visionary, committed, and skilled leaders, including chief executives. In Chapter One, Deborah D. Roberts concentrates on gubernatorial leadership. She forcefully argues that governors need to act as internal leaders, not just managers, of their executive branches.

Part Two concentrates on the workforce challenge, which centers on three issues: sustaining an adequate supply of high-quality human resources, implementing managerial strategies that emphasize quality and productivity, and organizing work to foster the first two goals. The authors wrestle with issues that go to the heart of the workforce challenge in state and local governments.

In Chapter Two, Carolyn Ban and Norma Riccucci argue that civil service systems and labor relations structures have accomplished important goals but are now frustrating the quest for efficiency and quality. They demonstrate that many jurisdictions are moving to reform those systems, at times by working cooperatively with public employee unions. They suggest an incremental package of six reforms that could yield tremendous benefits in workforce management at the state and local levels.

In Chapter Three, through an in-depth analysis of two states, James K. Conant and Dennis L. Dresang illuminate issues in recruiting and retaining high-quality professionals and senior managers in state and local governments. They conclude that at the state level, the problem may be less acute than some analyses suggest. Complementing this discussion, Chapter Four by Jorge Chapa emphasizes that the quest for top managers and professionals should not blind us to the indispensable role of state and local employees in nonprofessional positions.

The contributions of pay and diversity to the workforce challenge also receive attention. Steven D. Gold and Sarah Ritchie underscore in Chapter Five that true reform will require state and local governments to provide competitive compensation packages—and present a mixed picture of the degree to which current compensation practices meet this standard. Rita Mae Kelly emphasizes in Chapter Six that any answer to the workforce challenge must move beyond traditional equal employment opportunity and affirmative action to promote multicultural synergy.

Part Three probes two of the other management issues important to efforts to revitalize state and local public service—information technology and privatization. These two challenges differ in many respects, but both are linked to the workforce challenge. In Chapter Seven, James L. Perry and Kenneth L. Kraemer appraise the effects of new information technologies, both showing how these technologies can enhance performance and describing the human resource problems that they generate. Donald F. Kettl, in Chapter Eight, describes the pervasive use of private agents to deliver public services and the reasons this strategy makes good sense under some circumstances. He vividly documents, however, that privatization is hardly a panacea for government problems.

Part Four focuses on the health care challenge, which intertwines with the other challenges addressed in *Revitalizing State and Local Public Service*. The ability of chief executives to provide creative leadership often depends on their skill in solving health care problems. Health care issues also impinge on many workforce issues, including issues of personnel recruitment and retention, cultural diversity, information technology, and privatization.

In Chapter Nine, Michael Sparer and Lawrence D. Brown persuasively argue that Medicaid poses some of the toughest managerial challenges faced by state and local officials. Analyzing Medicaid in four states, the authors suggest that although program managers often develop resourceful strategies for greater efficiency and effectiveness, there are significant barriers to the success of such strategies. They question whether much revitalization can occur without basic reform of the country's medical care system. Because the enormous financial demands of health care programs greatly complicate the revitalization effort throughout state and local government, meeting this challenge may be a prerequisite to more general reform.

Part Five concludes the book. In Chapter Ten I return to the theme that progress can be made toward revitalization and even toward modifying the structural factors underlying the difficulties of state and local governments. I address five major themes that emerge from the previous chapters and the commission's hearings, and suggest some directions for future research.

The Appendix consists of the Report of the National Commission on the State and Local Public Service titled *Hard Truths/Tough Choices: An Agenda for State and Local Reform*.

Acknowledgments

Many people worked to keep this book on course. As usual, I benefited greatly from smart, supportive colleagues at the State University of New York, Albany. Richard Nathan served up his usual good advice at each stage of my work on this manuscript. Carolyn Ban, Helen Desfosses, Steven Gold, Robert Nakamura, Norma Riccucci, and Todd Swanstrom also offered sage comments.

Others helped as well. James Perry critiqued my chapters and helped me think about an overall strategy for the book. Jonathan Walters let me draw on his vast knowledge of state and local politics, as did Enid Beaumont. Advisers to the commission — Paul Light in the case of the main report, and Lawrence Brown and Michael Sparer in the case of health — assured a steady flow of intellectual nourishment.

The staff at Jossey-Bass also worked hard to improve this book. Alan R. Shrader, senior acquisitions editor, shaped the manuscript in important ways and showed just the right measure of impatience about its completion date. Lasell Whipple, project editor, masterfully coordinated the editing and production of the book.

The staff of the commission deserves a standing ovation. Miriam Trementozzi, the commission's project manager, made many useful suggestions, drawing in part on her prior experience with nonprofit agencies and the New York State Division of the Budget. She artfully managed the day-to-day life of the commission, giving me more time to focus on the book. Barbara Guinn of the commission staff commented on the manuscript, proved to be a skilled sleuth in tracking down needed information, and performed statistical analyses to support the research. Veronica Cruz, my research assistant, also helped. Mary Mathews and Echo Cartwright did superb work preparing the manuscript.

Finally, the tone Governor William Winter set for all commission activities undoubtedly benefited this book. To work with him is to understand why so many outstanding young people in Mississippi have chosen careers in public service after having met him.

All these helpful people should not be held accountable for any infirmities in the book—that responsibility falls to me. And ultimately, of course, the book reflects my views and those of the contributors, not necessarily the perspectives of commission members.

Albany, New York   Frank J. Thompson
July 1993

The Editor

Frank J. Thompson is executive director of the National Commission on the State and Local Public Service. He is also dean of the School of Public Affairs and associate provost of Rockefeller College at the State University of New York, Albany. He received his B.A. degree (1966) from the University of Chicago and his M.A. (1967) and Ph.D. (1973) degrees from the University of California, Berkeley, all in political science.

Thompson has written extensively on issues of health policy, policy implementation, public personnel policy, and administrative politics. His books include *Personnel Policy in the City* (1975), *Health Policy and the Bureaucracy* (1981), and *Public Administration: Challenges, Choices, and Consequences* (1990, with C. Levine and G. Peters).

Thompson is former president of the National Association of Schools of Public Affairs and Administration and has held offices in other professional associations. He has worked for the City of Oakland, California, and the U.S. Public Health Service. He has also served as consultant to various government agencies.

The Contributors

Carolyn Ban is associate professor of public administration in the Rockefeller College of Public Affairs and Policy, State University of New York, Albany. She received her B.A. degree (1964) from Smith College in government, her M.A. degree (1966) from Harvard University in Russian studies, and her Ph.D. degree (1975) from Stanford University in political science. Ban has written extensively on personnel reform and is coauthor of *Public Personnel Management: Current Concerns, Future Challenges* (1991, with N. Riccucci). She is currently working on a book about how federal line managers manage people.

Lawrence D. Brown is professor and head of the Division of Health Policy and Management in the School of Public Health at Columbia University. He received his B.A. degree (1969) in philosophy and his Ph.D. degree (1973) in government, both from Harvard University. He was previously on the faculty of the University of Michigan and the staff of the Brookings Institution. Brown writes on competitive and regulatory issues in health policy and on the politics of health care policymaking generally. He (and Catherine McLaughlin) evaluated the Robert Wood Johnson Foundation's Community Programs for Affordable Health Care and its Program for the Medically Uninsured. He was editor of the *Journal of Health Politics, Policy and Law* from 1984 to 1989.

Jorge Chapa is a faculty member at the Lyndon B. Johnson School of Public Affairs at the University of Texas, Austin. He received his B.A. degree (1975) from the University of Chicago in biology; and his M.A. degree (1979) in sociology, another M.A. degree (1983) in demography, and his Ph.D. degree (1988) in sociology, all from the University of California, Berkeley. Among Chapa's research interests are the means and methods of making government policies and practices more responsive to the needs of Latinos and more open to Latino participation in the formulation and implementation of those policies.

James K. Conant is associate professor of political science at the University of Oklahoma. He received his B.A. (1971), his M.A. (1973), and his Ph.D. (1974) degrees in political science from the University of Wisconsin, Madison. His research and writing focus on budgeting and financial management, executive branch organization and management, and management education and training in the states. He is coeditor of *Dollars and Sense: Policy Choices and the Wisconsin Budget, Volume II* (1991, with R. Hareman and J. Huddleston). His writings have appeared in *Public Administration Review, State and Local Government Review,* the *Handbook of Public Administration,* and other books and journals. Conant worked in the Office of the Governor and in the Wisconsin State Budget Office, and he was general manager of a private sector organization. He has served as consultant to environmental protection, transportation, human services, and education organizations.

Dennis L. Dresang is professor in the Department of Political Science and at the La Follette Institute of Public Affairs at the University of Wisconsin, Madison. He received his B.A. degree (1964) from the University of Wisconsin, Madison in international relations; and his M.A. (1965) and Ph.D. (1970) degrees from the University of California, Los Angeles in political science. He is the author of *Public Personnel Management and Public Policy* (1992), now in its second edition, and numerous articles and essays on a wide range of personnel management issues. Dresang has directed and participated in several task forces that have reformed personnel policies and practices in state and local governments.

Steven D. Gold is director of the Center for the Study of the States at the Rockefeller Institute of Government, the public policy research arm of the State University of New York. He is also on the faculty of the State University of New York at the Albany Graduate School of Public Affairs. He received his B.A. degree (1966) from Bucknell University in economics, and his M.A. (1964) and Ph.D. (1972) degrees from the University of Michigan in economics. Before moving to Albany in 1990, he was director of fiscal studies for the National Conference of State Legislatures. Gold has written or edited fifteen books, the most recent of which is *Public School Finance Programs of the United States and Canada, 1990–1992* (1992). He serves as adviser to the Policy

Economics Group of Peat Marwick and is chairman of the advisory board for the new weekly publication *State Tax Notes*.

Rita Mae Kelly is professor of justice studies, political science, public affairs, and women's studies at Arizona State University (ASU) and director of the ASU School of Justice Studies. She received her B.A. degree (1961) from the University of Minnesota in Russian language; and her M.A. (1967) and Ph.D. (1970) degrees from Indiana University in political science. Her recent books include *Advances in Policy Studies Since 1950* (1992), *The Gendered Economy: Work, Careers, and Success* (1991), and *Gender, Bureaucracy, and Democracy* (1989). Kelly is the recipient of the Distinguished Research Award of the American Society for Public Administration, Section on Women in Public Administration (1991) and of a Fulbright Fellowship to Brazil (1991).

Donald F. Kettl is professor of public affairs and political science at the University of Wisconsin, Madison, and he serves as associate director of the university's La Follette Institute of Public Affairs. He received his B.A. degree (1974) from Yale University as Scholar of the House; and his M.A. (1976), M.Phil. (1976), and Ph.D. (1978) degrees from Yale in political science. Kettl has consulted broadly for government agencies, including the House Budget Committee and the Food and Drug Administration, and he has served on a task force for the Secretary of Energy that examined the problems of radioactive waste disposal. He is the author of many works on public policy and administration, including *Sharing Power: Public Governance and Private Markets* (1993), *The Politics of the Administrative Process* (1991, with J. W. Fesler), and *Government by Proxy* (1988).

Kenneth L. Kraemer is professor in the Graduate School of Management and director of the Center for Research on Information Technology and Organizations at the University of California, Irvine. He received his B.Arch. degree (1959) from Notre Dame in architecture, his Master of City and Regional Planning degree (1964) from the University of Southern California, and his M.P.A. (1965) and Ph.D. (1967) degrees in public administration, also from the University of Southern California. Kraemer is coauthor of seven books on information systems, including *Managing Information Systems: Change and Control in Organizational Computing* (1989, with J. L. King, D. E. Dunkle, and J. P. Lane). His articles have appeared in *Public Administration Review, Communications of the ACM, Computing Surveys,* and *Telecommunications Policy,* among other journals. He currently conducts research on government policy and the diffusion of information technology in Pacific Asian countries and on advanced integrated manufacturing environments in U.S. companies.

James L. Perry is professor in the School of Public and Environmental Affairs, Indiana University, Bloomington. He received his B.A. degree (1970) from the University of Chicago in public affairs, and his M.P.A. (1972) and Ph.D. (1974) degrees from the Maxwell School of Citizenship and Public Affairs at Syracuse University in public administration. Perry's research focuses on public management and public personnel administration and has appeared in such journals as the *Academy of Management Journal, Administrative Science Quarterly, American Political Science Review,* and *Public Administration Review.* He has coauthored or edited four books, including the *Handbook of Public Administration* (1989). He is a recipient of the Yoder-Heneman Award for innovative personnel research and the Charles H. Levine Memorial Award for Excellence in Public Administration.

Norma Riccucci is associate professor of public administration and policy at the State University of New York, Albany. She received her B.A. degree (1979) from Florida International University in public administration, her M.P.A. degree (1981) from the University of Southern California, and her Ph.D. degree (1984) from the Maxwell School of Citizenship and Public Affairs at Syracuse University in public administration. She is the author of numerous journal articles and of *Women, Minorities and Unions in the Public Sector* (1990), and *Promoting and Valuing Diversity in Municipal Government Work Forces* (1992), and coauthor of *Public Personnel Management: Current Concerns, Future Challenges* (1991, with C. Ban).

Sarah Ritchie has been assistant director of the Center for the Study of the States at the Rockefeller Institute of the State University of New York since 1990. She received her two B.A. degrees (1988) from the University of Oklahoma in political science and history and in economics, and her M.A. (1989) and M.Phil. (1990) degrees from Yale University in political science. She is a doctoral candidate at Yale University and is currently completing a dissertation on bicameralism in the U.S. Congress.

Deborah D. Roberts is associate professor at the University of Virginia Center for Public Service, specializing in executive development and public policy. She consults extensively with state government. She received her B.A. degree (1973) from Syracuse University in political science and history and her Ph.D. degree (1982) from the Maxwell School of Citizenship and Public Affairs at Syracuse University in public administration. Her recent projects have focused on public ethics, managerial excellence, managing change, government efficiency, privatization, state personnel policy, strategic planning, intergovernmental relations, and growth management. Roberts teaches courses in executive leadership and public administration. She is director of the University's Mid-Career Executive Program, which provides executive development and graduate study for federal administrators.

Michael Sparer is assistant professor in the Division of Health Policy and Management in the School of Public Health at Columbia University. He received his B.A. degree (1977) from Beloit College in government and philosophy, his J.D. degree (1980) from Rutgers University School of Law, and his Ph.D. degree (1991) from Brandeis University in political science. Sparer sent seven years as a litigator for the New York City Law Department, specializing in intergovernmental social welfare litigation. He now studies and writes about the politics of health care, with an emphasis on the state and local role in the U.S. health care system.

Revitalizing
State and Local
Public Service

INTRODUCTION

Critical Challenges to
State and Local Public Service

Frank J. Thompson

State and local governance is like a kaleidoscope—very complex and shifting. There are nearly 87,000 of these governments across the United States; they grapple with an extremely broad and diverse range of issues; myriad, fluid, often conflicting forces buffet them, greatly affecting their capacity and performance. Citizens have a hard time understanding these governments, hold inconsistent views about what they should do, and frequently feel dissatisfied with their performance.

These governments are also vitally important to the well-being of the United States. Their performance affects our safety, our access to health care, the quality of our natural environment, our education, the adequacy of our roads and bridges, our prospects for economic growth, and much, much more. The state and local level is where the public sees government in action every day. More than fifteen million people work for these governments.

This book provides analytic work to help lay a foundation for those seeking to revitalize state and local governance. Webster's dictionary (1976, p. 992) tells us that *revitalization* implies giving new life and vigor to something. Of course, state and local governments across the country already manifest much energy, creativity, and downright success. Over the last quarter of a century, many of them have made remarkable strides toward efficient, effective, and democratically responsive governance. Despite the many success stories, however, we can ill afford complacency. As can be

1

expected, solutions to problems that bedeviled state and local officials in the past have generated new problems. To note the genuine progress ushered in by past reforms does not relieve us of the responsibility to seek further improvement.

This is a time of public ferment over how to enhance governance. "R" words — rebuild, reinvent, redesign, reinvigorate, revitalize — fill speeches, analyses, and even a book on the *New York Times* best-seller list (Osborne and Gaebler, 1992). The "R" words should not, however, become a mantra without conceptual content. In the case of this book, the hallmarks of revitalization deserve clarification at the outset.

Revitalized state and local governance would feature at least three main qualities. First, public agencies would perform better than ever. They would achieve greater efficiency and effectiveness in producing desired outputs (for example, more medical service) and outcomes (for example, better health) at reasonable cost. To succeed in this regard, these agencies would need to have adequate capacity — committed and capable personnel, information, physical infrastructure, funding, authority, organizational design, and management systems. Moreover, they would need to have plausible, coherent policies to implement. All the administrative capacity in the world will not ensure efficiency and effectiveness if policymakers pass laws that are rooted in poor theories of how to accomplish goals.

Second, public agencies would be more democratically responsive and accountable. They would be law abiding — operating within the scope granted by constitutions, charters, statutes, and ordinances; they would be sensitive to the lawful preferences of top policymakers. For their part, citizens would possess sufficient information and leverage to make reasonable judgments about the performance of state and local governments and to steer them in the right direction. Enough citizens would possess these characteristics to ensure that preferences more representative of broad segments of the public (as opposed to views held by more narrow interests) would receive weight in policy and administrative processes.

Third, citizens would perceive governments more favorably. People would feel connected to government, efficacious in dealing with it, and pleased with its performance. They would see state and local agencies as competent, responsive, and worth the money they pay in taxes. Their informed judgments would lead them to express confidence in these levels of the federal system.

Only Dr. Pangloss would suppose that doing better in these three areas will be easy. Progress in one does not ensure advancement in another. In fact, trade-offs often exist. Lots of emphasis on accountability and citizen responsiveness will not always be the recipe for greater efficiency and effectiveness. But at a bare minimum, revitalization implies a better profile of achievement on these three dimensions.

The thesis of this book is that prospects for revitalization will improve if we succeed in coping with certain challenges centering on leadership, the workforce, information technology, privatized service delivery, and health care. In this chapter, I briefly assess the nature of each of these challenges to set the stage for the contributions that follow. Prior to this, however, it pays to examine certain fundamental political and economic forces that form a critical backdrop for efforts to meet these challenges. In particular, I consider the American political legacy with its fragmentation and culturally embedded mistrust of public power, as well as the political economy of fiscal stress.

Two caveats deserve mention at the outset. I make no claim that the challenges considered in this book comprise the universe of those relevant to the revitalization of state and local public service, only that they are among the most important. It also deserves emphasis that, while the backdrop factors of fragmentation, mistrust, and fiscal stress are potent, persistent forces in American political life, they are not immutable. Indeed, the leadership challenge is in part about modifying them.

Political Legacy: Fragmentation and Mistrust

At the National Commission on the State and Local Public Service's hearing in Tallahassee, Eugene Patterson, a Pulitzer prize-winning editor emeritus, observed that the country's forefathers "created a chaotic system of government" based on the American notion that "people are probably a lot worse than they seem and you'd better watch it — especially if you are going to give them official power . . . . Somehow we have learned this from the very first. That is what the country is about."

As Patterson indicates, the United States has a very distinctive political tradition — one built on mistrust of government in general and centralized power in particular. This political culture, with its emphasis on individualism, combines with the separation of powers, federalism, the proliferation of governments, weak political parties, and other forces to fragment, even pulverize, public power in the United States. The forces unleashed by America's basic institutions and founding creed shape the challenges discussed in this book and the feasible responses to them.

Governments Galore

In one respect, and maybe one only, the United States is the most "governed" nation in the world (Anton, 1989, p. 4). Most of the other industrialized democracies far surpass the United States on such measures of being governed as tax rates, the proportion of the Gross Domestic Product spent by the public sector, and the number of civil servants per capita (Rose, 1991). If, however, one looks beyond dollars and public employees to the total number of governmental units, the United States looks very governed indeed.

Nearly 87,000 governments — state, county, municipal, township, school, special district — speckle the American landscape, as shown in Table I.1. This amounts to roughly one government for every 2,866 citizens. A

Table I.1. Number of State and Local Governments by Type, 1962–1992.

	1962	1972	1982	1992
State	50	50	50	50
County	3,043	3,044	3,041	3,043
Municipal	18,000	18,517	19,076	19,296
Township	17,142	16,991	16,734	16,666
School District	34,678	15,781	14,851	14,556
Special District	18,323	23,885	28,078	33,131
Total	91,236	78,268	81,830	86,742

Sources: U.S. Department of Commerce, 1991, p. 278; U.S. Bureau of the Census, 1992a.

typical citizen, of course, lives within the jurisdiction of several governments. Thanks to the consolidation of school districts from 1962 through 1992, the total number of governments declined by 5 percent over the last three decades (see Table I.1). But the trend downward stopped in 1972 when the census of governments approximated 78,000. A steady increase in the number of special districts — from just over 18,000 in 1962 to 33,000 in 1992 — largely accounts for this reversal. These districts are limited, usually single-function entities that provide services related to pollution control, fire protection, housing and community development, sewage, hospital and health care, cemeteries, parks and recreation, water supply, libraries, highways, airports, and more. They generally draw their sustenance from taxes they levy, bonding authority, grants from other governments, or charges for the services they deliver.[1] In contrast to special districts, general purpose governments have held constant at roughly 40,000 over the last thirty years.

What accounts for the rapid growth in special districts? Other things being equal, these districts more readily proliferate when the following hold: (1) a mismatch exists between the territorial jurisdiction of general purpose governments and the problem to be addressed; (2) annexation is inhibited by laws and the constituency calculations of local political elites (for example, reluctance by city officials to jeopardize their power base by absorbing the suburbs); (3) general purpose governments face more stringent legal limitations on the taxes they can impose and the debts they can incur; (4) the federal government provides incentive for their establishment, as in the case of soil conservation districts, and (5) top policymakers see general purpose governments as unduly hindered (for example, by cumbersome civil service systems) in delivering efficient and effective services (Bowman and Kearney, 1986).

Analysis of the sources of government proliferation cannot, of course, ignore the great differences embedded in American federalism. As Table I.2 indicates, states vary considerably in governmental density — the number of governments per 10,000 residents. North Dakota has provided the most fertile soil, achieving a density of 41.5 governments per 10,000; Hawaii offers the most barren turf with 0.2 per 10,000. In terms of sheer numbers of

Table I.2. Government Density in the Fifty States, 1987
(Density = State and Local Governments per 10,000 Population).

	Density	Number of state and local governments
1. North Dakota	41.5	2,788
2. South Dakota	24.8	1,763
3. Nebraska	19.8	3,153
4. Kansas	15.4	3,804
Montana	15.4	1,244
6. Vermont	12.3	674
7. Idaho	10.7	1,066
8. Wyoming	8.7	425
9. Minnesota	8.4	3,556
10. Maine	6.8	801
11. Iowa	6.7	1,878
12. Missouri	6.2	3,148
13. Arkansas	5.9	1,397
14. Illinois	5.7	6,628
Wisconsin	5.7	2,720
16. Oklahoma	5.5	1,803
Oregon	5.5	1,503
18. Indiana	5.1	2,807
19. New Hampshire	5.0	525
20. Colorado	4.8	1,594
21. Delaware	4.4	282
22. Pennsylvania	4.2	4,957
23. Washington	3.9	1,780
24. Kentucky	3.5	1,304
Entire U.S.	3.4	83,236
25. Alaska	3.3	173
Mississippi	3.3	854
West Virginia	3.3	631
28. Utah	3.2	531
29. Ohio	3.1	3,378
30. Michigan	2.9	2,700
31. Alabama	2.6	1,054
Texas	2.6	4,416
33. New Mexico	2.2	332
34. Georgia	2.1	1,287
New Jersey	2.1	1,626
South Carolina	2.1	708
37. Nevada	2.0	198
38. New York	1.9	3,303
Tennessee	1.9	905
40. Arizona	1.7	577
41. California	1.6	4,332
42. Connecticut	1.5	478
43. Massachusetts	1.4	837
North Carolina	1.4	917

Table I.2. Government Density in the Fifty States, 1987
(Density = State and Local Governments per 10,000 Population), Cont'd.

	Density	Number of state and local governments
45. Rhode Island	1.3	126
46. Louisiana	1.0	453
47. Maryland	0.9	402
48. Florida	0.8	966
49. Virginia	0.7	431
50. Hawaii	0.2	19

Source: U.S. Department of Commerce, 1991, pp. 20, 297.

state and local governments, Illinois leads with 6,628 and Hawaii again finishes last with 19. There appear to be some "economies of scale" in states with larger populations. Among the five most populous states, Pennsylvania ranks twenty-second with a density of 4.2 per 10,000, Texas thirty-first, at 2.6, New York thirty-eighth at 1.9, California forty-first at 1.6, and Florida forty-eighth at 0.8.

Other Fragmenting Forces

All these governments fit, of course, within the structure of American federalism. A very modest hierarchy exists. Washington constrains and directs state and local governments in certain ways; local governments exist and function at the pleasure of the states. However, any juxtaposition of "hierarchy" and "federalism" in the same sentence runs a big risk of missing the point. Relationships among governments at different levels of the federal system more frequently involve bargaining, negotiation, and mutual accommodation than authoritative decrees. To be sure, one level of government frequently imposes mandates on another. But even here, there is often substantial slippage between what the "higher" government requires and what the "lower" one does.

Nor is it appropriate to see the evolution of American federalism as a one-way street toward greater federal dominance of public policy (Nathan, 1990). Very few policy arenas are the exclusive preserve of one governmental unit or another. Fear of centralizing power in Washington has spawned a keen appreciation of intergovernmental grant programs as a vehicle for accomplishing public ends. The roles of federal, state, and local officials are typically blurred. Those who crave nice, neat assignments of functions to different levels of the federal system seem destined to go unsated in the American context. Federalism by definition means that the governments embedded in the system sustain substantial authority and powers to formulate policy, raise monies, and implement programs. Even when compared with other countries with federal systems, such as Germany and Austria, the United States stands out as a remarkably decentralized structure of governance.

To guard against abuse, the founding fathers also espoused another fragmenting mechanism — the separation of powers (really shared powers among institutions). Public managers in many jurisdictions face multiple bosses; state courts, legislatures, governors, and other elected executives often send conflicting signals to public agencies.

Citizen initiatives often add to the fragmentation brought on by the separation of powers and federalism. Sixteen states permit direct citizen initiatives to change their constitutions and eighteen to modify their statutes (Council of State Governments, 1992). The vast majority of these states are west of the Mississippi River with California being the foremost hotbed of these activities. (Although voting on charter and statutory alterations is also common at the local level, data are not readily obtainable on the degree to which citizens can directly place propositions on the ballot.) Direct initiatives can bypass corrupt or gridlocked institutions, but they also add to the dispersal of power, the complexity, and the uncertainty faced by policymakers and administrators. These initiatives typically ask voters to respond to single issues without much reference to how passage affects other important policy spheres. They at times impose conflicting statutory requirements on officials that make the balancing and aggregation of competing values into coherent public policy extremely difficult.

Too Much of a Good Thing

The splintering of public authority within the United States has produced many benefits. As the founders intended, it has reduced the risk of abuse of power by a central government, diffused conflict, and allowed government to be responsive to diverse preferences in various regions of the country. It affords opportunity for great amounts of experimentation and innovation. The fragmented structure also provides unusually great opportunities for access to the political system and public participation in it. For instance, nearly a half-million elected officials take part in state and local government, and countless other citizens receive part-time appointments to boards and other governing groups (Anton, 1989).

The conflict generated by the system often yields media coverage and, hence, information for the citizenry. Moreover, competition among jurisdictions sometimes brings out their best. Some suggest that the proliferation of governments facilitates democratic responsiveness by letting people vote with their feet. For instance, if a person does not like the schools in City A, he or she can move to Suburb B. Extrapolated to many different policy spheres, the possibility of exit from one jurisdiction to another allegedly creates a better match between what citizens want and what they get from state and local institutions. Moreover, it supposedly pressures these governments to pursue efficiency, effectiveness, and responsiveness because they do not want to lose citizens to other locales. Of course, not all citizens have the luxury of voting with their feet. The poor cannot as a rule move to affluent suburbs with superior local services. Nor can one assume that citizens will have enough information to make rational judgments or that competition will always have sanguine implications. Nonetheless, some advantages do undoubtedly accrue from competition born of fragmentation.

Much evidence indicates, however, that the United States has succumbed to too much of a good thing. James Bryce captured the nub of the problem more than a century ago when he wrote (1891, p. 295): "There is an excessive friction in the American system, a waste of force in the strife of various bodies and persons created to check and balance one another . . . . Power is so much divided that it is hard at a given moment to concentrate it for prompt and effective action." The current pattern of fragmentation raises genuine concerns about gridlock and drift, the ability to deliver programs efficiently and effectively, and accountability.

Fragmentation and Hard Choices

The United States faces many critical policy challenges in the 1990s. The globalization of the economy, sluggish economic growth, and pressing social needs often leave policymakers with hard choices. A fragmented political structure maximizes the opportunity for interests adversely affected by change to block new policies. Gridlock and drift can easily result.

Paradoxically, the reforms of the past may have helped fuel the problem. Over the past twenty-five years, the executive, legislative, and judicial branches have in general bolstered their capacity, among other things, employing greater numbers of more professionalized staff. They have also grown more assertive about their prerogatives. The problem is that in a system that constitutionally fragments political power, increasing the capacity of the parts need not produce a more coherent, well-functioning whole. In this regard, Murphy (1981, pp. 125, 135) points to a paradox of reform whereby the greater capacity of the subunits of government fuels "fragmentation, disarray, confusion, and lack of leadership." He suggests that the sheer number of increasingly sophisticated and interdependent participants taking part in state policymaking "has congested and slowed the process of government" and caused these governments to appear as "sluggish ineffective giants lacking leadership talent" (see also Ehrenhalt, 1992).

The friction induced by the formal separation of powers has been exacerbated by the public's tendency to divide control of the different branches of state government between the parties. Divided government increases prospects that state agencies will receive inconsistent policy directives concerning the implementation of programs. It heightens temptations to make the administrative arena a staging ground for allocating blame and scoring partisan points. Since 1978, most state governments have featured divided party control with the single exception of the 1982–1983 period (Fiorina, 1991; Council of State Governments, 1992).

The sense of gridlock created by conflict among the high-capacity subunits of government controlled by different parties can become acute. In his testimony before the commission in Sacramento, Barry Keene, senate majority leader in California, observed: "Some people argue that the problems of government are personal, rather than structural. They say our leaders don't lead, or they don't care, or they are crooks, or they're quitting. But these charges beg the question — *why* can even the *best* people in government accomplish so little? The reasons are partly societal . . . partly attitudinal . . . , but mainly structural." He noted that legislatures are often "particularly paralyzed" and went on to comment: "The Constitution of California, like that of the United States, virtually invites voters to elect legislative majorities of one philosophy and chief executives of another philosophy. And the voters accept the invitation regularly. Enacting policy that moves in one direction, while implementing it in the other, virtually guarantees stalemate . . . . Dispersion of power . . . may make sense for the federal government, which has great power. But the states copied it mindlessly, shackling themselves in their attempts to solve their problems . . . ."

The frustration conveyed by these remarks extends to many in the electorate as well. Voters can strike back in blunt terms: consider the movement to deprofessionalize state legislatures through term limits and radical reductions in legislative staffs. One effect of such efforts could well be to make the legislatures less of a player in the politics produced by the fragmentation of power.

Frictions fueled by the separation of powers have less impact on local governments. Many of these general purpose governments are formally nonpartisan and exist in smaller communities with more homogeneous outlooks. These governments tend to have only one legislative body filled with part-time officials who have very limited resources. Many mayors are also part time and enjoy modest staff support at most. Special districts are frequently ruled by a single governing board. For these local governments, other jurisdictions and the forces of federalism frequently do more to complicate governance than internal conflicts born of the separation of powers.

Fragmentation and Administration

The balkanization of public authority also creates problems for those involved in the day-to-day implementation of programs. Fragmentation often heightens transaction costs and complicates efforts at coordination. The endless discussion of service integration speaks volumes about the difficulties brought on by dispersed authority. DeAnn Friedholm, a special assistant in the lieutenant governor's office in Texas, captured the flavor of this concern when she told the commission in Austin: "In health care, the biggest issue other than resources is that it is so fragmented and broken up in terms of who is responsible for what that people don't know where to turn for assistance. When they do find someone, they get referred to many other places. No one is ever truly responsible . . . . If you try to diagram it, which I have done many times, Rube Goldberg would have a tremendous time trying to show you how complicated it is and how fragmented."

Moreover, the growing capacity and assertiveness of legislative bodies and the courts — especially when combined with divided party control — create problems for public managers. It often means that they face sharply conflicting expectations and outbreaks of micromanagement by these institutions. Oversight all too readily becomes a game of "gotcha" rather than an effort to learn and fix administrative problems. Indeed, one study suggests that local governments with part-time elected officials have a better chance of achieving creative innovation precisely because their elected leaders do not have the time to involve themselves in the nitty-gritty of administration (Light, 1992).

Fragmentation and Accountability

Splintered authority also raises issues of government accountability (a problem compounded by the frequent use of private agents to deliver public services). The complexity of the system imposes very high information costs on anyone seeking to learn enough to exert influence. Many individuals cannot identify the services provided by the governments around them, much less figure out exactly who is responsible for these services (Anton, 1989). Again in the words of DeAnn Friedholm, we risk that "when everyone is responsible a tiny bit, no one is responsible." Of course, all forms of government present information barriers to citizen competence. The sheer scale of government and the technical sophistication needed to make sense of a range of interconnected policies assures this (Gruber, 1987). But fragmentation usually contributes to the information barriers. Initial research at the local level has empirically documented that citizens living in more fragmented metropolitan settings make significantly more attribution errors than those living under more consolidated governments (Lyons and Lowery, 1989).[2] Attribution errors occur when citizens

- fail to recognize that government provides a particular service
- assume government or its agents perform some function when this is not the case
- hold one government responsible for service that another actually performs (Lowery, Lyons, and DeHoog, 1990).

The Quest for Public Confidence

A political culture built on mistrust of public authority not only encourages fragmentation, it directly affects state and local governance in other ways. It shapes the degree to which citizens have confidence in and feel satisfied with government — a key element of revitalization. It affects orientations toward accountability and managerial discretion. It compounds the leadership, workforce, management, and health care challenges.

If antigovernment sentiment were consistent across the board, public officials could at least take consolation in having to deal with a clear set of expectations. But while the populace tends to hold government in low esteem, it simultaneously pushes for activism in more and more policy spheres. Mistrust and disrespect have not bred a desire for massive program cutbacks. For instance, studies of citizens in California and Michigan who voted for tax limitation measures found that they were generally not voting for lower service levels. In fact, voters tended to express satisfaction with existing services and wanted more rather than less government (Anton, 1989).

Since the founding creed emphasizes a suspicion of centralized public authority in particular, it is not surprising that local governments tend to engender more trust than their state and national counterparts. For instance, in presenting an otherwise bleak picture of diminished citizen efficacy, a Kettering Foundation study found that this sense of political impotence did not so readily extend to the local level (Harwood Group, 1991). In similar fashion, a 1991 survey reported that more than twice as many people (35 percent) thought that local governments spend their tax dollars wisely as said this about the federal government (12 percent). A 1992 survey found that 60 percent expressed a great deal or a fair amount of confidence that local governments would do a good job in carrying out their responsibilities, 51 percent felt this way about the states, and 42 percent offered this view of the federal government.

It deserves note, however, that in the case of each government level, only about 5 percent expressed a "great deal" of confidence. Moreover, the survey found a decline in trust in the period from 1987 through 1992. Those expressing a great deal or a fair amount of confidence went down by twenty-six percentage points in the case of the federal government, by twenty-two points in the case of the states, and by thirteen points in the case of local governments (U.S. Advisory Commission on Intergovernmental Relations, 1992; see also Foster and Snyder, 1989). This slippage in public confidence reinforces the importance of pursuing governmental revitalization at all levels of the federal system.

Public Opinion Versus Judgment

Surveys, of course, often produce inconsistent findings. They do not, for instance, invariably indicate that the federal government fares worse than local, let alone state, governments in the peoples' minds. The U.S. Advisory Commission on Intergovernmental Relations has asked the following question nineteen times since 1972: "From which level of government do you feel that you get the most for your money?" Eleven times a plurality ranked the federal government first, seven times local government received this recognition, and one time federal and local governments tied. State government finished last eighteen out of the nineteen times. In 1991, the most recent year a sample responded to the question, 31 percent said that local government was the best deal, 26 percent the federal government, and 22 percent the state (Muste, 1992, Table 4).[3]

Inconsistencies in these findings about confidence no doubt spring from many sources, but much of the problem stems from the propensity of surveys to measure public opinion rather than judgment. Surveys can always elicit opinions from people. The question is whether these sentiments reflect considered judgment or shallow, off-the-cuff reactions. The latter often border on nonattitudes likely to fluctuate greatly in response to immediate stimuli from current events or questionnaire wording. Or they may also reflect knee-jerk, albeit more stable, reactions rooted in cultural stereotypes. Public judgment in contrast refers to views that respondents have thought about more. They have acquired more information, wrestled more with the consequences of their preferences, and reconciled them with other values they hold (Yankelovich, 1991).

The surveys focused on state and local government typically solicit opinion, but there are a few exceptions. Some research has probed the judgments of citizens based on their encounters with particular public bureaucracies. When pressed to talk about these encounters, most citizens express satisfaction with the performance of state and local agencies. This is especially true in the case of agencies that provide valued services such as workers' compensation or job training. Not surprisingly, regulatory agencies, such as police and motor vehicle departments, evoke less favorable responses among those who come in contact with them, although substantial numbers still express satisfaction (Katz, Gutek, Kahn, and Barton, 1975).

For political leaders, however, these judgments often matter much less than opinion. These leaders often cater to public opinion rather than work to create conditions for public judgment. For instance, Yankelovich (1991, p. 24) suggests that the frequent incantation that we can have more services and avoid paying more taxes by eradicating "waste, fraud, and abuse" is the quintessential example of poor quality opinion rather than judgment. It allows people to escape the consequences of their views. But this have-our-cake-and-eat-it-too opinion contributes greatly to difficulties in getting the public and political leaders to face hard, important choices about taxes and service levels. Stimulating and catering to opinion rather than judgment can vitiate opportunities for leadership and enhance prospects for gridlock.

Ultimately, of course, many forces shape the opinions and judgments of citizens about state and local governments. For those seeking revitalization of these institutions, however, one question looms particularly large: Will better performance by state and local agencies lead to greater citizen confidence in them?

Performance, Confidence, and Flypaper

More than two centuries ago, Alexander Hamilton observed: "It is not necessarily true that a numerous representation is necessary to obtain the confidence of the people. The confidence of the people will easily be gained by good administration. This is the touchstone" (Morone, 1990, p. 66). In fact, the relationship between "good administration" and public confidence is vastly more complex than Hamilton allowed. Performance plays a role in shaping public trust, but there is no one-to-one relationship.

Improvements in performance by state and local governments do not automatically trigger more favorable assessment of them in either specific or general terms. Studies frequently show that objective measures of service quality do not strongly correlate with citizen assessments of agency performance (DeHoog, Lowery, and Lyons, 1990; Parks, 1984). This could spring from methodological limitations to the studies, but it also drives home the point that improving on measures of quality defined by experts may fail to satisfy citizens. The pathway to greater citizen satisfaction requires agencies to focus on those aspects of performance that are most visible and matter most to the public. The pathway also involves publicizing agency accomplishments. Seasoned practitioners typically grasp this point. As a manager in the Michigan Department of Social Services observed: "Managers not only need to perform well, but they also must change the perception of that performance in the public's mind" (Bair, 1992, p. 8).

Of course, some citizens form impressions of public agencies through personal encounters with them. But to the degree that these encounters affect more general opinions about government, a flypaper effect may well apply where bad experiences stick more than positive ones. In their thorough and careful study of attitudes toward public agencies, Katz and his associates (1975, p. 126) found that while "general attitudes toward administrative agencies have little specific experiential basis and derive from the cumulative impact of the mass media and . . . culture . . . these stereotyped conceptions are not impervious to certain types of personal experiences." The bad news for government administrators is that "unpleasant occurrences result in lowered evaluations whereas pleasant encounters have little impact." Stated more formally, "bad experiences with specific agencies lower the individual's general appraisal of public offices, but good experiences do not raise it above the norm." Rising expectations could account for the more limited impact of positive encounters; citizens may respond to satisfying experiences with public agencies by raising their expectations of agency performance (Katz, Gutek, Kahn, and Barton, 1975). If so, the better public administrators do, the more citizens expect, and the greater the risk of disappointment.

The flypaper effect and the general climate of mistrust erode efforts to improve public administration. Policy implementation in the United States often features elaborate mechanisms to control administrative discretion even if this pursuit undermines efficiency and effectiveness. Mistrust encourages defensive, risk-averse, play-it-by-the-book management. The dictum seems clear: avoid experimentation and innovation because error will be viewed not as an opportunity to learn but as an occasion to blame and hold officials accountable. Thus, calls to deregulate public agencies to allow their executives greater freedom to manage and to be entrepreneurial face a very stiff headwind. The flypaper effect compounds the problem. If managers gain more discretion to experiment, they will on occasion err. If bad experiences stick more with citizens than positive ones, officials risk that the negative results of their experiments will be weighed more heavily by the public than the positive outcomes.

Opinion and Judgment in Perspective

In sum, a political culture of mistrust conditions contemporary judgments and opinions related to revitalizing state and local governance. Although surveys frequently suffer from methodological limitations, they suggest certain conclusions:

- A set of mistrustful, negative stereotypes about government deeply rooted in the nation's cultural legacy mingles with more volatile opinions and informed judgments about state and local governance.
- Citizens tend to express more confidence in local governments relative to the other levels of the federal system, although this does not translate into the view that local entities should have more power relative to the other levels (U.S. Advisory Commission on Intergovernmental Relations, 1991a, p. 12).
- Surveys suggest a moderate level of overall confidence in state and local governments, but this confidence appears to have eroded in recent years and citizens display great cynicism about certain aspects of the public sector's performance.
- Citizen judgments of the performance of specific agencies tend to be more favorable than their overall assessment of state and local governments; specific bad experiences with agencies may reinforce negative overall assessments much more than positive ones counteract these adverse impressions.

This backdrop of public sentiment as well as the attendant structural fragmentation comprise a big part of the leadership, workforce, management, and health care challenges that concern this book. Prior to turning to these challenges, however, it is critical to consider one other feature of the backdrop that profoundly shapes the revitalization effort — fiscal stress.

Fiscal Stress and Revitalization

Efforts to revitalize state and local public service in the 1990s will occur in a climate of substantial fiscal stress. Although it is hard to calibrate, stress generally refers to the excess of pressures for state or local spending over the dollars readily available to pay for it (Gold, 1992a). Pressures for expenditure spring from potent forces — the budgetary inertia of current programs, the desire to meet public demands for new or expanded services, and more. The degree to which money is readily available to pay for programs stems from such factors as the revenue flow generated by the existing tax structure, the degree to which antitax sentiment is pervasive, and the wealth of a jurisdiction.

Wellsprings of Spending

In 1990, state and local governments spent just over $2,500 per capita from their own sources (that is, excluding federal grants). Their 1990 expenditures per capita were double those of 1980 and roughly five times greater than 1970. These increases did not, however, signal great growth in state and local effort as a proportion of all economic activity. State and local expenditures as a proportion of the GNP have held about constant over two decades ranging from nearly 11 percent in 1970 to just over 10 percent in 1980 to just under 12 percent in 1990. Federal expenditures as a proportion of GNP are approximately double those of state and local governments (U.S. Advisory Commission on Intergovernmental Relations, 1991b).

Pressures to spend more will intensify during the 1990s with demographic trends doing much to fuel this development. As the proportion of the population over eighty-five increases, the demand for long-term care subsidized by Medicaid will probably rise sharply. At the other end of the spectrum, the children of the baby boom population are beginning to have children of their own leading to a projected growth in school enrollment of 13 percent in the 1990s (Gold, 1992b). As if these drains on the state and local purse were not sufficient, many jurisdictions face a growing need to repair deteriorating infrastructure (Rivlin, 1992).

Aside from demographics, relentless price increases in the medical sector seem destined to exacerbate state and local fiscal stress. From 1975 through 1990, annual increases in the medical care component of the consumer price index surpassed the general inflation rate in every year but two (1978–1979 and 1979–1980). During this fifteen-year period, prices for all items rose by 143 percent while the price of medical care soared by 243 percent (U.S. Public Health Service, 1992). The country's inability to restrain medical price hikes means higher Medicaid costs and greater government expenditures to insure their employees; it also contributes to the growing numbers of under- and uninsured whose care state and local governments often subsidize.

How Much Relief?

In the face of rising demands on state and local governments, three major factors could relieve stress: robust economic growth, greater federal assistance, and public receptivity to new taxes. None of them seems likely.

Economic forecasting is an inexact art and predictions vary, but the fact remains that few anticipate economic growth in the 1990s that would match the substantial rates present in the 1950s and 1960s (Rivlin, 1992).

Moreover, greater inelasticity in state tax systems makes the revenue boost of a more robust economy less potent than in the past. Elasticity becomes greater to the degree that a 1 percent growth in personal income results in a higher percentage increase in tax revenue. A movement toward less progressive income taxes in the late 1980s helped make state tax systems less elastic (Gold, 1992a).

Nor, given its massive debt, does the federal government seem likely to send out a rescue party. Federal aid is a tale of two decades — generosity in the 1970s and tightfistedness in the 1980s. Several snapshots convey this point. In constant 1982 dollars, federal grants to state and local governments grew rapidly in the 1970s from $61 billion to $106 billion, before declining to $101 billion in 1990. Measured in terms of federal aid per $100 of personal income, the pattern is even sharper — $2.83 in 1970, $4.08 in 1980, and $3.13 in 1990. From yet another vantage point federal aid as a percentage of all state and local expenditures increased from 18 percent in 1970 to 24 percent in 1980 before backtracking to 18 percent in 1990 (U.S. Advisory Commission on Intergovernmental Relations, 1991b; Gold, 1992a).

Although they capture a general pattern, these figures in many respects obscure the withdrawal pains experienced by many state and local governments. Federal aid is increasingly about Medicaid, leaving many other policy sectors starved for support. Medicaid, the federal entitlement program to provide nursing home and health care for the poor, grew from 22 percent of federal aid to the states in 1980 to 33 percent in 1990. Medicaid aid per $100 of personal income increased from 50 cents in 1970 to 67 cents in 1980 to 90 cents in 1990, an 80 percent boost. State officials became increasingly entrepreneurial in seeking ways to shift payment for programs to Medicaid in order to obtain federal matching funds. In contrast, federal aid for other areas, such as highways and education, was squeezed (Gold, 1992b). General revenue sharing, a program that had provided state and local governments with discretionary dollars, ceased to play a significant role in fiscal federalism in the 1980s.

Aggregate figures on federal assistance also mask the fact that local governments suffered more than states from Washington's cutbacks.[4] From 1970 to its highwater mark in 1978, federal aid to local governments rose sharply from $.34 per $100 of personal income to $1.21 — growth of well over 300 percent. Following 1978, however, direct federal aid to local governments spiraled downward, reaching $.42 per $100 of personal income in 1990. In contrast federal aid to the states rose and declined much less precipitously during the 1970–1978 and 1978–1990 periods (Gold, 1992a).

The predicament of many local governments has caused them to look to state capitals to mitigate fiscal stress. Local officials have demanded mandate relief as well as more dollars. In nominal terms, states have provided more assistance with state grants to localities, increasing from approximately $33 billion in 1971 to $83 billion in 1980 to $172 billion in 1989 (U.S. Advisory Commission on Intergovernmental Relations, 1991; U.S. Bureau of the Census, 1991b). The dependency of local governments on the states has clearly increased relative to their reliance on the federal government. For instance, in 1978, the highwater mark for federal aid, municipalities received 84 cents from the states for every dollar of federal assistance. By 1989, these jurisdictions received $2.75 from the state for every dollar from Washington. Some states have also tried to provide relief by taking over functions previously performed by local governments, with one analysis identifying eighteen states where this had occurred in the period from 1982 through 1987 (Gold, 1991).

The coming of the Clinton administration heightens prospects that state and local officials will have a more sympathetic ear in Washington concerning their fiscal problems. Major reform in the health arena, which is high on the Clinton agenda, could spell great relief. But the massive federal deficit casts a pall over prospects for federal assistance. As the discussion of the health care challenge later in this chapter indicates, Washington may not have the will to dispatch a major rescue party.

With the prospects for greater federal aid far from bright, the question naturally arises: Can state and local governments mitigate stress in the 1990s by boosting taxes? Ostensibly, these jurisdictions have room in which to maneuver. Tax rates in the United States tend to be lower than those in major European countries. Moreover, states and localities did not increase taxes at so rapid a rate over the last twenty years as to exhaust the potential to pursue this option. Taxes and charges per $100 of personal income among states and localities amounted to $14.14 in 1989 — about 7 percent greater than the comparable figure in 1980, but less than the tax burden in 1978 (Gold, 1991). Although state and local debt more than doubled during the 1980s, it still pales beside that of the federal government and has shrunk as a proportion of all government debt (U.S. Department of Commerce, 1991).

The extent to which citizens will tolerate additional tax hikes is uncertain, however. Policymakers in many states have been testing the limits to public tolerance. During 1991, for instance, thirty-four states raised taxes. But voters can, of course, bite back. The massive Republican realignment of both houses of the New Jersey legislature after Democratic governor James Florio pushed through tax increases testifies to the potential potency of the backlash. Wary of this resistance, policymakers have often proven at least as interested in reducing services as bolstering revenue. In 1991, for instance, twenty-nine states cut back spending below the level initially appropriated for the year, twenty-three provided no across-the-board salary increase for workers, twelve laid off employees, and seventeen cut welfare benefits (Gold, 1992a).

In considering tax hikes, state policymakers are typically constrained by fears that excessive rates will cause businesses and the more affluent to resettle elsewhere, thereby eroding the jurisdiction's tax base. Businesses have, of course, frequently used the threat of exit to influence state and local policies.

While at times this is an exercise in crying "wolf," state officials cannot safely dismiss the warning, especially in light of factors that have heightened the ability of firms to move in response to uncompetitive tax rates. According to Rivlin (1992, p. 138), these factors include

- Improvements in transportation and communication that greatly enhance the geographic mobility of people, goods, and services
- An economy dominated by large companies that operate in multiple locations and can easily shift activities and jobs from one place to the next
- The greater prevalence of service industries, which can more readily relocate and can often perform their activities at a substantial distance from their customers

Fiscal stress will not, of course, uniformly afflict state and local governments, because jurisdictions vary enormously in the factors that produce it. Consider inequalities in wealth among states. Other things being equal, richer states will be able to afford greater government capacity than their poorer counterparts. The playing field for revitalizing state and local public service will become more level to the degree that states become more similar in wealth. In fact, however, the trend over the last quarter century seems to be in the opposite direction. An analysis performed by the commission's staff found that in constant 1982 dollars, the standard deviations in per capita income among states increased from $1,474 in 1967 to $1,674 in 1980 to $2,146 in 1990.

Is fiscal stress a boon or barrier to the quest for more efficient and effective government? Some suggest that periodic austerity presents states and localities with the incentive and opportunity to make the tough decisions in setting priorities, achieving efficiencies, and spurring useful innovation. At a bare minimum, the absence of opportunities to expand programs often leaves policymakers with more time to focus attention on management issues. Unfortunately, however, hard times can lead to circumstances where the wheat gets thrown out with the chaff. Across-the-board cuts are popular. Furthermore, the boom and bust cycle in state and local finance makes it difficult for officials to plan and achieve continuity in service. Even more fundamentally, some jurisdictions are so impoverished as to stand little or no chance of revitalization. For them, the fiscal stress of the 1990s will overwhelm efforts to meet leadership, workforce, information, privatization, and health care challenges. It is to these challenges that we now turn.

The Leadership Challenge

Fragmentation, a culture of mistrust, and fiscal stress heighten the need for visionary, committed, and skilled leaders willing to tackle the tough issues of state and local governance. Leadership on behalf of a revitalized state and local public service occurs in myriad settings—in legislatures, deep within the bureaucracy, within public employee unions, in the courts, among citizen groups, and elsewhere. Without leadership from chief executives, however, it will be an uphill struggle to surmount the debilitating effects of the American backdrop; it will be hard to forge the coalitions needed to formulate, adopt, and implement sensible public policies; efforts to cope with the other challenges that concern this book will likely flounder.

In Part One of this book Deborah D. Roberts focuses on gubernatorial leadership. More than any other chief executive at the state and local level, governors shape the climate for public service. Roberts forcefully argues that governors need to see themselves not just as external leaders active in state politics and policy formulation; they should also be internal leaders (not managers) of the executive branch, including the civil service. This requires not only that they be dedicated, talented, and visionary; it also necessitates that they have an executive leadership system.

Significant as governors are, they still represent the tip of the iceberg in terms of executive leadership at the state and local levels. The activities of mayors, city managers, county executives, and other top officials are also critical. Most of the nearly 200 cities with more than 100,000 people place substantial authority with a city manager. Roughly 55 percent of these cities sustain a council-manager form of government while just over 40 percent have a mayor-council arrangement. In the twenty-three cities of at least a half-million residents, however, the mayoral form prevails; only five of these larger jurisdictions invest substantial formal powers in a city manager (Dallas, Phoenix, San Antonio, San Diego, and San Jose). The distinction between manager and mayor cities is muddled by the fact that over 60 percent of all city manager locales also feature elected mayors (International City/County Management Association, 1992; Ehrenhalt, 1990). Only a few cities with a population of 100,000 or more have clung to the commission model of government—a model that undercuts opportunities for integrative leadership. In pure form, this structure calls for each elected commissioner to be a legislator *and* the head of a city agency.

Those concerned with city governance have long wrestled with issues of how best to structure opportunities for executive leadership. The same cannot be said of county governments. More than any other level of the federal system, counties have provided barren soil for the flowering of strong executives. Among the more than 3,000 county governments, a commission or board consisting of a plural executive is the most common arrangement (Jeffery, Salant, and Boroshok, 1989; Herbers, 1989). In recent years, however, the infirmities of the commission system and the growing awareness of the vital tasks county governments perform have spurred movement to strengthen the hand of either an appointed or elected executive. Roughly 800 counties appoint a chief executive or manager, and close to 400 have elected executives (Gurwitt, 1989).

Whether at the state, county, or municipal level, chief executives vary greatly in their formal powers. In general, these leaders are institutionally stronger to the extent that at least the following apply:

- They are not subject to term limits.
- They possess more authority to appoint, remove, promote, demote, and transfer subordinates.
- They have control over budget submissions, enactments, and outlays.
- They can veto new legislation.
- They have the authority to issue orders changing government organization or modifying the administrative code that guides the actions of subordinate agencies.

Have the formal powers of chief executives increased over the last quarter century? We lack a handy scorecard to provide a definitive answer; available evidence, however, suggests some centripetal movement. At the state level, for instance, Beyle (1990) has traced a gradual increase in gubernatorial authority in the period from 1960 through 1990. Using an index that includes some of the factors specified above, he finds that the number of governors with strong or very strong "institutionalized powers" grew from fifteen to twenty-five during this period. When we examine the five most populous states, we find New York ranked as very strong in these gubernatorial powers. Pennsylvania as strong, California and Florida as moderately strong, and Texas as weak.

A focus on the formal powers of chief executives should not, of course, distract attention from the other important ingredients of leadership — energy, expertise, personality, sensitivity to symbols, skill, sound strategy, opportunity, and more. With enough of these ingredients, even executives with a weak institutional base can accomplish much on behalf of a revitalized public service. The chairman of the National Commission on the State and Local Public Service, William Winter, won kudos for just such a feat during his term as governor of Mississippi from 1980 to 1984 (Kaplan and O'Brien, 1991; Sigelman and Dometrius, 1988). Unable to succeed himself, possessing meager budgetary and personnel authority, and facing a recalcitrant legislature, Governor Winter appealed directly to the citizenry through public forums, phone banks, the creative use of the mass media, and a citizen petition drive. These efforts ultimately led to the "Christmas miracle" of December 1982 — legislative approval of major reform for Mississippi's public schools. Success stories such as this one should not, however, lull us into complacency. Such triumphs can occur, but chief executives with more formal powers will day-in, day-out be more able to provide leadership (Sigelman and Dometrius, 1988).

In considering the formal powers of chief executives, Roberts stresses the importance of personnel appointments. Her analysis suggests an interesting contrast between patterns present at the federal level — patterns that greatly concerned the Volcker Commission — and those in the states. The National Commission on the Public Service (1989) chaired by Paul Volcker concluded that presidents had excessively politicized the top levels of the bureaucracy and recommended reducing the number of positions available for presidential appointment by one-third. In this regard, the Volcker report reflected an ongoing concern about the quality of executive leadership in Washington. Heclo (1977) has described the nub of this concern in the following way. Political executives descend on Washington for brief (on average less than two-year) terms. Lacking supportive networks, these "birds of passage" form a "government of strangers." Often they acquire the programmatic and political knowledge they need to function effectively just about the time they leave office. Hence, the risk of amateur governance runs high. Drawing on a musical metaphor, Heclo suggests that the top levels of the executive branch have too few master violinists and too many kazoo players (p. 239).

In contrast, Roberts indicates that kazoo players may be less of a threat in state governments even in the face of growing numbers of positions exempt from civil service coverage and more subject to influence by the governor. To be sure, turnover rates at the apex of state agencies appear to be substantial — surely higher than those present in most legislatures. Turnover for agency heads approximated 50 percent every two years during much of the 1970s and early 1980s (Haas and Wright, 1989a, 1989b). The leaders of agencies with publicly controversial, difficult tasks may well exit with particular haste. For instance, the average corrections commissioner typically leaves within three years of taking the job (DiIulio, 1990); the average tenure of a mental health commissioner is about 2.6 years (Miller and Iscoe, 1990). Top state administrators who win national recognition for being unusually innovative often depart at an even higher rate as more lucrative and challenging job offers come their way. Their exit early in the implementation of the innovation can vitiate its staying power (Sapolsky, Aisenberg, and Morone, 1987).

Despite this fluidity, at least two factors usually make for something other than a government of strangers at the state level. First, exempt positions in state government do not as readily turn over when a newly elected governor takes office. Political executives in Washington almost all leave with the election of a new president from the party that has been out of power. By and large, states do not mirror this pattern. To be sure, new governors from the out party who possess substantial appointment authority tend to replace more senior executives than other governors during transitions. But even in these cases, many high-level administrators survive. Gubernatorial change of this kind is only modestly correlated with turnover at the top rungs of government (Haas and Wright, 1989b).

Second, top administrators in stage agencies usually have considerable experience in the public sector. According to a survey conducted in 1988, agency heads had on average spent thirteen years in state government, a figure virtually unchanged over two decades. At the time of their appointments as agency heads, 51 percent of them were already working in the same state government, 16 percent came from other governments (half from the local level), and 30 percent from the private sector. These data reinforce Roberts's point about state executives being in-and-arounders. In fact, the more pressing question is whether they are too ingrown. While over half of them have worked for more than one state agency, only 14 percent have held positions in other states (Wright, Yoo, and Cohen, 1991).

Are those who hold the top jobs in county and city agencies as experienced as those in state government? More fundamentally, have local chief executives also tried to acquire more authority to fill positions and remove personnel? The available data do not permit a precise response to these questions.

Clearly, however, many mayors, city managers, and county executives view greater discretion to hire and fire as central to their leadership. In testimony to the commission about her experience as mayor of Houston, for instance, Kathy Whitmire observed: "One of the problems department directors had in getting their departments to operate efficiently was the fact that all of their senior management people were covered by the civil service system. So they would have deputy directors and assistant directors of the department — all of whom had civil service protection, had been there a long time, and didn't want to change, and didn't want to carry out the mission of the newly appointed director." In response, Whitmire led a successful charter reform campaign in Houston that exempted up to 2 percent of the city's workforce from civil service protection. Other chief executives at the local level have fought for similar changes. Victories in enlarging their personnel authority seldom come easily, however. The Supreme Court has contributed to the challenge by making it more difficult for elected executives to hire and remove people for partisan political reasons — even for top policy jobs (Gurwitt, 1989; Katz, 1991; Thompson, 1991). Unions and other groups frequently fight any erosion of civil service coverage.

As for the work experience of agency executives in local government, anecdotal evidence, such as that provided by Whitmire, suggests a pattern quite the opposite of the "government of strangers" present in Washington. Local officials usually know each other and their communities very well. The question is whether they are too parochial and whether service in other jurisdictions would broaden their perspectives and hone their skills. Of course, as Roberts notes, city managers are a major exception in this regard because they typically serve several localities over a career.

The Workforce Challenge

Ray Marshall, a member of the National Commission on the State and Local Public Service, has called for a national economic policy based on human resource capitalism (with Tucker, 1992). His argument reflects well-known trends. In the face of intense international competition, the United

States has in recent years experienced sluggish economic growth, stagnant worker productivity levels, and declines in the real wages of workers. Human resource capitalism rejects the view that a country's natural resources provide the basic building block for a vital economy; it looks beyond such highly touted lubricants of economic progress as substantial consumer demand and the slow growth of the money supply. Instead, it calls for a competitive economy that maintains high incomes and full employment by placing the education, skills, organization, and management of the workforce at center stage. In a nutshell, human resource capitalism stresses (1) sustaining an adequate supply of high-quality human resources, (2) managerial strategies that emphasize quality and productivity, and (3) a pattern of work organization that fosters both of these goals (pp. 58–59).

These three elements also make up the essence of the workforce challenge in state and local governments. Ultimately the country's ability to compete in a global economy depends on high-performance organizations in the private and the public sector.

A Large and Growing State and Local Workforce

The sheer number of state and local workers alerts us to their overall role in a productive economy. State and local governments employ more than 80 percent of the public civilian employees in the United States — over 15.2 million in 1990, as shown in Table I.3. State governments alone have a civilian workforce (about 4.5 million) greater than that of the federal government (about 3 million). Most of those who work for state and local govern-

Table I.3. State and Local Government Employment
(Full- and Part-Time), 1960–1990.

Type of government	Employees (1,000)			
	1960	1970	1980	1990
State	1,592	2,755	3,753	4,503
County	725	1,229	1,853	2,167
Municipalities	1,692	2,244	2,561	2,642
Townships[a]		330	394	418
School districts	1,919	3,316	4,270	4,950
Special districts	581[a]	275	484	585
Total	6,387[b]	10,149	13,315	15,263[c]
State and local employees per 10,000 population	356	495	585	614

Notes:
[a]Available data combined townships and special districts in the same category.
[b]The column does not add precisely to the total because counts for particular types of local government are based on subsamples.
[c]Because of rounding, the column does not add precisely to the total.
Source: U.S. Bureau of Commerce, 1991, p. 305; 1961, p. 423; U.S. Bureau of the Census, 1991a.

ments provide one of the most critical services — education. As of 1990, approximately 37 percent of all state and local employees worked in elementary and secondary schools; another 15 percent staffed institutions of higher education. Two other service areas also engage particularly large numbers of public servants. About 11 percent of state and local employees work for hospitals and other health agencies, and over 10 percent provide public safety (police, fire, corrections). Other state and local workers are scattered among a range of settings — libraries, public welfare agencies, airports, park departments, housing authorities, sewer service agencies, highway departments, financial administration units, public liquor stores, and more (U.S. Bureau of the Census, 1991a).

Not surprisingly, states vary considerably in their propensity to employ these workers, as shown in Table I.4. Alaska tops the list with close to 800 full-time-equivalent state and local employees per 10,000 citizens, nearly double the rate of Pennsylvania, which comes in last. Among the five most populous states, New York sets the pace with 640 full-time equivalents per 10,000 (fifth among all states); Texas comes next with 547 (twentieth), followed by Florida at 507 (thirty-eight), California at 476 (forty-seventh), and Pennsylvania at 411 (fiftieth). What accounts for this variation? The answer lies beyond the purview of this study, but several possibilities suggest themselves. The variation could spring from the tendencies of governments in some states to rely more on privatization, to offer less ambitious programs, or to do better in achieving efficiencies. It deserves note that the variation does not appear to stem from the proliferation of governments. Analyses performed by the commission staff failed to find a meaningful correlation between government density (see Table I.2) and full-time workers per capita.

Employment in state and local government is also distinguished by its growth. In a political culture featuring mistrust of centralized authority, one would expect the public workforce at the state and local levels to increase more rapidly than that of the national government. This is in fact the case. While the federal civilian workforce per 10,000 population declined over the last thirty years from 135 in 1960 to 125 in 1990, the trend was quite the opposite in state and local governments. As Table I.3 indicates, full- and part-time state and local employment rose from 356 per 10,000 population in 1960 to 614 in 1990, an increase of over 70 percent. Growth occurred in each decade, although the rate was far smaller in the 1980s (from 585 to 614). State governments expanded slightly more rapidly than their local counterparts.

Even the recession of the early 1990s failed to halt increases in the state and local workforce. Although employment did decline in many states, the period from July 1990 through April 1992 witnessed overall growth in the number of civil servants at the state and local levels (Gold and Ritchie, 1992). As of October 1991 there were 15.5 million full- and part-time state and local employees, an increase of about 200,000 over the previous year (U.S. Bureau of the Census, 1992b).

Table I.4. Full-Time-Equivalent State and
Local Employment per 10,000 Population by State, 1990.

State	Rank Order Employment per 10,000
1. Alaska	786
2. Wyoming	778
3. Montana	645
4. New Mexico	641
5. New York	640
6. Kansas	621
7. Nebraska	616
8. Iowa	593
9. Georgia	590
Mississippi	590
11. Oklahoma	578
12. Louisiana	569
13. Hawaii	566
14. Delaware	564
15. Alabama	563
16. Colorado	560
South Carolina	560
18. Idaho	558
19. North Dakota	548
20. Texas	547
21. Vermont	546
22. Virginia	545
23. South Dakota	540
24. New Jersey	538
25. Oregon	537
26. Minnesota	534
27. North Carolina	529
Entire U.S.	526
28. Maine	524
Washington	524
30. Tennessee	521
31. Maryland	519
32. Indiana	515
33. Kentucky	514
West Virginia	514
35. Arkansas	512
36. Wisconsin	511
37. Utah	510
38. Arizona	507
Florida	507
Nevada	507
41. Michigan	494
42. Illinois	491
43. Ohio	483
44. Massachusetts	480

Table I.4. Full-Time-Equivalent State and
Local Employment per 10,000 Population by State, 1990, Cont'd.

State	Rank Order Employment per 10,000
45. Missouri	479
46. Connecticut	477
47. California	476
48. Rhode Island	470
49. New Hampshire	446
50. Pennsylvania	411

Source: U.S. Bureau of the Census, 1991a.

The steady growth in the state and local workforce per capita has prompted some observers to suggest that these governments are shrink-proof and prone to bureaucratic bloat (Walters, 1992). Rigid civil service systems and too many bureaucratic layers allegedly feed this pathology. But hard evidence to assess these claims is in short supply. Determining the optimal number of employees that agencies need to perform efficiently and effectively remains a matter of guesstimation rather than calibration. Some public agencies no doubt employ more people than they need to function efficiently, but the growth patterns must be kept in perspective.

As a proportion of the nation's total workforce, for instance, state and local employment gains do not look so large. The number of these workers rose from 9.7 percent of the total workforce in 1960 to 12.9 percent in 1970 to 13.4 percent in 1980 but fell back to the 1970 level at just under 13 percent in 1990 (U.S. Department of Commerce, 1991). Furthermore, compared to major European nations, governments in the United States employ an appreciably lower percentage of the overall labor force (Rose, 1991).

Much of the increase in the number of public servants stems less from some bureaucratic proclivity to feather nests than a responsiveness to citizen demands for service and new policy initiatives. The 1960s and 1970s witnessed movement toward greater government activism in many spheres. Even when the federal government initiated the programs, it often asked the states to implement them (for example, Medicaid, environmental regulation).

Analysis of employment trends in the major policy sectors—higher education, public safety, health and hospitals, and elementary and secondary education—provides some clues about the wellsprings of growth. From 1970 to 1990, higher education was a pacesetter with full- and part-time employment combined increasing by 76 percent. In the 1980s alone, the increase was 22 percent. This expansion largely reflects significant growth in enrollments in public colleges and universities from 6.4 million in 1970 to 10.7 million in 1990—a 67 percent jump (U.S. Bureau of the Census, 1971, 1981, 1991a; U.S. Department of Education, 1991; *Chronicle of Higher Education,* 1992).

The number of full- and part-time public safety workers also soared by 73 percent from 1970 to 1990 and 31 percent during the 1980s. Growing public sentiment to get tough with criminals, especially those involved in drug-related offenses, did much to fuel this trend. The number of corrections personnel alone soared by over 100 percent in the 1980s (U.S. Bureau of the Census, 1971, 1981, 1991a).

Employment in state and local health and hospitals also increased markedly, though not at the rate of higher education and public safety. From 1970 to 1990, this category grew by 49 percent; during the 1980s, however, growth fell to 7 percent. These aggregate figures mask significant shifts under way in this sector. From 1980 to 1990 the number of public hospital employees slightly declined, a trend that partly reflects a 20 percent reduction in the supply of short-stay public hospitals during this period (long-term hospitals also trended downward). In contrast, state and local health employees outside the hospital context increased their numbers by roughly 40 percent during the 1980s (U.S. Bureau of the Census, 1971, 1981, 1991a; U.S. Public Health Service, 1992).

Among the four major sectors, state and local employment in elementary and secondary education increased the least from 1970 to 1990, growing by 42 percent; in the 1980s alone, a 14 percent increase occurred. Unlike higher education, this growth did not parallel rising enrollments. In fact, the number of students attending public schools declined by over 10 percent during the decade of the 1970s before leveling off in the 1980s. In part, the expansion of employees in state and local public schools represents an effort to improve education by reducing class size (U.S. Bureau of the Census, 1971, 1981, 1991a; U.S. Department of Commerce, 1991).

Data on the large and expanding numbers of state and local employees make up only the tip of the iceberg in depicting the human resource challenge. Many of those involved in implementing state and local programs work for private nonprofit or proprietary entities that receive government grants or contracts to deliver some service or produce some good. The revitalization of state and local public service also depends on the success of these private organizations in managing their personnel.

Analytic Spotlight

Part Two of this book wrestles with issues that go to the heart of human resource capitalism and the workforce challenge in state and local governments. In Chapter Two, Carolyn Ban and Norma Riccucci argue that civil service systems and labor relations structures have succeeded in accomplishing important ends but that these systems currently do much to frustrate the quest for efficiency and quality. They demonstrate that many jurisdictions have made progress in reforming these systems, at times working collaboratively with public employee unions. They suggest an incremental package of six reforms that could yield a quiet revolution in workforce management at the state and local levels.

In Chapter Three, James K. Conant and Dennis L. Dresang zero in on two states to illuminate issues involved in recruiting and retaining high-quality professionals and senior managers in state and local governments. They argue that at the state level this problem may be less acute than some analyses suggest. Jorge Chapa in Chapter Four drives home the point that the quest to sustain the "best and brightest" managers and professionals in state and local public service should not blind us to the indispensable role played by employees whose jobs do not require college degrees. These "non-professionals" tend to staff the front lines of public agencies. They come in constant contact with the public and often spell the difference in any effort to improve service quality.

The contribution of pay and diversity to the workforce challenge also receives attention in Part Two. Steven D. Gold and Sarah Ritchie under-score in Chapter Five that reform efforts will flounder unless state and local governments provide competitive compensation packages. Their analysis presents a mixed picture of state and local pay and benefits. For her part, Rita Mae Kelly in Chapter Six emphasizes that any effort to meet the work-force challenge must move beyond traditional equal employment opportu-nity and affirmative action to promote multicultural synergy.

Whatever their agreements and disagreements, the authors in Part Two of this book clearly signal that the workforce challenge in state and local governments will be at least as formidable as that present in the pri-vate sector. This stems in part from the country's cultural legacy, which has devalued work in government relative to that in business. It is also because policymakers have asked civil service systems to address a much broader range of values than productivity and quality—the hallmarks of human resource capitalism. As Gloria Harmon, executive officer of the California State Personnel Board, expressed to the commission at its Sacramento hear-ing, "The bottom line to most civil service reform efforts that I'm familiar with is increased management flexibility. At the same time there is a com-peting pressure from employees and their representatives to enhance indi-vidual rights and protections. Other interests may be represented by the pub-lic, advocate groups, elected representatives, and the courts. And, of course, this is all overlaid by the fiscal realities and constraints under which we are operating." Coping with this thicket of competing values and concerns to tackle the workforce challenge will not be easy. But the chapters in Part Two provide hope.

Special Management Challenges

While the workforce challenge goes to the heart of efforts to revitalize state and local public service, other important management issues also loom large. Part Three probes two of them — information technology and privatized im-plementation. These two challenges differ in many respects. The former in-volves the quest for a technical fix—to harness hardware in a way that enhances organizational intelligence. The latter deals with whether to invite private players to government's administrative table, where to seat them, and what etiquette to apply to them.

Unique in many ways, the two challenges also have much in common. Both have been the subject of hype and oversell. Vendors often promise government officials revolutionary advances if they only buy more computers and software. They artfully play on the desire of administrators to be on the cutting edge of managerial practice—to be progressive, innovative, and (how can one be against it) more informed. They at times distract attention from the risk of computer-generated information glut, or overload. In Chapter Seven, James L. Perry and Kenneth L. Kraemer present a more balanced appraisal of the ups and downs of this technology. In turn, proponents of privatization have often depicted the approach as a surefire recipe for trim, efficient government. This view resonates with the culturally embedded suspicion of government power and cynicism about the capabilities of public bureaucracies. Privatization becomes a way of having cake and eating it too. One can have government programs and businesslike administration rooted in competitive market mechanisms. As Donald F. Kettl vividly documents in Chapter Eight, this portrait of privatization often bears faint, if any, resemblance to actual practice.

For all the hype, both information technologies and privatized administration have in fact profoundly penetrated state and local governance, often with sanguine consequences. Perry and Kraemer show how new information technologies frequently open the door to enhanced performance. From serving back-office support functions, such as payroll and accounts payable, computer applications have increasingly enabled front-line workers to perform the agency's core mission more effectively and efficiently. Developments here are often the stuff of innovation awards. For instance, the city of Los Angeles adopted a system called Automated Traffic Surveillance and Control to help it cope with clogged streets and highways. The system features roadway sensors and closed-circuit television to smooth the flow of vehicles through some 1,000 intersections, primarily through modifications in signal timing.

Computers can also become an arrow in the quiver of those who seek to overcome inefficiencies fueled by fragmentation. Lynn Presley, clerk of the chancery court and Jackson County board of supervisors in Mississippi, told the commission of his efforts to bring disparate county agencies into a computer network. Recounting an episode with the library in Jackson County, he noted:

> They wanted to buy a complete, total information system just for the library. If they had been allowed to do that, they would next want a person to run it, a programmer, they would have to pay maintenance costs, etc. After a lengthy exercise with our library board, I finally convinced them, with a great deal of

resistance, it was the smart use of money to join our computer system and let them be a user. They have and will tell you today that they thanked me for being so hard-nosed and pushing them into doing that. It has saved them tremendously.

For his part, Kettl describes the pervasive use of private agents to deliver almost every conceivable public service and how, under some circumstances, the strategy makes good sense.

Finally, information technology and privatized administration are indelibly linked to the workforce challenge. Perry and Kraemer hammer this point home as they describe the human resource problems generated by the proliferation of computer technology and options for coping with them. Privatized administration may well present a thornier dilemma for those grappling with workforce issues — the possibility of a reinforcing negative cycle. Undoubtedly, the rigidities in current civil service and labor relations structures heighten the allure of contracting with private entities. By the same token, the very presence of the privatization option reduces the incentive for state and local officials to put civil service reform on the front burner. In turn, the enduring, overly restraining management systems may make privatized administration all the more enticing. This cycle is not, of course, inevitable. Many states and localities have gone a long way toward revitalizing their human resource systems, at times in cooperation with unions.

The Health Care Challenge

The challenges of leadership, workforce, technology, and privatized service delivery are played out in a spectrum of policy sectors. In this regard state and local governments have long been in the crucible of efforts to protect the public's health. Their programs extend well beyond medical care. In fact, one of their biggest contributions to health stems from their role in ensuring that we have safe drinking water, proper sanitation, and other qualities of a safe, healthful environment. Over the last quarter century, however, quandaries of medical and long-term care have preoccupied state and local officials.

States and localities draw on an array of policy tools to shape the general capacity, organization, and practices of the health care sector. States, for instance, invest heavily in the education of medical students and other health professionals. Under the banner of quality control, they license physicians and other health care workers to practice. Through certificate-of-need programs, they determine whether a hospital can add to its physical plant. These and related programs greatly affect the supply, nature, and geographic distribution of human resources, facilities, and equipment in this sector. In varying degrees, states also mandate certain practices by private health insurance companies; encourage, or even require, employers to provide health insurance to their workers; regulate what hospitals can charge for their services; and make it more or less possible for proprietary hospitals and health maintenance organizations to prosper. States and localities also function as providers and insurers of medical and nursing home care, directly delivering care through public hospitals, health departments, and clinics. Through Medicaid and other programs, states pay providers to serve certain categories of people.

A focus on the health care challenge recognizes that the flavor of efforts to revitalize state and local public service varies from one policy sector to the next. But the justification for this focus extends well beyond its ability to provide instructive case material. No other policy sector has been such a potent source of fiscal stress at the state and local levels. By siphoning off resources from other policy spheres, health care greatly complicates the revitalization effort throughout state and local government. Indeed, success in meeting the health care challenge may well be a necessary (although not sufficient) condition for more general revitalization.

As indicated earlier, health care is the main policy area in which the federal government may send out a rescue party to mitigate the fiscal stress of states and localities. The escalating costs, gross inefficiencies, and troubling inequities of the medical care system have spawned broad public dissatisfaction and a demand that the federal government do something. The Clinton administration has pledged to try. Federal initiatives to guarantee insurance for all, to promote greater efficiency, to absorb a greater share of the funding for these programs, and to reduce certain mandates would markedly reduce fiscal strains at the state and local levels. Achieving health care reform will not be easy, however. This policy sphere is dense with multiple, powerful interests, many of whom benefit from the inefficiencies of the current system. The country's fragmented political structure provides ample opportunities for them to block reform. The culturally embedded mistrust of government may also help these opponents of change. Ultimately, this array of forces may keep Washington from dispatching much of a rescue party at all, or the party sent out to help the states may be better symbolized by the Chihuahua than the Saint Bernard.

Whatever the rescue attempt, state and local agencies will continue to play a major role in the health care drama. Efforts to enhance the capacity and performance of these agencies can add much to the revitalization effort. The lessons of Medicaid administration comprise one part of the primer for those seeking to improve health care management. Gary Clarke, assistant secretary for Medicaid in Florida, described Medicaid at the commission's Tallahassee hearing as the "program we love to hate." "For state legislators, the Medicaid program costs way too much. For health care providers, it is known as the program that pays way too little. For recipients, it is a difficult program to get eligible for and even more difficult to find willing providers. For lawyers, particularly rural legal services advocates, this is the program that constantly tramples the constitutional rights of its recipients. And for federal officials, it is perceived as the untended gold mine of federal funds which spendthrift state administrators continually raid."

In Chapter Nine, Michael Sparer and Lawrence D. Brown persuasively argue that Medicaid ranks near the top of *any* list of programs posing the toughest managerial challenges for state and local officials. Their analysis of Medicaid in four states suggests that the program's managers often demonstrate considerable ingenuity and creativity in developing strategies for greater efficiency and effectiveness. It identifies critical resources available to these managers in this effort. But Sparer and Brown also provide a sobering reminder of the barriers to the effective use of these strategies. They question whether much revitalization can occur without basic reform of the country's medical care system.

As the chapter on Medicaid indicates, the health care challenge intertwines with the other challenges that concern this book. The ability of chief executives to provide creative leadership often depends on their skill in dealing with health care problems. For instance, governors persistently face the issue of how to balance funding for Medicaid with support for public health departments and clinics, many of which provide the immunizations, well-baby visits, and other services that can do so much to prevent major illness. The National Commission on the State and Local Public Service repeatedly heard warnings at its hearings that Medicaid had driven out concern for the public health safety net — health departments, public hospitals, and community health centers.

In this regard, Dr. Alton Cobb, state health officer in Mississippi, told the commission at its hearing in Jackson:

> I think personally that we rely too heavily on access to health services — the non-public health services — to address our major health status deficiencies such as infant mortality. There is a prevalent mindset that availability of health insurance or Medicaid will solve all of the problems — just give somebody a card and all the problems are solved. Giving everyone access to the traditional medical care system is not a panacea for all of these problems. . . . Frankly, public health has been hurt in this country in the last years by the growing costs of Medicaid . . . I think all of our governors . . . tend to be captured by Medicaid and it becomes the health care issue and they tend to kind of forget about basic public health and the . . . interventions that can very effectively make a difference.

In a similar vein, DeAnn Friedholm, special assistant for health and human services in Texas, warned at the commission's Austin hearing: "Medicaid is a payment mechanism — it is not a health care program." She likened the relationship between Medicaid and the public health safety net to one group speaking "Greek" and the other "French."

Or as Pamela Brier, chief executive officer of Bellevue Hospital in New York City, pointed out at the commission's Philadelphia hearing: "We take care of more patients with tuberculosis than any hospital in the country. It is really staggering. And the fact that tuberculosis is with us again is disgraceful. Somewhere along the line, this notion of taking care of the public health of people got away from us, and the money went into tertiary hospital care. This has got to be redressed now. This is a tall order of business, but I would say you cannot talk about health care reform without talking about that."

The health care challenge also intermingles with many of the workforce issues discussed in Part Two of this book. Commission hearings repeatedly featured testimony about problems safety net institutions have in recruiting and retaining health care personnel (for example, nurses, allied health professionals). The travails produced by uncompetitive salaries and burdensome civil service systems often surfaced.

Nowhere did the commission hear more vivid testimony about the link between a culturally diverse workforce and the provision of quality service than with respect to public health departments and hospitals. Dr. David Werdegar, director of the Office of Statewide Health Planning and Development in California, said in Sacramento that "different languages, different cultures, ways of seeking care, health beliefs" contributed to problems of sustaining adequate access to quality care. In similar fashion, Pamela Brier of Bellevue Hospital Center in New York City stressed at the commission's Philadelphia hearing: "In the public sector, we have a special opportunity, and I think a special responsibility, to try to make sure that the people who take care of our patients in some way, shape or form reflect the diversity of those patients. I cannot imagine providing appropriate psychiatric services to largely Spanish- and Chinese-speaking patients if you cannot speak the language. We don't do a good enough job of recruiting these kinds of people." The problem of recruiting and retaining a diverse workforce extends to the executive levels. In discussing difficulties in attracting people of color to the top levels of the New York hospital system, Brier noted: "The problem of accomplishing that from a senior management perspective is we don't pay competitive salaries. And frankly, for people of color . . . there are lots of other job opportunities to make more than $128,000 a year, which is what I make. Not that that is a slouchy salary, but the CEO's in the voluntary hospitals make four times that amount, and their senior people accordingly."

The health care challenge also involves issues of information technology and privatized service delivery. For instance, Brown and Sparer describe how Medicaid managers strive to bring greater efficiencies to their operations through improved computer and data systems. However, considerable wheel spinning often occurs because of communication barriers between information experts and Medicaid managers. Moreover, while advancements in information technology can obviously enhance performance, they can also — as with the latest innovations in diagnostic medical technology — fuel price increases. As for privatized delivery of public programs, no sector presents a richer range of variation than the health care arena. Medicaid as well as other state and local health programs depend heavily on medical providers, nursing homes, nonprofit agencies, and other private parties to deliver services. Effectively working this boundary between the public and private requires highly skilled government managers.

Conclusion

Nearly everyone agrees that over the last quarter century the capacity and representativeness of state and local governments increased markedly (U.S. Advisory Commission on Intergovernmental Relations, 1985). The courts and other forces dealt one blow after another to patronage; staffs became more professionalized; government became more open, and legislative districts more equitably apportioned. Many jurisdictions planned, developed, and implemented new systems for purchasing, accounting, financial reporting, and other functions. Reorganizations to strengthen executive leadership occurred. Computers and other innovations for managing information spread far and wide.

Without doubt, the National Commission on the State and Local Public Service has a "better" set of problems to work on than a comparable commission would have had in the 1960s. But the new problems are nonetheless serious. State and local governments frequently fail to achieve the desired level of performance. Nor are they as responsive and accountable as many policymakers and citizens would like.

No doubt efforts at revitalization face some fundamental trade-offs. The quests for efficiency and for democratic control often bump up against one another in awkward ways. Better performance does not always ensure greater citizen satisfaction. But even recognizing these and other tensions, governments can do better. The stakes are high. There is a growing sense that we can revive the American dream only by revitalizing an array of social institutions, including our many governments. The ability of the country to swim the streams of global competition in the twenty-first century requires high-performance systems in the public as well as the private sector.

To a marked degree, efforts at revitalization will depend on success in meeting the challenges of leadership, the workforce, information, privatized service delivery, and health care. The fundamental backdrop of structural fragmentation, a mistrustful political culture, and fiscal stress will complicate efforts to deal creatively with these challenges. But resignation and defeatism should be shunned. Progress can be made toward revitalization, and even toward modifying the backdrop of state and local governance. We will return to this theme in the concluding chapter.

Notes

1. Many special districts are virtually shells with no employees. But even in this form, their proliferation further fragments authority.
2. Note, however, that the available evidence (which is meager) does not

permit us to conclude that citizens in more complex, fragmented governmental settings are less satisfied with public services than those in more consolidated contexts. Nor can one assume marked differences in the degree to which citizens feel politically efficacious in the two kinds of settings, although consolidated structures may enjoy a slight advantage (Lyons and Lowery, 1989).

3. To illustrate further the complexities of public opinion, a slight change in the wording of the question yields a different conclusion. When asked which level of government gives them the *least* for their money, the federal government comes out worst (U.S. Advisory Commission on Intergovernmental Relations, 1992).

4. These figures slightly overstate the magnitude of Washington's retreat from helping localities. To some extent, Reagan administration block grants converted direct federal-local aid to federal-state aid, with states routinely funneling the federal dollars to local governments.

References

Anton, T. J. *American Federalism and Public Policy: How the System Works.* New York: Random House, 1989.

Bair, L. A. Letter to the Editor. *Governing,* Aug. 1992, *5*(8).

Beyle, T. L. "Governors." In V. Gray, H. Jacob, and R. B. Albritton (eds.), *Politics in the American States.* Glenview, Ill.: Scott, Foresman, 1990.

Bowman, A. O., and Kearney, R. C. *The Resurgence of the States.* Englewood Cliffs, N.J.: Prentice-Hall, 1986.

Bryce, J. *The American Commonwealth.* Vol. I. New York: Macmillan, 1891.

Chronicle of Higher Education, Aug. 26, 1992, *36*.

Council of State Governments. *The Book of the States, 1992–93.* Lexington, Ky.: Council of State Governments, 1992.

DeHoog, R. H., Lowery, D., and Lyons, W. E. "Citizen Satisfaction with Local Governance: A Test of Individual, Jurisdictional, and City Specific Explanations." *Journal of Politics,* 1990, *52*, 807–837.

DiIulio, J. J., Jr. "Managing a Barbed-Wire Bureaucracy: The Impossible Job of Corrections Commissioner." In E. C. Hargrove and J. C. Glidewell (eds.), *Impossible Jobs in Public Management.* Lawrence: University Press of Kansas, 1990.

Ehrenhalt, A. "The New City Manager Is: (1) Invisible, (2) Anonymous, (3) Non-political, (4) None of the Above." *Governing,* Sept. 1990, *3*, 41–46.

Ehrenhalt, A. "The Need for a Few Good Hacks." *Governing,* Aug. 1992, *5*, 6–7.

Fiorina, M. P. "Divided Government in the States." *PS,* 1991, *24*, 646–650.

Foster, G. D., and Snyder, S. K. "Public Attitudes Toward Government: Contradiction, Ambivalence, and the Dilemma of Response." In *Rebuilding the Public Sector: Task Force Reports.* Washington, D.C.: National Commission on the Public Service, 1989.

Gold, S. D. "Changes in State Government Finances in the 1980s." *National Tax Journal,* Mar. 1991, *44,* 1–19.

Gold, S. D. *The Federal Role in State Fiscal Stress.* Albany, N.Y.: Center for the Study of the States, 1992a.

Gold, S. D. *The State Budget Context: How Medicaid Fits In.* Albany, N.Y.: Center for the Study of the States, 1992b.

Gold, S. D., and Ritchie, S. "State-Local Employment Resists Recession." *State Fiscal Briefs.* Albany, N.Y.: Center for the Study of the States, 1992.

Gruber, J. E. *Controlling Bureaucracies.* Berkeley: University of California Press, 1987.

Gurwitt, R. "Cultures Clash as Old-Time Politics Confronts Button-Down Management." *Governing,* Apr. 1989, *2,* 42–48.

Haas, P. J., and Wright, D. S. "Administrative Turnover in State Government: A Research Note." *Administration and Society,* 1989a, *21,* 265–277.

Haas, P. J., and Wright, D. S. "Public Policy and Administrative Turnover in State Government: The Role of the Governor." *Policy Studies Journal,* 1989b, *17,* 788–803.

Harwood Group. *Citizens and Politics: A View from Main Street America.* New York: Kettering Foundation, 1991.

Heclo, H. *A Government of Strangers: Executive Politics in Washington.* Washington, D.C.: Brookings Institution, 1977.

Herbers, J. "17th-Century Counties Struggle to Cope with 20th-Century Problems." *Governing,* May 1989, *2,* 42–48.

International City/County Management Association. Correspondence to staff at Rockefeller Institute, Nov. 23, 1992.

Jeffery, B. R., Salant, T. J., and Boroshok, A. I. *County Government Structure.* Washington, D.C.: National Association of Counties, 1989.

Kaplan, M., and O'Brien, S. *The Governors and the New Federalism.* Boulder, Colo.: Westview, 1991.

Katz, D., Gutek, B. A., Kahn, R. L., and Barton, E. *Bureaucratic Encounters.* Ann Arbor, Mich.: Institute for Social Research, University of Michigan, 1975.

Katz, J. L. "The Slow Death of Political Patronage." *Governing,* Apr. 1991, *4,* 58–62.

Light, P. "Surviving Innovation: Thoughts on the Organizational Roots of Innovation and Change." Paper presented at the Innovations and Organization Conference, Minneapolis, Minnesota, Sept. 1992.

Lowery, D., Lyons, W. E., and DeHoog, R. H. "Institutionally Induced Attribution Errors." *American Politics Quarterly,* 1990, *18,* 169–196.

Lyons, W. E., and Lowery, D. "Governmental Fragmentation Versus Consolidation: Five Public-Choice Myths About How to Create Informed, Involved, and Happy Citizens." *Public Administration Review,* 1989, *49,* 533–543.

Marshall, R., and Tucker, M. *Thinking for a Living.* New York: Basic Books, 1992.

Miller, G. E., and Iscoe, I. "A State Mental Health Commissioner and the Politics of Mental Illness." In E. C. Hargrove and J. C. Glidewell (eds.), *Impossible Jobs in Public Management*. Lawrence: University Press of Kansas, 1990.

Morone, J. A. *The Democratic Wish*. New York: Basic Books, 1990.

Murphy, J. T. "The Paradox of State Government Reform." *The Public Interest*, 1981, *64*, 124–139.

Muste, C. "Public Opinion and Democratic Governance in the U.S. Federal System: The Dimensions of Public Attitudes Toward State and Local Government." Paper prepared for the National Commission on the State and Local Public Service, Albany, New York, 1992.

Nathan, R. P. "Federalism—The Great 'Composition.'" In A. King (ed.), *The New American Political System, Second Version*. Washington, D.C.: AEI Press, 1990.

National Commission on the Public Service (Volcker Commission). *Rebuilding the Public Service: Task Force Reports*. Washington, D.C.: National Commission on the Public Service, 1989.

Osborne, D., and Gaebler, T. *Reinventing Government*. Reading, Mass.: Addison-Wesley, 1992.

Parks, R. B. "Linking Objective and Subjective Measures of Performance." *Public Administration Review*, 1984, *44*, 118–127.

Rivlin, A. *Reviving the American Dream*. Washington, D.C.: Brookings Institution, 1992.

Rose, R. "Is American Public Policy Exceptional?" In B. E. Shafer (ed.), *Is America Different? A New Look at American Exceptionalism*. New York: Oxford University Press, 1991.

Sapolsky, H., Aisenberg, J., and Morone, J. A. "The Call to Rome and Other Obstacles to State-Level Innovation." *Public Administration Review*, 1987, *47*, 135–142.

Sigelman, L., and Dometrius, N. C. "Governors as Chief Administrators: The Linkage Between Formal Powers and Informal Influence." *American Politics Quarterly*, 1988, *16*, 157–170.

Thompson, F. J. *Classics of Public Personnel Policy*. Pacific Grove, Calif.: Brooks/Cole, 1991.

U.S. Advisory Commission on Intergovernmental Relations. *The Question of State Government Capability*. Washington, D.C.: U.S. Advisory Commission on Intergovernmental Relations, 1985.

U.S. Advisory Commission on Intergovernmental Relations. *Changing Public Attitudes on Governments and Taxes, 1991*. Washington, D.C.: U.S. Advisory Commission on Intergovernmental Relations, 1991a.

U.S. Advisory Commission on Intergovernmental Relations. *Significant Features of Fiscal Federalism*. Vol. 2. Washington, D.C.: U.S. Advisory Commission on Intergovernmental Relations, 1991b.

U.S. Advisory Commission on Intergovernmental Relations. *ACIR News: Negative Opinions of Federal Government Increase in 1992 ACIR Poll*. Washington, D.C.: U.S. Advisory Commission on Intergovernmental Relations, 1992.

U.S. Bureau of the Census. *Public Employment in 1970*. Series GE-70-1. Washington, D.C.: U.S. Government Printing Office, 1971.

U.S. Bureau of the Census. *Public Employment in 1980*. Series GE-80-1. Washington, D.C.: U.S. Government Printing Office, 1981.

U.S. Bureau of the Census. *Public Employment in 1990*. Series GE-90-1. Washington, D.C.: U.S. Government Printing Office, 1991a.

U.S. Bureau of the Census. *State Government Finances: 1990*. Series GE-90-3. Washington, D.C.: U.S. Government Printing Office, 1991b.

U.S. Bureau of the Census. *Preliminary Report, 1992 Census of Governments*. Washington, D.C.: U.S. Government Printing Office, 1992a.

U.S. Bureau of the Census. *Public Employment in 1991*. Series GE-91-1. Washington, D.C.: U.S. Government Printing Office, 1992b.

U.S. Department of the Commerce. *Statistical Abstract of the United States, 1961*. Washington, D.C.: U.S. Government Printing Office, 1961.

U.S. Department of Commerce. *Statistical Abstract of the United States, 1991*. Washington, D.C.: U.S. Government Printing Office, 1991.

U.S. Department of Education. *Digest of Education Statistics, 1991*. Washington, D.C.: U.S. Government Printing Office, 1991.

U.S. Public Health Service. *Health, United States, 1991*. Hyattsville, Md.: National Center for Health Statistics, 1992.

Walters, J. "The Shrink-Proof Bureaucracy." *Governing,* Mar. 1992, *5,* 33–38.

Webster's New Collegiate Dictionary. Springfield, Mass.: Merriam, 1976.

Wright, D. S., Yoo, J., and Cohen, J. "The Evolving Profile of State Administrators." *Journal of State Government,* 1991, *64,* 30–38.

Yankelovich, D. *Coming to Public Judgment*. Syracuse, N.Y.: Syracuse University Press, 1991.

PART ONE

The
Leadership
Challenge

ONE

The Governor as Leader:
Strengthening Public Service
Through Executive Leadership

Deborah D. Roberts

"We are the chief executives of state government. . . .
We lead our political parties, symbolize our state's best hopes
for itself, and oversee the management of agencies,
which usually are larger than any private industry in our state."
— *Governor Lamar Alexander*
Remarks to National Governors' Association, February 23, 1986

As we look to the next century, states and their local governments will need to strategically transform their institutions and workforces as they assume even more importance in the American intergovernmental system. But state and local elected leaders and employees have been preoccupied with the painful 1990s.

Wealthy California issues billions in IOUs to employees and creditors until a compromise budget is finally passed. State government temporarily shuts down as governor and legislators haggle over workers' compensation in Maine and imposing a state income tax in Connecticut. New Jersey Governor Florio seeks to cut 8,000 out of 78,000 positions. Virginia's Governor Wilder orders all state employees to take a 2 percent pay cut to close a $2.2 billion biennium budget shortfall. Even after a lean decade of cutbacks, Michigan lays off another 2,000 workers. Frustrated by civil service and union inflexibilities, governors look to reorganization to do more with less. But downsizing, rightsizing, consolidating, and decentralizing all take a toll on their public service institutions in terms of morale, talent, capability, and flexibility for the future.

The 1990s are not business as usual for either government or the private sector. The common call for leadership is trite, but true. This chapter will argue that the needed executive "leadership" has two essential and interrelated parts: leaders such as governors and a leadership system.

What may have worked in the past may not suffice to remain competitive with a fast-paced and demanding environment. Both corporate and public CEOs (chief executive officers) are urged to act as leaders and to develop "people power" by positively viewing their employees as their most important asset. For Warren Bennis and Bert Nanus (1985, p. 93), great leaders "inspire their followers to high levels of achievement by showing them how their work contributes to worthwhile ends. It is an emotional appeal to some of the most fundamental needs — the need to be important, to make a difference, to feel useful, to be part of a successful and worthwhile enterprise." This is a different message than past calls to top executives to focus their efforts primarily on implementing management reforms that institute greater central control and efficiency.

Governors can have a profound impact on their state's public service. But whether that influence is negative or positive, temporary or enduring, depends on how governors view their public service — as a challenge, opportunity, resource, or obstacle. Governors have long aspired to be leaders, but they usually tend to see the external, public arena of politics and policy as where they can best exercise leadership. This chapter argues that governors need to see themselves as internal leaders of the executive branch, including the civil service.

However, it is not enough to have a few dedicated, visionary, or inspiring individuals at the top. The other half of executive leadership is the executive leadership system, which supports democratically elected leaders in both effective governance and delivery of government services to the public. The executive leadership system encompasses not only governors, elected officials, and their appointed officials, but the system also reaches down to the level of careerists integrally linked with the creation and conduct of public policy.

This chapter will explore four options governors and legislatures can choose from for organizing and staffing executive leadership systems: direct gubernatorial appointments, senior executive services, contract manager systems, and "exempt" systems (where positions are outside civil service protection due to their policymaking involvement). These systems need to develop and retain individuals who meet the very highest standards of competence, responsiveness, and representativeness. The complexity of state government and the enormity of its public missions cannot tolerate incompetence, ignorance, inflexibility, or exclusion in important posts.

The Governor as Leader of the Executive Branch

Little resembling its colonial weak-governor forebears, the modern governorship has greatly enhanced powers in tenure, personnel, budgeting, organization, and management as means to better consolidate and rationalize state government. Even presidents express envy of gubernatorial powers such as the line-item veto.

But the picture is not all rosy. The formal and legal powers vested in the governor vary widely across states and will affect the legislature's willingness to concede even more powers over the state bureaucracy to the governor (Beyle, 1968). All governors contend with many limits on the exercise of executive leadership, such as the fragmentation of political control over the administrative apparatus, fixed budgets and constrained resources, too little time to have initiatives bear fruit within the two- or four-year political cycle, and a system (not people) designed to be structurally inefficient. Governors do not stand atop a neat hierarchy over which they have clear command. For example, with over 107,000 state employees, Texas still has no central agency responsible for personnel administration; instead, personnel matters are left to 200 individual agencies to decide.

It would be difficult for the president of a corporation to understand, much less cope with or master, the skills governors must practice. As Wallace Sayre put it, government and business are alike in all the *unimportant* respects. Certainly the private and public sectors' leadership needs and actions are not the same. For instance, in state government, governors contend with public management that focuses on process instead of outcomes, as well as bureaucratic inertia, personnel constraints, and inflexible management structures (Behn, 1986).

Today's job description for governor lists an intimidating number of executive roles: chief legislator, party leader, chief intergovernmental negotiator, opinion leader, chief administrator, and ceremonial head (Dye, 1981). The first four are external executive roles facing outward that are seen as active, vibrant, and requiring leadership. By contrast, the last two are internal executive roles, relating to the institution of the executive branch itself. These roles have a more passive flavor — the governor as limited to "head" or administrator. They seem bland descriptions that fall far short of expectations for executive leadership.

The Governor as Just Chief Administrator

With the burgeoning growth of state government, governors have been urged to increasingly focus on administrative and management matters, using tools such as budgeting, reorganization, decision systems, and central management controls. In the late 1970s, governors reported that the single greatest use of their time was devoted to "managing the state" (National Governors' Association, 1978). Far from an unavoidable obligation, governors like to propose management reforms. A 1982 survey conducted by the National Governors' Association, the Council of State Planning Agencies, and the Duke University Governors' Center reported that "the overwhelmingly favorite area for innovation for governors in 1982 was fiscal and administrative policy" (Cheek, 1983, p. 53).

Based on the Florida experience of the 1980s, Polivka and Osterholt argue for a very activist and influential governor-as-manager who orchestrates budgeting, comprehensive planning, policy priority process, executive office staff, and performance agreements with agencies all into one grand management score. Yet they concede that, in order to remain vital and responsive, agencies "must be allowed substantial autonomy, particularly in terms of day-to-day program management and the formulation of the many small- and medium-range program policies required for the agency to operate effectively" (Polivka and Osterholt, 1985, p. 101).

How well has this chief administrator model worked in reality? Are enhanced budget and appointive powers really enough to give governors qualitative control as chief administrator? Abney and Lauth think not. They see governors as having three administrative "hats": they are in charge of management, program development, and external relations. They measured governors' influence from the vantage point of 778 administrators in all fifty states. Only 38 percent of agency heads chose the governor as the most influential political actor affecting their agency decisions. Abney and Lauth conclude (1983, p. 48) that governors "are apparently personally incapable or disinclined to use those (administrative) powers that they do possess. Governors appear to be more inclined to seek to be managers rather than policy leaders." But is it the fault of the governors that they seek to be managers when this is precisely what they have been urged to do in order to have better control over state government?

Undoubtedly, a governor should have a conscious, active strategy for administration. As noted by Don Stone (1986, p. 2), if an individual governor does not actively welcome an administrative leadership role, he or she will inevitably deal "with political brush fires, inter-agency squabbles, program failures, disgruntled personnel, and the insatiable pressures of special interest groups." But the governor should not personally act as an administrator or manager. One reason is tactical, that micromanagement is costly and cannot be done well and even may be counterproductive to achieving the governor's substantive agenda. A more important reason is strategic — that it should not be done. The governor needs to play a qualitatively different and critical role as leader of the executive branch, not supermanager.

As for real-world tactics, Herzik argues, "At both the presidential and gubernatorial level, the expression of executive authority in day-to-day management appears to be, at best, a zero-sum game" (1985, p. 358). In a look at the strong-governor states of New York, New Jersey, and Massachusetts, Lockard, Schuck, Gleason, and Zimmerman conclude (1976, p. 98) that "the fallacy of much of the gubernatorial reform literature lay in a mistaken assumption that management was the key to success," with an implicit assumption that "policy objectives were a given to be manipulated through the right management techniques."

Lessons Drawn from the Experience of the Presidency

The model closest to the American governorship is not the private corporation leader; it is the presidency. The American governorship served as the model for the presidency. As James MacGregor Burns (1978, p. 385) notes, the constitutional founders, who had reason to be very leery of strong power figures, intended the president to "be a chief *executive* . . . but he was not to be an executive *leader*." Just as the governorship has changed dramatically, 200 plus years have revolutionized the presidency, so that the most pronounced demand today *is* for leadership.

Many of the enhanced presidential powers of the twentieth century were argued for as management tools that would be instrumental to strong, effective leadership. During the activist-government 1930s, the presidentially appointed Committee on Administrative Management, led by management expert Louis Brownlow, extolled the strong executive as an indispensable part to make democracy work. When added to by the 1949 Hoover Commission, the stress was on organization, management, and accountability. Two parts were the *accountability of* the executive (preferring the single executive to headless commission forms of governance) and *accountability to* the executive with a clear chain of command from the bottom to the top officer, the president, who would be assisted by top staff.

From the national level come many caveats on a president, as chief executive, flexing detail-oriented management muscle. For example, Thomas Cronin (1975, p. 10) argues: "Presidents have made a serious mistake, starting with Roosevelt, in asserting that they are the Chief Managers of the federal government." In reality, most have been "atrocious managers," who should have better spent their energies as chief political officer of the United States, making a few significant decisions. In *Organizing the Presidency,* Stephen Hess (1976) advises presidents to be wary of the operational trap of the day-to-day affairs of the bureaucracy.

In his work on *The Administrative Presidency,* Richard Nathan argues that an administrative strategy is instrumental and critical to accomplishing the political executive's policy objectives. He argues that "a political executive should be just what the name indicates—*political and executive.* The basic premise is that management tasks *can and should* be performed by partisans" (1983, p. 7). This is the very opposite of arguing that political leaders should *become* administrators. J. M. Burns also emphasizes the inherently political and individual nature of executive leaders (1978, pp. 371–372): "The distinguishing characteristics of executive leaders, in contrast with party or parliamentary leaders, are their lack of reliable political and institutional support, their dependence on bureaucratic resources such as staff and budget, and most of all their use of themselves—their own talent and character, prestige and popularity, in the clash of political interests and values."

Governors as Internal Leaders of Careerists

Today's governors are looked to for leadership vitality, direction, and vision. Sabato's pointed whimsy of *Goodbye to Good-Time Charlie* (1983) and the work of many others demonstrate that modern governors are far better equipped than their predecessors to be both savvy and assertive as public CEOs with the personal qualities critical to lead a successful large enterprise. Regina Brough, from Duke University's Governors' Center, stresses the personalized nature of the governorship: "(N)either a state's constitution nor its statutes tell the entire story. The effectiveness of the governor in identifying goals, focusing resources, getting results, and making them stick is also a function of the incumbent's personality and drive. Equally important are the public's expectations about what the governor should do and accomplish" (1986, p. 13).

Leadership as exercised by an individual is not interchangeable with formal authority. Governors Romer and Lamm of Colorado demonstrate that the governor can exercise substantial leadership initiative even under a formal weak-governor system that allows only twenty-six gubernatorial administrative appointments out of a 55,000 workforce and where referendum proposals to increase appointment powers have gone down to defeat twice in recent years. For instance, Governor Romer has used executive orders for sweeping human resource management changes.

Few gain from bureaucrat-bashing at the state level. Hostility to the public service can be especially demoralizing and can damage the institutional credibility of both the governor and the public service, as novice Evan Mecham showed in Arizona. A governor who has served as a state legislator (for example, Baliles of Virginia, Engler of Michigan) or in another statewide elected post (for example, Richards of Texas, Wilder of Virginia, Miller of Georgia, Edgar of Illinois) already knows many agency heads and may be able to artfully bend the bureaucratic process. These individuals make a sharp distinction between the system's limits and the abilities of the people working within the system.

During the 1970s, governors were the innovators who brought in private sector executives on blue-ribbon commissions to increase the efficiency of government operations. The Reagan administration copied the model with the federal Grace Commission. Starting in the 1980s, governors again led the way in looking for more cooperative public-private partnerships to advocating positive reforms like quality management and empowerment of employees. For instance, Governor Lawton Chiles of Florida, a strong supporter of public service, has focused on changing the system. One of his first acts in office was to charge his Governor's Commission for Government by the People, chaired by Orlando Mayor William Frederick, with reinventing government. Proponents of greater empowerment, the Frederick Commission (State of Florida, 1991, p. 4) likens existing state bureaucracies to dinosaurs: "They are too slow; they are too rigid; and they are too distant from the real problems our people experience in their day-to-day lives. They are filled with good people, but those people are tied up in rules and red tape." Realizing that the 130,000-strong civil service also would need to be transformed, Chiles charged a task force of state employees to make recommendations for its complete overhaul.

Like Lawton Chiles, governors need to have a career orientation to their state system, not just opinions about the capabilities and motivations of individual public servants they know personally. The Volcker Commission and the National Academy of Public Administration have shown that the systemic problem in the federal government is top leaders and political appointees who despise "bureaucrats" on principle but praise the "fine civil servants" they actually know. Governors first need to articulate a general philosophy as to how goals should be accomplished through the effective use of people. Second, governors should have respect and understanding of the expertise, knowledge, experience, and insight of people who have dedicated their careers to the state. Third, governors need a long-term perspective for good governance beyond their own term.

In the 1920s, the burgeoning leadership literature sought to define traits of outstanding leaders. Munson (1921) defined leadership as the creative and directive force of morale. In the field of public administration, Philip Selznick (1957) carefully distinguished administration ("organizational engineering," or what today we often call management) from leadership. The leader has four major responsibilities: defend institutional integrity, define institutional mission, gain institutional commitment, and order internal conflict. For a governor, all four needs involve reaching and motivating state employees as persons, rather than as technicians or functionaries.

Responsible and creative leadership is the equivalent to statesmanship, according to Selznick (1957). This is a role that should appeal to governors. We need to make a more attractive and compelling argument to governors that they should view their states' public service as human resources of immediate and strategic importance. Governors also need to hear this message from citizens. Public education first needs to reinforce that citizens expect and want a strong, viable public service workforce.

In conclusion, the governor is not the only major player in state government, but each governor can be highly influential in his or her effect on morale in state government. If the governor will not assume leadership, few other single individuals (not institutional bodies such as the legislature or courts) can fill the vacuum. The governor also sets the tone for his or her appointees who will direct and lead their state agencies. Governors can empower and urge their key appointees to adopt a similar positive philosophy.

Executive Leadership Systems:
Strategic Choices for Governors and Elected Leaders

"It is dangerous to let the effectiveness of any of our government institutions depend on a single individual," Abramson and Scanlon argue (1991,

p. 20). Indeed, no organization can rely only on "star" top leadership. A leadership system implies responsibility spread deep throughout government. Abramson and Scanlon articulate five dimensions needed for the complete organization: hierarchical leadership (downward management), subordinate leadership (upward management), collegial leadership (peer management), public leadership (environmental management), and process leadership (administrative management).

Beginning at the top with the governor and key agency appointees, the executive leadership system continues to reach down to the level of careerists integrally linked with the creation and conduct of public policy. Or as Abramson and Scanlon would define it, the careerist province of subordinate, collegial, and process leadership. This system must be viable before a governor can move to "penetrate" the bureaucracy to accomplish substantive policy priorities.

Civil service systems focus on how to staff state government at the mass rank-and-file levels. A state's civil service system, no matter how good, cannot give a governor or other elected leaders the system for filling the top posts in government. This is because civil service systems are set up mainly to deliver neutral competence that can be objectively determined and ascertained through standardized means.

The job criteria for posts at the very top of the state government hierarchy are different. They require savvy and responsive individuals who are highly competent *and* have the trust of their political superiors. Staffing these sensitive positions is akin to corporate headhunting. This government headhunting needs to be flexible and sophisticated, because what is being looked for are elusive and complex qualities, such as leadership and judgment, that cannot be measured by solely objective criteria. Today, the choice of the system for selection of top-level public officials has never been more important. The complexity of state government and the enormity of its public missions cannot tolerate either incompetence, ignorance, inflexibility, or exclusion in top posts.

In recent decades, governors have been making steady arguments for increased, selective personnel powers to fill these sensitive posts, and state legislatures have been granting their wishes. Staffing options are increasingly seen as means to augment elected leaders' personnel powers and substantive control over the administrative branch so that their policy objectives can be realized.

State elected leaders select and shape their state's executive leadership system through both statutory and executive action, choosing among four major options: direct gubernatorial appointments, senior executive services, contract manager systems, and "exempt" systems (where positions are outside civil service protection due to their policymaking involvement).

Option One: The Top Kingdom of Direct, Gubernatorial Appointees

Envisaged by our constitutional founders, this is the traditional and essential patronage power of elected leaders to choose individuals for subordinate posts to assist them in the discharge of their official duties. Of course, this is an option that is used in every state government. But how far can it be taken and still work effectively?

After a long, hard-fought campaign and the exhilaration of winning the election, the new governor has a few short months for the transition. Among the hundreds of strategy topics is one of people—how to most effectively use the appointment power. The press reports the tally of cabinet officer, agency head, and possibly deputy appointments. These are the political appointees to top policymaking and staff positions that are directly appointed by the governor. States do not vary widely in the number of direct full-time administrative appointments given to governors. For example, the Connecticut governor appoints fifty commissioners and deputies, the Arizona governor about one hundred, and the governor of Kentucky seventy-one. The number of cabinet officer and agency head appointments will depend on the degree of centralization, the structure of state government, and the sharing or division of appointment powers with other authorities such as statewide elected officers or policy boards, such as in Texas, Florida, and South Carolina. As at the national level, many of these posts may require legislative confirmation.

Although this may seem the easiest way to extend the governor's personnel powers, there are many arguments against radically expanding the numbers of direct, top-down appointments. Quality appointments are far more potent than the quantity of appointments.

First, there is the question of the governor's comfort with and knowledge about appointees. For "known quantity" candidates, the governor's recruiters have personal knowledge of the individual, his or her track record, and some assurance of loyalty to the governor's policies and priorities. Obviously, it is harder to realize this criterion as the scale escalates, and as the position in question is located further down in the hierarchy, far removed from the office of the governor. Since the bulk of these appointments are made in the early months of the transition, they must be filled before getting on with the governor's policy agenda.

Second, there are significant stakes at risk for a governor and his or her "policy and management team." Suppose that instead of a hundred posts, a governor had a thousand direct appointments for administrative posts. Or is it a thousand chances to make mistakes that might end up in scathing newspaper editorials? Sheer scale would mean the governor (or close staff) would have little quality control over those selected but would be blamed for a questionable appointment gone wrong, whether the cause be incompetence, conflict of interest, corruption, or impropriety.

Third, governors place a higher priority for their precious time on making an impact on their extensive citizen board and commission appointments, which can number in the thousands. The governor of New York has 8,000, and the governor of California makes 2,200 appointments to over 300 state councils and commissions. Ann Richards has made it her priority in Texas to raise ethical standards and to bring in women and minorities for her 4,000 appointments. It is a significant logistical victory to run a careful selection process that considers qualifications, geographic and interest group balance, professional and technical knowledge, and fair representation of women and minorities. Governors would overreach if they attempted to replicate this Herculean effort in direct staffing for the bureaucracy.

Fourth, radically increasing political appointments could endanger the credibility, legitimacy, and effectiveness of gubernatorial appointees within their agencies. As Ingraham and Ban (1988, p. 7) note, "tension exists between democratic theory, which values openness and change, and administrative theory which values predictability and stability." And to agency personnel, the living embodiment of that sometimes threatening openness and change are the new governor and political appointees. Careerists have their own high standards that they expect political appointees to meet. A longtime state government practitioner, himself technically a political appointee, refers to his commissioner of a large agency as a "1,000-day wonder"—somewhat suspect for not devoting a lifetime to his post or a specific state government, even though he has his doctorate in public administration and has extensive experience in the subject and technical fields most essential to his specific post. The popular adage is a "nine-day wonder." By comparison, 1,000 days of hard work and overtime, constantly dealing with crises and criticisms—in other words, the typical job of an agency head—should not qualify one as a flash-in-the-pan dilettante. But this attitude expresses careerists' skepticism about the qualifications, rightness, seriousness, or staying power of political appointees.

For these and many other reasons, substantially expanding the number of political appointees directly picked by the governor has not been pursued in many states. The opposite option is to create an upward extension of the civil service system, emphasizing careerism but paired with more explicit responsiveness to a select number of gubernatorial appointees.

Option Two: Senior Executive Services with Lofty Hopes But Modest Success

Twelve states have created senior executive services. Four states—California (1963), Minnesota (1969), Wisconsin (1973), and Oregon (1977)—preceded the Carter administration's 1978 formation of the national senior executive service. A spurt of states adopted senior executive services (SES) systems shortly after: Connecticut (1979), Florida (1980), Iowa (1980), Michigan (1980), Washington (1980), and Pennsylvania (1981). Both Tennessee and New Jersey passed their laws in 1986. A thirteenth state, Massachusetts, gives the governor the statutory authority to set up a career management service, but Governor Weld is the first to show any implementation interest.

First advocated by the Second Hoover Commission (1955) as part of much-needed reforms in national administration, SES systems were conceived as an elite corps of generalists to give responsive yet neutral competence to democratically elected and appointed superiors. However, the idea runs contrary to many American preferences. Thomas Jefferson's urgings that public officials be given "drudgery and subsistence only" underscores a belief that public office ought to involve sacrifice, not facilitate a permanent executive establishment inhabited by career administrators. Sherwood and Breyer (1987, p. 415) note that the idea runs against the "strong Jacksonian cast to American political ideology," and Mosher (1982) illustrates how American public administration has never been able to sell a British or continental elite model of attracting the best and brightest to permanent high-level posts in government.

"The Governor admires the British system of permanent under secretaries, but it doesn't require 475 people in Michigan state government to do this." This acerbic comment by a top Engler official (from a personal interview with the author) is typical of disillusionment with SES systems as a panacea for a host of ills. In theory, these elite manager corps promise exciting career, mobility, and leadership opportunities to entice top talent to join and remain in state government. Like civil service, SES systems spell out and coordinate formal personnel policy on entry, selection, work contracts, performance evaluation, salary, and individual rights. However, as Sherwood and Breyer (1987, p. 415) note, "Little in the 24-year history of executive personnel systems in the states suggests that they have come to occupy a highly significant role in the processes of governance."

Why such disappointment? The reasons are many. State SES systems contain too many lofty and contradictory goals that cannot all be satisfied. These contradictions revolve around incentives, membership quandaries, and diversity among the important players:

- Give careerists real leadership as close and trusted advisers of top policymakers, yet also give political appointees (who may be strangers to the system and its capabilities) more power to make careerists more vulnerable to their wishes.
- Using performance-driven evaluations, increase rewards (which in reality turn out to be meager or nonexistent), but also increase SES members' risks of being reassigned, demoted, or penalized by political superiors.
- Be a select elite, yet a big enough class to act as a powerful motivator for those lower in the ranks aspiring to move up; also defend elitism and excellence in a system geared to egalitarianism.
- Promise a highly mobile SES with transferable abilities, when most people have advanced through the ranks as either subject or technical specialists.
- Balance the mix between the careerist core and lateral entry by those with significant leadership and managerial talent, without degenerating into another patronage route.
- Identify, attract, retain, and enhance the skills of candidates, without substantial commitments of time, training, or development; but expect results immediately.

- Convince many audiences — governors, appointed agency heads, legislators, personnelists, interest groups, potential candidates, and the rank-
  and-file civil service — of the merits without offending or damaging any
  of their separate interests.

These are challenges that most SES systems have not surmounted. Existing systems are undergoing painful retrenchment and redirection, and few states appear willing to adopt new SES initiatives.

Option Three: Exempt from Civil Service Protection Those with Policy Involvement

In many states hundreds and even thousands of full-time positions are exempt from civil service protection because of their policymaking or confidential nature. They are sometimes referred to as "unclassifieds," but this chapter will use "exempt" as a generic term.

This personnel policymaking growth industry of the last twenty years has been a bonus for many governors. Since 1970, at least twenty-eight states have made significant policy changes regarding these positions, almost all in the direction of increasing the number of exempt top managers and policymaking careerists from civil service protection and giving governors and appointed administrative superiors more personnel discretion (Roberts, 1988). For instance, states that have either created new exempt classes or set up new means for determining exemptions from civil service protection based on "policymaking involvement" include Indiana, Kentucky, Minnesota, Mississippi, Missouri, New Jersey, North Carolina, North Dakota, Tennessee, Virginia, West Virginia, and Wisconsin. Policy involvement means determining or publicly advocating substantive program policy, providing legal counsel, or having a direct, confidential working relationship to a key official.

This option accelerated after 1979 when the federal government expanded exemptions under the Intergovernmental Personnel Act (IPA) regulations for merit system standards in personnel administration for state and local agencies receiving federal grants-in-aid (U.S. Office of Personnel Management, 1979). With few guidelines and reliance on states to certify their own compliance, state decision makers, often led by the governor's office, have been eagerly experimenting with extending the reach of executive leadership over more key agency personnel.

The main justification for extending the reach of executive leadership farther down the hierarchy has been to increase accountability. Many governors and their subordinate agency heads now have a greatly expanded "management team," analogous to that of a private CEO, which hopefully will promote policy confidentiality, coordination, loyalty, and greater responsiveness to the governor's initiatives. Although the total count of federal political appointees has grown as layers were added to the hierarchy to accommodate them (Heclo, 1977), at the state level, these changes have often transformed the character of existing layers at the heart of policy and operations.

These people fill the top line and staff agency level, often reporting directly to the agency head, with titles like deputy commissioner, division head, special assistant, or bureau chief. They are key players in agency policy and execution, and they are the contacts to and direct superiors of the civil service members. These people can be removed "at will" from their posts by their political superior without cause (although many retain rights to "fall back" to the civil service).

Although many governors share in common enhanced personnel powers over top agency positions, each governor inherits a system distinctive to his or her state—with intricacies that an outsider to state government would be hard pressed to understand. Some states have "civil service" systems in name only that actually function as spoils systems (such as Illinois during the 1980s), while many other states have legally exempt staff that are in many ways as professional and careerist in their orientation as protected civil servants. Because many of these provisions are so new, their occupants can be seen as "chameleons," and their behavior will reflect their state institutional environment, including executive leadership, civil service tradition, political influence, the legal rights of public employees, and agency factors (Roberts, 1991).

Confusing the matter are the many ways state policymakers decide two questions: "Who is a manager?" and "Which managers are involved in policymaking?" The extremes range from Colorado, where out of 5,000 employees considered to be managers only two dozen agency heads are exempt due to their policy roles, to the Massachusetts Weld administration's proposal that *every manager in state government* (some 3,500 people), even down to the supervisory level, should be considered as involved in policy and part of the administrative exempt team.

There is no consensus on where to draw the line between positions appropriate for appointees and those reserved for careerists. Seven states restrict noncivil service personnel to the top level only; fourteen states extend down to the second level; eighteen states extend to the third level, and three states go four or more levels down (Roberts, 1991). The impact of exempt positions also depends on the size, number, and functions of agencies.

State practices vary as to who decides what positions will be exempted from civil service coverage and what criteria will be used. The continuum ranges from informal, laissez-faire approaches to strict, constitutional provisions. For example, Michigan's 1964 constitution limits each department to a maximum of six political appointments. Some legislatures may either impose statutory caps on the total numbers of exempts, as North Carolina does; spell out exempts via individual authorizing bills for agencies, as do Minnesota, Vermont, and Washington; or even specify every specific position, as Maine does to limit its governor.

By contrast, other state legislatures are content to give either the governor or his appointee approval authority. For example, Maryland has no legal procedures, and the agency head has the discretion to exempt, subject to approval of the governor and personnel board. This may be one reason why Maryland ranked first among states in the governor's relative influence, as measured by 91 percent of agency administrators voting for the governor as the most influential actor (Abney and Lauth, 1983). Although the appointing authority may be the agency head or commission, an administration may first require clearance from the governor's office, especially before taking any adverse action. Some states use multiple criteria, for example, in West Virginia an agency head petitions the Civil Service Commission, which will exempt a position if it satisfies all three requirements of (1) being in charge of a major organizational unit, (2) reporting directly to a department head, and (3) setting policy for the department.

Governors have attracted public ire for going too far in expanding exempt positions, such as in Wisconsin, Georgia, and North Carolina. Once positions are exempted, how much discretion a governor has in filling positions varies. It may be easier to fire, but it is not necessarily easier to hire, since some states, such as Virginia and North Carolina, lay out qualification criteria for hiring, often as strict as those for civil service hires.

Option Four: Experimental Sunset and Contract Manager Systems

These can be used in addition to or as a substitute for exempt policymaking systems or senior executive services. Sunset management contracts were adopted by Massachusetts in 1981 for its top eight of twelve management levels and by Illinois's 1982 change to automatically fire middle managers whose four-year contracts are not renewed by agency officials (within-term firings must show cause). The Illinois term contracts have been upheld by the courts and seem to be working satisfactorily so far.

At first opposition centered around fears that the sunset provisions would be used categorically to clean house, with little regard for an individual's performance. According to an Illinois official, "firings have been used selectively for a very few who have become complacent." However, this experience only covers the period of the long-term Thompson administration and one same-party transition. Also, as the *Rutan* v. *Republican Party of Illinois* case makes apparent, during this time, there was a far more massive avenue for patronage under the governor's hiring freeze exceptions. As noted by Anne Freedman, an expert on Illinois political appointments, "They (the managers with term appointments) have been kept on because they are the ones who make government work" (personal interview).

Whether these contract managers will remain off limit from partisan abuse is not clear. The Supreme Court's *Rutan* ruling that promotion, transfer, recall, and hiring decisions for 60,000 nonpolicymaking executive branch employees cannot be decided on the basis of party affiliation and support will surely redirect partisan politics to expanding exempt policymaking posts.

The Edgar Illinois administration may convert many of these contract posts into the 4,000 exempt positions they want. But the Massachusetts Weld administration's consideration of widescale attempts not to renew contracts for managers suggests otherwise.

In Georgia, contract management services have been used to hire people (3,000 in the Department of Human Resources alone) for a variety of positions, for reasons such as having employees not fall under state liability coverage. The advocates of privatization have not taken time to consider political personnel abuses through contracting, as states consider extending contracting to sensitive manpower areas such as facility management teams for prisons, hospitals, or mental health treatment centers. Most of the emphasis has been on freedom from civil service coverage over personnel matters, not on how accountability over key managers exercising discretion will be achieved.

In the past, states have used noncompetitive classes for blue-collar trades where skill cannot be measured by standardized written tests. This class designation, apart from the civil service, can also be used for employing managers as New York state has done. In addition to about 2,500 exempt employees (of which 40 percent are in managerial positions), New York also has about 900 noncompetitive managers who were selected by elected or appointed officials using training and experience as selection criteria, thus avoiding the competitive appointment process. These employees serve a five-year term before being granted tenure. Although most are recruited from the career ranks, this option, plus the extensive use of exempt hirings, gives political appointees extensive hiring flexibility.

Ohio has a loophole for "administrative staff" (especially of boards and commissions) that allows agencies to pay much higher salaries (over $230,000 in one case) because *no* rules apply. However, the lack of rules and guidelines also means that the legal status and rights of these administrative staff are unclear. In Arkansas, tight pay compression led agency employers to "beat the system" by hiring under unclassified provisions so that salaries could stay competitive with the private sector. These well-meaning proemployee attempts have potential for later abuse against the employee.

Building Strong Executive Leadership Institutions

In summary, the preceding section showed how many governors and their subordinate agency heads now have more options to increase their personnel control over the career bureaucracy, especially at the critical levels of agency decision making and policy implementation.

But can these systems be used in the most productive way, assuring both policy flexibility, a high level of competence, and able leadership? With the exception of the SES systems, these novel systems are defined by *what they are not* (not protected civil service). What they all share is that they are evaders that can maneuver around the worst bureaucratic features of the civil service. Far less attention has been given to positively define *what they are and should be.*

Flexibility and change are the prime goals of these systems for staffing and decision-making relationships at the top levels of government. Still, a degree of stability is required for their implementation. The next section will look at forces of instability that need to be addressed, including the political arena, the dynamics of policy and agency considerations, and the inadequate understanding on the part of major actors as to how their state's executive leadership system is operating and ought to perform. These top personnel classes are often unstable because they are closely tied to the political cycle and process, with its most dramatic manifestation in a change-of-party gubernatorial transition or split-party control between the executive and the legislative branch.

Merit Versus Patronage Dynamics

Merit systems were first adopted in the late 1800s by some states, but many states remained under political machine control and a spoils system through the early to mid 1900s (Van Riper, 1958). Exempt management posts may be more political in states that have only recently achieved broad civil service coverage. For instance, on the inauguration day of Ohio Governor Celeste, over 2,500 pink slips went out to exempt employees. During the last two years of the Celeste administration, hundreds of these unclassified positions were "blanketed into" classified status. The Illinois Commission on the Future of the Public Service (1991, p. 5) has called on newly elected Governor Edgar to "pledge to end the era of excessive patronage at the state level," affecting 60,000 executive branch jobs.

A strong party apparatus and broad use of patronage employment will increase pressures to politicize exempt posts as political plums. A few states first clear candidates for unclassified management posts through state and county party offices. For example, Governor Cuomo's office has stopped seeking job recommendations from the New York Democratic Party (Katz, 1991). Party officials may have a significant say as to qualifications sought, the extent of turnover when administrations change, and to whom managers feel a debt of gratitude.

Administrative Transitions — Particularly Risky Times

New governors want to have an immediate impact, not just in making appointments but in preparing budget revisions and policy initiatives for the legislative session. Everyone is vulnerable and at risk during the transition. The governor's team needs to gear up quickly, master the running of government, and set the desired policy tone.

Many agencies suffer policy drift and paralysis during transition months, demoralizing even for the lowest employees. Little moves ahead as speculations abound as to the agency head's fate. Usually only after the decision has been made as to who the agency head will be can the fate of those at lower deputy and assistant levels be decided. Meanwhile all the exempt employees are in limbo about their fates.

An unusual case is the 1990 election of Republican William Weld in Massachusetts, where the cabinet turnover was 100 percent, many agency heads were not retained, and serious consideration is being given to letting go of many of the 2,500 middle managers. Most states' experience with senior executive services and exempt systems, however, at least so far, has been considerable retention across administrations at the exempt ranks. Yet there is considerable instability, at least temporarily, because for every person that will lose a position, scores imagine that they might.

Continuity seems to be the norm, but many states with expanded classes of policy-exempt employees are just beginning to experience either a change in party control or split party control. For example, Virginia has had two Democratic successors to the Robb administration that first exempted nearly 500 careerists; since then there has been remarkable continuity among agency heads. Even with no upheavals, Democratic legislative leaders have attempted to return these careerists to protected status.

On the other hand, the recent elections pose severe tests of executive leadership systems in Ohio, Wisconsin, Massachusetts, Florida, and Illinois. Beyond partisan wrangling, economic hard times will pose the major threat in the near future. In the face of unprecedented budget deficits, in states such as New Jersey, Michigan, Florida, Massachusetts, and Connecticut, governors' reorganization proposals for downsizing, rightsizing, consolidating, and decentralizing all will have substantial impact on their state's public service, with exempt positions at the middle and upper levels of hierarchies being especially vulnerable.

Dynamics of Policy and Agency

Obviously, not all agencies are alike in the eyes of governors. Some agencies are of greater political consequence and sensitivity, so that governors will want to be assured of some measure of meaningful control and influence. But how is this best achieved? Some states' specific statutory listings may exempt from civil service protection prison wardens and directors of mental health and mental retardation facilities. For instance, the genesis for Virginia's exempting of nearly 500 top careerists was Governor Robb's fury over a death row breakout from Mecklenburg prison. Other states will specifically require that these same posts be career protected, reasoning that ensuring neutral professionalism is the best insurance against politically embarrassing incidences.

States also take different stances toward the status of professions in strategic central management functions such as budgeting, personnel, accounting, policy analysis, and administration. For example, the Office of Management and Budget equivalent may be in the governor's office and therefore unclassified. This does not mean that all posts will turn over with a new administration. On the other hand, who occupies top sensitive posts sends symbolic and political messages. For example, the head of the Illinois Department of Central Management Services during the latter part of the Thompson administration has been appointed by Governor Edgar to be chairman of the state Republican Party.

If there is a high degree of political consensus over the "policy space" of what the agency policies should be and how they should be implemented, there will likely be more deference to the agency's jurisdiction and neutral careerists (Downs, 1967). Agencies with polarized interest groups and controversial policy implications, such as environment or transportation, can expect that their discretion will be tempered with closer involvement by higher officials.

Agency structural factors such as size and task complexity affect how deep political influence will want to penetrate. In highly technical functions, such as those found in health departments, people much farther down in the hierarchy may be active in policy decisions but given career protection because of their neutral, technical expertise. In agencies with tall hierarchies, fewer managers may have a direct confidential relationship with an agency head, and so fewer may be exempted. Tall hierarchies also have intervening deputy layers, some without line responsibilities, that work to insulate the operating levels of the bureau and division directors. The current call for downsizing and streamlining, which is usually accompanied by cutting out middle layers of managers and pseudomanagers (due to grade creep inflation), will have dramatic impacts on the agency and its corps of managers.

The respect for formal authority and subordination to superiors' orders also affects people's behavior. The paramilitary state police will comply voluntarily with superiors' authority, but in agencies with high turnover and devotion to occupation or profession, agency heads may wish for more ways to exact ready cooperation with their dictates.

Symbolic Leadership and Individual Agency Heads

During the last ten years, the leadership field has turned to focusing on leaders as shapers of their organizations' cultures and values. According to Edgar Schein (1985), symbolic leadership can embed and transmit culture, by means such as creating systems for reward, promotion, status, retirement, and excommunication that are consistent with the leader's values. A qualitative change can come to the bureaucracy, if these exempt policymakers and managers (including career executive services) come to be seen as the positive role models that other employees admire and wish to emulate.

Although a governor can set the symbolic tone, the leader who is closest — the agency head — will have the most day-to-day influence. It is up to the individual agency head to fire, retain, trust, delegate, and set the tone for the work relationship. Much depends on quality appointees who are capable, competent, activist, and knowledgeable about state government. Agency heads who have risen up through the ranks will more likely feel kinship with civil servants, sharing their career and programmatic orientation. "In-and-outer" political appointees serving in a number of posts across administrations or coming from the private sector are more likely to identify primarily as members of the governor's team. Compared to the federal government, political appointees in state government are less likely to be novices, since there is significant carryover across administrations as high as agency head, and more are professionals making a career in politically appointed posts.

Legitimizing Executive Leadership Systems for Employers, Participants, and Future Candidates

Buffeted from without by political winds, these systems are also plagued from inside the executive branch by major actors' lack of system understanding, support, continuity, and confidence. There are a number of critical actors, such as the governor, legislature, and the courts, but the basic three are (1) the employers of exempt and SES employees (usually agency heads), (2) the incumbents of these posts, and (3) the pool of prospective candidates. The major obstacle is that these systems need to be better designed personnel institutions that command respect and perform in a consistent fashion.

States have no equivalent of the city manager system. City managers have contracts and can be (and often are) fired or encouraged to leave by their governing councils. Although it may look like an unstable and risky career path for individual city managers, it does seem to be a stable and workable system, even if it lacks theoretical purity (Sherwood, 1990; Stillman, 1980). The city manager system (and similar county and town equivalents) works for three basic reasons. One, while a city council may become very negative about their last city manager, they still believe in the system principles and hire another manager. Two, leaving a jurisdiction does not prevent the city manager from finding a new post elsewhere—it is a mobile profession without an oversupply of good, tested practitioners. Three, prospective city managers know about the risks up front, can get valuable work experience in these systems before stepping up to their first post as city manager (often working as an assistant city manager or department head), and consciously choose a career as a city manager.

These three conditions—employers who are committed to the system, job mobility to balance employment risks, and a training ground for potential practitioners to get experience and credibility—are often missing at the state level for exempt systems, as well as for senior executive services and other personnel options.

The agency head "employer" may be both new to the system and temporary if administrations turn over; thus the employer may be ill informed and suspicious of an SES or exempt system. Political appointees therefore need experience and education about the state's executive leadership system. This is another reason for not significantly expanding the number of political appointees, thereby diluting their quality overall.

States need to enhance mobility across state government. Mobility is often limited in state government, especially across functional areas, because mobility is not expected or appreciated. Most state careerists are not hired as supergeneralists, not because they lack the capability but because most states do not have the breeding grounds to allow such talents to flourish and to recognize and reward them. Most careerists are promoted because of technical and subject specialization.

Even if a person really is a supermanager, it may not lead to job offers and promotions across government. Other agencies (which tend to be territorial and insular) may not be convinced that such skills are valuable or that the individual could still be as effective in a new setting. Another barrier is limited lateral entry into state government service, restricting the pool of candidates to people who came in at lower levels. To break down these barriers, professional training and executive development programs can both impart skills and create networks across agency lines. Finally, cross-state mobility is even more restricted, with exceptions of the rare individual or in highly specialized technical fields like mental health or corrections where there is a nationwide professional network. Mobility is also discouraged by compensation and pension packages.

States need to define new professional roles so that participants in these executive leadership systems share an understanding of their role and careers as connected to the system. As Marvick (1954, p. 24) notes, "Career orientation . . . determines what personal interests will preoccupy administrative and policymaking employees who work in the setting of the highest bureaucracy." In other words, these people need to see themselves as executive leadership system professionals. Much of their specialty is based on their extensive knowledge of their state and its government and practitioners. They cannot see themselves as technical-area professionals (managers, economists, psychologists, or whatever) who just happen to work at the top levels of state government.

Like their political appointee superiors, these careerists need to come up with a positive career orientation that acknowledges their responsiveness, flexibility, and accountability to political leaders as the basic premise of what it means to be a "professional careerist" involved in policymaking. One impediment is the traditional notion of a politics-administration dichotomy that "good public servants" must be strictly neutral and must stay far away from politics. But politics is an inevitable part of policymaking.

State governments can invest in these executive leadership systems to give them legitimacy and to increase their likelihood of success. For example, a state can sponsor professional peer networking and education, such as through improved executive development and training offerings. By encouraging professional networking and communications across agencies, the state encourages its most promising people to stay for interesting and varied careers in state government, and it also improves its capacity for problem solving and cooperation.

Stable Government of Acquaintances

The Volcker Commission wrestled with the many negative impacts on the public service brought about by Washington's "government of strangers" at the appointee ranks (Heclo, 1977), but many states are shielded from this problem of transient executive leadership. Many people in policy posts in state government are seasoned veterans: governors themselves, political appointees who serve more than once, career executive services' participants, exempt officials with solid professional reputations, and civil servants filling tours of duty in policymaking slots.

State government is better described as "government by acquaintances" at the highest levels. Many governors themselves qualify for the label of "in-and-arounders." Although some governorships have been won by true outsiders who have never held political office, most successful gubernatorial candidates benefit from some kind of insider reputations — as state legislators, local mayors, statewide elected officers (such as lieutenant governor, attorney general, treasurer), or even state-appointed officeholders. Being labeled an insider first requires an intimate knowledge of state government. For example, the 1991 transitions of former senators, now governors Lawton Chiles (Florida), Pete Wilson (California), and Lowell Weicker (Connecticut), who all brought in appointees from their Washington networks and staffs, have many veteran state government officials guessing where the governors' interests lie, and transitions were slow.

Many political appointees have *horizontal career paths* with more than one term of state experience during their lives. Unlike their Washington counterparts, they remain close to home while serving, and their posts more closely relate to the remainder of their careers, often revolving around the state halls of power. For example, Michigan Governor Engler (R) has brought in many people who served in the earlier Milliken and Romney administrations, as well as moving appointees from the Blanchard administration up and around. In contrast, Governor Blanchard (D), who had been a congressman, brought in far more outsiders for his top team.

In New York, which has had only one party change turnover in the last thirty years (Hugh Carey's defeat of Malcolm Wilson), many people have had whole careers moving among posts within government, across agencies, and across the executive and legislative branches (Benjamin and Hurd, 1985). Such networks of friends and acquaintances undoubtedly make governments more intimate and workable than the sheer size of government and employee ranks (over 288,000) would indicate. Similarly, many of the same people have moved in administrative and legislative staff circles in Virginia, going back not only three Democratic terms but to the last Republican term of Governor John Dalton.

Governors and the best interest of their states can also be served by networks of "known quantity" proven professionals within the state bureaucracy who pursue *vertical career paths*. These can be quality exempt and senior executive service participants that have credibility among all parties for getting the work done. An added solution that many states have come up with for how to increase both flexibility and capability is to distinguish between the position, which is flexible, and the incumbents' rights, which are firm. Just because a new agency head prefers another person for an exempt policymaking post does not mean the previous incumbent will be out on the streets. The system preserves choice for top decision makers and expands mobility choices for people who intend to devote their careers to state government.

Frederick Mosher (1982) points out that we need to connect politics and administration, not to artificially segregate their practitioners. There need to be close working relationships between political appointees and careerists. His observation for the federal government also holds true for many state governments — the crucial presence of mixed echelons with traits of both careerists and appointees. But to have such an interweaving, people, not positions, need to move. Careerists are often encouraged to take assignments among political appointees. In such positions they can offer advice, stability, and continuity — especially at the later stages of an administration when few high-quality outsiders can be enticed to serve.

An important factor to allow exempt systems to flourish with positive benefits to both superiors and participants is a tradition of mobility between appointed posts and the career civil service, which was encouraged by the 1979 IPA federal regulations. One such option is for careerists to take leaves of absence in order to fill exempt policymaking positions, which will be encouraged by generous reemployment rights. For example, a personnel official noted that her husband is a civil servant, but the last five jobs he has held are exempt policy posts. This anecdote illustrates the point that many career professionals in government "trade" posts both up and across the hierarchy.

Many states have reemployment rights (the right to return to their civil service job when they leave an appointed post) but with limitations, such as if a slot is open (Kentucky, Washington, Utah), if their old position still exists (Minnesota), if the careerist remains in the same job (Maine), or if the careerist has so many years of state service (Rhode Island, Maryland, North Carolina).

California, Connecticut, Michigan, New Jersey, New York, Pennsylvania, Kansas, and Wisconsin have guaranteed full reemployment rights, even to the point of bumping those with less seniority or creating a position to accommodate a manager who is removed from an exempt post. Layoffs lead to ripple effects; for example, a New York exempt manager during 1990 bumped down to the job that he had held a dozen years before, pushing out the incumbent who had held the job "temporarily" for over ten years.

In Montana, New Hampshire, and Virginia, employees have no reemployment rights once in exempt posts. This rigid glass ceiling may keep valuable people from ever taking a promotion to a higher agency post, since they cannot afford the risks. In states where exempts have no reemployment rights, as a fallback practice, many exempts that are not retained by a new agency head will have the experience and technical qualifications to find new jobs either in exempt or lower civil service openings, presuming favorable economic conditions. Most states converting positions from a career to exempt status will "grandfather in" the incumbent or allow generous reemployment rights.

A minority of states (Texas, Alabama, Alaska, Utah, and South Dakota) still maintain rigid divides between political appointees and careerists who might have much to offer. This artificial glass ceiling both limits potential career advancement for the best careerists and increases the gulf between appointees and the permanent bureaucracy.

Conclusion

Just as the leadership literature has matured from an early focus on single, great leaders to stress leadership as a relationship and function that can be performed by many throughout an enterprise (Bass, 1981), our thinking about executive leadership in state government also needs to deepen. A general with neither field commanders nor troops cannot succeed. No governor can single-handedly "lead" his or her state without support from others in the executive branch who are committed to public service and share a vision of what their state can aspire to be, both now and in the future.

Executive leadership is at its core a manpower issue. Each state needs to fashion a workable executive leadership system to support top elected officials to achieve the American ideal: a democracy that works and that delivers quality services. The executive leadership system sits atop the operating levels of state government and cuts across the institutional boundaries of agencies that focus more narrowly on "their" functional and policy areas.

The fifty states are indeed laboratories of democracy. Each builds its own system, civil service, and merit traditions. Some may be exemplary, while others are in crisis. Unlike the federal government, which, despite all its size and sprawl, can be defined as one system of public service, fifty different state systems must be considered. In general we do not see the crisis of confidence over how top government operates as was detailed by the Volcker Commission. However, many of the state executive leadership systems have been significantly modified and are still experimental. There is still room for considerable improvement and probably more optimistic chances for their progress, *if* elected leadership makes positive reform a priority.

We need to be justifiably concerned with the capacity and qualifications of individuals in top posts of government, but a larger concern is the capacity of the system (under which these individuals work) to attract, recognize, teach, groom, and reward a wide pool of quality candidates. Many rising incumbents now view these systems — exempt, unclassified, contract, and senior executive services — not as a distinct general career but as just the means one must put up with to get a challenging job or one's own continued employment. They do not share esprit de corps pride in belonging to an executive system that consciously and consistently provides leadership for their state.

Although many states have time-honored practices of government of acquaintance, so that there are many seasoned veterans serving within state government, there are also inherent risks that could undermine what many state officials now may take for granted. Because state governments may have benefited from "in-and-arounders," are these now becoming old-timers? How many governors today inspire legions of bright young people to come into government for the challenge as Nelson Rockefeller did in New York? Will future governors and other state leaders be able to depend on new generations of talent with equivalent career paths and opportunities to contribute to their public service?

References

Aberbach, J. D., Putnam, R. D., and Rockman, B. A. *Bureaucrats and Politicians in Western Democracies.* Cambridge, Mass.: Harvard University Press, 1981.

Abney, G., and Lauth, T. P. "The Governor as Chief Administrator." *Public Administration Review,* 1983, *1,* 40–49.

Abney, G., and Lauth, T. P. *The Politics of State and City Administration.* Albany: State University of New York Press, 1986.

Abramson, M. A., and Scanlon, J. W. "The Five Dimensions of Leadership: Organizations Cannot Depend Only on 'Star' Leadership." *Government Executive,* July 1991, 20–25.

Adams, J. D. *Transforming Leadership: From Vision to Results.* Alexandria, Va.: Miles River Press, 1986.

Alexander, L. Remarks from work session "The Governor as CEO." Made at the annual meeting of the National Governors' Association, Washington, D.C., Feb. 23, 1986.

Appleby, P. *Big Democracy.* New York: Knopf, 1945.

Appleby, P. *Morality and Administration in Democratic Government.* Baton Rouge: Louisiana State University Press, 1952.

Ban, C., and Riccucci, N. (eds.). *Public Personnel Management: Current Concerns — Future Challenges.* New York: Longman, 1991.

Bass, B. M. *Stogdill's Handbook of Leadership: A Survey of Theory and Research.* (2nd ed.) New York: Free Press, 1981.

Bell, C., and Price, C. *California Government Today: Politics of Reform.* Homewood, Ill.: Dorsey, 1980.

Behn, R. "A Curmudgeon's View of Public Administration: Routine Tasks, Performance, and Innovation." Paper presented at the national conference of the American Society for Public Administration, Anaheim, Calif., Apr. 14, 1986.

Benjamin, G., and Hurd, T. N. (eds.). *Making Experience Count: Managing*

Modern New York in the Carey Era. Albany, N.Y.: Nelson A. Rockefeller Institute of Government, 1985.

Bennis, W. G. *Why Leaders Can't Lead: The Unconscious Conspiracy Continues.* San Francisco: Jossey-Bass, 1989.

Bennis, W. G., and Nanus, B. *Leaders: Strategies for Taking Charge.* New York: HarperCollins, 1985.

Beyle, T. L. "The Governor's Formal Powers: A View from the Governor's Chair." *Public Administration Review,* 1968, *19,* 540–545.

Beyle, T. L. "The Governor's Power of Organization." *State Government,* 1982, *55*(3), 79–87.

Blair, D. K. "The Gubernatorial Appointment Power: Too Much of a Good Thing?" *State Government,* 1982, *55*(3), 88–92.

Bodman, L., and Garry, D. B. "Innovations in State Cabinet Systems." *State Government,* 1982, *55*(3), 93–98.

Brough, Regina K. "The Powers of the Gubernatorial CEO: Variations Among the States." *Journal of State Government,* July–Aug. 1986, *59,* 58–63.

Brough, R. K. "The Governors Center — Exploring a New Role for Governors." *Popular Government,* Fall 1987, *53,* 32–37.

Buchanan, P. C. (ed.). *An Approach to Executive Development in Government: The Federal Executive Experience.* Washington, D.C.: National Academy of Public Administration, 1973.

Burns, J. M. *Leadership.* New York: HarperCollins, 1978.

Cheek, S. K. "Gubernatorial Innovations." *State Government,* 1983, *56*(2), 53–57.

Cleveland, H. *The Future Executive: A Guide for Tomorrow's Managers.* New York: HarperCollins, 1972.

Cohen, S. *The Effective Public Manager: Achieving Success in Government.* San Francisco: Jossey-Bass, 1988.

Commission on the Organization of the Executive Branch of the Government (Second Hoover Commission). *Task Force Report on Personnel and Civil Service.* Washington, D.C.: U.S. Government Printing Office, 1955.

Commonwealth of Virginia. *Project Streamline: 1990 Interim Report.* Richmond, Va.: Office of the Governor, 1990.

Cronin, T. E. *The State of the Presidency.* Boston: Little, Brown, 1975.

Downs, A. *Inside Bureaucracy.* Boston: Little, Brown, 1967.

Dye, T. R. *Politics in States and Communities.* (4th ed.) Englewood Cliffs, N.J.: Prentice-Hall, 1981.

Freedman, A. "Doing Battle with the Patronage Army: Politics, Courts, and Personnel Administration in Chicago." *Public Administration Review,* 1988, *5,* 847–859.

Gardner, J. W. *On Leadership.* New York: Free Press, 1990.

Heclo, H. *A Government of Strangers: Executive Politics in Washington.* Washington, D.C.: Brookings Institution, 1977.

Herzik, E. B. "The President, Governors and Mayors: A Framework for Comparative Analysis." *Presidential Studies Quarterly,* Spring 1985, *15,* 353–376.

Hess, S. *Organizing the Presidency*. Washington, D.C.: Brookings Institution, 1976.

Huddleston, M. W. "Background Paper." In Twentieth Century Fund Task Force on the Senior Executive Service, *The Government's Managers*. New York: Priority Press, 1987.

Illinois Commission on the Future of the Public Service. "Excellence in Public Service: Illinois' Challenge for the '90s." ICFPS preliminary report. Chicago: Chicago Community Trust/Government Assistance Project, Jan. 1991, 1–7.

Ingraham, P. W., and Ban, C. "Politics and Merit: Can They Meet in a Public Service Model?" *Review of Public Personnel Administration*, 1988, *8*(2), 7–19.

Kallenbach, J. E. *The American Chief Executive: The Presidency and the Governorship*. New York: HarperCollins, 1966.

Katz, J. "The Slow Death of Political Patronage." *Governing*, Apr. 1991, *4*, 58–62.

Light, P. C. "When Worlds Collide: The Political-Career Nexus." In G. C. Mackenzie (ed.), *The In-and-Outers*. Baltimore, Md.: Johns Hopkins University Press, 1987.

Lockard, D., Schuck, V., Gleason, E. J., and Zimmerman, J. "A Mini-Symposium on the Strong Governorship: Status and Problems." *Public Administration Review*, 1976, *1*, 90–98.

Marvick, D. *Career Perspectives in a Bureaucratic Setting*. Ann Arbor: University of Michigan Press, 1954.

Mosher, F. *Democracy and the Public Service*. (2nd ed.) New York: Oxford University Press, 1982.

Munson, E. L. *The Management of Men*. New York: Holt, Rinehart & Winston, 1921.

Nathan, R. P. *The Administrative Presidency*. New York: Wiley, 1983.

National Governors' Association. *Governing the American States*. Washington, D.C.: National Governors' Association Center for Policy Research, 1978.

Newland, C. A. (ed.). *Professional Public Executives*. Washington, D.C.: American Society for Public Administration, 1980.

Osborne, D. *Laboratories of Democracy: A New Breed of Governor Creates Models for National Growth*. Cambridge, Mass.: Harvard Business School Press, 1990a.

Osborne, D. "Ten Ways to Turn D.C. Around." *Washington Post Sunday Magazine*, Dec. 9, 1990b, 19–43.

Polivka, L., and Osterholt, B. J. "The Governor as Manager: Agency Autonomy and Accountability." *Public Budgeting and Finance*, Winter 1985, 91–104.

Roberts, D. D. "State Civil Servants Who Serve at the Will and Pleasure of Political Superiors." *University of Virginia News Letter*, 1987, *63*(7). Charlottesville, Va.: Center for Public Service.

Roberts, D. D. "A New Breed of Public Executive: Top Level Exempt Managers in State Government." *Review of Public Personnel Administration*, 1988, *8*(2), 20-36.

Roberts, D. D. "A Personnel Chameleon Blending the Political Appointee and Careerist Traditions: Exempt Managers in State Government." In C. Ban and N. Riccucci (eds.), *Public Personnel Management: Current Concerns — Future Challenges*. New York: Longman, 1991.

Rohr, J. *Ethics for Bureaucrats*. New York: Dekker, 1978.

Rutan v. *Republican Party of Illinois*, 58 Law Week 4872, 1990.

Sabato, L. *Goodbye to Good-Time Charlie: The American Governorship Transformed*. Washington, D.C.: Congressional Quarterly, 1983.

Schein, E. H. *Organizational Culture and Leadership*. San Francisco: Jossey-Bass, 1985.

Selznick, P. *Leadership in Administration*. Evanston, Ill.: Row, HarperCollins, 1957.

Sensenbrenner, J. "Quality Comes to City Hall." *Harvard Business Review*, Mar.-Apr. 1991, *69*, 64-75.

Sherwood, F. P. "The Sad Decline of Florida's Civil Service: An Old Problem for a New Governor." *Governing Florida*, Winter 1990, 8-11.

Sherwood, F. P., and Breyer, L. J. "Executive Personnel Systems in the States." *Public Administration Review*, 1987, *47*(5), 410-416.

State of Florida. "Governor's Commission for Government by the People: A Prescription for Florida's Future." 1991, 1, 4.

Stillman, R. J. II. "The City Manager: Professional Helping Hand, or Political Hired Hand?" In C. A. Newland (ed.), *Professional Public Executives*. Washington, D.C.: American Society for Public Administration, 1980.

Stone, D. C. "Orchestrating Governors' Executive Management." *State Government*, 1985, *58*(1), 33-39.

Stone, D. C. *The Governor's Management Improvement Program: How to Do It*. Coalition to Improve Management in State and Local Government. Pittsburgh, Pa.: School of Urban and Public Affairs, Carnegie-Mellon University, 1986.

Sylvia, R. "Merit Reform as an Instrument of Executive Power." *American Review of Public Administration*, Summer-Fall 1983, *17*, 115-120.

U.S. Office of Personnel Management. "Intergovernmental Personnel Act Programs. Standards for a Merit System of Personnel Administration." *Federal Register*, Feb. 16, 1979, 44:10238-10248.

Van Lare, B. "Reorganization and Management Improvement Initiatives: An Essay of State Experience." Washington, D.C.: National Governors' Association, 1986.

Van Riper, P. P. *History of the U.S. Civil Service*. Evanston, Ill.: HarperCollins, 1958.

PART TWO

The
Workforce
Challenge

TWO

Personnel Systems and Labor Relations:
Steps Toward a Quiet Revitalization

Carolyn Ban
Norma Riccucci

For many state and local government managers, civil service systems and unions are seen primarily as constraints, as something that gets in the way of their ability to manage their organizations and thus limits performance. As one author put it, "civil service . . . is now clearly associated with inefficiency, rigidity, and indifference to performance" (Ukeles, 1982, p. 17).

Certainly, the main goal of civil service and labor relations systems was not to improve efficiency in government. Civil service systems, based on the concept of a merit system, were introduced as a way to eliminate the "spoils system," that is, the reliance on patronage as a basis for selecting people for employment. While basing selection on individuals' qualifications for the job might indeed improve organizational performance (although not all political appointees are unqualified "hacks"), civil service systems do, indeed, reduce management discretion in hiring, promotion, and removal of employees.

Labor relations systems, too, came into being for reasons other than improving efficiency. Their main goal is to protect the rights and interests of employees. Thus, they, too, can limit managerial flexibility in areas such as setting pay, assigning work, and laying people off or firing them. Nonetheless, as will be seen later, management working with labor can have positive organizational payoffs.

These goals continue to be important. In the federal government, after over 100 years of a merit system, abuses, such as hiring political cronies or one's friends for career jobs, continue to occur. The rate of perceived abuses varies sharply by agency (Ban and Redd, 1990). Certainly, an empirical study would uncover sharp variations between states and cities on the extent to which the civil service is still politicized. As Lee (1979, p. 26) observed, "Some local personnel systems may be nominally merit but practically political." And, absent an organized system for the representation of workers' interests, some managers would indeed treat their employees unfairly.

The challenge for those who would reform these systems, then, is how to introduce more management flexibility without sacrificing the protections provided by civil service systems and labor unions. This chapter examines two closely related topics: civil service systems and labor relations in state and local governments. It focuses on new and creative approaches to the challenges of civil service and labor relations that can lead to improved organizational performance.

One problem we encountered in writing this chapter is the dearth of good empirical research on personnel and labor relations systems at the state and local levels. What little research is available is often quite narrow, such as a report on the efforts of a single jurisdiction. True comparative literature is lacking, and even broad descriptive work describing the range of practices in states and localities is missing. Although this discussion does not pretend to be a comprehensive examination of the civil service and labor relations systems of all states and cities, the authors have examined four states and two cities that present a range of models of civil service and labor relations systems. On the one hand, both New York state and New York City have very formal civil service systems with limited flexibility and strong unions that play an active role in personnel issues. On the other extreme, both the state of Virginia and the city of Indianapolis have abandoned formal centralized merit systems in favor of decentralized personnel systems. Unions play little role in these systems. In the middle, California and Minnesota have developed civil service systems with considerable flexibility, in some cases with the cooperation of unions. In addition, we present examples drawn from the literature that describe innovative practices in other jurisdictions.

The State of Civil Service Systems

While the size of the federal workforce has remained level in recent years, the number of people employed by state and local governments has continued to climb. As of 1990, the states employed about 4.5 million workers and local governments nearly 11 million. This comprises an enormous investment by governments in human resources. Improving the way these resources are managed is central to improving the quality of services offered by these governments.

Trends in the Development of Civil Service Systems

The federal government adopted a merit system with the passage of the Pendleton Act in 1883, but diffusion of civil service systems to state and local governments has been gradual and uneven. New York passed a similar law the same year, and Massachusetts followed suit the next year (Lee, 1979). Several cities also joined the bandwagon. Ironically, Albany and Chicago, famous for retaining patronage systems well into the 1980s, were among the first to pass laws establishing civil service systems, pointing up once again the gap between official and actual practice.

Although several other states moved to merit systems in the period before World War I, the process of diffusion proceeded by fits and starts, with some states even adopting systems that were then gutted or repealed. For example, Connecticut passed a civil service law in 1912, weakened it, repealed it in 1921, and then started again with a broader act in 1937 (Mosher and Kingsley, 1941). Some states, including Virginia, have more recently abandoned their merit systems, and a few states, including Texas, have never adopted a civil service system (Rodriguez, 1992).

Municipal governments moved more rapidly. By 1940, almost all large cities were using some kind of merit system, and this use has gradually spread to smaller cities, as well (Mosher and Kingsley, 1941; Stahl, 1983). County governments remain backward in this respect. Except for a few large counties, and for counties in the few states that require merit systems, merit systems remain rare at the county level (Stahl, 1983).

The federal government has played an important role in encouraging the adoption of civil service systems by state and local governments, as have the federal courts. The first major impetus for state and local governments to adopt civil service systems was the Social Security Act of 1935, and especially the amendments of 1940, which required state and local government employees administering health, welfare, and employment programs funded by the federal government to be under merit systems (Mosher and Kingsley, 1941). As Cayer (1980, p. 47) points out: "A large part of the intent of the new requirements was to insulate the programs and personnel from direct political involvement so that money could not be used by elected state and local officials to build political machines for their own benefit."

As a result of this legal requirement, states were forced to develop merit systems for at least some of their employees. Some chose to develop systems covering *only* those employees, while others developed parallel systems, with a separate system (presumably meeting stricter standards of merit) for grants-in-aid employees. As of 1969, as Table 2.1 shows, nine states still had systems covering only grants-in-aid employees and six states had dual systems.

The second federal influence on the development of state and local civil service systems was the Intergovernmental Personnel Act (IPA) of 1970. It encompassed a number of positive functions, including funding for em-

Table 2.1. Civil Service Coverage — 1969 to 1981.

1969		1981	
Dual System	Grant-in-Aid	Dual System	Grant-in-Aid
Arkansas	Indiana	Arkansas	Texas
Mississippi	Missouri	Montana	West Virginia
Pennsylvania	Montana	Nebraska	
South Dakota	Nebraska	Pennsylvania	
Virginia	North Dakota	Wyoming	
Wyoming	South Carolina		
	Tennessee		
	Texas		
	West Virginia		

Sources: Council of State Governments, 1970, 1982.

ployee training programs, provision of technical assistance and grants to improve personnel methods, and a streamlining of merit system standards. It also included a mobility program that allowed state and local employees to spend time working in the federal government and vice versa (Stahl, 1983; Cayer, 1980). Throughout the 1970s, the IPA programs had a clear effect in "upgrading public personnel systems and public employee skills" (Cayer, 1991, p. 4). Unfortunately, in 1981 the Reagan administration cut all funding for the IPA, eliminating both the positive programs and on-site oversight of state and local merit systems.

U.S. Supreme Court decisions have also played a major role in changing state and local personnel systems, particularly those decisions bearing on patronage systems. Two cases are particularly important. In *Elrod* v. *Burns* (1976), the Court overturned the time-honored patronage practices of Cook County, Illinois, ruling that firing nonpolicymaking, nonconfidential employees solely because of their political beliefs was unconstitutional.

The Court followed four years later with a decision (*Branti* v. *Finkel*, 1980) ruling that two assistant public defenders in Rockland County, New York, could not be dismissed solely because of their partisan affiliation but only if they make partisan policy. In 1990, the Court extended the limits on use of patronage to cover hiring, promotions, or transfers of lower-level employees (*Rutan* v. *Republican Party of Illinois*). It is too early to tell whether the Court's actions will lead to the development of more formal civil service systems at the local level.

By 1990, most states had modern civil service systems covering most personnel functions. Table 2.2 summarizes the structure and functions of these state systems.

The State of Labor-Management Relations

Although creation of legal frameworks to govern labor relations at the state and local levels of government is relatively recent, labor unions have had a long presence on the state and local government scenes (Kearney, 1992). And, although formal collective bargaining laws did not exist until recently, bargaining and conferring between labor and management have been taking place since the 1800s. In New York state, for example, labor representatives of the Civil Service Employees Association (CSEA) had been regularly meeting with management representatives since the early 1900s, yet the Taylor Law, which established a collective bargaining framework for unions and the state, was not enacted until 1967. In New York state as well as other state and local jurisdictions where unions or associations are present, there have been bitter battles over a host of issues, in particular wages.

Trends in Labor Law

Today, virtually every state in the union has some type of statute or administrative edict to regulate the system of labor relations at the state and local levels of government. Even in those states where no statute exists, collective bargaining or meeting and conferring may nonetheless take place. Table 2.3 illustrates the variance in degree to which state and local government employees are allowed to engage in collective bargaining. Table 2.4 provides a brief description of the thirteen states that allow state and local employees some "modified" right to engage in strikes.

It should be noted that although the legal right of public employees to strike is extremely limited, as Table 2.4 shows, public employees continue to engage in strikes or other types of work stoppages or slowdowns (for example, work-to-rule). Table 2.5 illustrates the rise in the number of worker days lost to employee strikes at the state and local levels of government from 1970 to 1980. (Because the latest data available on public employee work stoppages are from 1980, the reader would, with caution, need to extrapolate in order to get an idea of the number of worker stoppages in more recent years.)

The legal right of public employees to engage in strikes continues to be debated. Because of the great resistance on the part of management, it is unlikely that there will be a significant increase in the number of states that allow state and local government employees some modified or limited right to strike.

Trends in Union Membership

Public sector union membership has, overall, been more stable than in the private sector. As Table 2.6 shows, other than an increase from 1987 to 1988, public sector union membership over the past several years has hovered around 38 percent. Table 2.7 shows variation by state. Table 2.8 shows the fluctuation in labor union membership at the federal, state, and local levels of government. (Also see Table 2.9, which provides a breakdown of local government union membership.) Notably, union membership at the state

Table 2.2. State Personnel Administration: Structure and Functions.[1]

State or other jurisdiction	Legal basis for personnel department	Organizational status — Separate agency	Organizational status — Part of a larger agency	Human resource planning	Classification	Recruitment	Selection	Performance evaluation	Promotion	Employee assistance and counseling	Human resource development and training	Affirmative action	Labor and employee relations	Grievance and appeals	Compensation	Retirement
Alabama	C,S	★	—	—	●	★	—	★	★	—	●	★	★	★	★	—
Alaska	C,S	—	★	—	●	●	—	●	★	—	●	★	—	—	●	—
Arizona	S	—	★	—	★	●	★	●	●	—	★	—	—	—	★	—
Arkansas	S	—	★	—	●	●	—	●	—	—	●	—	●	●	●	—
California																
State Personnel Bd.	C,S,E	★	—	—	★	●	●	—	★	—	—	●	★	●	—	—
Dept. of Personnel Admin.	S	★	—	—	★	—	—	★	—	—	—	—	★	★	★	—
Colorado	C,S,E	★	—	★	●	★	★	★	—	—	★	★	★	★	★	—
Connecticut	S	—	★	★	●	★	★	★	★	★	★	★	★	★	●	—
Delaware	S	★	—	—	●	★	●	★	●	—	★	●	★	★	●	●
Florida	S	★	—	●	●	●	●	●	●	●	●	●	★	●	●	—
Georgia	C,S	★	—	●	★	●	★	—	—	★	★	★	★	★	★	★
Hawaii	C,S	★	—	★	●	●	★	★	★	★	●	★	●	★	★	—
Idaho	S	★	—	★	●	★	★	★	—	—	—	★	—	★	★	●
Illinois	S	—	★	—	●	★	★	★	—	★	★	★	★	★	★	—
Indiana	S	★	—	●	★	★	●	★	★	●	★	—	●	★	★	★
Iowa	S	★	—	●	★	●	●	★	●	★	●	★	★	★	★	★
Kansas	S	—	★	—	★	●	★	★	—	—	—	—	●	★	●	—
Kentucky	S	★	—	★	●	★	★	★	●	★	★	●	—	★	●	—
Louisiana	C	★	—	—	●	★	●	●	—	—	●	●	★	★	●	—
Maine	S	★	—	—	●	★	●	●	—	●	★	★	—	●	●	—
Maryland	S	★	—	★	●	★	●	★	★	★	●	●	★	●	●	—
Massachusetts	S	★	—	★	●	★	●	★	—	—	●	—	★	—	★	—
Michigan	C	★	—	★	●	★	●	★	●	★	●	●	●	★	●	—
Minnesota	S	★	—	●	●	★	●	★	●	★	●	●	●	●	●	—
Mississippi	S	★	—	●	●	★	●	★	●	★	●	★	—	●	●	—
Missouri	C,S	—	★	★	●	●	★	★	★	●	●	★	●	●	●	—

State	Type														
Montana	S	—	★	—	—	•	•	•	•	•	—	★	(c)	•	•	—
Nebraska	S	★	•	★	•	•	•	★	★	★	—	★	★	•	★	—
Nevada	S	★	—	—	—	•	•	•	•	—	•	★	—	—	•	—
New Hampshire	S	—	★	—	—	•	•	•	•	★	•	—	★	★	•	—
New Jersey	C,S	★	—	★	★	•	•	•	•	★	•	★	•	★	•	★
New Mexico	S	★	—	★	★	•	•	•	★	•	★	—	—	•	•	—
New York	C,S,E (b)	★	—	★	★	•	•	★	—	★	★	★	•	★	•	•
North Carolina	S	★	—	•	•	•	•	★	★	•	•	—	★	★	★	★
North Dakota	S	—	★	—	—	•	•	—	★	★	—	★	★	★	•	—
Ohio	C	—	★	—	—	•	•	•	★	—	—	•	—	—	•	★
Oklahoma	S	★	—	★	★	★	★	•	•	★	•	★	•	•	•	—
Oregon	S	—	—	★	•	•	•	★	★	★	★	★	★	★	•	—
Pennsylvania																
Civil Service Comm.	S	★	—	★	—	—	—	★	—	—	—	★	—	—	•	—
Bur. of Personnel	E	—	★	•	•	•	•	•	★	•	★	—	★	•	•	•
Rhode Island	S	—	★	•	★	★	★	•	★	•	—	•	—	—	★	•
South Carolina	S	—	★	—	—	★	★	★	—	★	—	•	•	★	•	—
South Dakota	S	—	—	•	•	★	★	•	•	•	•	•	(c)	★	★	★
Tennessee	S	★★	—	•	•	★	★	★	•	★	★	★	★	★	—	•
Texas														(c)		
Utah	S	★	—	★	★	•	•	•	•	★	—	•	★	★	•	•
Vermont	S	—	★	★	★	•	•	•	•	—	—	—	•	•	•	•
Virginia	S	★	—	★	•	•	•	★	★	★	★	★	•	•	★	•
Washington	S	★	—	—	•	•	•	★	★	★	★	★	•	•	★	•
West Virginia	S	★	—	—	★	•	•	•	•	•	★	•	★	★	•	•
Wisconsin	S	★	—	—	—	•	•	•	•	•	•	—	—	•	•	•
Wyoming	S	—	★	★	—	—	—	•	—	—	—	—	•	—	•	—
Guam	S	★	—	★	★	•	•	★	★	★	★	★	★	★	★	★
Puerto Rico	S	★	—	•	•	•	•	•	•	•	—	—	—	—	•	•

Notes: [1]Information derived from survey of state personnel offices conducted by the Council of State Governments (March 1986) for the National Association of State Personnel Executives.

C = Constitution; S = Statute; E = Executive order.

(a) In these columns: ★ = function performed in agency personnel department; • = function performed in a centralized personnel agency/department; (b) also, Civil Service Commission regulations; (c) decentralized system.

Source: Council of State Governments, 1990.

**Table 2.3. State Collective Bargaining Provisions
Established by Legislation or Administrative Fiat.**[a]

State	Employees covered				
	State	Local	Police	Firefighters	Teachers
Alabama	—	—	—	Y	Y
Alaska	X	X	X	X	X
Arizona	Y	Y	Y	Y	Y
Arkansas	—	—	—	—	—
California	X	X	X	X	X
Colorado	—	—	—	—	—
Connecticut	X	X	X	X	X
Delaware	X	X	X	X	X
Florida	X	X	X	X	X
Georgia	—	—	—	X	—
Hawaii	X	X	X	X	X
Idaho	—	—	—	X	X
Illinois	X	X	X	X	X
Indiana	X	X	X	X	X/Y
Iowa	X	X	X	X	X
Kansas	Y	Y	Y	Y	X
Kentucky	—	—	X	X	—
Louisiana	—	X[b]	—	—	—
Maine	X	X	X	X	X/Y
Maryland	—	X	—	—	X
Massachusetts	X	X	X	X	X
Michigan	X	X	X	X	X
Minnesota	X/Y	X/Y	X/Y	X/Y	X/Y
Mississippi	—	—	—	—	—
Missouri	Y	Y	—	Y	—
Montana	X	X	X	X	X/Y
Nebraska	X	X	X	X	Y
Nevada	—	X	X	X	X
New Hampshire	X	X	X	X	X
New Jersey	X	X	X	X	X
New Mexico	X/Y	—	—	—	—
New York	X	X	X	X	X
North Carolina	—	—	—	—	—
North Dakota	Y	Y	Y	Y	X
Ohio	X	X	X	X	X
Oklahoma	—	X	X	X	X
Oregon	X	X	X	X	X
Pennsylvania	X/Y	X/Y	X	X	X/Y
Rhode Island	X	X	X	X	X
South Carolina	—	—	—	—	—
South Dakota	X	X	X	X	X
Tennessee	—	—	—	—	X
Texas	—	—	X	X	—
Utah	—	—	—	—	—
Vermont	X	X	X	X	X
Virginia	—	—	—	—	—
Washington	X	X	X	X	X
West Virginia	Y	Y	Y	Y	Y
Wisconsin	X	X	X	X	X
Wyoming	—	—	—	X	—

Notes: X = collective bargaining provisions; Y = meet and confer provisions; Y/X = collective bargaining on some issues, meet and confer on others. [a]For example, civil service regulation, executive order, or attorney general opinion. [b]Public transit workers only.

Sources: Adapted from Kearney, 1992. Updated by *Labor Relations Reporter,* 1989–1990.

Table 2.4. State and Local Government
Employees with the Right to Strike, as of 1990.

State	Employees covered
Alaska	All public employees except for police and firefighters
California	All but police and firefighters, *providing* a court or California PERB does not rule that striking is illegal[a]
Hawaii	All public employees
Idaho	Firefighters and teachers
Illinois	All public employees except for police, firefighters, and paramedics
Minnesota	All public employees except for police and firefighters
Montana	All public employees
Ohio	All public employees except for police and firefighters
Oregon	All public employees except for police, firefighters, and correctional officers
Pennsylvania	All public employees except for police, firefighters, prison guards, guards at mental hospitals, and court employees
Rhode Island	All public employees
Vermont	All public employees except for correctional officers, court employees, and state employees
Wisconsin	All public employees except for police, firefighters, and state employees

Note: [a]The California State Supreme Court, in *County Sanitation District* v. *L.A. County Employees Association* (699 P.2d 835, 1985), said that unless expressly prohibited by statute—or case law—striking by public employees is not illegal. Firefighters are prohibited by statutory law, police by case law.

Sources: Adapted from Kearney, 1992. Updated by *Labor Relations Reporter,* 1989–1990.

and local levels of government grew rapidly between the early 1950s and the mid 1970s, and again in the mid 1980s. This increase is due to the combination of rapid growth in state and local governments with stagnation and decline in the private sector (Troy and Sheflin, 1984). The growth of labor union membership at the state and local levels peaked in 1976. Then, after a slight dip from 1976 to 1982, it soared to 33.5 percent in 1986. The large increase may be attributed to the increased growth in such unions as the American Federation of State, County, and Municipal Employees (AFSCME).

Trends in the Labor-Management Relationship

It goes without saying that the nature of the labor-management relationship has been and continues to be thought of in adversarial terms. From the perspective of management, labor unions often are seen as thwarting efforts aimed at making civil service systems more flexible, such as moving away from the rule of three or permitting lateral entry from outside government. Problems notwithstanding, the relationship between labor and management in many cases has actually evolved beyond the point of strict antagonism.

Table 2.5. Work Stoppages by State and
Local Government Employees, 1970–1980 (in Thousands).

	State			Local		
Year	Number of stoppages	Workers involved	Days idle	Number of stoppages	Workers involved	Days idle
1970	23	8.8	44.6	386	168.9	1,330.5
1971	23	14.5	81.8	304	137.1	811.6
1972	40	27.4	273,7	335	114.7	983.5
1973	29	12.3	133.0	357	183.7	2,166.3
1974	34	24.7	86.4	348	135.4	1,316.3
1975	32	66.6	300.5	446	252.0	1,903.9
1976	25	33.8	148.2	352	146.8	1,542.6
1977	44	33.7	181.9	367	136.2	1,583.3
1978	45	17.9	180.2	435	171.0	1,498.8
1979	57	48.6	515.5	536	205.5	2,467.1
1980	45	10.0	999.0	493	212.7	2,240.6

Source: Finkle, 1985, p. 398. Reprinted courtesy of Marcel Dekker Inc.

And in some cases, as will be seen in this chapter, unions have been willing
to permit the easing of civil service constraints. So, while labor and management must — at least in theory — be seen as adversaries (to promote credibility among the rank and file), a good deal of cooperation is taking place
either formally or behind the scenes. Indeed, formal cooperative measures
have become more common, particularly in the wake of fiscal crises. Although
such issues as wages may not feasibly lend themselves to cooperation, a number of states and localities have reported successes with joint ventures over
a host of issues. It seems that, in jurisdictions that have collective bargaining, the support and participation of labor is key if state and local governments seek to make effective changes in civil service systems, since unions
and the employees they represent perceive these systems as protections against
management abuses.

Table 2.6. Union Membership in Public and Private Sectors, 1977–1989 (Percent).

	Public (all levels)	Private
1977[a]	32.1	23.3
1980[a]	33.8	22.3
1986[b]	38.0	15.6
1987[b]	38.3	15.2
1988[b]	40.3	14.6
1989[b]	38.9	14.2

Sources: [a]Calculated from the U.S. Department of Labor, Bureau of Labor Statistics, Earnings and Other Characteristics of Organized Workers, 1979 and 1981. [b]Tabulated from the Current
Population Survey (CPS), U.S. Bureau of the Census, Mar. 1986–1989.

Table 2.7. Percentage of Private and Public Sector Employees
Organized, by State, 1975, 1982, and 1988.

State	1975[a]			1982[a]			1988[b]		
	Private	Public	Total	Private	Public	Total	Private	Public	Total
Alabama	18.9	42.3	23.9	14.2	32.4	18.2	12.8	28.7	16.1
Alaska	39.7	44.9	41.2	30.3	30.7	30.4	15.0	50.3	26.4
Arizona	16.4	35.8	20.9	10.1	24.0	12.8	5.6	23.8	8.6
Arkansas	16.3	27.0	18.4	11.2	21.6	13.2	10.0	19.1	11.6
California	34.1	35.8	34.5	23.8	32.9	25.4	14.2	59.4	21.4
Colorado	19.2	39.4	23.6	14.8	32.1	18.0	8.3	28.9	12.3
Connecticut	22.1	60.0	27.7	14.1	51.6	18.9	13.7	66.4	20.3
Delaware	19.4	55.1	25.8	14.2	50.6	20.3	11.4	46.5	16.6
Florida	12.4	28.4	15.6	7.2	21.4	9.6	5.6	39.1	10.6
Georgia	11.5	25.6	14.4	11.0	19.6	12.7	9.9	24.7	12.3
Hawaii	28.1	53.8	34.3	24.7	54.6	31.4	23.9	61.3	32.8
Idaho	15.0	33.9	19.4	13.3	26.1	16.1	10.6	24.8	13.4
Illinois	35.9	30.9	35.1	26.9	30.6	27.5	18.6	48.6	23.0
Indiana	31.8	30.7	31.6	24.4	28.6	25.1	20.8	30.9	22.3
Iowa	19.9	38.2	23.4	16.9	35.0	20.4	13.1	40.5	18.2
Kansas	12.6	28.8	16.0	9.2	22.9	12.0	11.6	25.2	14.1
Kentucky	22.9	31.3	24.6	17.5	32.8	20.4	16.6	26.6	18.1
Louisiana	17.5	28.5	19.8	11.8	22.5	13.8	8.3	22.5	11.0
Maine	12.8	50.3	20.7	11.2	47.7	18.5	11.1	58.6	18.3
Maryland	20.9	46.5	27.5	14.3	32.4	18.6	12.3	37.3	18.6
Massachusetts	18.8	53.7	24.3	14.4	52.5	19.7	12.5	61.4	19.3
Michigan	41.0	47.1	42.2	30.2	49.6	33.7	22.7	60.2	28.3
Minnesota	25.7	43.7	29.0	20.7	43.5	24.5	15.7	56.8	22.2
Mississippi	11.3	16.8	12.6	8.1	13.4	9.3	7.4	15.7	9.0
Missouri	36.3	20.6	33.4	26.7	26.1	26.6	16.1	32.8	18.7
Montana	32.3	30.5	31.8	20.7	25.0	21.7	12.3	41.6	19.9
Nebraska	15.0	33.9	19.3	12.4	30.8	16.3	10.9	42.7	16.8
Nevada	35.5	46.5	37.4	19.4	38.0	22.1	17.2	43.4	20.8
New Hampshire	11.2	46.4	16.9	7.5	41.4	12.3	7.4	48.0	12.1
New Jersey	25.2	43.5	28.4	17.5	31.6	19.9	19.4	61.0	25.9
New Mexico	15.5	20.8	17.0	11.2	17.4	12.8	8.5	17.4	10.8
New York	39.3	59.6	43.2	31.2	56.9	35.8	20.3	71.0	29.7
North Carolina	5.9	38.5	11.0	4.8	28.6	8.9	5.2	21.8	7.6
North Dakota	13.3	36.0	19.4	9.5	29.0	14.2	8.8	36.0	15.4
Ohio	34.8	43.2	36.1	25.3	38.4	27.4	19.5	49.8	24.1
Oklahoma	15.0	34.5	19.5	9.9	25.7	12.9	8.1	22.5	11.0
Oregon	30.5	46.6	33.8	25.5	35.1	27.5	16.2	60.6	23.6
Pennsylvania	32.3	44.4	34.3	23.6	46.2	27.0	18.1	55.1	23.1
Rhode Island	21.0	52.8	26.3	12.1	61.1	19.4	12.6	68.0	20.4
South Carolina	3.9	17.7	6.8	3.9	13.7	5.8	5.1	13.8	6.6
South Dakota	9.0	25.3	13.3	6.2	23.1	10.3	5.8	30.5	10.8
Tennessee	17.9	38.5	21.7	14.0	33.0	17.3	11.0	33.3	14.7
Texas	12.4	31.8	16.0	9.6	27.3	12.5	6.1	21.7	8.9
Utah	14.0	47.6	22.4	9.4	42.3	16.8	6.9	41.7	15.1
Vermont	8.6	48.5	16.3	6.5	37.3	11.9	6.7	54.5	14.0
Virginia	11.4	23.9	14.4	8.1	20.1	10.9	8.9	20.6	11.4
Washington, D.C.	48.8	14.9	33.0	45.3	18.0	33.4	13.1	28.9	19.2
Washington	46.1	39.7	44.7	33.1	32.4	32.9	21.7	53.9	28.2
West Virginia	37.5	35.5	37.1	28.5	30.2	28.9	21.1	29.0	22.8
Wisconsin	28.5	46.3	31.5	20.3	44.8	24.5	16.6	53.6	22.3
Wyoming	16.1	43.8	22.6	11.5	31.4	15.6	12.0	27.2	16.2
United States	26.3	39.6	28.9	19.0	35.1	21.9	13.8	43.4	18.8

Sources: [a]Troy and Sheflin, 1985. [b]Curme, Hirsch, and MacPherson, 1990.

Table 2.8. Union Membership in the Public Sector, 1929–1989 (Percent).

	Federal*	State and local**
1929[a]	43.3	0.7
1940[a]	33.7	2.6
1950[a]	26.4	4.7
1962[a]	26.9	9.8
1970[a]	39.6	16.6
1976[a]	41.5	20.6
1982[a]	37.2	18.6
1986[b]	30.9	33.5
1987[b]	28.1	31.9
1988[b]	31.2	34.7
1989[b]	35.9	34.3

Notes: *Includes postal service; **excludes education.

Sources: [a]Adapted from Troy and Sheflin, 1984, p. 22. [b]Tabulated from the Current Population Survey (CPS), U.S. Bureau of the Census, Mar. 1986–1989.

The Challenge of Reform

A number of factors have led to increased pressure for reform of civil service systems and labor-management relations in state and local government. First, both civil service systems and public sector labor unions share a common problem — a negative image on the part of many citizens. To some extent, that is a function of the negative image that many citizens have of government employees, which impedes recruitment to governments at all levels. This problem may have a differential effect; some local government positions, such as police and firefighters, are not usually seen as "bureaucrats" and may be viewed more positively (see, for example, the poll results cited by Goodsell, 1985, Chapter 2). But, as Holzer (1991) makes clear, the images of government work as poorly paid and lacking in challenge and of the underworked, uncaring bureaucrat are constantly reinforced by the mass media. There is some evidence that people view state and local governments more favorably than they do the federal government (National Commission on the Public Service, 1989).

Table 2.9. Local Government Union Membership by Sector, 1977–1982 (Percent).

	County	Municipal	Township	Special district	School district
1977	34.6	53.1	58.9	34.9	59.9
1978	34.5	53.8	58.5	36.5	60.3
1979	34.1	53.5	56.1	35.9	59.9
1980	34.9	53.9	58.6	37.8	60.2
1982	35.1	52.7	62.4	36.4	53.8

Source: Adapted from Freeman, Ichniowski, and Zax, 1988, p. 379.

The public image of labor unions in general is also very low. Unions tend to be seen by the citizenry (as well as elected officials) as a major source of such problems as bloated budgets, out-of-control government spending, waste, and corruption. It is common knowledge that some unions have certainly contributed to such problems, but the poor image created in such isolated cases extends to all unions, whether private or public (federal, state, or local).

Both civil service systems and labor unions have been seen as rigid, archaic, and antithetical to good management. (See, for example, Osborne and Gaebler, 1992.) The remainder of this chapter examines the status of civil service systems to see if this stereotype is still valid. We focus particularly on examples of successful reforms in state and local governments.

New Approaches to Staffing and Classification

A major contributor to the negative image of the public service is the popular impression that governments at all levels are strangled by red tape. This image dominates the view of public personnel systems. One critic has noted that "the most pervasive and persistent problems of public personnel administration are the impersonal, slow, unresponsive, rigid, and expensive personnel processes" (Newland, 1976, p. 529).

This section explores the extent to which this image still holds. Where are the problems in the areas of staffing and classification, and have some jurisdictions found useful solutions to these problems? We begin by exploring the methods used to recruit new employees, and we then move to testing and selection procedures and to the process of classifying jobs.

Recruiting

Probably the most important thing that state and local governments can do to improve the efficiency of their workforce is to improve the quality of the people they hire. The process of hiring new employees encompasses several steps, starting with recruiting people to apply for positions and moving through testing and then actual selection of the person to be hired. Each of these steps in the process needs to be examined to see where there is room for improvement.

Recruiting is the critical first step; if good people do not apply, by definition they cannot be hired. This is an area that needs improvement. Most public employers have traditionally relied on a passive recruiting strategy: they have simply posted vacancies, usually within the agency and at employment offices, and expected applicants to find them. Any recruiting was likely to be simply by word of mouth (Ukeles, 1982), which was adequate when government jobs were attractive and when large numbers of people usually applied. Now state and local governments are in increasing competition with other sectors, particularly for people with scientific, technical, and medical expertise. A recent report on the civil service of Michigan pointed out the limited supply of applicants in technical and professional fields and the need for active recruitment in these areas. However, it noted that "responsibility for active recruitment in technical and professional fields does not appear to be clearly defined" (Citizens Research Council of Michigan, 1988, p. 31). Michigan is not alone in facing this problem.

To be sure they can meet their workforce needs, organizations need to have an explicit human resource plan, in order to anticipate future needs (Ban, 1991) and to explore active and creative ways to get the word out about opportunities in government to all potential employees, including those in underrepresented groups. One of the most successful approaches is to develop internship or apprenticeship programs, which can be used to bring people into the workforce, often while they are still in school. Such "stay-in-school" or "co-op programs" are in place in a number of jurisdictions, including New York state and the federal government. They link education, job training, and recruitment, giving students real job experience and often ensuring them a job when they finish high school or college, while ensuring the government agency a supply of trained workers who can be carefully evaluated during the training period before they are hired as civil service employees.

At a higher level, New York state's Public Management Internship program, similar to the federal government's Presidential Management Internship program, brings in people with masters degrees in public administration, public policy, and related subjects. The two-year internship includes rotations that complement the permanent job assignment, either within the agency or to other agencies (such as from an operating agency to a central staff agency, or vice versa). This prestigious program is perceived as a fast track to upper-level management positions.

New Approaches to Testing

When most people think of civil service testing, they think of rows of people sitting in a room taking a written test, which may take months to score. Further, traditional selection from tests has depended on the "rule of three." That is, in an effort to prevent abuse, the manager trying to hire a new employee is restricted to selecting from a list of the people with the top three scores on the civil service test. Both the content and the scoring of civil service tests have come in for considerable criticism. (For a discussion of the "traditional" model and some of the variations from it, see Ban, 1991.)

State and local governments are trying out new approaches to the content of the tests, how they are administered, and how they are scored. Improving the quality of selections is critical to improving government performance. Burke and Pearlman (1988, p. 98) point out that "optimal recruitment, selection, and classification procedures can, by themselves, contribute substantially to increased individual productivity, often at comparatively little cost to the organization and typically with minimal change or disruption of existing organizational structures and processes."

Improving the quality of testing methods can simultaneously meet the goals of selecting people who better fit the job and opening up jobs to underrepresented groups, such as women and minorities. In spite of some stereotypes, the two goals are not necessarily in conflict (Riccucci, 1991).

Test Content. We use the term *testing* broadly to mean any formal method used to screen applicants for employment. Many jurisdictions are now utilizing a wide array of testing methods, ranging from improved written tests to biodata (forms assessing aspects of a person's life experience), rankings of training and experience, oral interviews, and simulations or role-playing exercises.

Some jurisdictions, such as New York City, still rely heavily on written tests both for entry-level positions and for promotions. Although New York state still makes heavy use of written tests, it often combines them with structured oral interviews. Similarly, California uses Qualifications Appraisal Panel (QAP), a scored interview, sometimes in conjunction with a written examination, for such positions as corrections officer.

Minnesota uses written tests most often for entry-level positions. For more technical positions, experience and training are considered, in one of a number of ways. This may be pass-fail, in the case of a requirement for licensure. (You either have the necessary license or not.) It can also be an entry standard followed by a job-element questionnaire, asking applicants to describe their experience or accomplishments, which is rated by a panel of experts.

On the other hand, some jurisdictions have responded to the stringent requirements for test validation imposed by the federal government by dropping written tests altogether. Our interviewee in Virginia told us, "There is no civil service or merit system in Virginia. There was at one time, until about ten years ago." This does not mean a return to patronage but rather a decentralized system where individual agencies are free to decide how to recruit and select their employees, within guidelines from the central personnel agency. Few written tests are used, because of validation requirements. The criteria of selection include record of experience, references, and, in some cases, writing or other work samples.

Similarly, Indianapolis reported that it uses no written tests, largely because of validation requirements. Selection is partly centralized and partly left up to each department. The central personnel agency advertises positions and screens for minimum requirements, then individual supervisors in the agencies make selections primarily based on interviews. In both Virginia and Indianapolis, formal skills tests have been retained for clerical workers. Lana Stein, in her survey of ten cities, found wide variation, with all cities making at least limited use of written tests but only three (St. Louis, Baltimore, and Dallas) relying heavily on them (Stein, 1992).

Access to new technologies has also changed how the tests are administered. Some jurisdictions are moving to computerized testing, which can greatly speed the scoring of tests and thus speed up the hiring process. Many jurisdictions use test forms that can be optically scanned for scoring. In the newest technology, the test is actually delivered via microcomputer or computer terminal, with the individual directly interacting with the computer. This allows for use of "decision trees" in which the question presented may depend on the response to the previous question. It also permits instantaneous scoring and could thus be used along with "on-the-spot" hiring authority by recruiters on college campuses, for example.

Some of these changes are beyond the budgets of small jurisdictions, but improved test quality does not have to be expensive. One route is for small jurisdictions to form consortia to share resources for test development and validation. And as the cost of computer equipment continues to drop, wider use of computerized testing will become possible; in fact, as of 1987, thirty-two states planned to automate testing and/or certification (National Association of State Personnel Executives, 1987).

Test Scoring. The standard image of test scoring in civil service systems has been the rule of three mentioned before, in which tests were scored numerically, often to several decimal points, and managers could choose only among the top three scorers. Many observers, even those who strongly supported the validity of written tests, recognized that making the assumption that someone with a score of 98.51 was more qualified than another person with a score of 98.50 was unwarranted. Further, such restrictive scoring often made it difficult to reach protected class members who were quite qualified but not at the very top of the list.

In fact, few jurisdictions that we examined still use this restrictive method of scoring. New York state and New York City both still rely on the rule of three. In New York City, for some examinations, particularly in the uniformed services, tests are scored down to decimal points. In fact, in the uniformed services, selection is made based on a rule of one, with people taken off the list in rank order.

In New York state, the Department of Civil Service, which conducts examinations and maintain lists of candidates, refers the top three scorers, plus any people who tie with them. This often results in more than three people being referred. In fact, there may be twenty or more people on one score, depending on the size of the competition. New York City sometimes refers all those with tied scores but sometimes uses Social Security numbers to randomly break ties.

Minnesota uses a rule of ten for internal hires and a rule of twenty for external and also has a policy of "expanded certification." If protected classes are not represented on the list, the list is expanded to reach the top two passing protected-class candidates, which can bring the list to as many as twenty-eight people. Stein (1992) found that, of ten cities, only two (St.

Louis and Cleveland) always applied the rule of three. Some cities had rules of five or ten, but four of the cities had no such restriction.

California reports that the rule of three, with the top three names and scores rounded to the nearest hundredth, was uniformly used in the past but was replaced about ten years ago by a rule of three ranks. This means that scores are rounded to three top scores (for example, 95, 90, and 85), and all people with these scores can qualify. This is typically used for higher-level positions. In the case of entry-level exams that result in a very large pool, random certification is sometimes used to reduce the numbers.

California is not the only jurisdiction to have moved to zone scoring, which is analogous to giving candidates scores of A, B, and C rather than specific numerical scores. Illinois does precisely that: the top 25 percent get a rating of A, the next 30 B. New Jersey divides the list into deciles, permitting managers to select from one-tenth of the applicants at a time (International Personnel Management Association Assessment Council, 1989; Ban, Faerman, and Riccucci, 1992).

Zone scoring obviously increases flexibility. But, if the zones are too broad, managers who previously had two few choices now receive so many choices that they are overwhelmed. For example, a citizen's committee reviewing Michigan's civil service system reported that since the state moved to a broad-band certification process in 1979, managers have complained that they "are forced to consider an excessive number of persons on employment lists, and that many of these are marginally qualified for the opening, or are not seriously interested in the vacancy" (Citizens Research Council of Michigan, 1988, p. 30). In some cases the lists contained 100 or more names.

Michigan has not changed its certification process, which is based on the standard error of measurement of the examination, but since the 1988 report it has requested applicants to identify which positions they would actually be interested in and has thus somewhat reduced the number certified. But it reports that, depending on the location of the opening, the number certified still ranges anywhere from 5 in a small county to probably 100 in the Detroit area.

The fire department in Menlo Park, California, provides a good example of how broadening test scoring can improve representation of protected classes. The department moved from the rule of three to the rule of the list: that is, anyone who passed the test was deemed qualified and could be hired. This was combined with an aggressive recruitment strategy, which involved all current employees in recruiting women and men of color, and with a series of workshops for employees on discrimination and harassment. The results were impressive; the department moved from one African American and no women to about 14 percent female and persons of color (Lee, 1988).

Union Response to More Flexible Hiring Methods. The standard image of the role of unions is that they oppose introducing more flexibility into the civil service system because they mistrust management and fear that it will lead to abuse. This has certainly been the stance of unions in New York state. When the Department of Civil Service attempted to move to broadband certification, the union successfully challenged it in court. We should note that the bands in this case were very broad; it is not clear what the union position would be if narrower bands were used.

But other jurisdictions with strong unions have not faced the same opposition. In the past fifteen years, as California has moved away from heavy reliance on written tests and away from the rule of three to broader certification plans, the unions have generally been neutral about these changes. Similarly, in Minnesota, unions have not opposed increased flexibility, and, indeed, union members sat on the blue-ribbon panel that recommended changes. Virginia faced no union opposition for the simple reason that it has no recognized unions.

Opening Up the Civil Service at All Levels

Many civil service systems limit the ability of people from outside the system to enter any place but at the bottom. Typically, people come into entry-level positions and move up the ladder. Often higher-level jobs are open only to those who are already in the system, or the requirements are written so narrowly that the de facto effect is the same. The organizational effects of limiting lateral entry can be negative, making it difficult to bring in "new blood," with new ideas or skills. This is a particularly serious problem in highly technical areas, where the needed skill mix changes rapidly over time. In some cases, managers find ways to "get around" this limitation by bringing people in through alternative routes, such as temporary or provisional appointments, but bypassing the system rather than changing it can have negative results on morale and turnover (Ospina, 1992).

In New York City in recent years, attempts to get around the system were so widespread that there was a de facto system that was very different from the official system. This de facto system relied upon hiring provisional employees. Over the past ten years, the number has increased dramatically; currently there are roughly 40,000 provisionals. As our interviewee told us, the Department of Personnel just stopped giving a lot of tests and allowed the agencies to do whatever they wanted to. Not surprisingly, hiring from outside was common in the absence of lists. Now, as a result of a lawsuit, the city is being forced to return to the official system, and hiring from outside will be very difficult. The result will probably be pressure to remove some positions from the competitive class, which will be opposed vigorously by the city unions.

Opening up the system to outside hiring beyond the entry level needs to be handled carefully. Wholesale hiring of outsiders for mid- and high-level positions can reduce the opportunities for promotion of those already in the system and can harm morale.

The jurisdictions we studied showed a wide range of practices. Those jurisdictions with formal civil service systems and strong unions tend to have more limited lateral entry. Thus, on the one hand, in California, lateral entry is at the discretion of the hiring department, but in practice, lateral entry occurs only rarely and generally only in areas that are hard to fill from within, such as in technical or professional fields. In New York, where there is a clearly established career line with an opening at the top, promotion from within is relied on, but there are instances where people are brought in from the outside for high-level jobs. In contrast, in Virginia and Indianapolis, lateral entry is quite common. In Virginia, agencies will often recruit both within and outside of state government to get a larger and more diverse pool, and recruitment nationwide for higher-level positions is common. Similarly, in Indianapolis it is quite common to bring in people with appropriate experience from other cities for higher administrative positions, and probably about 50 percent of hires for middle and upper positions are from outside.

Stein (1992) found a mixed pattern on lateral entry among ten cities; none totally restrict it, but several give preference to current employees. Two cities (Pittsburgh and St. Louis) give no such preference but rather give credit for training and experience.

This is an area where unions have often been actively involved, since they define their role as protecting the job opportunities of current members. Unions have also traditionally been staunch supporters of seniority. Thus, for example, in Minnesota, there is a seniority in appointment provision for eligible lists for AFSCME—covered bargaining units. So if there are two or more candidates on a list, the most senior is expected to be appointed unless there is a very clear difference between them. If there is a sole internal candidate, it is hard to select an external candidate, and such a choice would certainly be challenged by the unions. Therefore, lateral entry is easier for exempt positions. This may help explain why, when we interviewed Nina Rothchild, the former commissioner of the Department of Employee Relations in Minnesota, she said: "My specific recommendation is to unclassify all managerial jobs. It does away with the concept that an unclassified manager is a political appointee. It gets away from the idea that a new administration comes in, and you lose good people. Second, I really think the new administration should have the right to select the people you want. . . . I don't know if that would work in all states. We don't have a lot of patronage here."

Veterans Preference: Finding a Better Balance

The goal of opening up government may also conflict with traditional civil service procedures such as veterans preference. Veterans preference is a controversial issue because it challenges the core value of hiring based on merit and because it pits one group, veterans, against another, women, who are frequently disadvantaged by strict veterans preference. But it remains a

serious limitation on managers' ability to hire. All fifty states, as well as the
federal government, have provided some kind of veterans preference (Tompkins, 1985), and some provide for absolute preference. That is, if a veteran
meets the minimum qualifications for the job, he or she must be chosen.
Most jurisdictions have shied away from trying to eliminate or reduce veterans preference because veterans are well organized and vocal, and most
courts have upheld its legality. See *Personnel Administrator* v. *Feeney,* 422 U.S.
256 (1979). Nonetheless, some states, including Oregon, Maine, and Louisiana, have succeeded in changing veterans preference laws. Montana's
amended veterans preference law limits preference to the initial hiring decision, not to promotions or reductions in force, and provides preference only
as a "tie-breaker" between substantially equally qualified candidates, not as
an absolute preference. For nondisabled veterans, preference is extended
only for fifteen years after separation from service. There is no time limit
for disabled veterans (Tompkins, 1985). In short, some jurisdictions have
succeeded in finding a balance between the desire to give veterans a "hand
up" into public service and to open the public service to other groups as well.

Classification: In Need of Reform

Closely linked to hiring is the traditional position classification system. The
tendency for classifications to proliferate and to become overspecific ham-
pers management flexibility in both the hiring process and the assignment
of work. As Table 2.10 shows, the number of separate classifications in the
states varies widely, from 510 in South Dakota to an astounding 7,300 in
New York.

Some states and cities have made efforts to reduce the number of
separate job titles. In New York state, after an outside review, secretarial
titles were consolidated. In Indianapolis and Virginia, there were reductions in the number of agency-specific titles. However, as Nina Rothchild
told us about Minnesota, "We talk all the time about cutting back, but all
the pressures are to expand. . . . It's managers who want to test for very
specific job skills, and changes in jobs as a result of computerization."

A 1984 study reported that 56 percent of the cities surveyed had consolidated some job titles (West, 1984, p. 329). Stein (1992) found a wide
range in the number of classifications; of the ten cities, the range was from
350, in Charlotte, to 1,300, in Baltimore. None of the cities had plans for
title reduction.

In the 1970s, New York City consolidated titles. But now that they
are under pressure to reduce the heavy use of provisional appointments by
offering more tests, there is pressure to break titles apart and make them
as narrow as possible. This will both ensure that the people on the hiring
lists have the necessary skills for a specific position and provide a greater
chance that the lists will be short and thus more quickly exhausted, permitting a return to hiring provisionals until the test can be given again.

Recently, the National Academy of Public Administration (NAPA) recommended that the federal government as a whole move to a simplified classification system using broad classifications and pay bands (National Academy of Public Administration, 1991). States and local governments should consider whether major reforms of the classification systems would have positive effects.

Experimenting with New Approaches: The Minnesota Experience

In the federal government, as we saw above, the ability to conduct demonstration projects trying out new approaches has led to some exciting proposals for reform. In the federal case, the Civil Service Reform Act of 1978 contained a provision permitting the Office of Personnel Management to suspend civil service law, under some specific guidelines, for agencies wishing to conduct such demonstration projects.

Minnesota is the only state we know of to have received statutory authorization to suspend law or regulation in order to conduct experiments in the staffing area, with reporting to the legislature, and with "meet and confer" with the unions (Vickmanis, 1990). Several of the experiments have been quite creative. For example, when an agency was hiring off a list that was over one year old and that had been used more than ten times, the number of people certified was doubled (that is, from ten to twenty or from twenty to forty). This "met management need for fresh faces and more names . . . without engendering the work and animosity of reopening the exam or removing nonselected candidates from the list" (Vickmanis, 1990, p. 3).

Permitting civil service law to be suspended requires a high level of trust that this authority will be used responsibly. But where it is politically feasible, such experiments may lead to creative solutions to staffing and other personnel problems.

Improving Motivation and Work Performance

Recruiting and hiring good people is the critical first step, but once they are on board, how do you motivate them to achieve the highest level of performance? This section examines several approaches to improving motivation and performance, including merit pay and performance appraisal, productivity bargaining, quality of work life programs, and total quality management.

Pay for Performance and Performance Appraisal

For many years, the standard approach to improving motivation and productivity has been to adopt a reward system linking pay to performance. As the recent report of the National Research Council of the National Academy of Sciences pointed out, "adoption of 'pay-for-performance plans' has been

Table 2.10. Classification and Compensation Plans: 1986.[1]

State or other jurisdiction	Classification plan				Legal basis for compensation plan
	Legal basis for plan	Current number of classifications	Requirement for periodic comprehensive review of plan (a)	Date of most recent comprehensive review	
Alabama	(b)	1,340	★/5	1982	S,R
Alaska	S	1,000	—	1985	S
Arizona	S,R	1,450	—	1987(c)	S,R
Arkansas	S	2,100	—	1980	S
California	C,S	4,400	★/2	—	S
Colorado	C,S	1,600	—	1975(d)	C,S
Connecticut	S	2,500	—	1986(c)	S,CB
Delaware	S	1,100	—	1986	S
Florida	S	1,651	—	1985	S
Georgia	S	1,500	—	1978	S
Hawaii	S,R	1,605	—	1987	S,R
Idaho	S	1,100	★/2	—	S
Illinois	S	1,620	—	1987(c)	S
Indiana	S	1,525	—	1986(c)	S
Iowa	S	1,116	—	1985	S,CB
Kansas	S,R	1,200	—	1986(c)	S,R
Kentucky	S,R	1,442	—	1982	S,R
Louisiana	C	3,764	—	1987	C
Maine	S	1,497	★/10	1982	CB
Maryland	S	3,000	—	1982	S
Massachusetts	S	1,000	—	1987	S,CB
Michigan	C	1,766	—	1980	C
Minnesota	S	1,600	—	1986(c)	S,CB
Mississippi	S	1,700	—	1987(c)	S
Missouri	S,R	1,080(e)	—	(f)	S
Montana	S,R	1,500	—	1985	S,R

State		Number	Review	Year	
Nebraska	S	1,300	—	1969	S
Nevada	S	1,200	★/5	1986(c)	S
New Hampshire	S	1,470	—	1987	S
New Jersey	S,R	6,500	—	1986(c)	S,R
New Mexico	S	800	—	—	S
New York	S	7,300	—	1954	S
North Carolina	S	3,012	—	1949	S
North Dakota	S	960	—	1986(c)	S
Ohio	S	1,832	—	1987–88	S
Oklahoma	S	1,136	—	1981	S
Oregon	S	1,185	—	(c)	S
Pennsylvania	S,R,E	2,700	—	1970	S,R,E
Rhode Island	S	1,500	—	1957	S
South Carolina	S	2,400	—	1979	S
South Dakota	S,R	579	—	1986	S,R
Tennessee	S	1,451	—	1984	S
Texas	S	1,288(e)	★/1	(g)	S
Utah	S	2,100	★/ (c)	1986(c)	S
Vermont	S	1,063	—	1986(c)	S
Virginia	S	2,100	—	1980	S
Washington	S	2,400	—	1986(c)	S
West Virginia	S	950	—	1986	S
Wisconsin	S	2,011	—	1947	S
Wyoming	S	1,375	—	1976	S
Guam	S	900	★/2	1984	S,R
Puerto Rico	S	1,131	—	1986(c)	S

Notes: [1]Information derived from survey of state personnel offices conducted by the Council of State Governments (March 1986) for the National Association of State Personnel Executives.

C = Constitution; S = Statute; R = Regulation; E = Executive order; CB = Collective bargaining.

(a) In this column, number after slash represents frequency (in years) of required review; (b) authorization from state personnel board rules; (c) ongoing review. In Illinois, ongoing since 1949; (d) incremental reviews have been conducted, based on 1975 comprehensive review; (e) legal limit on number of classifications. Missouri – 1,100; Texas – 1,288; (f) no comprehensive review; only reviews of sections of plan; (g) in Texas, budget reviewed biennially by classification compensation salary administration.

Source: Council of State Governments, 1990.

highly publicized as a means for improving U.S. labor productivity" (Mil-kovich and Wigdor, 1991).

The popularity of pay-for-performance (PFP) systems is reflected in the statistics on their use. As of 1987, twenty-two states had a PFP system "in which employees with a performance rating above that of satisfactory receive[d] a higher raise or bonus than those with only a satisfactory rating" (Lawther, Bernardin, Traynham, and Jennings, 1989, p. 8). The International City Management Association (ICMA) reported that, as of 1986, 82 percent of local officials who responded to a survey said that their jurisdiction had a formal performance appraisal system, and 76 percent stated that performance appraisal ratings were tied to wage increases. This contrasts with Stein's findings; none of the ten cities in her sample had linked pay to performance across the board (three had merit pay only for managers). The ICMA study found use of PFP less frequent in the Northeast, probably because of the strong influence of unions in that region.

Of the jurisdictions we examined, all utilize some kind of performance appraisal system. Several, including New York and Virginia, use Management by Objectives (MBO), a system with goals, or, in Virginia's terms, "expectations," set in advance. In New York, unions have played an active role in this area, in bargaining over the terms of performance appraisal and even in determining the forms to be used. California still uses a trait-based system, ranking employees on such qualities as task skills, knowledge, work habits, relations with people, and so on. Minnesota's system is quite decentralized, with each agency choosing its own system. The central personnel agency (the Department of Employee Relations) offers a model and provides technical support but does not mandate a specific form.

There is also considerable variation in linkages to pay. New York state implemented a pay-for-performance system in the early 1980s but then dropped coverage for bargaining unit employees. Virginia recently attempted to link pay to performance via an incentive pay plan that was scheduled for implementation in 1990–1991, but the general assembly did not provide the necessary funds. The failure to implement the plan has been the source of some morale and motivation problems.

Union response to pay-for-performance plans has often been negative, since unions tend to question whether such systems will be used fairly. However, in Minnesota, several bargaining units have negotiated achievement awards — sizable bonuses for special achievements. More typically, in California and Indianapolis, PFP plans cover only nonbargaining unit employees. California recently surveyed its higher managerial employees, and preliminary reports indicate that in some departments, in order to avoid morale problems, the bonuses are being rotated so that everyone gets one over a period of years.

The tendency to rotate bonuses is only one of the problems that arise in administering PFP programs. As Perry (1991, p. 75) points out, state and local PFP systems have not been extensively evaluated, but "[i]n-depth evaluations of specific plans have identified significant limitations." Research on PFP, and on the performance appraisal systems on which they are based, has pointed out a number of problems. First, there are concerns about the perceived validity and fairness of almost all performance appraisal systems. In fact, the search for a purely objective rating system is probably a chimera, because the process of rating is by nature a subjective process. Second, the amounts of pay or bonus given by PFP systems are usually too little and too late to have any significant effect on motivation or performance. The net result is that employees often do not perceive a real link between pay and performance. Many critics of current PFP plans point out that they reward individual rather than group behavior, thus increasing competition rather than fostering cooperation and team effort.

In short, most studies have failed to demonstrate a clear link between PFP systems and agency effectiveness (Milkovich and Wigdor, 1991). Yet organizations continue to adopt them, raising perplexing questions about the relationship of research to practice in the field.

Low Productivity and Fiscal Stress

The fiscal stress that many states and localities are encountering places constant pressure on them to utilize all types of resources in a more efficient, effective manner. Because personnel costs represent the lion's share of state and local government budgets (about 70 percent), pressures to reduce spending invariably entail the movement (for example, transfers and demotions) and layoff of government workers. Productivity improvement strategies have become extremely popular during such periods of shrinking resources. Whatever strategies or programs are pursued to combat them, fiscal crises create tensions between labor and management. Labor seeks to protect its turf, in particular its workers, from layoffs and other regressive employment actions. Management, on the other hand, feels hamstrung by unions and impeded in its attempts to control spiraling spending.

In the 1970s, the city of Orange, California, and the City of Orange Police Association engaged in what is known as "productivity bargaining." This concept refers to efforts that directly link salary increases to observable increases in productivity. Although many unions are skeptical of productivity bargaining because its threat to increase productivity may thereby result in layoffs, some public sector unions have found it to be desirable and effective.

Under the labor-management program in Orange, salary increases were tied to reductions in four areas of crime: rape, robbery, burglary, and auto theft. It was the first agreement of this nature in the country involving police. This one-time effort was aimed at controlling increases in the crime rate in the above-mentioned categories, while containing police costs.

As Staudohar (1985, pp. 261–263) reports: "The plan's monetary incentive has had some effect in motivating police to be more effective . . . and employee morale is high . . . . Experience with the police performance incentive plan in Orange indicates success in reducing the reported total of four target crimes."

The experience at New York City's Bureau of Motor Equipment (BME), which is housed in the Department of Sanitation, similarly represents a unique joint effort to improve productivity. The BME repairs and maintains the department's fleet of vehicles, which includes collection trucks, mechanical sweepers, and salt spreaders, just to name a few.

In the late 1970s, the BME was plagued with management, leadership, and labor problems to the point where one-half of the main equipment was unusable each day, leading to staggering overtime costs, because vehicles had to be used during the evening to complete collection routes. BME addressed these problems by forming a top-level Labor Committee, whereby "[u]nion representatives joined with the Bureau's top management group to form a special Executive Committee, thereby including labor in the planning, strategy formulation and implementation process throughout the organization" (Contino, 1986, p. 171). Through observation and communication with employees, formal "improvement programs" were developed and implemented with the aim of improving working conditions. Once the Labor Committee proved that its voice was heard among management and that it was not simply a token gesture on the bureau's part, employees began to offer suggestions for enhancing efficiency and productivity. Contino (1986, p. 174) notes that the efforts led to a "$16.5 million cost avoidance . . . within the first two years . . . along with dramatic improvements in service quality." The BME case represents a good illustration of how effective joint ventures can be when labor and management take the concept of cooperation seriously.

In an effort to address the fiscal crisis and foreboding layoffs in New York state in the mid 1970s, labor and management joined forces. The state and the Civil Service Employees Association (CSEA), which represents over 105,000 blue-collar workers in the state, formed the Continuity of Employment Committee (CEC). The CEC studied the impacts of worker displacement, made recommendations that would minimize layoffs, and developed and implemented reemployment programs for those workers who were displaced prior to the formation of the CEC (Jick, 1978; McKersie, Greenhalgh, and Jick, 1981). The committee's work was successful insofar as no massive layoffs of employees took place. Moreover, as McKersie, Greenhalgh, and Jick (1981, p. 219) point out, "The state subsequently adopted attrition programs as standard operating procedure for work force reductions. Thus, in a very important sense, the work and thinking of the Committee has been adopted by state decision-makers." (It should be noted that even today, New York state seeks to rely on attrition, but layoffs have simply been unavoidable during certain economic downturns.)

Quality of Work Life and Labor-Management Cooperation

An ongoing concern for both labor and management is the quality of the working environment for individual employees. Under quality of work life (QWL) programs, which are employed with as well as without union participation, employees are given opportunities for personal accomplishment and participation in organizational decision making (Gold, 1986). QWL programs generally came on the scene in the early 1970s and flourished well into the 1980s. As we move into and beyond the 1990s, there will be a growing demand for such programs, particularly in light of the forecasted changes in work and work technology.

In 1976, the city of Columbus, Ohio, started one of the largest municipal experiments with joint labor-management cooperation. AFSCME and the city entered into an agreement creating the Columbus/AFSCME Quality of Working Life Program, aimed at improving not only the quality of the work environment but the quality of city government services as well. In addition to a steward-level committee comprised of the mayor of Columbus and top officials of AFSCME, working-level committees exist within various departments or facilities. Decision-making power rests with these working-level committees (Midwest Center for Public Sector Labor Relations, 1979). The program has allowed the parties to reach the source or cause of various problems and rectify them; it has improved overall communication between the parties and has led to a reduction in the number of grievances filed by city employees; it has raised skill levels in such areas as techniques of leadership and interpersonal relations.

Another major concern to both labor and management today is health care, and particularly its rapidly rising cost. As Carswell (1991, p. 1) notes: "The spiraling cost of health services, now approaching two billion dollars a day, has driven the cost of insurance up and forced millions of working Americans into the ranks of the uninsured." Several jurisdictions have dealt creatively with this challenge. Minnesota's approach to rising health costs is noteworthy because of active union involvement. Minnesota has had a series of labor-management committees with its largest union, AFSCME, for some time, addressing such issues as safety, child care, parking, and VDTs. On the question of health insurance, which affected all state employees, they engaged in coalition bargaining with all ten state unions simultaneously. The result was significant cost savings through development of a statewide network of preferred providers, which has resulted in national recognition for the state's efforts.

In the early 1980s, labor and management officials of Clackamas County, Oregon, formed a labor-management committee for the sole purpose of health care cost containment (Barrett, 1985). The primary strategy pursued by the committee to contain the costs of health care while maintaining its quality is referred to by the committee as "market pressure." As

Barrett points out, about 90 percent of all health care costs are paid by insurance companies and other third parties. As such, the consumer has very little knowledge of or information about health care costs. The Clackamas Committee, working with employees and citizens, disseminates information about and provides public education on health care costs with the ultimate goal of placing pressure on the county's two hospitals and 300 doctors to reduce costs. The committee also conducts studies of cost issues and emphasizes wellness, safety, and screening programs. The success of the committee has led to the formation of similar committees around the country as well as to a national-level committee between the U.S. Conference of Mayors and AFSCME (Barrett, 1985).

Total Quality Management

The newest approach to improving motivation and performance, in both the public and private sectors, is total quality management, or TQM. TQM is a management system that emphasizes customer satisfaction, involving all the employees in improving work processes, and statistical measurement to monitor performance. The approach usually relies heavily on problem-solving teams thus building on earlier approaches such as quality circles. Several states and local governments are now trying a TQM approach. Walton (1990) describes in detail a "Quality First" project in the tri-cities area of Kingsport, Johnson City, and Bristol, Tennessee, that involved a public-private partnership with leadership from the mayor and city manager of Kingsport, the Chamber of Commerce, and business leaders. Joseph Sensenbrenner (1991) has written about his pathbreaking attempts to instill the values of TQM in a city workforce while he was mayor of Madison, Wisconsin.

In most of the jurisdictions we examined, TQM is in the early stages of implementation. Indianapolis is perhaps farthest along. They developed a program called TQS (total quality service), which has been in place since 1990. It involves TQS teams throughout the city to deal with issues employees face on a daily basis. Teams develop and implement improvements for getting work done. Their program was modeled after the private sector (particularly Florida Power and Light and Eli Lilly). TQS is obviously very new but is regarded as successful so far both in improving the quality of service and improving cost-effectiveness or efficiency in the city's administration of its programs.

New York state is in the early stages of implementing what it calls QtP (Quality through Participation). Some agencies in both Minnesota and California are adopting a TQM approach, particularly the Department of Transportation in Minnesota and the Department of Motor Vehicles in California, which experienced a great improvement in the quality of performance using TQM.

TQM is a potentially exciting approach to improving government performance. A few caveats should be kept in mind, however. Because TQM is still relatively new, we have no studies that demonstrate its effect over the long term. There is some evidence that its effectiveness is dependent on top management commitment; it thus may be difficult to institutionalize so that it can survive changes in leadership. For example, Walton (1990, p. 121) points out that Sensenbrenner's reforms in Madison were "highly dependent on Sensenbrenner's patronage . . . and bogged down when political power changed hands."

Second, the values of TQM stress group participation and group rewards, which is in conflict with the values underlying traditional pay-for-performance systems. If such a system is already in place, as is the case in many public sector jurisdictions, that conflict needs to be addressed.

Third, most of the TQM literature does not address the role of unions; it is typically pictured as a management effort. We need to look more at whether TQM, like quality circles, can operate effectively in a unionized environment, and what role unions should play in the TQM process. In the jurisdictions we studied, the union role varied. New York state is still developing QtP and, although it has consulted the unions, it is too early to say with assurance what role the unions will play. In Indianapolis, there is no official union role in the TQS program, although individual members participate and serve as team leaders.

Conclusion

When we presented the initial draft of this chapter at a planning conference for the commission, one of the comments was that the civil service system was so unwieldy that it was not salvageable. It should just be blown up. That may or may not be desirable, but it certainly is not politically feasible. It is the contention of this chapter that these systems *can* be reformed, that some changes, which have been made successfully in some states and local governments, can significantly improve the functioning of these systems. The chapter discusses reforms in three areas: personnel systems, motivational systems, and training and development.

A number of jurisdictions have introduced needed flexibility into their personnel systems without abandoning the concept of merit. We see six areas as central to reform in personnel systems.

- Improving active recruiting, linked to human resource planning
- Exploring alternatives to written tests for some occupations
- Moving away from the rule of three for selection
- Increasing opportunities for lateral entry
- Limiting veterans preference
- Consolidating job titles

State and local governments also need to improve motivation and productivity. We conclude that they should use pay-for-performance systems with caution, understanding their limitations. We also explore ways state and local governments have improved productivity with union involvement, using such approaches as productivity bargaining, quality of work life programs, quality circles, and TQM.

In sum, we hope this chapter has served to break some widely held myths about civil service systems and labor relations. We have presented some positive examples of ways in which state and local governments have used and adapted these systems to improve their organizational performance. The lesson, then, is that these systems *can* be reformed. Rather than simply tolerating them, gaming them, or trying to circumvent them by contracting out work, state and local politicians and administrators need to explore ways to improve efficiency and increase management flexibility without sacrificing the original goals of both the civil service and labor relations.

References

Ban, C. "The Realities of the Merit System." In C. Ban and N. Riccucci (eds.), *Public Personnel Management: Current Concerns — Future Challenges.* New York: Longman, 1991.

Ban, C., Faerman, S. R., and Riccucci, N. M. "Productivity and the Personnel Process." In M. Holzer (ed.), *Public Productivity Handbook.* New York: Marcel Dekker, 1992.

Ban, C., and Redd, H. C. III. "The State of the Merit System: Perceptions of Abuse in the Federal Civil Service." *Review of Public Personnel Administration,* 1990, *10*(3), 55–72.

Barrett, J. T. *Labor-Management Cooperation in the Public Service: An Idea Whose Time Has Come.* Washington, D.C.: International Personnel Management Association, 1985.

Branti v. *Finkel,* 445 U.S. 506 (1980).

Burke, M. J., and Pearlman, K. "Recruiting, Selecting, and Matching People with Jobs." In J. P. Campbell, R. J. Campbell, and Associates, *Productivity in Organizations: New Perspectives from Industrial and Organizational Psychology.* San Francisco: Jossey-Bass, 1988.

Carswell, J. "Pepper Report Excludes VA System." *Public Administration Times,* Jan. 1991, *1*(3).

Cayer, N. J. *Managing Human Resources.* New York: St. Martin's Press, 1980.

Cayer, N. J. "Local Government Personnel Structure and Policies." In *The Municipal Yearbook, 1991.* Washington, D.C.: International City Management Association, 1991.

Citizens Research Council of Michigan. *An Evaluation of the Michigan Civil Service System.* Report no. 288. Detroit: Citizens Research Council of Michigan, 1988.

Contino, R. "Productivity Gains Through Labor-Management Cooperation at the N.Y.C. Department of Sanitation Bureau of Motor Equipment." In J. M. Rosow (ed.), *Teamwork: Joint Labor-Management Programs in America.* New York: Pergamon Press, 1986.

Council of State Governments. *The Book of the States, 1970–1971.* Lexington, Ky.: Council of State Governments, 1970.

Council of State Governments. *The Book of the States, 1982–1983.* Lexington, Ky.: Council of State Governments, 1982.

Council of State Governments. *The Book of the States, 1990–1991.* Iron Works Pike, Ky.: Council of State Governments, 1990.

Curme, M. A., Hirsch, B. T., and MacPherson, D. A. "Union Membership and Contract Coverage in the United States, 1983–1988." *Industrial and Labor Relations Review,* 1990, *44,* 5–33.

Elrod v. *Burns,* 427 U.S. 347 (1976).

Finkle, A. L. "State Government Unionism." In J. Rabin and D. Dodd (eds.), *State and Local Government Administration.* New York: Marcel Dekker, 1985.

Freeman, R. B., Ichniowski, C., and Zax, J. "Collective Organization of Labor in the Public Sector." In R. B. Freeman and C. Ichniowski (eds.), *When Public Sector Workers Unionize.* Chicago: University of Chicago Press, 1988.

Frucher, M. S. "Director of the Governor's Office of Employee Relations." In J. Benjamin and N. Hurd (eds.), *Making Experience Count: Managing New York in the Carey Era.* Albany, N.Y.: Nelson A. Rockefeller Institute of Government, 1985.

Gold, C. *Labor-Management Committees: Confrontation, Cooptation or Cooperation?* Ithaca, N.Y.: ILR Press, 1986.

Goodsell, C. *The Case for Bureaucracy.* (2nd ed.) Chatham, N.J.: Chatham House, 1985.

Holzer, M. "Attracting the Best and the Brightest." In C. Ban and N. Riccucci (eds.), *Public Personnel Management: Current Concerns — Future Challenges.* New York: Longman, 1991.

International City Management Association (ICMA). "Performance Appraisals in Local Government." *Baseline Data Report,* 1986, *18*(1), 1–13.

International Personnel Management Association Assessment Council (IPMAAC). "Recent Innovations in Public Sector Assessment." A paper presented to the National Commission on Testing and Public Policy, 1989.

Jick, T. "Labor-Management Panel Seeks to Help Laid-Off State Workers." *Monthly Labor Review,* July 1978, pp. 92–94.

Kearney, R. *Labor Relations in the Public Sector.* (2nd ed.) New York: Marcel Dekker, 1992.

Labor Relations Reporter. "State Labor Laws." Washington, D.C.: Bureau of National Affairs, 1989–1990.

Lawther, W. "The State of State Training." *PM,* July 1987, pp. 16–19.

Lawther, W., Bernardin, H. J., Traynham, E., and Jennings, K. "Implications of Salary Structure and Merit Pay in the Fifty American States." *Review of Public Personnel Administration,* 1989, *9*(2), 1–14.

Lee, R. D. *Public Personnel Systems.* Baltimore, Md.: University Park Press, 1979.

Lee, R. M. "One Fire Department's Approach to Affirmative Action Hiring." *Western City,* Oct. 1988, pp. 23 + .

McKersie, R. B., Greenhalgh, L., and Jick, T. D. "The CEC: Labor-Management Cooperation in New York." *Industrial Relations,* Spring 1981, pp. 212–220.

Midwest Center for Public Sector Labor Relations. *Labor-Management Committees in the Public Sector.* Bloomington: Indiana University Press, 1979.

Milkovich, G., and Wigdor, A. *Pay for Performance: Evaluating Performance Appraisal and Merit Pay.* Washington, D.C.: National Academy Press, 1991.

Mosher, W., and Kingsley, J. D. *Public Personnel Administration.* New York: HarperCollins, 1941.

National Academy of Public Administration. *Modernizing Federal Classification: An Opportunity for Excellence.* Washington, D.C.: National Academy of Public Administration, 1991.

National Association of State Personnel Executives (NASPE) and the Council of State Governments. *State Personnel Office: Roles and Functions.* Lexington, Ky.: Council of State Governments, 1987.

National Commission on the Public Service (Volcker Commission). *Rebuilding the Public Service: Task Force Reports.* Washington, D.C.: National Commission on the Public Service, 1989.

Newland, C. "Legalistic Reforms vs Effectiveness, Efficiency, and Economy." *Public Administration Review,* 1976, *36,* 529–537.

Osborne, D., and Gaebler, T. *Reinventing Government.* Reading, Mass.: Addison-Wesley, 1992.

Ospina, S. "'Expediency Management' in Public Service: A Dead-End Search for Managerial Discretion." *Public Productivity and Management Review,* Summer 1992, *15*(4), 405–421.

Perry, J. "Linking Pay to Performance: The Controversy Continues." In C. Ban and N. Riccucci (eds.), *Public Personnel Management: Current Concerns — Future Challenges.* New York: Longman, 1991.

Personnel Administrator v. *Feeney,* 422 U.S. 256 (1979).

Riccucci, N. M. "Merit, Equity, and Test Validity: A New Look at an Old Problem." *Administration and Society,* 1991, *23*(1), 74–93.

Riccucci, N. M., and Wheeler, G. R. "Positive Employee Performance: An Innovative Approach to Employee Discipline." *Review of Public Personnel Administration,* Fall 1987, pp. 49–63.

Rodriguez, V. "Texas Government." Briefing paper prepared for the National Commission on the State and Local Public Service, 1992.

Rosenbloom, D. H., and Shafritz, J. M. *Essentials of Labor Relations.* Reston, Va.: Reston Publishing, 1985.

Rutan v. *Republican Party of Illinois,* 58 Law Week 4872, 1990.

Sensenbrenner, J. "Quality Comes to City Hall." *Harvard Business Review,* Mar.-Apr. 1991, *69,* 64–75.

Shafritz, J., Riccucci, N. M., Rosenbloom, D., and Hyde, A. *Personnel Management in Government.* (4th ed.) New York: Marcel Dekker, 1992.

Stahl, O. G. *Public Personnel Administration.* (8th ed.) New York: HarperCollins, 1983.

Staudohar, P. D. "An Experiment in Increasing Productivity of Police Service Employees." In M. J. Levine (ed.), *Labor Relations in the Public Sector: Readings and Cases.* (2nd ed.) Columbus, Ohio: Grid, 1985.

Stein, L. "Municipal Administrative Reforms: Hope or Reality?" Paper prepared for the National Commission on the State and Local Public Service, 1992.

Tompkins, J. "Employment Preference for Veterans: Montana's Restrictive Approach." *Review of Public Personnel Administration,* 1985, *6*(1), 1–10.

Troy, L., and Sheflin, N. "The Flow and Ebb of U.S. Public Sector Unionism." *Government Union Review,* Spring 1984, pp. 1–149.

Troy, L., and Sheflin, N. *U.S. Union Sourcebook.* West Orange, N.J.: Industrial Relations Data and Information Services, 1985.

Ukeles, J. B. *Doing More with Less: Turning Public Management Around.* New York: AMACOM, 1982.

Vickmanis, J. "A Statutory Authorization for Selection Experimentation." Paper presented at IPMAAC Symposium, June 26, 1990.

Walton, M. *Deming Management at Work.* New York: Putnam's, 1990.

West, J. "City Personnel Management: Issues and Reforms." *Public Personnel Management,* Fall 1984, *13*(3), 317–334.

THREE

Retaining and Recruiting
Career Professionals

James K. Conant
Dennis L. Dresang

The condition of the public service at the national level was the focus of the National Commission on the Public Service (Volcker Commission). The findings from that commission were published in a 1989 report titled *Rebuilding the Public Service*. As the title of the report implies, the commission's general finding was that the national public service is a troubled institution. In this chapter, we make an initial attempt to determine whether the perceived troubles of the public service extend beyond the national level to the states. The focus of the investigation is on career professional retention, morale, and recruitment in the states. A related topic—education and training for career professionals—is briefly discussed as part of our conclusions because it is relevant to our findings. A systematic examination of this important topic is, however, beyond the scope of our analysis.

Most career professionals fill positions that require a university un-

Additional financial support for this research was provided by the Fund for New Jersey, the Robert M. La Follette Institute of Public Affairs at the University of Wisconsin, Madison, and the Wisconsin Department of Administration. Lauren McHargue, Suzanne Piasta, and Jutta Joachim served as project assistants for the study. Important contributions to the study were also made by the staff of the University of Wisconsin Extension Survey Research Lab, the Commissioners and Secretaries of the New Jersey and Wisconsin executive branch departments examined in this study, the 1,150 managers and staff people in those departments who filled out surveys or participated in other ways in the research, and James Perry and Paul van Rijn.

dergraduate degree or graduate degree, and most are hired into the civil service system. Because they are trained in disciplines like chemistry, engineering, social work, biology, public affairs, business, medicine, or law, career professionals have been described as the "conveyer belts between knowledge and theory on the one hand, and public purpose on the other" (Mosher, 1968, p. 103). At the core of the Volcker Commission report was the view that the public service was unable to retain or recruit the career professionals (human resources) needed to function effectively.[1] The principal cause of the problem was presumed to be the public sector's inability to compete with the private sector for this human resource.[2]

Other dimensions of the troubles noted in the Volcker Commission's final report and subcommittee reports include *low morale* among senior managers and among career professional employees and *underinvestment in skill development* for both groups. Morale problems for both groups were perceived to be a function of several factors, including the ongoing government-bashing by Ronald Reagan and other elected officials. No particular reason was given for the underinvestment in skill development.

Senior Executive Retention and Morale in the States

The most visible sign of the national government's troubles in the late 1970s and early 1980s was the low morale and high rate of exit among the government's 7,000 senior managers. Between July of 1979 and March of 1983, more than 40 percent of the managers in the senior executive service (SES) left government (Levine, 1986). Additionally, 72 percent of the senior managers who responded to a Merit Systems Protection Board study said that they would not recommend a career in government to their children (Federal Executive Institute Alumni Association, 1984). Do the troubles of the national government's senior executive service extend to the states? In order to facilitate the development of an answer to this question, we develop a model that can be used to explain the high rate of exit at the national level. We then use the model to make predictions about senior manager morale and retention at the state level. Next, we test those predictions with data drawn from two states: New Jersey and Wisconsin.

Specifying the Relationship Between
Morale Problems and Exit Decisions

One of the first, and we think most useful, models of turnover was developed by March and Simon (1958). In their model, turnover (which includes exit from an organization as well as movement within an organization) is a function of two general factors: (1) the desirability of movement (from or within an organization) and (2) the ease of movement. According to March and Simon, the key factor in the (perceived) desirability of movement is job satisfaction — or morale. The key factor in the ease of movement is the condition of the economy.

The model we have developed for this study was informed by March and Simon's work. Our decision to develop our own model is not, by any means, an implied criticism of their work but rather, our intent was to develop a model that allowed us to map or define more closely key relationships and key variables we wanted to examine. Our model—and our perspective on the morale/exit relationship—is outlined in Figure 3.1.

Figure 3.1. The Morale/Exit Relationship.

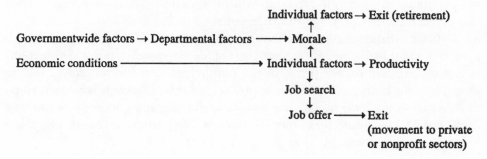

Our assumptions about the general relationship between morale and exit are (1) that negative conditions within the government or within individual departments create morale problems, (2) the most direct and immediate effect of morale problems is likely to be a negative effect on productivity, but (3) the negative conditions that create low morale also motivate some (senior managers) to search for alternative employment opportunities, and these conditions (4) enhance the prospects that job offers from outside government will be accepted.[3] We also assume that some (small) portion of SES members will leave government for jobs in the private or nonprofit sector regardless of governmentwide or departmental circumstances. The rate of departure, however, is likely to depend to some extent on the condition of the economy.

It is possible, of course, that for some senior managers the link between negative governmentwide or negative departmental conditions and the decision to exit is direct and immediate. After all, those factors may have a sharp, personal impact on some senior managers. For example, in a case where departmental circumstances are negative, a senior manager might not be invited to meetings with political appointees in which policy, program, or budget decisions that affect his areas are being made. Or she may be invited but not allowed to speak or, if allowed to speak, treated with disdain.

Even in the face of such excruciating circumstances, however, senior managers are unlikely to resign immediately because they need an alternative source of income. Consequently, either the retirement option or some other source of employment is, for most, a necessary condition for exit.[4]

On these grounds alone, one would not necessarily predict exit rates above the norm even with most or all of the governmentwide and departmental variables in the negative column. All of this, however, makes even more striking the fact that more than 40 percent of these senior managers left the federal government between July 1979 and May 1983.

Specifying the Parameters of the Morale/Exit Model for the SES

The specific assumptions of our model of senior manager morale and exit are (1) the top-level managerial jobs in the SES are highly desirable positions,[5] (2) the holders of these positions are not likely to give them up lightly, (3) normal turnover, which includes both exit from government (retirement, movement to private sector, and so on) and movement within or between departments (promotions, transfers, and so on) is likely to be in the range of 5 to 8 percent a year—or 25 to 40 percent over a five-year period, with (4) approximately one-quarter of that annual turnover (1 to 2 percent) showing up as movement within government and three-quarters (4 to 6 percent) showing up as exit decisions. Finally, we assume that two-thirds (3 to 4 percent) of the exit decisions will involve retirement; one-third (1 to 2 percent) will involve movement to jobs outside of government.

This is the proposition or hypothesis we want to test.

> Morale problems for the senior manager group as a whole and exit rates above the normal rate of 4 to 6 percent per year are generated *primarily* by negative circumstances within the national government.

In preparation for testing our hypothesis, we will provide some additional background information on our model. Specifically, we will describe the three general variables or parameters in our model of morale/exit and the specific components of each. The three variables are *governmentwide factors, departmental factors,* and *individual factors.* The potential effects these factors have on morale and exit are displayed in Figure 3.1.

A key to the governmentwide climate is presidential leadership. Presidential leadership, in turn, has several dimensions that can positively or negatively influence morale and exit rates. A change in presidential leadership—particularly if it includes a change in party—might stimulate exit among senior managers who worry about being associated with the opposition party. Likewise, a chief executive with an antigovernment ideology might create morale problems and stimulate exit—particularly if that ideology is accompanied by government-bashing and a budgetary strategy aimed at shrinking the size and role of government. Presidential leadership (and ideology) also come into play in terms of appointments to the top posts in the executive branch departments and agencies. An antigovernment president is likely to appoint people who have a similar ideology and who distrust or have disdain for career managers. Last but not least is the fiscal climate of the times. A negative fiscal climate (recession) creates impetus for cutbacks and thus makes the senior executive's job less attractive.

Factors that might affect the departmental climate senior managers encounter include rates of turnover in departmental leadership (secretaries, deputy or assistant secretaries); the policy positions taken by the secretary and deputy or assistant secretaries; the management style of the political appointees; the degree of opportunity for advancement within the department; and the level or type of opportunity managers within the department have for skill development or personal growth. For example, high levels of leadership turnover create uncertainty and risk for a senior manager, which might create stress—which in turn might create morale problems and ultimately lead to turnover. Likewise, a deep-seated disagreement with a political appointee on an important policy issue could create a very difficult working circumstance. On the other hand, stability in departmental leadership and congruence on key policy issues might mitigate negative governmentwide factors.

Finally, individual variables that might influence exit rates include the age of the senior manager (retirement), opportunities for employment in the private sector, or opportunities for employment in other public or nonprofit organizations. For example, a senior manager may decide to retire at age sixty-two or sixty-five, regardless of whether governmentwide factors are positive or negative.

Testing the Model with SES Data

All of the governmentwide factors were negative during the Reagan years; on this basis alone, one might predict low morale and high exit rates. Furthermore, where some or all the departmental factors were negative, they amplified the negative aspects of the governmentwide factors and thus increased the prospects for low morale and high rates of exit. Do the SES data fit our model and our predictions about morale and exit in the SES between 1979 and 1983? Generally speaking, they do.

As we would predict, given the negative governmental climate and departmental variables, morale was very low during this period. Second, as we would predict, the rate of exit from the SES was above the normal rate of departure. Indeed, the imputed five-year exit rate was 53 percent—more than double the predicted normal rate. Of those who exited between 1979 and 1983, approximately 47 percent retired, 5 percent took other public or nonprofit positions, and 48 percent moved to the private sector. For half or more of those who fit into each of these groups, we think there is good reason to believe that the decision to leave was not made independent of the negative conditions in government or their departments at the time. In sum, we think we have a model that works reasonably well for predicting senior manager exit rates and morale. We will now use that model to make predictions about the states.

Using the Model to Make Predictions About the States

If governmentwide conditions are strongly negative in a state, we predict that they will have a negative effect on the morale of most senior managers and thus set the conditions for above-normal rates of exit from government. At the same time, we predict that where governmentwide conditions are positive, exit rates will fall within the normal range of 4 to 6 percent a year or 20 to 30 percent over five years. We also predict that two-thirds of the annual exit decisions will be for retirement when exit rates fall within the normal range.

Likewise, we predict that where conditions in specific departments are strongly negative, they will have a negative effect on the morale of most senior managers in those departments and thus set the stage for rates of exit above the norm. In turn, higher-than-normal exit rates could contribute, depending on the size of the department, to an above-normal exit rate on a statewide basis.

In order to do a direct comparison with the SES, we need data from the 1980s on the circumstances or experience of states that have a senior executive or career executive service. A potential source for such data is the literature on these systems and states. Although it is not large, that literature does contain useful information about the origins, goals, and characteristics or design of these systems.[6] For example, we know that in 1987, twelve states had executive personnel systems, that their formal or stated goals paralleled those of the national SES, and that a "rich variety" of approaches were taken in designing these systems (Sherwood and Breyer, 1987).

Unfortunately, the literature does not contain data on exit rates or morale of the states' senior managers. This situation highlights the pressing need for such research, and it provides an inducement to look elsewhere for data on exit rates and morale. In this case, we will look at data collected as part of studies conducted in New Jersey and Wisconsin by the principal investigator for this study. The studies in the two states were designed for other purposes, but turnover data—including exit data—can be culled from them.[7]

Using the Model to Make Predictions for New Jersey and Wisconsin

Both the New Jersey and Wisconsin studies were designed to be studies of the states' management skill development activities. The New Jersey study was conducted from late 1989 through the spring of 1990 but includes data on turnover for the five-year period from December of 1984 through December of 1989. The Wisconsin study was conducted between late 1990 and the summer of 1991, and provides a five-year window on turnover and exit for the period March of 1986 through March of 1991.

Both studies focused on a subset of the states' executive branch departments and agencies. In New Jersey, the departments were Environmental Protection, Health, Labor, and Treasury. These departments had 35 percent of the state's employees and the same percentage of the state's managers. In Wisconsin, the departments were Administration, Natural Resources, Revenue, and Transportation, which had 30 percent of the state's employees and a similar percentage of the state's managers.

Some additional background on the two two states might be useful contextual material. New Jersey had approximately 80,000 state employees in 1989, with approximately 70 percent (54,000) working in the nineteen executive branch departments and agencies. Most of the remaining 30 percent worked in the state's universities and colleges. Approximately 11,250 supervisors and managers worked in the executive branch departments and agencies, and approximately 4.8 percent (540) of those managers were senior managers.

Wisconsin had approximately 60,000 employees in 1991, with approximately 53 percent (32,000) employed in the thirty-eight executive branch departments and agencies. Most of the remaining 47 percent worked in the state's universities and colleges. There were approximately 5,900 supervisors and managers in the executive branch departments and agencies, with approximately 6 percent (350) holding senior manager positions.

To develop predictions about morale and exit rates in New Jersey and Wisconsin, we need to know something about the two general factors that are likely to have a powerful governmentwide effect on them. Specifically, we want to know whether there are reasons to predict an exit rate higher than the expected normal rate. In both states, the general answer is no.

During the years 1985 to 1989, New Jersey enjoyed a combination of stable and exceptional gubernatorial leadership and rapid economic growth. Tom Kean was elected governor in November of 1981, was reelected by a huge margin in November of 1985, and held office through early January of 1989. He was very much committed to developing the capacity of the New Jersey state government and took a host of initiatives to develop both its infrastructure and its human resources. The principal blemish on this otherwise positive climate for senior managers was their emerging concerns in 1989 about the upcoming election and about the state of the economy. Many of the senior managers interviewed for the study believed that they would be vulnerable if the Democratic candidate won the election, assuming that their current working relationships with their Republican superiors would make the Democrats suspicious of them. They were also concerned about the signs of economic slowdown and its potential effects on state revenues. In short, at least at the end of this five-year time period, the strains of the forthcoming political and economic transition were showing up. The parameters of the model for New Jersey and Wisconsin are summarized in Table 3.1.

Like its northeastern counterpart, Wisconsin also experienced a period of political stability and strong economic growth during the mid and late 1980s. Indeed, the transition period for the state occurred just before the five-year segment examined here, rather than at the end as it did in New Jersey. A change in governors and parties occurred at the beginning of 1986,

Table 3.1. Causes of Exit Among Senior Managers.

	National Government 1979–1983	New Jersey 1984–1989	Wisconsin 1986–1991
Governmentwide variables			
Presidential/gubernatorial leadership			
Leadership change (election)	X		X
Party change (election)	X		X
Ideology: antigovernment	X		
Government-bashing	X		
Budgetary cutback strategy	X		
Political appointees			
Ideology (antigovernment)	X		
Negative attitude toward career managers	X		•
Fiscal climate: recession	X		
Departmental variables			
Turnover in leadership	•	•	•
Style of leadership	•	•	•
Policy positions of leadership	•	•	•
Little opportunity for advancement	•		
Limited opportunity for skill development/growth	•		
Individual variables			
Promotion, lateral move, transfer	•		
Retirement	•	•	•
External opportunities (private sector)	•	•	•
External opportunities (public, nonprofit)	•	•	•

Note: X means variable has widespread and potentially significant impact; • means variable may come into play in specific circumstances.

with Republican Tommy Thompson replacing Democratic incumbent Anthony Earl. Some perceived Thompson to be in the Reagan tradition, and most viewed him as a conservative Republican, but, in contrast to Ronald Reagan, he neither publicly bashed government nor attempted to severely curtail government activity. Like his counterpart at the national level, however, Thompson aggressively used his appointment powers to put his own people at the top of the governmental agencies. Since many of these appointees were drawn from business, and since some were perceived to be antigovernment, the process did raise some concerns.

In short, with most of the governmentwide factors positive, we predict that the five-year exit rate in Wisconsin's senior management corps will be within the normal range of 20 to 30 percent. Given the fact that one governmentwide factor was negative, however, and the fact that some of the departmental factors might be negative or at best neutral, we predict that the exit rate will fall toward the upper end of the normal range (20 to 27 percent). With respect to New Jersey, the senior managers' concerns about a sharp political and economic change might lead one to expect a somewhat higher-than-normal exit rate in the range of, say, 30 to 35 percent.

Testing the Model

Given the predictions stated above, the raw data for both the New Jersey and Wisconsin surveys provide a big surprise—indeed a shock. The data show that in New Jersey 75 percent of the senior managers in the four departments were in their current positions for five years or less. This seems like an extraordinary level of change or turnover in the top-level managerial ranks. It might also indicate that there is an extraordinary degree of instability in the state's executive branch departments. The data for Wisconsin are somewhat less dramatic but seem to show a similar pattern. In that state, 54 percent of the senior managers in the four departments were in their positions for five years or less.

How do the New Jersey and Wisconsin figures compare to the SES figures? Since we have exit data for the SES but not turnover data, we cannot make a direct comparison at this point. However, we can use the imputed five-year exit rate in the SES (53 percent) as a rough measuring stick. On this basis, the turnover in the senior management corps in Wisconsin appears to be about the same as the exit rate in the SES. The turnover rate in New Jersey, however, appears to be substantially higher.

From these data, one might draw the conclusion that the troubles of the public service at the state level are equally severe or even more severe than those of the national public service. Additionally, since the conditions in both states were positive for all or most of the key governmentwide factors during the five-year segments examined, one might conclude that private sector competition is the underlying cause of the states' troubles. Upon closer inspection, however, neither conclusion holds up. The key information for Wisconsin, including the statewide totals and the data for each of the four departments included in this study, is provided in Table 3.2.

The Wisconsin data show that 53 of the 103 (52 percent) senior managers who held their positions in March of 1991 had been in those jobs for five years or less. In the case of 6 of those 53 positions, however, this was a function of a newly created position within the five-year period, rather than turnover of an incumbent. Consequently, the imputed statewide turnover rate for senior managers during the period was 46 percent rather than 52 percent, only slightly above the upper end of our predicted normal rate. Of the remaining 47 senior managers, 15 were in positions where the incumbent moved up or laterally within the department, 2 were in positions where the previous manager moved to another state government department or another executive branch department; 30 were in positions where the incumbent left state government. In short, the five-year exit rate for senior managers in Wisconsin is only 29 percent (30/103).

We forecast a rate at the upper end of the predicted normal rate of 20 to 30 percent, and the actual exit rate (29 percent) is within that forecast. At the same time, the actual exit rate is far below the five-year imputed SES exit rate of 53 percent. Equally important, the data in Table 3.2 show that almost all of the senior managers who left Wisconsin state government re-

Table 3.2. Background Information on Senior Manager Turnover in the Executive Branch Departments in Wisconsin.

Agency*	DOA	DNR	DOR	DOT	Department totals
Number of senior manager positions in 1991	14	44	6	39	103
Number of senior managers who held jobs less than five years	12	16	2	22	52
Number holding new positions (created between 1986 and 1991)	6	0	0	0	6
Number holding positions where incumbent was promoted or moved within the department	0	8	1	6	15
Number holding positions where incumbent transferred to another state agency	0	1	1	0	2
Number of senior managers who left government	6	7	1	16	30
Retired	2	6	1	16	25
Other public or nonprofit	3	1	0	0	4
Private sector	1	0	0	0	1

Note: *DOA is Department of Administration; DNR is Department of Natural Resources; DOR is Department of Revenue; DOT is Department of Transportation.

tired. Specifically, of the thirty senior managers who decided to exit, twenty-five retired, four took positions in public or nonprofit organizations outside of state government, and only one moved to the private sector. These data seem to show quite convincingly that the allure of higher private sector salaries did not play a significant independent causal role in the exit rate of Wisconsin's senior managers.

Still open, however, is the question of why the exit rate was at the upper end of the predicted normal rate. Since almost all of the exit was connected to retirement, we need to ask whether something unusual was happening in Wisconsin during this time period. As it turns out, the rate of retirement during this time period seems to be largely a function of two factors: demographics and state policy. In terms of demographics, the career professionals who entered state service in the years immediately following the end of World War II were reaching retirement age. In terms of state policy, Wisconsin offered its employees an early retirement option that was in effect between June of 1988 and July of 1989.

The effects of both factors are highly visible in the Department of Transportation, where the turnover rate for senior managers was 56 percent and the exit rate was 41 percent. The early retirement policy by itself, however, may have resulted in 20 to 25 percent of the total retirements. In any case, the departmental turnover and exit rates probably exceed what would be found for any previous five-year period, and probably exceed what will be found in any future five-year period.

Having determined that Wisconsin fits our model of senior manager decision making and turnover, we can turn our attention to New Jersey. Unfortunately, we are not able to provide the kind of departmental data for New Jersey that we did for Wisconsin, but we can speculate about the components of those data. Between 1985 and 1989, there was substantial growth in New Jersey state government. Indeed, that growth was particularly pronounced in two of the four departments included in the study.[8] Consequently, we estimate that 20 to 25 percent of the senior managers were in positions created during that five-year period. In turn, this means that the statewide senior manager turnover rate was probably 50 to 55 percent, rather than 75 percent.

This still leaves a turnover rate substantially above the predicted normal rate, and it probably means that the exit rate was above the predicted normal rate too. We think the variation from the predicted normal levels for both can be explained largely by three factors in New Jersey that did not come into play in Wisconsin: (1) rapid growth in government, (2) a superheated regional and state economy, and (3) worries about the upcoming political and economic transition.

The rapid growth in government not only led to the creation of many new positions but also to higher-than-normal levels of promotions and lateral moves within and between departments. In the Department of Environmental Protection, for example, the workforce expanded by almost 25 percent during the time period we are considering. Thus the opportunity for senior managers to move laterally or gain promotions within their own departments was very high. Opportunities to move to other departments were probably unusually high, too.

Likewise, we suspect that extraordinary opportunities for movement from the public to the private sector were created by the powerful cycle of economic growth in the region and the state. The rapid economic growth probably created an unusually strong need on the part of private firms for engineers, scientists, accountants, lawyers, and other professionals. For some of those firms, senior managers within government may have been very attractive recruits.

Finally, the worries about the upcoming political and economic transition may have had an effect on a number of senior managers — particularly in terms of motivating a search for employment outside of state government. As noted above, the rapid economic growth in the region probably made this initiative seem more palatable and enhanced the prospects of finding alternative employment. In sum, even though the New Jersey turnover and exit rates are probably 15 to 20 percent above our predicted normal rates, we think that the three factors identified here can account for almost all of the above-normal turnover and exit. Consequently, we think the New Jersey case, like the Wisconsin case, provides support for our predictions and our model.

Predictions About Senior Manager Turnover in Other States

We end our examination of senior manager turnover and exit in New Jersey and Wisconsin confident that the model does specify key cause-and-effect relationships. We also think that we have succeeded in identifying what normal turnover and exit rates look like — and what factors are likely to push those rates up. We think that the normal annual turnover rate is 5 to 8 percent; the normal five-year rate is 25 to 40 percent. We think that the normal exit rate is three-quarters of the turnover rate, which means 4 to 6 percent on an annual basis and 20 to 30 percent on a five-year basis.

We could make predictions for each state about whether the statewide turnover and exit rates will be within or above the normal range by defining the parameters of the model. For example, in states where election decisions brought in a new chief executive, particularly from the opposition party, we would expect to see a negative effect on morale and turnover. We would also expect to see exit rates somewhat above the normal rate. Additionally, in the states where that chief executive's ideology was antigovernment, where he or she made a practice of bashing government, appointed agency heads who were of similar disposition, and took a budgetary cutback strategy, we would expect to find even higher rates of senior manager turnover and exit. In states where the governmentwide variables were positive or neutral, no early retirement plan was in effect, and the regional and state economy was not superheated, we would expect to see normal rates of turnover and exit.

Career Professional Retention and Morale

In this section we shift our focus from the top of the organizational hierarchy and senior managers to the base of the executive branch departments and the career professional employees. The national public service's troubles during the early and mid 1980s were perceived to include morale and retention problems. The morale problem was generally thought to be a governmentwide phenomenon. The Reagan administration's government-bashing and its attempts to shrink the size and role of government were presumed to be the principal causes of the problem (Johnson, 1986). The retention problems may also have had a governmentwide dimension, but the principal focus of concern seemed to be on the exit rate among scientists and engineers. The presumed cause of the exit problem among these two professional groups was private sector competition (Packard, 1986).

*Specifying the Relationship Between
Morale and Exit of Career Professionals*

Given the perspective provided above, one might assume that two different paths or models of career professional exit were operating in the national public service during the late 1970s and early 1980s. One model, especially applicable to scientists and engineers, emphasizes the role of attractive job opportunities in the private sector as the source of exit. A second model focuses on negative governmental circumstances as a cause of low morale, and, ultimately, exit. Both of these simple models are useful starting points for a discussion of morale and exit problems among career professionals in the national and state governments. The point to emphasize here, however, is that turnover that consists of both exit and movement within government takes place independent of governmentwide circumstances. When negative governmental conditions occur, they are, in effect, superimposed on "normal" circumstances. The trick here is to figure out just what effect the negative factors have.

In Figure 3.2 we present an expanded version of the model we introduced in Figure 3.1 as part of our discussion on senior manager retention and morale. In Figure 3.2, we define five key factors that drive or effect rates of turnover (exit and movement within government) for career professional employees: (1) economic circumstances, (2) labor market factors, (3) governmental circumstances, (4) departmental factors, and (5) individual factors. Our principal concern is exit, rather than movement within government, but the same general factors may come into play for both.

The top (horizontal) line in Figure 3.2 is the expanded element of our model. Economic conditions and labor market forces are listed on that line. The general condition of the economy is likely to be the single most important factor in determining turnover rates for career professionals (March and Simon, 1958). The overall level of business and government activity defines rates of job growth or contraction—and thus the overall level of demand for workers in both the public and private sectors. At the same time,

Figure 3.2. Career Professional Morale and Exit.

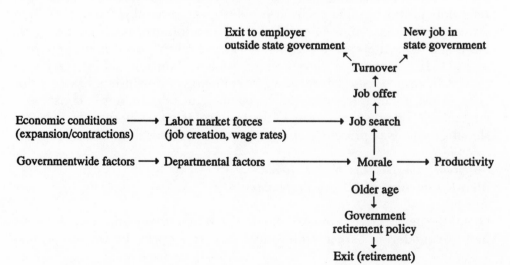

labor market forces, including the supply of and demand for particular types of professionals, may give some professionals greater opportunity for mobility than others.

Among the things we want to underscore here is that some career professionals — and particularly those in "hot" occupations — will be conducting a job search independent of governmentwide circumstances. Although negative governmentwide circumstances may accelerate the level of that activity somewhat, other (individual) factors may play an even more important role. For example, some career professionals reach retirement age every year, and they decide to retire regardless of all other circumstances. Others may decide that they do not like the work they are doing, do not work well with their supervisor, find workloads too heavy or too light, and so on. As a result, they may decide that they want to make a change. If they decide to conduct a job search, they may look within government or outside of government; in either case, a search that yields a job offer may result in turnover. If the job offer is accepted and it is from a private sector firm or nonprofit organization outside of government, exit occurs.

Governmentwide and departmental factors are displayed in the second horizontal line in Figure 3.2. Since these factors, as well as individual factors, were discussed in our presentation on Figure 3.1, we will not review them here. We do want to note, however, that the second horizontal line can be viewed as highlighting the circumstances for most employees in most career professionals groups. Most of these employees will *not* undertake a job search in a given year, regardless of the external governmental circumstances. Positive work-related factors, such as the work itself, friends in the workplace, promotional opportunities, and so on, come into play here. Negative factors, such as fear of the unknown, a desire to avoid relocation, or fear of exams or interviews, may also come into play.

In sum, the most direct and immediate effect of negative governmental (or departmental) circumstances is on morale and productivity. The primary determinants of exit decisions will be economic conditions, market forces (competing job offers), and age (retirement). Negative governmental circumstances and morale problems may push up exit rates in both cases incrementally. Unless those circumstances are very severe, accompanied by an early retirement policy or by extraordinary economic circumstances, however, we do not expect the effect to be very visible.

Specifying the Parameters of the Morale/Exit Model for Career Professionals

The underlying assumptions for our model of career professional morale and exit are that (1) career professional positions in government are desirable positions to have,[9] (2) the holders of these positions are not likely to give them up lightly, consequently (3) normal (annual) turnover for *most* professional positions will be in the range of 5 to 8 percent, with exit accounting for three-quarters (4 to 6 percent) of that turnover and movement within government accounting for one-quarter. Finally, we assume that retirement will account for two-thirds of the exit activity (3 to 4 percent); movement to employment outside government will account for one-third (1 to 2 percent).

These are the propositions or hypotheses that we want to test.

1.   Where morale is low across professional groups in government, negative governmentwide factors will be the principal cause.
2.   Where turnover and exit rates for specific professional groups are 10 percent or more, economic and labor market factors will be the principal cause of those high rates.
3.   Where turnover rates and exit rates across most professional groups are 10 percent or more within a particular department, negative departmental factors will be the principal cause.

Given the high level of private sector demand for scientists and engineers during the 1980s, we expect to find high turnover and exit rates among this group. Specifically, we expect to see annual turnover rates between 10 and 15 percent and annual exit rates between 6 and 10 percent. Similar labor market forces seemed to be working for management information specialists, such as computer programmers and so on, during the 1980s. Consequently, we expect to find high rates of turnover and exit for this professional group, too. Again, we expect the annual turnover rates to be in the range of 10 to 15 percent and the annual exit rates to be in the range of 6 to 10 percent.

Using the Model to Make Predictions About Wisconsin

In order to use the model of career professional morale and exit to make predictions about morale, turnover, and exit rates in a particular state, the parameters of the model—or the conditions in that state—have to be specified. Specification involves thre principal elements: (1) economic and labor market factors, (2) governmentwide factors, and (3) departmental factors. With respect to economic conditions and labor market factors, the critical issue is whether economic conditions and labor market factors in a particular state or region vary significantly from national conditions. If the regional or state economy is operating below the national level, opportunities to move from government to the private sector might be constrained even for key professional groups like scientists and engineers.[10] If it is exceptionally strong, such opportunities may be enhanced.

As noted in the previous section, economic and labor market conditions during 1988–1990 were somewhat better than national conditions. On this basis, we predict that turnover or exit rates across all professions might be in the upper end of the normal range—say 5 to 8 percent and 4 to 6 percent respectively. Given national labor market conditions, however, we expect higher rates of turnover and exit for scientists, engineers, and computer-related positions. Specifically, we expect turnover to be in the range of 10 to 15 percent and exit to be in the range of 6 to 10 percent.

The critical issue with respect to governmentwide factors and departmental factors is whether they are positive, neutral, or extremely negative. The principal effect we expect to see from negative factors is on morale and productivity; in extreme circumstances, however, some incremental effect on exit rates might be expected. Most of the governmentwide factors that came into play in Wisconsin were positive; only one was perceived to be negative. Some departmental factors were thought to be negative, others neutral or positive.

Testing the Model

Three key questions need to be examined in order to test our predictions about Wisconsin: (1) What was the morale of career professionals in Wisconsin state government during 1988–1990? (2) What were the turnover and exit rates among key professional groups? and (3) What were the turnover and exit rates in particular departments or agencies during that time period? The survey data needed to answer the question about morale were not available, and we did not attempt to undertake original research on the question. We faced similar circumstances with respect to the other two questions. There were no statewide data on turnover among professional groups, and there were no published data on turnover and exit in the departments and agencies.

In order to collect the data we needed, we decided to focus our efforts on the fifteen most heavily populated professional positions in Wisconsin state government. Those positions and the number of full-time equivalent employees in each are listed in Table 3.3.

Even though time and resource constraints prevented us from assembling the statewide data on turnover in the fifteen most heavily populated positions, we did construct a portrait of turnover in the ten most populous positions in five of Wisconsin's executive branch departments. Before outlining those data, however, a brief comment on the data in Table 3.3 is needed. These data not only define the structure of the state's professional ranks but also provide a portrait of the concentrations of professions.

For example, the data show that engineer, rather than social worker, nurse, job service specialist, attorney, and so on, is the most heavily populated professional group. The data also show that the number of professionals exceeds 1,000 in only three types of positions (engineers, nurses, and management information specialists). Furthermore, it exceeds 500 in only four types of positions.

The data on the top fifteen professional positions also give us a valuable perspective on the scope, scale, and potential impact of turnover and exit rates that range from normal (5 to 8 percent and 4 to 6 percent respec-

Table 3.3. Fifteen Most Populous Positions in Wisconsin State Government: 1989.

Rank	Title	Number of full-time employees
1	Engineer	1,800
2	Nurse	1,407
3	Management information specialist	1,187
4	Social worker	678
5	Teacher	426
6	Administrative officer	410
7	Auditor	305
8	Attorney	301
9	Natural resource specialist	284
10	Job service specialist	277
11	Environmental specialist	276
12	Program and planning analyst	261
13	Vocational rehabilitation counselor	222
14	Unemployment benefit specialist	207
15	Medical technologist	145

tively) to high (10 percent or more and 7 to 8 percent or more). For the state's most heavily populated statewide professional position (engineers), a 5 percent annual turnover rate would mean that 90 engineers left their positions for other jobs within government, retirement, or other employment opportunities. A 10 percent statewide exit rate among engineers would mean that 180 left their positions for employment outside of government and for retirement. In the least heavily populated of the top fifteen professional positions, medical technologists, the exit rate would hit 5 percent if 8 retired or departed for jobs outside of government. The rate would hit 10 percent if 15 employees left their positions.

Finally, the statewide picture provides a background perspective for the turnover and exit data collected for this investigation. The data were collected from five executive branch departments: Administration, Health and Social Services, Natural Resources, Revenue, and Transportation. These departments have more than 50 percent of all of Wisconsin's executive branch employees, and they have all but a small portion of the state's career professionals. The five departments include significant concentrations of thirteen of the state's fifteen most heavily populated professional positions. The only positions not covered in these five departments are job service specialist and unemployment benefit specialist. Almost all of the employees for both types of positions are located in one department not included in this study — Industry, Labor, and Human Relations.

In Tables 3.4 to 3.8, we show the ten most heavily populated professional positions in the departments of Administration, Health and Social Services, Natural Resources, Revenue, and Transportation. We also show the turnover rates for each of those positions for fiscal year (FY) 1990. If turnover exceeded 10 percent in any of those three years in any professional position, it was so designated. This does not mean, however, that the turn-

Table 3.4. Department of Administration (DOA)
Turnover in Ten Most Populous Positions: Fiscal Year 1987–1990.

Rank	Title	Number of full-time employees	<10%	10–14%	15–19%	20+%
1	Administrative officer	48		X		
2	Management information specialist	29		X		
3	Administrative assistant	29	X			
4	Budget analyst	27		X		
5	Engineer	22		X		
6	Construction representative	20	X			
7	Architect	11	X			
8	Accountant	11			X	
9	Superintendent of buildings and grounds	10		X		
10	Program/planning analyst	8	X			

Table 3.5. Department of Health and Social Services
(DH and SS) Turnover in Ten Most Populous Positions: Fiscal Year 1987–1990.

Rank	Title	Number of full-time employees	<10%	10–14%	15–19%	20+%
1	Nursing	356	X			
2	Vocational rehabilitation counselor/specialist	225	X			
3	Teacher	204	X			
4	Management information specialist	179				X
5	Social worker	166	X			
6	Social service specialist	151	X			
7	Therapist	119	X			
8	Administrative assistant	115	X			
9	Accountant	102	X			
10	Disability determination specialist	97	X			

Table 3.6. Department of Natural Resources (DNR)
Turnover in Ten Most Populous Positions: Fiscal Year 1987–1990.

Rank	Title	Number of full-time employees	<10%	10–14%	15–19%	20+%
1	Natural resource specialist	271	X			
2	Environmental specialist	220	X			
3	Engineer	148		X		
4	Conservation warden	144	X			
5	Hydrogeologist	72	X			
6	Ranger	55	X			
7	Administrative assistant	50	X			
8	Management information specialist	48			X	
9	Program/planning analyst	44	X			
10	Community service specialist	20		X		

Table 3.7. Department of Revenue (DOR)
Turnover in Ten Most Populous Positions: Fiscal Year 1987–1990.

Rank	Title	Number of full-time employees	<10%	10–14%	15–19%	20+%
1	Revenue auditor	260	X			
2	Revenue agent	124	X			
3	Property assessment specialist	87	X			
4	Management information specialist	49	X			
5	Revenue tax specialist	21	X			
6	Attorney	14	X			
7	Excise tax investigator	11	X			
8	Tax conferee	8	X			
9	Economist	5	X			
10	Budget and planning analyst	4	X			

Table 3.8. Department of Transportation (DOT)
Turnover in Ten Most Populous Positions: Fiscal Year 1987–1990.

Rank	Title	Number of full-time employees	<10%	10–14%	15–19%	20+%
1	Civil engineer	358				X
2	Management information specialist	144		X		
3	Program/planning analyst	96				X
4	Administrative officer	88			X	
5	Real estate agent	45				X
6	Administrative assistant	18	X			
7	Budget and management analyst	12				X
8	Accountant	8	X			
9	Auditor	8	X			
10	Attorney	7	X			

over exceeded 10 percent in all three — or even two of the three — years. Our approach here may overstate turnover rates somewhat, but we thought it was useful to have data that extended beyond a single year. The data in Tables 3.4 to 3.9 show that turnover fell within the normal range for thirty-four of the fifty departmental positions examined here. The positions where turnover exceeded 10 percent in any of the three years (FY 1987–1988, 1988–1989, 1989–1990) are listed in Table 3.9.

How did our predictions fare? The data in Tables 3.4 to 3.9 allow us to draw conclusions on three levels: (1) for the fifty positions we examined here, (2) for the state's most populous positions, and (3) on a departmentwide basis. With respect to the fifty positions examined here, our general conclusion is that turnover of 10 percent or more appears to be the exception rather than the rule. Turnover rates were within the predicted normal range for more than three-fifths of the positions.

The data we were able to collect on the thirty-four positions where

Table 3.9. Positions with 10 Percent or Greater Turnover: Fiscal Year 1987–1990.

Rank*	Title
	DOA
1	Administrative officer
2	Management information specialist
4	Budget analyst
5	Engineer
8	Accountant
9	Superintendent of buildings and grounds
	DOT
1	Civil engineer
2	Management information specialist
3	Program and planning analyst
4	Administrative officer
5	Real estate agent
7	Budget and management analyst
	DNR
3	Engineers
8	Management information specialist
10	Community service specialist
	DOR
0	No positions
	DH and SS
4	Management information specialist

Note: *Original rank from the listing of ten most populous positions.

turnover was below 10 percent also show that our predictions about the components of normal turnover are reasonably good. In the Department of Revenue, for example, approximately 20 percent of the turnover in 1989 was the result of movement within the department or movement to other departments within state government; 80 percent was the result of exit. Of those who exited, approximately two-thirds retired and one-third took employment outside of government. Although we were not able to secure all of the data needed for all departments, the profile of turnover within the Department of Revenue's top ten professional positions appears to be similar in the other departments. The one significant difference seems to be a lower rate of movement within and between departments for Revenue career professionals as compared to the employees in the other four departments. Since that is the only area where the data from Revenue did not fit our predictions about the components of turnover, we think the predictions themselves hold up pretty well.

With respect to the state's most populous professional positions, the data in Tables 3.4 to 3.9 show that turnover reached or exceeded 10 percent in only two of the thirteen positions examined here: engineer and management information specialist. On the basis of the data we were able to gather, we conclude that mobility inside of government and outside of government is higher—or even substantially higher—for employees in these professional positions than it is for others. Furthermore, movement to the private sector does make up a somewhat larger portion of exit than it would in our predicted normal rate, but it is not substantially larger than the one-third portion we predict. Indeed, among engineers, retirement (especially in the Department of Transportation) seems to be the key to the high exit rates. In sum, in these areas, the data seem to fit our predictions reasonably well.

There is, however, one area where we were rather far off the mark. The rates of turnover and exit substantially exceeded our upper-end prediction for engineers and management information specialists in several departments. We did not envision any circumstances where turnover would exceed 20 percent of a particular professional group, but that is what we found. The most noteworthy of these exceptions is the engineer position in the Department of Transportation. Again, demographics, or age, played a key role here. Many of the department's engineers came on board in the years right after World War II and were reaching retirement age. The other factor operating here was the state's early retirement policy. As it did for senior managers in this department, the policy seems to have increased the retirement rate at least 20 to 25 percent above what it would have been without the policy.

Moving from the statewide picture to the departmental picture, we find that our predictions also worked reasonably well. In three of the five departments, the turnover rates in most or all the ten most heavily populated professional positions fell within the normal rate of 5 to 8 percent. In the Departments of Administration and Transportation, however, the turnover rate was equal to or exceeded 10 percent in six of the departments' ten most populous positions.

Why was the turnover rate high for so many positions in these two departments? Using our model, a natural point for investigation would be the departmental factors. Specifically, it would be important to see whether they were negative or even very negative in either or both of these departments. Unfortunately, our data did not provide a means to make this check. There are other factors that could be examined here, however, including the types of positions themselves. In both departments, two of the positions (engineers and management information specialists) on the high-turnover list were on the high-turnover list in other departments. In short, high turnover in these two positions is not unique to Administration or Transportation.

The positions on the high-turnover list in both Administration and Transportation also include administrative officer and budget analyst. For both of these positions, the turnover largely reflects movement within departments and between departments. At least three explanations could be offered for this phenomenon: (1) these two professional positions provide a relatively high level of mobility that results from competing offers within or across departments, (2) people in these positions are vulnerable to changes in the preferences or styles of the immediate superiors of these position holders and must be ready to move at any time to another position, or (3) both competing offers and vulnerability occur across these positions simultaneously.

With respect to the remaining two positions in each department where turnover exceeds 10 percent, we think a number of factors come into play. These factors range from private sector competition to high rates of retirement. For example, private sector competition seems to be important to turnover for real estate agents in the Department of Transportation. Retirement seems to be a key to the high turnover among accounts in the Department of Administration.

Predictions About Career Professional Retention and Exit in Other States

On the basis of the Wisconsin findings described above, we are prepared to predict that high turnover in the other forty-nine states' most populous professional positions will be the exception, rather than the rule. We are also prepared to predict that in some departments, turnover above 10 percent may be found for half or more of the ten most populous departmental positions. Where the high rates of turnover occur, they may be a function of negative departmental factors. It is more likely, however, that they will be a function of other factors included in our models, such as age (demographics and retirement), inter- and intradepartment mobility, and, to a lesser extent, opportunities in other public, nonprofit, or private sector organizations.

We make these predictions knowing our initial test of the model may not provide data from "typical" or "average" states. This does not, in our view, present any particular problem, since a good model ought to work for most states. Nevertheless, it does provide an inducement to specify some caveats to our prediction. Specifically, there may be at least two variables that did not show up in Wisconsin that could make a significant difference in turnover and exit rates for career professionals in the states.

The two variables are (1) the size of the gap between public and private pay scales in the states' major metropolitan areas and (2) the working conditions for state employees. Where the public/private pay gap is large for professionals, we would expect to see turnover rates exceed our predicted normal rate in more than a small proportion of the professional positions. Additionally, where a substantial number of career professionals work in severely crowded, unpleasant, or unsafe working environments, we would also expect to see turnover above the norm in a higher number of professional positions.

Career Professional Recruitment

In many respects, recruitment is the flip side of retention: where there is turnover, recruitment is the key to filling a vacancy. Indeed, the process of hiring to fill vacancies is particularly important in career professional positions where there are high rates of turnover. This examination of career professional recruitment or hiring follows a similar path to the examination of turnover and morale for senior managers and career professional employees. The general issue for investigation is whether the troubles of the national public service extend to the states in the area of career professional recruitment. We begin the investigation with a brief review of the troubles of the national public service, then we develop some predictions about the process of hiring career professionals in the states. Finally, we test the predictions with data from a case study of career professional recruitment in Wisconsin that was designed specifically for this investigation.

Recruitment Troubles in the National Government

The national government's perceived inability to attract (recruit) the talent it needed was a principal concern of the Volcker Commission and others who wrote about the national public service during the 1980s. Three general types of concerns were raised in the published materials: (1) inability to recruit highly qualified engineers and scientists, (2) inability to recruit the "best and brightest" college graduates, and (3) general concerns about the national government's ability to attract qualified college graduates.

Concerns about the national government's ability to hire highly qualified science and engineering graduates were highlighted by the Packard Commission in 1985 and 1986. Concerns about the national government's ability to hire the best and brightest college graduates in all types of professional fields were raised in 1982 by Mosher, in 1986 by Levine, and in 1988 by the Volcker Commission. Studies conducted by the Merit Systems Protection Board (1988) and Sanders (1990) provide strong support for both concerns. Indeed, the general conclusion of the two studies is that very few of the best and brightest are willing to consider a career in government.

The general concern about the national government's ability to recruit capable college graduates was raised in 1986 by Conant and Brademas. It was also raised in 1988 by the Merit Systems Protection Board. The focus of the concern here was not limited to the best and brightest; the concern was about the general and very dramatic shift in the preferences of college students and college graduates away from the public service to the private sector. The shift in career preferences was visible among students in all university disciplines, including public administration and public affairs programs.

The principal explanation the Packard Commission advanced for the difficulties with recruiting highly qualified engineering and science graduates was private sector competition. Levine offered the same explanation for the difficulties of hiring the best and brightest in other professional fields. Both Packard and Levine viewed the public/private pay gap as the key to college student preference for the private sector, but both also listed the cumbersome civil service hiring process and better private sector working conditions as contributing factors. In the most recent work on the best and brightest recruitment problems, however, Sanders provided a very different perspective. He argued that pay is the least important of ten job and organization factors that are key to the employment preferences; the most important factor, he maintained, is the negative image of government.

According to Conant and Brademas, the general problem of hiring qualified college graduates was the result of political, economic, sociocultural, educational, and administrative factors. Political factors included government-bashing by the president and other elected officials. Economic factors included rapid employment growth in the private sector, small employment growth in the public sector—and particularly the national government—and the public/private pay gap. Sociocultural factors included a set of values that emphasized personal rewards. The educational factors included the explosive growth of enrollments in business schools and the negative image of government that faculty in these schools and other professional schools communicated to their students. The administrative factors included the demise of the examination for screening applicants for professional positions (PACE) and the lack of recruitment activity by the Office of Personnel Management (OPM) and the executive branch agencies.

The latter factor is particularly important with respect to the analysis we are conducting here. Since it appears that so little recruiting is being done at the national level, describing the problem as a "recruitment" problem may be a misnomer. Consequently, throughout the remainder of this section, the problem is referred to as a hiring problem, rather than a recruitment problem.

Specifying the Model of the Career Professional Hiring Troubles

The perceived sources and results of the national government's hiring problems are defined in Figure 3.3. The model can also be used for developing some general predictions about career professional recruitment in the states during the 1980s. The predictions are that (1) the size of the applicant pool for career professional positions is not likely to be large, (2) the quality of the applicant pool is not likely to be very strong, and (3) the hiring process will move very slowly.

Before the predictions can be tested in the states, they must be more clearly defined. Specifically, it is essential to define "small" pool of applicants, "low and moderate quality," and "a long time" to fill positions. A small number of applicants could mean five, ten, or twenty to some and thirty, forty, or even fifty to others. Likewise, operational definitions of "low quality" and "long time" might differ considerably from person to person.

Figure 3.3. Sources and Results of Hiring Problems.

Sources of Problem	Results
Political	
Bashing of government	
Economic	
Public/private salary gap	
Little public employment growth	
Substantial private employment growth	
Sociocultural	Application pool:
Negative image of government	Small number of applicants
Value structure: Me generation	Applicant quality low/moderate
Educational	Long time to fill position
Dramatic growth in business school enrollments	
Negative attitude of faculty in business	
and other professional schools toward government	
Administrative	
Demise of professional, administrative, and clerical examinations	
Cumbersome hiring process	
Little recruitment activity	

For purposes of this model, a small number of applicants will be defined as twenty or fewer. "Long time to hire" will mean 90 to 180 days; "very long time" will mean 181 days or more. Quality is the most difficult of the three factors to define, in part because a host of difficult issues is involved in setting a benchmark. For purposes of this model, however, moderate quality will mean grade point averages between 3.3 and 3.0 and exam scores between 90 and 85 percent; low will mean grade point averages below 3.0 and exam scores below 85 percent. These definitions or benchmarks are listed in Figure 3.4 below.

Predictions About the Career
Professional Hiring Process in the States

The national variables listed in our model are likely to provide the general background or topography on which the state hiring process works. That

Figure 3.4. Expected Results of Hiring Problems.

Number of applicants for professional positions:	Small = <20
Quality of applicants:	Moderate = 3.3 – 3.0 GPA and 90 – 85 percent exam score
	Low = <3.0 GPA and <85 percent exam score
Time to fill vacant position:	Long time = 90 – 180 days
	Very long time = >180 days

topography is likely to have state-specific contours, however, that can make a significant difference in the hiring process itself. For example, the effects of the government-bashing done by Jimmy Carter and Ronald Reagan during their electoral campaigns and their time in office undoubtedly spilled over into the states. Nevertheless, a number of states had chief executives and legislators who did not bash government during the 1980s — indeed, in some states elected officials actually highlighted the positive dimensions of government. New Jersey and Governor Thomas Kean serve as excellent examples.

With respect to economic factors, national data show that there was very little job growth during the 1980s in the national government's non-defense-related agencies. At the same time, the employment growth rate in the private sector was substantial. The data also show a public/private wage gap for most professional positions. At the state level, however, aggregate employment growth was somewhat higher than it was at the national level. Furthermore, in some states, like New Jersey, government employment grew fairly rapidly. Likewise, in New Jersey, professional salaries for many key positions were actually better during the mid and late 1980s than they were for comparable positions in the national government.

Sociocultural factors, such as the negative image of government, could also be mitigated somewhat in states that had a positive image of government deeply ingrained in their history and culture. Likewise, with respect to educational factors, faculty in states where there has traditionally been a close working relationship between the state and the university might not be so negative about government. Minnesota and Wisconsin are such states.

With respect to administrative factors, the variation could be substantial. One need not assume that all states experienced the demise of their principal screening exam for career professional applicants. Likewise, it is possible that some states not only have a decipherable application process but also have effective statewide — or at least some agency — recruitment activity.

Finally, at least one very important factor must be added to the list of key variables that affect results of the hiring process. That variable is geography. Working for the national government is likely to mean working far away from home and leaving friends and family. Additionally, since only a small fraction of college students live in or have traveled to Washington, D.C., the national government is likely to seem remote, and prospects for success in the application process seem dim. In contrast, working for state government may mean being within driving distance of family and friends, and prospects for success in the application process may seem relatively good. These factors may be particularly important in states where large universities are located in the state capital. Minnesota, New York, Oregon, Texas, and Wisconsin are examples of states that fit these circumstances.

Testing the Predictions in the States

Although we knew that the variables described above could make a difference — even a significant difference — in some states, we began our investigation with the assumption that the perceived career professional hiring troubles of the national public service could be found in *most* states. The effort to test this assumption and our model of career professional hiring in the states started with a literature search. We were unable to find the kind of data we needed in academic journals or books — or any other published source. Apparently the investigation of such topics has not been high on the agendas of scholars or the states. This situation is probably explained in part by the fact that empirically based research on these topics can be both time consuming and costly.

Indeed, the only published material we were able to locate was a report by the Illinois Commission on the Future of the Public Service (1991). The report lists a series of concerns about the career professional hiring process in Illinois state government that parallel the findings of the Volcker Commission. For example, the report notes that the Illinois application process is viewed as bewildering and time consuming — that those who do apply for a career professional position might have to wait for three to six months just to receive a response to their application.

Other elements of the report provide equally striking commentary, and the study is certainly a wake-up call for those who think human resource questions are not important for the states. Furthermore, it provides general support for the notion that the troubles of the national government do extend to the states. Consequently, the report provides a useful benchmark for our investigation, even though it does not contain the kind of information we need to test our model.

Some additional benchmarks for our study were located through a half-dozen telephone conversations we had with personnel officials in five states: Minnesota, New Jersey, Oklahoma, Oregon, and Wisconsin. In those conversations, we laid out our general predictions about the career professional hiring process in the states (small applicant pool, low quality of applicants, and slow-moving hiring process) and asked whether the predictions fit those states. Overall, we got mixed responses to our predictions. More important than the overall response, however, was the perspective provided by a Minnesota official.

"Our problem," this official said, "is not too few applicants or too few good applicants. Our problem is that we have so many applications for most positions that we cannot process the paperwork in a timely fashion." One result, this official conceded, might be the loss of some of the best applicants for career professional positions. Nevertheless, the official was confident that both the size and quality of the applicant pool was sufficient to guarantee that the career professional positions were being filled with highly qualified applicants.

The response left us with two questions. Did the perception of the official actually reflect the real situation there? If so, was Minnesota unique or were there some other states in a similar, enviable position? The questions highlighted the need for research on the topic. Additionally, the Minnesota official's response provided support for the notion that there was variation in the hiring process in the states and that the range of variation in that process might be much wider than we had initially expected. Finally, the Minnesota case, like the Illinois case, confirmed our belief that our model could provide an effective means for organizing the research process and utilizing its results.

Using the Model to Make Predictions About the Hiring Process in Wisconsin

Our general predictions about the hiring process in Wisconsin were more favorable than the predictions generated from existing work on the national public service. We expected to find (1) moderate to large applicant pools for most professional positions, (2) good to very good applicant quality, and (3) a moderate length of time to fill vacant positions. The predictions are based on positive or relatively positive dimensions in all of the variables included in our model.

Government-bashing has not been a popular sport for Wisconsin gubernatorial candidates or chief executives. Public sector wages fall within or in a few cases exceed private sector wages for comparable professional positions. A positive view of government's role in society is part of Wisconsin's heritage. The link between the state and the university has traditionally been very strong. The state is known for having a strong administrative apparatus. Finally, in terms of geography, the University of Wisconsin, Madison is located in the state capital, and the state's second largest university (University of Wisconsin, Milwaukee) is located in the only large metropolitan area.

On the basis of these factors, we predicted that the appliant pool for most professional positions would be in the range of forty to eighty applicants, test scores for the applicants would be above average to very good, and time to fill vacant positions would be in the range of ninety days.

Testing the Predictions and the Model

Our study of career professional recruitment in Wisconsin consisted of three steps: initial interviews, the collection of information through a questionnaire, and the collection of data on specific hiring processes. The initial interviews provided some rich material. In almost all of the half-dozen interviews conducted with Wisconsin personnel officials, we heard that there were some problems — even serious problems — in the hiring of career professionals.

The two principal reasons generally given for these problems were private sector competition (salaries) and the civil service hiring process itself. We thought that these perceptions about the existence of recruitment problems and the causes of those problems provided an important starting point for the investigation. One of our objectives for the study was to compare the perceptions with the data we collected.

The questionnaire on the hiring of career professionals, like the questionnaire on career professional retention, was distributed to and filled out by personnel officers and staff in five departments: Administration, Health and Social Services, Natural Resources, Revenue, and Transportation. The questionnaire focused on the ten most populous positions in each department. Specifically, we asked personnel officers and staff in five departments to designate the positions for which they thought they were having recruitment difficulties. We also asked the personnel officers to define the cause or causes of any recruitment problem they identified. The results of that survey effort are listed in Table 3.10.

Several things stand out in the information provided in Table 3.10. First, four of the five departments had career professional positions that were viewed as problem areas with respect to hiring. Second, in three of the five departments, problems were identified in four of the ten most heavily populated positions. Third, two of the problem positions, engineer and management information specialist, were positions where turnover exceeded ten percent.

What were the problems? It is important to remember that problems are usually defined by people from their own vantage points. A personnel

Table 3.10. Positions with Recruitment Difficulties: Fiscal Year 1987–1990.

Rank*	Title
	DOA
1	Administrative officer
2	Management information specialist
5	Engineer
8	Accountant
	DOT
1	Civil engineer
2	Management information specialist
5	Real estate agent
11	Attorney
	DNR
3	Engineers
8	Hydrogeologist
	DOR
0	No positions
	DH and SS
1	Nursing
4	Management information specialist
7	Therapist
10	Accountant

Note: *Original rank from the listing of ten most populous positions.

officer's definition of a recruitment problem is likely to be heavily influenced by the fact that line managers want to have vacancies filled as quickly as possible so workflow and workloads are not negatively impacted. In any case, the problem definitions seemed to have three principal dimensions: numbers, time, and quality. The numbers for some positions were believed to be too small, the hiring process was generally viewed as taking too long, and there were concerns about applicant quality for some positions.

What were the causes of the problems? The written responses matched up very closely with the initial interview responses. The two main causes of the problem were defined as private sector competition (salaries) and a cumbersome hiring process. The data we collected seemed to show that the perceptions of the personnel officers and staff had a factual basis, but not in the way we expected. The time problem, which can be controlled largely by the departments themselves for most positions, seemed to come into play primarily for positions that were lightly populated. "Custom" recruitments were required for these positions—there was no continuous statewide application or examination process and thus no standing register of applicants. For most of the positions that fell into a department's ten most heavily populated list, however, the time needed to hire did not seem to be a significant problem.

The quality and quantity factors seemed to come into play in two areas: hiring for upper-level positions and hiring processes that were not open recruitments. As we will demonstrate, there is a correlation between the two. We have the data needed to provide some perspective on the numbers issue; we have to rely on opinions of the personnel officials as our "data" on the quality issue.

The number of applicants for positions listed as open recruitments appeared to be higher, or even significantly higher, than for positions listed as "servicewide recruitments" (applications limited to current state employees). Additionally, the number of applicants for entry-level positions appeared to be significantly higher than for upper-level positions in almost all of the ten most populous departmental positions.

Some perspective on these circumstances, and a more direct link to our predictions and our model, can be provided with some examples that appeared to us to be typical of the hiring processes for open recruitments in the five departments. The examples are listed in Table 3.11.

The data in Table 3.11 show that in "open" hiring processes for entry-level positions, the circumstances look very favorable with respect to number of applicants, quality of applicants, and time to fill vacant positions. Indeed, the results exceeded our predicted levels in each of the categories. Furthermore, the data also showed that even for upper-level positions, open recruitments were likely to yield results that fit within or exceeded our predicted (favorable) levels. The one type of position in our case examples where this did not seem to fully hold up is the management information specialist. Even here, however, the numbers looked relatively good.

A brief review of two examples may help to amplify our general conclusion on this issue. In both cases, the applicant pool was large, and there

Table 3.11. Hiring Process for Professional Positions.

Position level	Engineer (DOT)	Management information specialist (DH and SS)	Accountant (DOA)	Natural resources specialist (DNR)
Entry level				
Applicants in pool	150	104	300	150
Quality of applicants	good	good	good	good
Time to fill vacancies	60 days	60 days	45 days	45 days
Advanced level				
Applicants in pool	70	23	56	26
Quality of applicants	good	average	good	good
Time to fill vacancies	60 days	45 days	90 days	60 days

were many highly qualified candidates. We begin with the natural resource specialist in the Department of Natural Resources, the department's most populous position, with 271 professionals currently employed. It is also the ninth most heavily populated position on a statewide basis (284). Since the exit rate for this position is low, around 3 to 5 percent per year, the number of recruits needed is not very large — the number may run around six to thirteen positions a year.

For these positions there will be fierce competition. The applicant pool for each of the positions will consist of 100 to 400, and most of those applicants will have very good undergraduate or graduate records. In short, for a college graduate who has prepared to be — and really wants to be — a natural resource specialist, the likelihood of securing such a position is not very high. From the department and the state's perspective, however, the odds are all to the good: the numbers alone should make it possible to hire recruits who are highly qualified.

Even in positions listed as recruitment problem areas, the circumstances are not necessarily different. Let's take an example of a recent recruitment process the Department of Transportation (DOT) ran for a budget analyst. In this process, there were ninety applicants who made the register for the position. The pool contained so many qualified applicants that interviews were conducted with approximately thirty of them. From this group of thirty, one person was picked for the position. Here again, the odds for the applicants were long; the odds for the state and the department were highly favorable.

Neither these examples nor any of the findings in this section are meant to imply that there are no problems with respect to numbers of applicants for professional positions, quality of applicants, or time to fill vacant positions. Clearly there are some problems in each of these areas. Additionally, none of our findings should be misconstrued to suggest that the "best" candidate for each professional position is hired. Such concerns, while important, are beyond the scope of this investigation.

Our general view of the matter, however, is that the hiring process for career professionals in the state is better than many might have predicted. Additionally, we have learned that, at least for entry-level positions, the data seem to fit—indeed exceed—our predictions for the state. We have also learned that for upper-level positions where recruitment is not open, the process does not seem to be as favorable. In short, we may have to make our model a two-level (entry and advanced) and two-process (open, not open) model.

Conclusion

The general issue discussed in this chapter is whether the reported troubles of the national public service extend to the states. Our investigation of this issue was conducted with an eye toward developing remedies or prescriptions for the problems identified. The long-term objective we assume to underlie this type of work is to ensure that the public service at the state level is healthy and capable of contributing to effective governance. The natural starting point for this investigation was the Volcker Commission's report *Rebuilding the Public Service* and the writings of others whose work preceded the commission's report. The principal problem identified in all of these works was the national government's inability to retain and attract the talent it needed to function effectively.

To focus and operationalize our research, we divided the investigation into three topical areas: senior manager retention and morale, career professional retention and morale, and career professional recruitment. For each area, we used models to define key relationships. We also used the models to define what "normal" rates of exit would look like for senior managers, what normal rates of exit would look like for career professionals, and what normal hiring patterns might look like for career professionals. Once this difficult task was accomplished, we concentrated our attention on attempting to determine how much variation from the norm occurred in a given state in each of these areas. We also attempted to determine why the variation occurred.

Our research on senior manager retention showed that turnover and exit rates in Wisconsin were at the upper end of the normal range. Turnover rates in New Jersey exceeded the upper bounds of the predicted normal rate. Demographics (aging) and an early retirement policy pushed turnover and exit rates up in Wisconsin; a superheated regional economy and demographics seemed to be the key causal factors in the high turnover rates in New Jersey. Since neither the aging process nor regional economic growth rates can be controlled by government, we were unable to prescribe a policy response that seemed likely to bring the turnover and exit rates down.

In our investigation of career professional exit and morale in the states, we found that turnover and exit rates in Wisconsin were within the predicted normal range in thirteen of the state's fifteen most heavily populated professional positions. We also discovered, however, that circumstances varied considerably from department to department. In two of the five departments, high turnover exit rates were found in more than half of the departments' ten most heavily populated positions. We were able to explain the statewide pattern with our model, and we were able to account for a substantial portion of the departmental variation with that model. The findings do not lead, however, to any straightforward prescriptions. Market forces do seem to be key to a factor in the high turnover and exit rates of engineers and management information specialists. The effects of such forces are not easy to ameliorate. Increasing pay at the upper ranges of these positions may help, but we are not confident enough about it to make such a recommendation at this point.

In our investigation of career professional hiring in the states, we found that the pool of applicants for virtually all entry-level positions in Wisconsin was large and strong.[11] We also found that the applicant pool for upper-level positions was not as large and was not perceived to be as strong as the pool for entry-level positions. Most of the hiring processes for upper-level positions were restricted — only current state employees could apply. Thus, the size and perceived quality of the applicant pool seems to be correlated to the type of hiring process used. Finally, we found that timely filling of vacant positions seemed to be occurring in Wisconsin. The exceptions to this rule seem to be in position types where the numbers of applications are small. Like our findings about career retention, these findings about hiring do not lead to any obvious prescriptions. The efficiency with which the agencies and the personnel departments conduct their hiring activities seems to be a key to timely hiring, and the type of hiring processes used seems to have much to do with the size and quality of the applicant pool for upper-level positions. We could recommend that open hiring processes be used for all positions, but this recommendation would run headlong into the notion of career development.

To sum up, we think we can draw three general conclusions from our research: (1) in some cases the circumstances in the states parallel the troubles of the national government and in others they are very different, (2) the circumstances themselves are likely to vary from state to state and for a variety of reasons, and (3) it is important to define what is (and what is not) a problem before one attempts to develop prescriptions for enhancing or rebuilding the public service in the states. All of this highlights, we think, the importance of conducting additional research on retention, morale, and recruitment in the states. This research can provide the basis for additional testing of the models we have developed, supply information about the range of variation in the states, and provide a clearer portrait of whether the states have some common troubles in the areas of career professional retention, morale, and recruitment that need to be addressed.

When the findings from the three areas — senior manager retention and morale, career professional retention and morale, and career professional recruitment — are added together, there seems to be good grounds for advancing at least one general prescription. The prescription is that the states should upgrade the investment they make in management education and training as well as training and development for career professionals. Existing research shows that state investment in management education and training, as well as training and development for career professional employees, is likely to be very modest (Conant, 1990, 1992).[12] Yet, the high rate of turnover among senior managers documented in this chapter shows how pressing the need is to have an effective management development program in place for new senior managers. In turn, an effective training program is needed for the managers who are promoted to middle management as replacements for the new senior managers. Our research also shows that most career professionals who elect to work in state government remain in government throughout their careers. Consequently, providing programs that give them the opportunity to upgrade their skills and to keep their skills current with new technology, new job requirements, and so on is a necessary condition for maintaining and enhancing individual, group, department, and state government productivity and effectiveness.

Notes

1. Opinions on turnover differ. The traditional view, one implicit in the work of the Volcker Commission, holds that turnover is undesirable. Others, however, emphasize the benefits of turnover (for example, Dalton and Tudor, 1979).
2. For analysis and commentary on the condition of the public service that preceded the Volcker Commission's report, see Mosher, 1982; Cleveland, 1982; Rosen, 1983; Packard, 1986; Johnson, 1986; Levine, 1986; Brauer, 1986; Brauer and Karp, 1986; Conant, 1986; Huddleston, 1986; Kline, 1986; and U.S. Merit Systems Protection Board, 1988. Work on this topic published after the release of the Volcker Commission report includes Conant, 1989; U.S. Merit Systems Protection Board, 1990a, 1990b; Lane and Wolf, 1990; Lewis, 1991.
3. We also assume that the departure of some from government contributes to the morale problems of those who have not yet elected to exit.
4. This is not to say that none of these managers would resign on the basis of principle, beliefs, and so on. Rather it is simply an acknowledgment of the importance economic considerations play for most people in such decisions. For a classic discussion of this issue, see Albert Hirschman, *Exit, Voice, and Loyalty,* 1970.
5. Among the reasons they are highly desirable are (1) an impressive package of pay and benefits and (2) exceptional status and influence within their departments.
6. A list of sources can be found in Ban, 1988, and Sherwood and Breyer, 1987.

7. The New Jersey study was conducted from the fall of 1988 through the end of 1989, and the Wisconsin study was conducted in 1991. The purpose of the studies was to examine each state's efforts to provide management skill development for its executive branch managers. In both of the states, the studies were focused on four departments.

8. The two departments were Environmental Protection, where the growth rate exceeded 25 percent, and Treasury, where the growth rate was similar.

9. This assumption is based on two factors: (1) the work itself is desirable and (2) the pay and benefits of these positions are viewed as attractive by many professionals.

10. The assumption we are making here is that there is a geographic or regional dimension to the labor market, that is, that movement from the public to private sector is likely to take place within a community, state, or region.

11. Indeed, we discovered that the size of the applicant pool itself may actually create a problem of timely processing of paperwork. This situation may, in turn, create frustration on the part of many applicants.

12. Indeed, the investment is unlikely to equal 1 percent of a state's or a department's operating expenditures (Conant, 1990, 1992).

References

Ban, C. "The Diffusion of Innovation in Personnel Reform: The Case of the Senior Executive Service." Unpublished manuscript, 1988.

Brademas, J. "The Value of Public Service." Paper presented at the Brookings/American Enterprise conference on The Public Service in the Year 2000, Washington, D.C., 1986.

Brauer, K. "The Quiet Crisis in the Public Service." Paper prepared for the Brookings/American Enterprise conference on The Public Service in the Year 2000, Washington, D.C., 1986.

Brauer, S., and Karp, J. "Shunning the Job-Hunt Maze: Civil Service Loses Career Appeal for Recent College Graduates." *The Washington Post,* August 7, 1986, p. A17.

Cleveland, H. "The Character of the Institution." *Public Administration Review,* 1982, *42,* 310–313.

Conant, J. K. "Universities and the Future of the Public Service." Paper prepared for the Brookings/American Enterprise Institute conference on The Public Service in the Year 2000, Washington, D.C., 1986.

Conant, J. K. "Universities and the Future of the Public Service." *Public Administration Quarterly,* 1989, *13,* 342–374.

Conant, J. K. *Management Education and Training in New Jersey: A Description, an Appraisal, and Recommendations for Improvement.* East Orange, N.J.: Fund for New Jersey, 1990.

Conant, J. K. *Management Education and Training in Wisconsin: A Description, an Appraisal, and Recommendations for Improvement.* Madison, Wis.: Wisconsin Department of Administration, 1992.

Dalton, D., and Tudor, W. T. "Turnover Turned over: An Expanded and Positive Perspective." *Academy of Management Review,* 1979, *4,* 225–235.

Federal Executive Institute Alumni Association. Draft report, 1984.

Hirschman, A. *Exit, Voice, and Loyalty.* Cambridge, Mass.: Harvard University Press, 1970.

Huddleston, M. "Whither the SES?" Unpublished manuscript, 1986.

Illinois Commission on the Future of the Public Service. "Excellence in Public Service: Illinois' Challenge for the '90s." ICFPS Preliminary Report. Chicago: Chicago Community Trust/Government Assistance Project, Jan. 1991, 1–7.

Johnson, H. "U.S. Customs Service Tries to Do More with Less: Mission Grows but Staff Shrinks." *The Washington Post,* August 24, 1986, pp. 1A, 12A.

Kline, R. "Contemporary Problems of the Public Service: What Should Be Done; How to Be Ready." Unpublished manuscript, 1986.

Lane, L., and J. F. Wolf. *Human Resource Crisis in the Public Sector: Rebuilding the Capacity to Govern.* New York: Quorum Books, 1990.

Levine, C. H. "The Federal Government in the Year 2000: Administrative Legacies of the Reagan Years." *Public Administration Review,* 1986, *46,* 195–206.

Lewis, G. "Turnover and the Quiet Crisis in the Federal Service." *Public Administration Review,* 1991, *51,* 145–155.

March, J., and Simon, H. *Organizations.* New York: Wiley, 1958.

Mosher, F. *Democracy and the Public Service.* New York: Oxford University Press, 1968.

Mowday, R., Porter, L., and Steers, R. *Employee-Organization Linkages: The Psychology of Commitment, Absenteeism and Turnover.* Orlando, Fla.: Academic Press, 1982.

Packard, D. "The Loss of Government Scientific and Engineering Talent." *Issues of Science and Technology,* Spring 1986, p. 128.

Rosen, B. "Effective Continuity of U.S. Government Operations in Jeopardy." *Public Administration Review,* 1983, *46,* 207–214.

Sanders, R. P. "The Best and Brightest: Can the Public Service Compete?" Manuscript prepared for the National Commission on the Public Service, Washington, D.C., 1990.

Sherwood, F. P., and Breyer, L. J. "Executive Personnel Systems in the States." *Public Administration Review,* 1987, *47,* 410–416.

U.S. Merit Systems Protection Board. *Attracting Quality Graduates to the Federal Government: A View of College Recruiting.* Washington, D.C.: U.S. Merit Systems Protection Board, 1988.

U.S. Merit Systems Protection Board. *Who Is Leaving the Federal Government?*

An Analysis of Employee Turnover. Washington, D.C.: U.S. Merit Systems Protection Board, 1989.

U.S. Merit Systems Protection Board. *Who Is Leaving Federal Government? An Analysis of Employee Turnover.* Washington, D.C.: Merit Systems Protection Board, 1990a.

U.S. Merit Systems Protection Board. *Working for America: A Federal Employee Survey.* Washington, D.C.: U.S. Merit Systems Protection Board, 1990b.

FOUR

Rebuilding Public Trust:
The Vital Role of
Nonprofessional Public Servants

Jorge Chapa

American government is facing an expanding crisis of approval, credibility, and legitimacy. The Volcker Commission tackled the problem of how to rebuild the reputation and performance of federal managers and professionals. In an effort to address a similar set of questions for state and local governments, this chapter will focus on the issues that pertain to the employment and performance of the nonprofessional and paraprofessional employees. The factors that bear upon these employees must be seen as an important part of any effort to improve the perception and performance of state and local government, if only because they comprise 79 percent of all employees at these two levels. In addition to the importance that comes from constituting the large majority of the state and local workforce, these nonprofessionals and paraprofessionals play an important role in shaping the public impression of government because many of these workers directly interact with public clients (for example, license clerks or receptionists) or provide a service that is directly observed by the public at large (for example, waste removal, street sweeping, or road maintenance). Both direct contact and the provision of public services create opportunities for these workers to greatly influence the public's perception of *their* government and the basis for drawing generalizations regarding *all* state and local governments. In fact, both because of their much larger proportion and because of the nature of their duties, it seems certain that the public is much more likely to interact with nonprofessional workers than it is with state or local managers or professionals. (See Foster and Snyder, 1989; Prottas, 1979).

The Volcker Commission report was released and discussed during the time that the superheated economies of the Northeast were reaching the crest of an extended period of economic growth. This boom of the late 1980s resulted in pronounced labor shortages in which many relatively low-paying positions in the private and public sector could not be filled. Now the crest of this wave of growth has passed, leaving many governments floundering in a recessionary trough that will require reductions in force and layoffs. In addition to the impact of the recession, the diminishing amount of the federal contribution to state and local needs, along with increasing demands for services and a widespread, tenacious resistance to higher taxes have jointly resulted in the worst state and local government financial situation in a decade. Thirty states are facing extensive budgetary shortfalls and cities are said to be in a "death spiral" of higher property taxes, decreased services, and population flight that leaves only the very poor behind (deCourcy Hinds, 1991). The recent changes in the fortunes of state and local government and their ability to attract or retain workers suggest that it is wrong to assume that state and local governments will invariably face only boom or bust. Cyclical changes in the economic bases of state and local governments seem likely to endure. This chapter will focus on the current status and likely future of nonprofessional and paraprofessional employees abstracted from the turbulence caused by this type of cyclical change. Rather than taking either cyclical economic extreme as the status quo, it might be more useful to see how this cyclicality itself constrains the ability of the government and willingness of its employees to optimize their performance and productivity.

Instead of examining the effects of these relatively short-term cycles on the availability of personnel for these nonprofessional positions, this chapter will pay more attention to the potential consequences of a longer-term "sea change" in the nature of the American economy and in the demographic composition of future labor force entrants. After providing a descriptive overview of state and local workers compared to federal and private sector employees, this chapter will examine how the current attributes of the nonprofessional and paraprofessional employees of state and local governments might interact with the projection that the American economy will increasingly demand workers with high skill levels during a period in which a majority of new labor force entrants will be women or minorities (Johnston and Packer, 1987). This analysis will form the basis for a discussion of various goals and issues regarding the optimal performance of state and local nonprofessional and paraprofessional employees. In particular, I posit that many of the goals that were formulated by the Volcker Commission as means of improving the federal executive also apply to the state and local nonprofessional as well. The goals most relevant to the nonprofessional workforce include the following: decentralize government management, rebuild student interest, increase the representation of minorities, provide competitive pay and competitive performance, increase government productivity, provide the training to succeed, improve the government workplace (National Commission on the Public Service, 1989). The purpose of this chapter will be to provide suggestions as to how these general goals can be applied to the specific situation of nonprofessional workers in state and local government.

The State and Local Nonprofessional Workforce

Three dimensions are of particular importance to this analysis of nonprofessional employees: demographics, educational attainment, and occupational distribution. In order to put these characteristics in perspective, the recent demographic changes in the size and composition of the state and local workforce will be briefly reviewed. Then this chapter will focus on the educational background and occupational makeup of the workforce in the state-local, federal, and private sectors. This analysis will compare the distribution of these characteristics between these sectors and also evaluate any recent changes in the distribution of characteristics in the different sectors.

Table 4.1a establishes two facts that are important points of reference. First, the number of state and local employees is more than three times greater than the number of federal employees. Second, the number of employees in each sector has increased substantially between 1980 and 1987. Table 4.1b shows that the proportion of state and local employees who are women or minorities has increased since 1975.

The comparison between the employees of the three sectors can be made by referring to Table 4.2a, which presents the distribution of employees by major occupational groups for each sector for 1980 and 1988. In 1980, at the state and local level, clerical and service workers were the two largest occupational categories, with professional and technical workers being a close third. Managers and administrators made up 11 percent of the state and local workforce compared to 16 percent of the federal workforce and 9 percent of the private sector. The largest category by far among federal workers is the clerical occupations. However, it should be noted that most postal workers fall into this category, and they account for a large part of it. The

Table 4.1a. Number of Federal, State, and Local Government Employees, 1975, 1980, and 1987 (Excluding School Systems and Educational Institutions).

	1975	1980	1987
Federal employees	2,890,000	2,898,000	3,091,000
% change from previous		.3%	6.7%
State and local	8,115,000	9,045,000	9,570,000
% change from previous		11.5%	5.8%

Source: U.S. Bureau of the Census, 1990, Table 487.

Table 4.1b. Distribution of State and Local Government Full-Time Employees
by Selected Characteristics (Excluding School Systems and Educational Institutions).

	1975	1980	1987
State and local	100%	100%	100%
Male employees (% of total)	62%	59%	58%
Female employees (% of total)	38%	41%	42%
White, non-Hispanic (% of total)	80%	79%	74%
All minorities (% of total)	20%	21%	26%
Blacks (% of total)	15%	16%	18%
Hispanics (% of total)	4%	4%	6%
Other minorities (% of total)	1%	2%	2%

Source: U.S. Bureau of the Census, Table 489.

federal workforce also has a smaller proportion of service workers than either
the state-local or private sectors. The private sector workforce has the smallest
proportion of managers or administrators and professional or technical employees. The general distribution among these categories was about the same
in 1988 as in 1980. One trend that is suggested by the changes between 1980
and 1988 is that the proportion of managerial and professional employees
is increasing in all sectors. The 1988 percentage of managers, administrators, professional, and technical workers was at least 1 percent higher in
all cases. The change, when considered in light of the increase in the number of government employees shown in Table 4.1a, probably reflects a long-
term trend that will be discussed in more detail later. The other notable
change is the sharp decrease in the proportion of the state-local workforce
employed in service occupations from 21 percent in 1980 to 16 percent in
1988. Although a number of factors were doubtlessly reflected in this change,

Table 4.2a. Distribution of Employees by Occupational Group in the State and
Local Government, the Federal Government, and the Private Sector, 1980 and 1988.

	1980			1988		
	State and local	Federal government	Private sector	State and local	Federal government	Private sector
Manager or administrator	11%	16%	9%	12%	18%	10%
Professional or technical	19%	19%	11%	20%	21%	12%
Sales	1%	1%	11%	1%	2%	13%
Clerical	22%	36%	16%	23%	39%	16%
Service	21%	8%	14%	16%	5%	14%
Protective service	9%	2%	1%	11%	2%	1%
Farm laborer	2%	1%	2%	2%	1%	3%
Craft worker	5%	8%	13%	6%	7%	12%
Operatives	7%	5%	17%	6%	4%	13%
Laborers	3%	3%	6%	2%	3%	6%
	100%	100%	100%	100%	100%	100%
Sector as percent of total	11%	4%	85%	10%	3%	87%

Table 4.2b. Distribution of Employees by Educational Group in the State
and Local Government, the Federal Government, and the Private Sector, 1988.

	1980			1988		
	State and local	Federal government	Private sector	State and local	Federal government	Private sector
High school	56%	57%	66%	52%	45%	62%
Some college	22%	22%	20%	23%	26%	20%
College graduates	22%	21%	14%	25%	29%	18%
	100%	100%	100%	100%	100%	100%

Sources: Tabulations from the 1980 Public Use Microdata Sample (PUMS) machine-readable data file and from the March 1988 Current Population Survey machine-readable data file. U.S. Bureau of the Census, 1988.

it is possible that part of this decrease may reflect the impact of the privatization or contracting-out for the provision of some services.

The bottom row of Table 4.2a shows the share of the total labor force found in each sector. Between 1980 and 1988 the three sectors grew numerically, but the growth of the private sector outstripped both government sectors, making them slightly smaller parts of this total.

Table 4.2b shows evidence on the related issue of the distribution of and changes in the educational levels of employees in each sector. The comparison of state-local and federal employees in 1980 shows that the distribution of each of these sectors was about the same in terms of the distribution of employees with a high school education, those who had completed between one and three years of college, and those with a bachelor's degree or more education beyond that. Both government sectors had a sizably larger proportion of college graduates than did the private sector. The comparison of the 1980 figures with those for 1988 shows an across-the-board increase in the proportion of college-educated workers. The largest increase in this dimension is in the percentage of federal workers who are college graduates — 29 percent in 1988 compared to 21 percent in 1980. The apparent contradiction between this increase in federal workers with college degrees and the concerns of the Volcker Commission may well be due to a change in the workforce through the aging and retirement of older, less educated federal workers and a subsequent increase in the proportion of relatively younger, college-educated federal workers. Many of the concerns of the Volcker Commission focused on successfully recruiting new young employees and retaining senior executives. The information shown here does not directly address these issues.

The defining criterion of a nonprofessional or paraprofessional employee used here is employment in positions that do not typically require a college degree. In order to identify these occupations and recent employment trends, the joint distribution of educational attainment levels and occupational categories is presented in Tables 4.3a through 4.3c.

Table 4.3a. Distribution of State and Local Workforce by Education and Occupation.

	1980				1988			
	High school	Some college	College graduates		High school	Some college	College graduates	
Manager or administrator	39%	21%	40%	100%	33%	26%	41%	100%
Professional or technical	20%	21%	59%	100%	15%	19%	66%	100%
Sales	*	*	*	100%	*	*	*	100%
Clerical	56%	31%	13%	100%	55%	32%	12%	100%
Service	80%	15%	5%	100%	80%	16%	4%	100%
Protective service	51%	35%	14%	100%	51%	32%	17%	100%
Farm laborer	*	*	*	100%	*	*	*	100%
Craft worker	79%	17%	4%	100%	78%	18%	4%	100%
Operatives	84%	13%	3%	100%	85%	12%	3%	100%
Laborers	83%	14%	4%	100%	83%	14%	3%	100%
Overall distribution	57%	22%	21%	101%	52%	23%	24%	100%

Table 4.3b. Distribution of Federal Workforce by Education and Occupation.

	1980				1988			
	High school	Some college	College graduates		High school	Some college	College graduates	
Manager or administrator	37%	23%	39%	100%	25%	27%	47%	100%
Professional or technical	26%	22%	52%	100%	15%	19%	67%	100%
Sales	60%	24%	16%	100%	50%	23%	28%	100%
Clerical	62%	27%	11%	100%	56%	32%	12%	100%
Service	82%	14%	4%	100%	80%	14%	5%	100%
Protective service	42%	22%	37%	100%	57%	21%	23%	100%
Farm laborer	71%	20%	8%	100%	55%	27%	18%	100%
Craft worker	74%	22%	4%	100%	65%	29%	6%	100%
Operatives	80%	18%	3%	100%	69%	26%	5%	100%
Laborers	77%	16%	6%	100%	78%	13%	9%	100%
Overall distribution	55%	23%	22%	100%	45%	26%	29%	100%

Table 4.3c. Distribution of Private Sector Workforce by Education and Occupation.

	1980				1988			
	High school	Some college	College graduates		High school	Some college	College graduates	
Manager or administrator	39%	27%	35%	100%	32%	24%	44%	100%
Professional or technical	25%	29%	47%	100%	17%	26%	57%	100%
Sales	*	*	*	100%	*	*	*	100%
Clerical	65%	26%	10%	100%	62%	27%	11%	100%
Service	78%	17%	5%	100%	81%	14%	5%	100%
Protective service	*	*	*	100%	*	*	*	100%
Farm laborer	*	*	*	100%	*	*	*	100%
Craft worker	78%	16%	6%	100%	78%	17%	5%	100%
Operatives	86%	11%	3%	100%	84%	12%	4%	100%
Laborers	83%	14%	3%	100%	84%	14%	2%	100%
Overall distribution	66%	20%	14%	100%	62%	20%	17%	100%

Note: *Sample too small for reliable estimates of subgroups.

Source: Tabulations from the March 1988 Current Population Survey machine-readable data file. U.S. Bureau of the Census, 1988.

Table 4.3a presents the distribution of educational attainment levels within each major occupational category for state-local employees in 1980 and 1988. If we interpret the defining criteria, *usually* not having a college degree, to mean that a *majority* of the employees in each category are not college graduates, then all the state-local employees except those in the professional or technical occupational category qualify as nonprofessionals. Each of these ten occupational categories is composed of the aggregation of a total of 512 different occupational titles. The first point that can be culled from Table 4.3a is that it will be necessary to use the more narrow and specific job titles as a basis for sorting the nonprofessionals from the professionals. Distinguishing between professional and nonprofessional job titles will be particularly important for the administrative and managerial group. This aggregate category includes many different specific occupations. Many of the specific occupations within the larger category of managers and administrators are filled with people who typically have a college degree. However, there are some occupations placed within this group that are usually held by employees who do not have a college degree. For example, property and real estate managers and construction inspectors are counted in the larger category of managers and administrators, but the incumbents of these positions do not typically have a college degree (see U.S. Bureau of the Census, 1988). Therefore, the identification of nonprofessional workers for this chapter will be done on the basis of specific occupations. This topic will be discussed in more detail later.

Inspecting the percentage of state and local managers or administrators with college degrees in 1980 and 1988 shows only a very slight increase from 40 to 41 percent. Both the federal government and private sectors, Tables 4.3b and 4.3c, had lower proportions of college graduate managers in 1980, but by 1988 both sectors exhibit a substantial increase in the proportion of college graduate managers or administrators to levels exceeding that at the state and local level. This comparison of the state-local with the federal sector hints that the management and leadership problems that the Volcker Commission directly addressed also pertain to the state-local level. Most pertinent are the appointment process, the ultimate prospects for career employees, management decentralization, and the partnership between elected officials and career employees. The proportion of professional and technical employees who were college graduates increased in all three sectors, with the largest increase occurring among federal employees.

In contrast to management and professionals, the remaining occupational groups at the state and local level seem to be filled with employees with about the same educational levels in 1988 as in 1980. The only exception to this might be seen in the increase in the percentage of protective service providers who were college graduates. Again, the state-local absence of an increase in the educational levels of employees in the nonmanagerial and nonprofessional categories stands in contrast to the federal pattern where we can see an increase in the percentage of college graduates in all groups and an increase in the percentage of college attendees in several of these groups. Proportionally, more college-educated people are working for the federal government at all levels, but the same is not true for states and localities.

The preceding discussion has helped establish a precise operational definition for identifying the nonprofessional and paraprofessional employees. The procedure used was to determine the specific occupational title of each state or local government employee in the 1988 Current Population Survey data set and to calculate the proportion of each specific occupational title composed of people who did not have college degrees. All of the employees of the resulting list of job titles were said to be nonprofessional or paraprofessional employees regardless of their own educational level. As the previous tables might have suggested and the subsequent one will show, some nonprofessional employees have earned a college degree. However, these people will be listed as nonprofessionals because most of the people with such jobs do not have college degrees. Table 4.4 lists the nonprofessional and

Table 4.4. Distribution of Nonprofessional Employees of State and Local Governments by Occupation and Women Employees as a Percentage of Each Occupational Group, 1988.

	Percentage of total	Women as percentage of group
Other office workers	12.8%	83%
Police, sheriffs, correctional officers, and guards	12.5%	13%
Secretaries, stenographers, and typists	11.6%	99%
Cleaning and building services	7.4%	31%
Inspectors and management-related occupations	7.0%	48%
Food service	5.5%	80%
Construction and crafts	5.4%	7%
Clerks	5.3%	82%
Bus and truck drivers	5.0%	42%
Health aids	3.9%	81%
Laborers	2.9%	5%
Mechanics and repairers	2.9%	2%
Machine operators and material movers	2.8%	22%
Other service workers	2.7%	81%
Firefighters	2.6%	3%
Sales workers	2.4%	64%
Health technicians	1.9%	71%
Groundskeepers	1.4%	9%
Administrative support supervisors	1.3%	56%
Technicians other than health	1.3%	39%
Computer operators	1.0%	67%
Recreational and related workers	.5%	36%
	100%	52% of all state and local nonprofessional employees are female.

Source: Tabulations from the March 1988 Current Population Survey machine-readable data file. U.S. Bureau of the Census, 1988.

paraprofessional occupations identified in this manner. In order to avoid referring to this long list of specific titles, Table 4.4 presents information for groups
composed of job titles with similar characteristics all meeting the defining
criteria. For example, the largest group found among state-local nonprofessionals is listed on Table 4.4 as "other office workers" and includes duplicating machine operators, messengers, and telephone operators along with several
additional specific, similar occupational titles. The employees with these titles make up 12.8 percent of all state and local nonprofessionals. Table 4.4
also indicates that 83 percent of these other office workers are women. Although
women make up little more than half, 52 percent, of all nonprofessional workers, Table 4.1 indicates that in 1987, 42 percent of all state and local employees
were female. Therefore, women are relatively concentrated in these nonprofessional occupations compared to the rest of the state-local occupations.

Table 4.5a condenses the occupational distribution of the nonprofessional state and local workers by expressing their distribution in the major
occupational categories used earlier and compares this to the distribution
of professionals and all state and local employees. This makes it easy to see
that clerical workers are about a third, 32 percent, of nonprofessionals and

Table 4.5a. Distribution of State and Local Nonprofessional Employees by Occupational
Group Compared to Professional and All State and Local Government Workers, 1988.

	All state and local workers	Professional state and local workers	Nonprofessional state and local workers
Manager or administrator	12%	25%	7%
Professional or technical	20%	66%	4%
Sales	1%		2%
Clerical	23%		32%
Service	16%	9%	17%
Protective service	11%		15%
Craft worker	6%		8%
Operatives, laborers, and groundskeepers	10%		15%
Percent of all state and local workers	100%	21%	79%

Table 4.5b. Distribution of State and Local Nonprofessional Employees by Educational
Level Compared to Professional and All State and Local Government Workers, 1988.

	All state and local workers	Professional state and local workers	Nonprofessional state and local workers
High school	52%	20%	60%
Some college	23%	13%	25%
College graduates	25%	67%	15%
	100%	100%	100%

Source: Tabulations from the March 1988 Current Population Survey machine-readable
data file. U.S. Bureau of the Census, 1988.

the largest group by far. The percentages of service workers, operatives, and protective service among nonprofessional state and local employees are approximately similar, roughly 15 percent each. As suggested above, Table 4.5a shows that there are many nonprofessional occupations in the terms defined here that fall into the Census Bureau's managerial, professional, and technical grades. A total of 11 percent of all nonprofessionals fall into these categories. All together, nonprofessionals make up 79 percent of the state and local non-education-related workforce. The remaining 21 percent are professionals, defined here as those working in occupations held by people who typically have a college degree.

Table 4.5b compares the distribution of education levels for all state and local workers, professionals and nonprofessionals. It is worth noting that 25 percent of the nonprofessionals have completed at least one year of college and 15 percent have a college degree.

Skill Levels, Economic Change, and Demographic Trends

The Hudson Institute's report, *Workforce 2000,* created a stir in public discussion by questioning the capacity of our future workforce to acquire the skills necessary to contribute to the competitiveness of our economy. The authors argued that the following trends would have a great impact on America's economic future: (1) the continuing growth of service employment and continuing decline in manufacturing; (2) an increasing demand for more highly educated workers; (3) as the population ages, the majority of a decreasing pool of future labor force entrants consisting of women and minorities; (4) inadequate child care and other support systems, limiting the potential productivity of women; and (5) ineffective educational institutions, limiting the potential productivity of minorities. One major potential consequence of the interaction of these trends is a future shortage of well-educated workers in comparison to the requirements of newly created jobs (Johnston and Packer, 1987).

Civil Service 2000 extended the analysis of *Workforce 2000* to explore the potential impact of these trends on the federal workforce, which will also require increasingly more well-educated administrators and professionals. The authors assert that the federal government will require a proportion of employees with the highest math and verbal skill ratings three times as large as that of the private sector. Even though this publication also notes the recent increase in the number of federal employees with college degrees, a trend also shown in Tables 4.2 and 4.3 above, the crisis in morale, low pay, concentration of federal jobs in areas with high costs of living, and frustrating administrative practices suggests that the federal government will not be able to compete with the demand from the private sector for the most highly qualified workers (Johnston and others, 1988).

How do these considerations apply to the future quality and supply

**Table 4.6. Distribution of State and Local Nonprofessional
Employees by Occupation and Skill Rating for Each Occupation.**

	% of all state and local nonprofessionals	Language skill rating	Math skill rating	Total skill rating

Manager or administrator
    Inspectors and compliance officers
    Management-related occupations
	7.0%	4.4	4.2	8.6

Professional or technical
    Other technicians
    Health technicians
    Recreational and related workers
	3.7%	4.0	3.9	7.9

Sales
    Cashiers
    Sales workers
    Sales supervisors
	2.4%	3.6	3.3	6.9

Clerical
    Secretaries, stenographers, and typists
    Miscellaneous administrative support
    Record clerks
    Administrative support supervisors
    Dispatchers and schedulers
    Information clerks
    Office machine operators
    Eligibility clerks
	32.0%	2.9	2.7	5.6

Protective services
    Police
    Firefighters
    Guards, excluding crossing guards
	15.1%	4.0	3.2	7.2

Service workers
    Cleaning and building services
    Food preparation
    Health service occupations
    Groundskeepers
	17.0%	2.6	2.2	4.8

Craft workers
    Carpenters, electricians
    Painters, plumbers
    Equipment repairers
    Vehicle mechanics
    Construction supervisors
    Plant and system operators
	8.3%	2.9	2.8	5.7

Operators and laborers
    Bus drivers
    Truck drivers
    Construction laborers
    Other laborers
    Operating engineers
	14.5%	1.6	1.5	3.1

Total Percent and Weighted Average	100%	3.0	2.7	5.7

Sources: Tabulations from the March 1988 Current Population Survey and machine-readable data file, U.S. Bureau of the Census, 1988; skill ratings from Johnston and others, 1988, pp. 11–15.

of nonprofessional and paraprofessional employees in state and local governments? Table 4.6 shows the distribution of these employees by occupational
category, along with the average language, math, and total skill rating scores
used in the Hudson Institute reports. These ratings are based on the General
Education Development Score used by the U.S. Department of Labor to
measure math, language, and reasoning skills on a scale from 1 through
6. A job with a math rating of 6, the top score, would require the ability
to use calculus, econometrics, or other highly developed mathematical abilities. A job at the bottom of the scale would have a score of 1 and require
only the ability to add and subtract two-digit numbers. The opposite extremes of the language scale also reflect large differences in ability. Jobs with
high language skill scores require employees with the ability to read and
write scientific, technical, financial, or legal publications and documents.
Occupations with the lowest language skill ratings require the ability to read
or deliver simple messages, follow oral instructions, fill out forms, and so
on (Johnston and Packer, 1987; Johnston and others, 1988). Typical nonprofessional job titles are listed below each category in Table 4.6 to give
an indication of what types of jobs are covered by these categories. Almost
a third of nonprofessional employees have occupations with low skill requirements—service workers or operators and laborers. Approximately another
third are clerical workers with intermediate skill levels. In sum, Table 4.6
shows that most nonprofessional employees are in jobs that have relatively
low skill ratings and low educational levels. Of course, the low educational
levels follow directly from the procedure used to identify these jobs. If the
economy is requiring an increasing supply of highly trained and skilled workers, does this mean that the skill requirements of all jobs will likewise increase? Also, what do these matters portend for state and local nonprofessional employees? Will the predicted mismatch between the educational
requirements of new jobs in the future and our inadequate educational system create a relative surplus of workers with low or medium skill levels?
Will the services now performed by nonprofessionals soon be provided by
college graduates?

     Some of the apparent differences between the projected supply and
demand for highly educated workers in the future workforce come from comparing the needs of jobs with the fastest growth rates to current levels of
educational attainment. Even if many or most of the newly created jobs of
the future will indeed require highly educated workers, this does not mean
that many or most of *all* jobs will have such requirements. Even though many
new jobs, including those in state and local government, require highly educated workers, the foreseeable future includes a need for the services of many
nonprofessional and paraprofessional state employees. Even if there were
a steady trend that acted to increase the proportion of professionals and to
decrease the proportion of nonprofessionals in state and local government,
it would take a long time for such a trend to reduce the 79 percent share
of nonprofessional state-local employees to an insignificant figure.

The report of the National Center on Education and the Economy (1990), *America's Choice: High Skills or Low Wages,* provides a very helpful complement to *Workforce 2000.* The fact that the new jobs created by economic growth and change generally do require higher educational levels, as *Workforce 2000* indicates, does not mean that the skill requirements for existing jobs are increasing. The authors of *America's Choice* argue that these new jobs stand on the stable strata of the large majority of jobs with low formal educational requirements and no indication of a demand for change. In their analysis, America's workforce is employed in three groups of approximately similar sizes. The first consists of jobs that require no more than an eighth-grade-level competency in math and language, the requisite physical ability to do the work, and an agreeable personality. The service workers and operators and laborers listed in Table 4.6 are examples of this group. The second workforce group comprises jobs that require specialized training beyond basic literacy and numeracy but not a four-year college degree. Many of the clerical and craft occupations from Table 4.6 are examples of these jobs. The third category encompasses the occupations that do require college degrees and thus are not of direct concern here. The skill shortage that was identified in *America's Choice* consisted of a shortage or lack of interpersonal skills, reliability, communications ability, and other work-related attitudes and manners (National Center on Education and the Economy, 1990).

America's Choice emphasizes that our present and future workforce needs good training, but it does not need a workforce exclusively composed of Ph.D.s or other very highly trained workers. A large proportion of jobs in the future will require workers with basic cognitive and work skills. The same seems to be true of state and local government employees. *America's Choice* also makes some important suggestions for school-to-work transition programs and life-long learning, which will be discussed later. It also describes the characteristics of "high-performance work organizations." The topic of productivity and high performance will be discussed next.

Restructuring the State and Local Government Organization

The Volcker Commission specified a set of goals that also apply to an effort to rebuild public regard for and trust of state and local governments. The only way in which a related subset of these goals can be met is by a restructuring of the organization of state and local government and a drastic change in the role of nonprofessional employees in these structures. This subset of interrelated goals includes increasing productivity, decentralizing management, providing training, and rebuilding student interest.

One of the enduring themes of academic and public policy discussion since the mid 1970s has been the causes and consequences of the decline of the manufacturing sector of the American economy and the rise of the service sector. The issue of how to measure the productivity of service workers has been debated for an even longer period of time (Holzer, 1976). State and local governments are, first and foremost, service providers. The call for increasing the productivity of government is usually met with the response that since the productivity of these service providers cannot be reliably measured, the determination of productivity increases will be arbitrary and unreliable. It is possible to recognize the difficulty of measurement and still insist that increased productivity means simply doing more with the same or fewer resources (National Commission on the Public Service, 1989). The authors of *Workforce 2000* call for the removal of the competitive barriers in the services, including government-provided services, and for investment in technologies that would increase service productivity (Johnston and Packer, 1987). The suggestions made in *America's Choice* for "high performance work organizations" involved greatly increasing the ratio of front-line workers to support staff and the budget for worker training. The management of a high-performance organization would also delegate much more responsibility and control to these better trained front-line workers. In an example drawn from a computer manufacturing plant, the initiation of this new work organization increased productivity by 200 percent, quality by 500 percent, and total production by 600 percent (National Center on Education and the Economy, 1990, pp. 34–35).

Because of the duties they perform and because they constitute about four out of every five state-local workers, the nonprofessionals must be seen as playing major roles in the provision of government services and in any prospect for increasing the productivity of government workers. These workers also need to be integrally included in the creation of high-performance work organizations. One major current in the literature on reorganizing public sector work and making it more productive revolves around the topic of quality circles.

The concept of quality circles is an element of the management of Japanese manufacturing plants. The idea of quality circles was popularized in the United States by William Ouchi's 1981 bestselling book, *Theory Z: How American Business Can Meet the Japanese Challenge.* American manufacturing and service companies, such as banks, hospitals, and insurance companies, adopted quality circles and provided examples of how this innovation might be adopted by government agencies (Boyce, 1985). In essence, quality circles are a means of multiplying an organization's productivity and quality through employee participation in the decision-making process. The improvements come from the assumption that the employees' intimate familiarity with the task creates a basis for useful suggestions and that their participation increases their commitment to suggested changes (Blair, Cohen, and Hurwitz, 1982).

Quality circles have been found to result in dramatic increases in the quality and quantity of output in private sector manufacturing firms, service companies, and in the public sector as well. The city-owned water utility in Fort Collins, Colorado, was able to increase the amount of pipe installation by 450 percent because quality circles gave the workers an opportunity to choose the equipment, techniques, and schedules they would use to get the job done (Hefland, Bachmann, and Campbell, 1984). The Missouri state government has extensively implemented quality circles with very favorable results. In one example, the data entry staff at the Tax Division implemented a new way of checking for errors and posting deposits that resulted in less worker stress, fewer errors, and the quicker deposit of tax receipts—all with savings to the state. In another example, the quality circle of press operators at the printshop suggested that the state buy some metal shelves for storing print stock in an organized and easy-to-retrieve manner. This suggestion was estimated to save more than 1,000 hours of staff time a year (Denhart, Pyle, and Bluedorn, 1987). Note that in these cases the suggestions came from nonprofessional staff members. In fact, the conceptualization of quality circles is such that they are oriented toward increasing input from line staff rather than managers and professionals. Theory Z and quality circles are now part of at least one textbook on public management. As this text suggests, the popularity of quality circles and their widespread adoption and institutionalization can be seen as an expression of a growing trend toward worker participation (Starling, 1986). In addition to the value of the specific suggestions and the increased commitment to the jointly reached decision, participation in the decision-making process indicates that the employees and their ideas are valued. All of these factors can be sources of productivity improvements.

Quality circles cannot be taken to be a universal panacea. They have been implemented in thousands of government agencies with many successes and some failures. A detailed analysis of quality circles in Florida has pointed to three major problem areas. First, they can be implemented as a "program fad"—the bromide or buzzword that is used in response to a crisis situation without a long-term commitment to the implementation or evaluation of quality circles. If they are to work, they must be seen as part of a new way of doing business. A second problem area lies in organizational philosophies that are at odds with the inclusive, participatory thrust of quality circles. The organizational philosophy that sees circles as "simply something that the top told the middle to do to the bottom" not only assumes that productivity and quality problems are caused by staff and supervisors rather than managers, but it also negates the sources of the productivity improvement inherent in quality circles. Finally, quality circles may conflict with formal and informal aspects of labor relations, particularly in unionized workplaces. These and many other factors may indicate situations where quality circles may not be effective. However, this need not be a matter of speculation. The success or failure of this organizational innovation can be determined through evaluations (Bowman, 1989).

While quality circles do seem to be useful means of improving productivity and worker participation, the types of changes and improvements they produce are not likely to inspire a strong positive reaction from the public. Many of the innovations introduced through quality circles have a dual message. They say that bureaucrats are doing things much more efficiently now, but they also say that they were doing things very inefficiently before and that the principal source of the inefficiency was bureaucratic rigidity. In a context of a crisis of public confidence in public servants and services, quality circles seem more like a first step toward the organizational restructuring of public sector work and productivity than like an ultimate solution that will effectively respond to the exigencies government services are now facing.

Two recent books dealing with the organizational restructuring of private sector manufacturing and service firms provide some useful suggestions for improving public sector productivity: Tom Peters's *Thriving on Chaos* and *Service Breakthroughs* by James Heskett, Earl Sasser, and Christopher Hart. Most of the ideas I will cull from these books focus on improving productivity, but they are also closely linked to several other Volcker Commission goals, including decentralizing management, providing training, improving the workplace, providing competitive pay, and receiving competitive performance.

Both of these books start by insisting on the absolute necessity of making the delivery of superior service the number one organizational goal. The restructured organization must have a clear vision of who it is serving and what it must do to serve them well. For the state and local agencies that provide direct service to the general public, such as utilities, street maintenance, waste collection, and the dispensing of unemployment benefits, establishing the focus should be relatively straightforward. The support staffs that have an internal function can still develop a vision focusing on providing the highest-quality service, be it data processing, audits, duplicating, or printing services. The inability to identify the "customer" and goals may well be an indication that this staff should be redeployed when the ratio of front-line to support staff is increased.

Keeping the ultimate goal of these reforms in mind may also suggest where to start. The ultimate goal here is to rebuild the public regard for state and local government by improving the quality of the service and the productivity of the workforce. This restructuring should begin where it can have the greatest positive impact on the public regard. As mentioned above, points of direct contact between government worker and the general public are one place to start. Other priority areas could be determined through systematic evaluation of the effectiveness and perceptions of service delivery (Hatry and others, 1977). A conspicuous improvement in the quality of services in an area where the public has low expectations could have a big impact on the perceived quality of government services overall. For example, one recent book presents the following simple relationship between perceived quality, expected service, and actual service (Heskett, Sasser, and Hart, 1990, pp. 5–10).

Quality = Actual Service – Expected Service.

Peters makes a similar point, which can be expressed with a slightly different formula (Peters, 1987, pp. 118–120):

Quality = Actual Service / Expected Service.

Although the form of the relationship between the terms is different than above, the basic idea is the same. Also similar are the implications for a situation where low expectations are exceeded by high-quality service; an unexpected improvement in actual service will yield a high value for perceived quality. Both authors emphasize the subjective nature of the perception of quality and that it is evaluated on the basis of expectations. A slight improvement from a previously poor service provider will be perceived positively. A slight slip from an otherwise high-quality provider will be perceived as decreased service quality. How can this be done and how does it involve nonprofessional employees? These two books sugggest that the answer for service industries is the same as that suggested in *America's Choice* for high-performance manufacturing: maximize the proportion of well-trained front-line staff with sufficient authority to take control and take responsibility for the outcomes of their actions. I am suggesting that state and local government services can benefit from these ideas as well. Furthermore, the components of this change are largely similar to those called for in the Volcker Commission goals but now applied to the large majority of nonprofessional state and local workers who were not covered by the original report.

The goal of improving the productivity and the quality of public services calls for increasing service-providing personnel and decreasing support and supervisory staff. Peters calls this "flattening the organizational structure" (Peters, 1987, pp. 430–465). This will tend to improve the quantity of the personnel available to provide the service and, through this, probably lead to an improved perception of service quality. As shown previously in Table 4.2a, 12 percent of all state and local employees were managers and administrators in 1988, compared to 18 percent of the federal workforce and 10 percent of the private sector. Even though the state proportion is not too much higher than the private sector, Peters suggests that even the private sector level of managers is too high. Flattening the organizational structure would mean decreasing these percentages. Increasing the ratio of service providers to support staff would also involve this change in organizational structure and reassigning or redeploying some of the 32 percent of the nonprofessional workforce that are administrative support clerical workers (Table 4.6) as well, along with ensuring that a higher proportion of service, craft, and other workers directly deliver services rather than support those who do. This type of organizational change might well cut off career ladders in the situations where they exist for nonprofessional workers. Employee loyalty and performance would have to be sought with pay increases, performance rewards, and increased responsibility and control.

One of the ideas behind the success of quality circles is that the people doing the work know much about how to do it. The people who do the work are also those in contact with the public, and they are also knowledgeable about how it might be made better in terms the public appreciates. However, these people are rarely those who make the decisions about what they do or how to it better. Management has to be decentralized to the point where the service providers can make decisions. Middle managers would be communication facilitators instead of guardians of the rules (Peters, 1987). Staff jobs have to encompass some aspects of management and control responsibilities in order to give workers the opportunity to respond to problems and opportunities as they occur.

It may well be true that the jobs of the future will require more technically sophisticated, well-informed, and self-reliant workers. It could also be true that no more than a third of the jobs available in the near future will require a college degree. Yet the majority of all workers and particularly the nonprofessional state and local employees could meet some of the increasing technical needs of future jobs through on-the-job training. All of the works I have cited so far call for a great increase in the amount of training available to staff over the course of their employment. Peters (1987) lists several aspects of the type of training program that would be necessary to implement the order of changes that are suggested here:

1. Have extensive entry-level training.
2. Treat all employees as potential career employees.
3. Retrain regularly.
4. Be generous with time and money for training.
5. Use on-the-job interaction as a form of training.
6. Don't assume limits to what can be learned.
7. Make training meet the needs of the front line.
8. Use training to share vision, values, and skills.

A training program such as this in a restructured organization could give people with an eighth-grade education the necessary skills and judgment to respond to the specific opportunities and challenges they confront in their daily tasks and make informed, responsible decisions.

An example of a similar emphasis on training, and on several of the other issues raised above, can be seen in the report of the Task Force on the New York State Public Workforce in the 21st Century (1990). They begin the report with a recognition of the importance of human capital and that external forces such as a high dropout rate; a workforce where many lack basic reading, writing, computational, and reasoning skills; and a rapidly changing workplace technology all call for the state to implement an education and training program for its employees. Specifically following some of Peters's suggestions regarding training, they recommend that the state provide remedial education, including basic literacy and English instruction.

They also urge that staff training and development focus on the ability of workers to cope with change in the workplace (Task Force on the New York State Workforce in the 21st Century, 1990).

The types of changes suggested can stretch the abilities of current employees. How can a high school dropout with minimal literacy skills be expected to take a degree of control over his or her work? If it is not expected, it will not happen, and without this major improvement in the abilities of workers, the possibilities for rebuilding the public service will be limited.

The Volcker Commission Task Force on Education and Training made a number of suggestions for high school and college-based programs designed to attract young people into civil service careers. All of these outreach activities are good ideas, and state and local governments have the advantage of propinquity in working with schools in efforts like these. Another school-based program where state and local government could provide an example of innovation for the private sector is in school-to-work transition programs. One of the great problems with our educational system is its failure to provide high school graduates with an institutionalized connection with employers. High school would be a natural place for state and local governments to recruit nonprofessional staff members. At least half of the nation's high school students do not go to college. Class presentations, summer employment, and recruitment of graduating seniors into entry-level positions could help governments find good employees and, properly structured, such a program could possibly motivate potential dropouts to stay in school. The relationship between high school classes and necessary job skills could be made much more direct by changes in the curricula and in the hiring practices of government employers. Grades earned in a work-skills-based high school course seem to be legitimate and meaningful employee selection criteria. Attendance records might also be used to select employees. The idea behind both of these suggestions is to reinforce performance in high school with the tangible opportunity of employment in state and local government.

Conclusion

The comparison of the characteristics of state and local nonprofessional and paraprofessional employees with demographic and economic trends suggests that local and state governments will continue to need large numbers of these employees in the future. The main challenge to these governments will not be to find new employees but to mobilize all resources, particularly human resources, to increase productivity, the public evaluation of the quality of government services, and the confidence of the public that their local and state governments are serving them well. Following some recent literature on service-oriented businesses, I argued that an obsession with the delivery of top-quality services should be the goal of organizational restructuring.

Nonprofessional and paraprofessional employees have to be a major part of any effort to achieve these ends because of the nature of their jobs and because they are the preponderance of state and local employees. Many of the suggested reforms may be unrealistic or impractical. However, there is one undeniable core to this argument: any hope of rebuilding the public service and the public trust will fail unless it permits and enables these non-professionals and paraprofessionals to maximize their contribution to the organizational goals.

Appendix: Description of Data Sources and Analysis

The tables in this report are based on three sources of data: the 1980 Census Public-Use Microdata Sample (PUMS), the March 1988 Current Population data file, and published Census Bureau tabulation based on the Census of Governments, the Survey of Governments, and the tabulation of administrative records and reports.

The PUMS data used here consist of a 1-in-1,000 sample of the coded responses to the Census Bureau's detailed questionnaire for the entire population in 1980. The total sample size from this data set was about 225,000 respondents (see U.S. Bureau of the Census, 1983).

The Current Population Survey (CPS) is a monthly survey of approximately 53,000 households across the nation. The CPS is conducted by the U.S. Bureau of the Census to determine employment levels and other labor force and economic characteristics. Each CPS questionnaire also contains a set of supplemental questions asked on a rotating or ad hoc basis. The March 1988 CPS contains the information used in the annual demographic file (see U.S. Bureau of the Census, 1988). The major problems with CPS data are that they are relatively tricky and complicated to use, as is the case with weighted data drawn from a complex sample. Also 53,000 households is, in some cases, a relatively small sample size for discussing the characteristics of population subgroups.

The analyses of both of these data sets began by excluding all teachers, including preschool, K-12, postsecondary, educational administrators, and teacher aides, from the sample of all public employees. The farm laborers occupational category in state and local and federal employment consists almost entirely of groundskeepers. The farm laborer group was used in Tables 4.2 and 4.3 in order to make the comparison between the public and private sectors more consistent. In the subsequent tables presenting data on state and local workers, groundskeepers were grouped with operatives and laborers. The data from the published reports excluded employees of school districts and educational institutions.

The tabulated statistics are based on samples of the following sizes:

	1980	1988
State and local employees	16,230	6,563
Federal	6,627	2,544
Private sector	18,610	11,954

The private sector sample is a 20 percent random subsample of the records available in the data sets. The large size of the private sector made it unnecessary and inefficient to process all records. These are fairly large samples, and numerically small differences in proportions would probably be statistically significant at commonly used confidence levels.

References

Blair, J., Cohen, S., and Hurwitz, J. "Quality Circles: Practical Considerations for Public Managers." *Public Productivity Review,* 1982, pp. 9–18.

Bowman, J. "Quality Circles: Promise, Problems, and Prospects in Florida." *Public Personnel Management,* 1989, *18,* 375–403.

Boyce, M. "Can Quality Circles Be Applied in the Public Sector?" *Journal of Collective Negotiations,* 1985, *141,* 67–75.

deCourcy Hinds, M. "Strapped, Big Cities Take Painful Steps." *New York Times,* January 6, 1991, p. A9.

Denhart, R., Pyle, J., and Bluedorn, A. "Implementing Quality Circles in State Government." *Public Administration Review,* 1987, *47,* 304–309.

Foster, G., and Snyder, S. "Public Attitudes Towards Government: Contradictions, Ambivalence, and the Dilemma of Response." In *Rebuilding the Public Service: Task Force Reports.* Washington, D.C.: National Commission on the Public Service, 1989.

Hatry, H., and others. *How Effective Are Your Community Services?* Washington, D.C.: Urban Institute and the International City Management Association, 1977.

Hefland, G., Bachmann, R., and Campbell, J. "The Applicability of the Japanese Model to the U.S. Public Sector." *Public Productivity Review,* 1984, pp. 127–136.

Heskett, J. L., Sasser, W. E., Jr., and Hart, C. *Service Breakthroughs: Changing the Rules of the Game.* New York: Free Press, 1990.

Holzer, M. *Productivity in Public Organizations.* Port Washington, N.Y.: Kennikat Press, 1976.

Johnston, W. B., and Packer, A. H. *Workforce 2000: Work and Workers for the Twenty-First Century.* Indianapolis, Ind.: Hudson Institute, 1987.

Johnston, W. B., and others. *Civil Service 2000.* Indianapolis, Ind.: Hudson Institute, 1988.

National Center on Education and the Economy. *America's Choice: High Skills or Low Wages.* Rochester, N.Y.: National Center on Education and the Economy, 1990.

National Commission on the Public Service (Volcker Commission). *Rebuilding the Public Service.* Washington, D.C.: National Commission on the Public Service, 1989.

Ouchi, W. *Theory Z: How American Business Can Meet the Japanese Challenge.* Reading, Mass.: Addison-Wesley, 1981.

Peters, T. *Thriving on Chaos.* New York: HarperCollins, 1987.

Prottas, J. *People Processing.* Lexington, Mass.: Lexington Books, 1979.

Starling, G. *Managing the Public Sector.* (3rd ed.) Chicago: Dorsey Press, 1986.

Task Force on the New York State Public Workforce in the 21st Century. *Public Service Through the State Government Workforce: Meeting the Challenge of Change.* Albany, N.Y.: Nelson A. Rockefeller Institute of Government and the State Academy for Public Administration, 1990.

U.S. Bureau of the Census. *Census of Population and Housing, 1980: Public Use Microdata Samples Technical Documentation.* Washington, D.C.: Data Users Services Division, Bureau of the Census, 1983.

U.S. Bureau of the Census. *Current Population Survey, March 1988: Technical Documentation.* Washington, D.C.: Data Users Services Division, Bureau of the Census, 1988.

U.S. Bureau of the Census. *Statistical Abstract of the United States, 1990.* Washington, D.C.: U.S. Government Printing Office, 1990.

FIVE

Compensation of
State and Local Employees:
Sorting Out the Issues

Steven D. Gold
Sarah Ritchie

Duuring the last decade, the scope of state and local government policies and the size of their budgets have increased dramatically. Under mounting pressure of federal deficits, federal aid to states and localities has dropped 38 percent during the 1980s. Simultaneously, many new mandates have been placed on states and localities (Nathan, Doolittle, and Associates, 1987; Conlan, 1988; Gold, 1990). Expanding policy responsibilities makes it imperative that state and local agencies recruit and retain well-trained, productive employees. The level of compensation is critical to employee job satisfaction and, hence, the successful administration of public policies.

The magnitude of the public sector compensation issue is highlighted by the fact that state and local employees are paid more than $336 billion per year. If they work full time, they earn on the average more than $29,000 per year, not including the cost of their benefits, which is more than 22 percent of their salaries and wages.[1]

This chapter provides an overview of patterns of compensation from various perspectives. Analyzing compensation is difficult because of problems in comparing jobs, compensation arrangements, and living costs in different places. Although the research provides some useful national perspectives, it cannot be used to draw definitive conclusions about which states pay their employees best and worst. Conclusions about the adequacy of compensation in a particular state require a more detailed analysis than can be provided by a fifty-state study. A good example of a study that *did* perform such an analysis was published by the Urban Institute (Dickson and Peterson, 1980). Despite its relatively large budget and substantial resources, Urban Institute researchers were able to compare compensation for only seven jobs in twelve large cities. The Urban Institute project demonstrated that valid comparisons can be made, but only with a large research investment.

This chapter provides a good framework for considering compensation issues in particular states. It should be especially useful in identifying (1) pitfalls that can mar comparisons among states, and (2) areas where data are lacking or are of questionable validity. Our goal is not to answer all of the questions that need to be addressed but rather to provide a road map that will be helpful in sorting out the issues from a particular point of view.

The chapter deals with three major questions:

- What is the variation in the compensation of state and local employees among the states?
- How does compensation for high-level positions compare to that for jobs requiring less skill and experience?
- How has the compensation of state-local employees fared relative to inflation and to the compensation of private sector workers in the last decade?

Since these issues are multifaceted, it has been necessary to limit the study in several ways. First, more of the research covered relates to state than to local employees. Second, considerably more attention focuses on workers who are not involved with education, either at the elementary-secondary or postsecondary levels. These emphases shift the analysis away from the majority of the employees of state and local governments. As of October 1990, 52 percent of state and local government employees were involved in education. Approximately 70 percent of employees worked for local governments. In other words, the primary focus here is on the 2.5 million state workers who are not involved in the education sector. By comparison, there were a total of 15.3 million state-local employees in October 1990. The compensation of local and education employees is not completely neglected. Their earnings are discussed in the next section, and their fringe benefits are covered in a later section of this chapter.

The limitations of this analysis are necessary because of the great diversity among local governments. It is difficult enough to make comparisons among the fifty states, but the information needs to expand enormously if localities are also covered. There are more than 80,000 local governments in the United States. Even if the focus is limited to large governments, the data problems are great. There are 306 cities with a population over 75,000 and 412 counties with a population over 100,000. Since the issues that arise in comparing local compensation are essentially the same as those involved in comparing state compensation, this analysis is useful in establishing a framework for research at both levels.

This chapter has seven parts: aggregate earnings comparisons among states, disaggregated earnings comparisons among states by occupation, comparisons of public and private earnings, fringe benefit comparisons, cost-of-living adjustments, changes in earnings over time, and conclusion.

Aggregate Earnings Comparisons Among States

Table 5.1 compares the average earnings of full-time state and local employees in each state in October 1989. While these figures are of some interest, they have two serious limitations. First, because of the severe fiscal problems that have afflicted many state and local governments recently, some of the patterns may have changed in the interim. Second, interstate comparisons of public employee earnings are not as meaningful as intrastate earnings comparisons for similar jobs in the public and private sector. Interstate comparisons are plagued by differences in regional living costs and variations in the composition of the workforce among occupations.

There is a great deal of diversity in average earnings, with Alaska's employees receiving more than twice as much as those in Mississippi. After Alaska, the highest earnings were in California, New York, Connecticut, Michigan, Minnesota, Maryland, New Jersey, Rhode Island, and Massachusetts. Except for South Dakota, all of the ten states with the lowest earnings were in the Southeast and the Southwest.

Large differences in earnings exist among regions. For example, for state employees, the Middle Atlantic, New England, and Great Lakes states had the highest average earnings, with the Far West ranking next highest. The averages of monthly salaries for states in each region are as follows:

Region	Salary
New England	$2,467
Middle Atlantic	2,480
Great Lakes	2,466
Plains	2,176
Southeast	1,991
Southwest	2,083
Rocky Mountain	2,139
Far West	2,404

There is a fairly close relationship between earnings at the state and local levels. State employees usually have higher average earnings than local employees, but states that are high or low at one level also tend to be high or low at the other. In thirty-six states, the ranking at the state level is within nine places of the ranking at the local level. The exceptions, where state workers are paid considerably more than local workers, are Alabama, Colorado, Idaho, Indiana, Iowa, and Kentucky; and the states where local workers are paid considerably more than state workers are Delaware, Florida, Hawaii, Missouri, Nevada, Utah, and Wyoming.[2]

Table 5.1. Average Monthly Earnings of State and Local Employees, October 1989.

	Total	Rank	State	Rank	Local	Rank
New England						
Connecticut	$2,744	4	$2,888	3	$2,657	4
Maine	1,938	36	2,114	29	1,840	38
Massachusetts	2,452	10	2,569	11	2,399	13
New Hampshire	2,112	25	2,117	28	2,109	24
Rhode Island	2,500	9	2,542	12	2,471	8
Vermont	2,107	26	2,847	25	2,042	26
Mid-Atlantic						
Delaware	$2,258	18	$2,157	26	$2,375	15
Maryland	2,592	7	2,508	12	2,638	5
New Jersey	2,595	5	2,658	7	2,570	6
New York	2,758	3	2,826	4	2,734	3
Pennsylvania	2,275	17	2,252	19	2,283	18
Great Lakes						
Illinois	$2,408	11	$2,485	13	$2,384	14
Indiana	2,032	28	2,335	17	1,910	33
Michigan	2,593	6	2,769	5	2,523	7
Ohio	2,199	21	2,353	16	2,147	22
Wisconsin	2,322	15	2,389	15	2,299	17
Plains						
Iowa	$2,127	24	$2,602	9	$1,918	32
Kansas	1,945	34	2,025	37	1,908	34
Minnesota	2,525	8	2,739	6	2,444	10
Missouri	1,950	33	1,908	43	1,968	30
Nebraska	1,995	31	2,026	36	1,981	28
North Dakota	2,067	27	2,037	34	2,088	25
South Dakota	1,725	46	1,895	46	1,634	48
Southeast						
Alabama	$1,783	44	$2,054	32	$1,650	46
Arkansas	1,607	50	1,822	48	1,492	50
Florida	2,149	23	2,083	31	2,170	21
Georgia	1,859	39	2,021	38	1,796	39
Kentucky	1,794	43	2,034	35	1,657	45
Louisiana	1,723	47	1,878	47	1,644	47
Mississippi	1,610	49	1,794	49	1,530	49
North Carolina	2,030	29	2,250	21	1,937	31
South Carolina	1,827	41	1,898	45	1,782	40
Tennessee	1,890	38	2,004	40	1,842	37
Virginia	2,164	22	2,240	23	2,125	23
West Virginia	1,693	48	1,696	50	1,692	42
Southwest						
Arizona	$2,389	12	$2,275	18	$2,429	12
New Mexico	1,830	40	1,987	41	1,732	41
Oklahoma	1,770	45	1,922	42	1,687	43
Texas	1,955	32	2,149	27	1,897	35
Rocky Mountain						
Colorado	$2,321	16	$2,628	8	$2,214	20
Idaho	1,814	42	2,102	30	1,680	44
Montana	1,927	37	2,046	33	1,870	36
Utah	1,945	35	1,904	44	1,976	29
Wyoming	2,019	30	2,014	39	2,021	27
Far West						
Alaska	$3,336	1	$3,252	1	$3,427	1
California	2,938	2	3,101	2	2,891	2

Table 5.1. Average Monthly Earnings of State and Local Employees, October 1989, Cont'd.

	Total	Rank	State	Rank	Local	Rank
Hawaii	2,252	19	2,186	24	2,469	9
Nevada	2,384	13	2,250	20	2,440	11
Oregon	2,235	20	2,246	22	2,230	19
Washington	2,378	14	2,391	14	2,371	16
National Averages	$2,160	NA	$2,260	NA	$2,119	NA

Source: U.S. Bureau of the Census, 1989a.

Table 5.2 reports average earnings for workers who are not involved in education. In most, but not all, states the average earnings of noneducation employees are similar to the earnings of all employees. There are only eight states where the average earnings of all employees were 10 percent or more higher than the average earnings of noneducation employees. In only five states, noneducation employees earned more than the average of all employees.

Data on average earnings is helpful in that they provide an overall indication of differences in how well employees are compensated. They also suggest that the more intensive study of state employees' earnings in this chapter is not irrelevant to local employees' earnings, and likewise the neglect of education workers' earnings is not as serious as it would be if there were no relationship between the earnings of education workers and others.

The aggregate data in Table 5.1 have four serious flaws.

- The data ignore differences in the composition of the workforce. For example, states where higher education faculty represent an above-average proportion of total employment tend to have higher average salaries because faculty are typically paid more than the average state worker. To overcome this problem, it is necessary to compare salaries for people with the same occupation and responsibilities, as is done in the next section of this chapter.
- They ignore fringe benefits. Employees in some states may receive a larger proportion of their compensation as fringe benefits rather than as wages and salaries. This issue is discussed in the fourth section of this chapter.
- They ignore differences in the cost of living among states. This issue is discussed in section five of this chapter.
- They ignore differences in how many years workers have been employed. If two places have exactly the same pay scales and the composition of their workforces is identical, they may still have significant differences in average earnings because more experienced workers are paid more.

Earnings Comparisons for Similar Jobs

To overcome some of the problems in interpreting statewide differences in average earnings, data have been assembled from a variety of sources to

Table 5.2. Average Monthly Earnings of State and
Local Employees Not Involved with Education, October 1989.

	Total	Rank	State	Rank	Local	Rank
New England						
Connecticut	$2,678	3	$2,867	3	$2,444	7
Maine	1,933	29	2,038	25	1,788	35
Massachusetts	2,466	6	2,510	8	2,431	8
New Hampshire	2,046	25	1,984	30	2,103	20
Rhode Island	2,274	14	2,492	10	1,993	25
Vermont	2,038	27	2,649	22	1,963	27
Mid-Atlantic						
Delaware	$2,051	23	$2,006	29	$2,174	17
Maryland	2,343	12	2,340	13	2,345	10
New Jersey	2,366	11	2,535	7	2,261	14
New York	2,634	4	2,769	4	2,567	3
Pennsylvania	2,096	19	2,161	18	2,052	22
Great Lakes						
Illinois	$2,340	12	$2,377	11	$2,324	12
Indiana	1,711	43	1,933	33	1,596	44
Michigan	2,453	8	2,724	5	2,273	13
Ohio	2,045	25	2,226	17	1,971	26
Wisconsin	2,116	18	2,250	16	2,065	21
Plains						
Iowa	$2,050	23	$2,339	14	$1,832	30
Kansas	1,915	30	2,060	23	1,803	34
Minnesota	2,412	9	2,602	6	2,327	11
Missouri	1,838	35	1,786	43	1,876	29
Nebraska	1,976	28	1,888	36	2,029	24
North Dakota	1,755	41	1,868	40	629	50
South Dakota	1,645	47	1,721	46	1,566	45
Southeast						
Alabama	$1,742	42	$1,873	39	$1,657	39
Arkansas	1,548	48	1,684	48	1,404	48
Florida	2,093	20	1,972	31	2,153	18
Georgia	1,839	34	1,883	37	1,813	32
Kentucky	1,688	45	1,720	47	1,650	40
Louisiana	1,653	46	1,758	44	1,557	46
Mississippi	1,543	49	1,596	49	1,502	47
North Carolina	1,856	32	2,018	28	1,743	37
South Carolina	1,692	44	1,746	45	1,630	41
Tennessee	1,838	36	1,876	38	1,817	31
Virginia	2,083	21	2,039	24	2,121	19
West Virginia	1,465	50	1,490	50	1,343	49
Southwest						
Arizona	$2,310	13	$2,113	20	$2,403	9
New Mexico	1,801	38	1,843	42	1,755	36
Oklahoma	1,771	39	1,861	41	1,687	38
Texas	1,914	31	1,944	32	1,899	28
Rocky Mountain						
Colorado	$2,273	15	$2,496	9	$2,184	16
Idaho	1,836	37	2,106	21	1,628	42
Montana	1,766	40	1,916	34	1,613	43
Utah	2,041	26	2,038	25	2,044	23
Wyoming	1,853	33	1,907	35	1,807	33
Far West						
Alaska	$3,308	1	$3,271	1	$3,366	1
California	2,926	2	2,984	2	2,905	2

Table 5.2. Average Monthly Earnings of State and Local
Employees Not Involved with Education, October 1989, Cont'd.

	Total	Rank	State	Rank	Local	Rank
Hawaii	2,209	16	2,033	27	2,469	6
Nevada	2,489	5	2,368	12	2,557	4
Oregon	2,181	17	2,121	19	2,233	15
Washington	2,453	7	2,327	15	2,539	5
National Averages	$2,075	NA	$2,142	NA	$1,998	NA

Source: U.S. Bureau of the Census, 1989a.

compare salaries for workers with similar jobs, both for low- and middle-level jobs and also for heads of agencies and executive departments.

A survey by the National Association of State Personnel Executives (NASPE) and the Council of State Governments (CSG) reported 1989 salaries for forty-nine job titles in eleven employment areas in forty-eight states.[3] This information provides a good basis for states to evaluate how their own compensation compares to that in other states, at least for jobs below the top-tier executive level. For example, Table 5.3 shows how this research was used by the Federal Reserve Bank of Boston in a study of Massachusetts's compensation of state employees (Henderson, 1990). The data in the table reveal that although Massachusetts's compensation is relatively high in some job categories, it is relatively low for a greater number of jobs.

The Federal Reserve study compared Massachusetts to sixteen states that it considered to be relatively similar to it in terms of the nature of their economies. For the present study, the Center for the Study of the States analyzed the NASPE data for the entire nation, comparing the unweighted average of salaries in each state with the national average. Table 5.4 summarizes the results of that analysis.

The NASPE/CSG data reveal some broad patterns that are similar to those described in the previous section. According to this study, the five states with the highest overall salaries were Alaska, California, Minnesota, Michigan, and Connecticut. In regional terms, New England, Middle Atlantic, Great Lakes, Plains, and Far West states tended to have above-average earnings. The following list shows the regional variations in average earnings.

Region	Overall difference from average salary
New England	9.13%
Middle Atlantic	1.64
Great Lakes	6.09
Plains	1.63
Southeast	−7.58
Southwest	−6.65
Rocky Mountain	−2.68
Far West	15.15

Table 5.3. Median Monthly Wage for Selected
Occupations in Massachusetts and Other State Governments, June 1989.

	Massachusetts	Range for sixteen states	Massachusetts difference from sixteen-state average
Office and allied service			
Stenographer clerk	$1,425	$1,092–1,823	–1%
Junior clerk	1,229	968–1,546	–1
Offset duplicating			
Machine operator	1,485	1,210–1,900	–2
Custodian and food services			
Cook	1,367	1,028–2,059	–11
Janitor	1,189	968–2,160	–15
Maintenance and construction			
Laborer, heavy	1,367	968–2,224	–6
Truck driver, heavy	1,425	1,319–2,514	–18
Plumber	1,654	1,482–3,513	–21
Electrician	1,654	1,587–3,456	–21
Carpenter	1,564	1,482–3,250	–22
Machinist	1,564	1,587–3,289	–27
Stationary engineer	1,425	1,495–3,217	–31
Data processing			
Key punch operator	1,270	1,235–1,860	–13
Systems analyst	2,407	2,014–3,507	–16
Computer operator	1,425	1,533–1,949	–19
Fiscal management			
Auditor	2,071	1,769–2,717	–13
Legal			
Administrative law judge	3,036	2,444–6,043	–25
Education and library			
Librarian	1,425	1,462–2,989	–34
Agriculture inspection			
Agricultural inspector	1,642	1,482–2,790	–17
Engineering and allied services			
Junior engineer aide	1,571	968–2,154	+10
Assistant engineer	2,643	2,216–3,351	+1
Chemist	2,283	1,796–2,975	–2
Medical and medical support			
Registered nurse	2,550	1,894–2,792	+13
Laboratory technologist	2,283	1,587–2,904	+10
Pharmacist	2,906	1,881–3,851	+9
Staff psychologist	3,569	2,357–3,898	+9
Speech pathologist	2,550	2,033–3,343	0
Physical therapist	2,250	2,014–2,904	–8
X-ray technician	1,425	1,404–2,308	–18
Vocational nurse	1,425	1,587–2,042	–20
Master of social work	1,833	1,948–2,904	–24

Source: Henderson, 1990, p. 219.

Table 5.4. Average Difference from Mean Salary for 49 Specific Job Titles.

States	Average Deviation from Salary Mean	Rank
New England		
Connecticut	15.83%	6
Maine	23.74	4
Massachusetts	NA	
New Hampshire	NA	
Rhode Island	1.91	18
Vermont	–4.96	30
Mid-Atlantic		
Delaware	–7.53	36
Maryland	1.08	21
New Jersey	12.13	9
New York	NA	
Pennsylvania	0.89	22
Great Lakes		
Illinois	1.32	20
Indiana	–9.92	38
Michigan	25.41	3
Ohio	3.10	16
Wisconsin	10.53	10
Plains		
Iowa	–1.51	26
Kansas	–4.66	29
Minnesota	23.74	5
Missouri	–6.59	33
Nebraska	–0.81	25
North Dakota	–0.35	23
South Dakota	NA	
Southeast		
Alabama	2.00	17
Arkansas	–19.23	45
Florida	–17.09	44
Georgia	–0.64	24
Kentucky	–11.73	40
Louisiana	–5.75	31
Mississippi	–19.53	46
North Carolina	14.31	8
South Carolina	–1.99	27
Tennessee	–16.53	43
Virginia	1.70	19
West Virginia	–16.48	42
Southwest		
Arizona	3.81	15
New Mexico	–7.25	35
Oklahoma	–13.71	41
Texas	–9.45	37
Rocky Mountain		
Colorado	14.72	7
Idaho	–6.49	32
Montana	–11.68	39
Utah	–3.23	28
Wyoming	–6.74	34
Far West		
Alaska	37.05	1

Table 5.4. Average Difference from Mean Salary for 49 Specific Job Titles, Cont'd.

States	Average Deviation from Salary Mean	Rank
California	34.07	2
Hawaii	3.82	14
Nevada	5.37	12
Oregon	5.70	11
Washington	4.91	13

Note: NA means data not provided in document.
Source: Calculated from survey by National Association of State Personnel Executives (NASPE) and Council of State Governments (CSG).

Although the findings of the NASPE/CSG survey are similar to those described in the previous section, the disaggregated data do reveal some differences. For example, there is agreement that Alaska, California, Connecticut, and Michigan have high salaries, while most southeastern states have low salaries. For Maine, on the other hand, the two sources provide opposite indications, one suggesting that salaries are high and the other indicating that they are relatively low.[4] Nevertheless, the NASPE/CSG survey is useful in that it considers how earnings compare for various low- and middle-level positions in state government.

In addition to the national data provided by NASPE and the CSG, several regional groups of state personnel officials have collected extensive salary data that cover numerous high-level employment positions. Information published by the Central States Salary Conference in 1989 indicates that there is some consistency among compensation in various occupational areas and at different levels. In particular, states that tend to have higher salary levels among professionally trained employees will likely pay above-average wages to nonprofessional workers. Greater salary variability exists in rankings among lower-paying states.[5]

Finally, some observers have expressed concern about the salary levels for upper-management and executive officials at the state level (Witt, 1988). In this regard, 1989 salaries for governor and seven cabinet-level positions (directors of budget, personnel, social services, transportation, mental health, labor, and education departments) were reviewed for each of the fifty states (Council of State Governments, 1990). The overall average salaries for the respective positions were as follows:

Position	Salary
Governor	$79,537
Budget director	65,973
Personnel director	63,109
Social services director	66,503

Transportation director	71,405
Mental health director	65,479
Labor director	59,410
Education director	75,506

There is substantial variation among states in the salaries of directors of departments, as Table 5.5 demonstrates. However, the levels of executive salaries appear to be closely related to a state's population size and per capita income. In fact, two indicators — a state's population and its per capita income — account for 59 percent of the variation in average salaries.[6] Of the ten states with the highest average salaries, seven are among the ten with the largest populations.

State	Average salary
*New York	$105,164
*California	92,127
Virginia	87,812
*Texas	86,392
*New Jersey	82,970
*Michigan	81,411
*Illinois	80,730
*Florida	78,829
South Carolina	78,608
Delaware	78,116

*Among the ten most populous states in the United States.

Comparison of Public and Private Earnings

Comparisons between public and private earnings levels are a difficult but very significant indicator of the level of overall compensation. Comparisons such as those in the previous section, for similar jobs in different states, do not take account of differences in the cost of living or the amenities of various places. Besides, state and local governments must compete with the private sector for employees, so public-private comparisons are more important than interstate comparisons for similar jobs.

The most important conclusion about differences in employee earnings between the state-local and the private sectors is that there is a major distinction between low-wage and high-wage workers. As the amount of skill and training involved in a job increases, state-local salaries tend to become less competitive with the private sector.

For example, the Hay Group (1984) has shown that state government salaries tend increasingly to lag behind private salaries as one progresses up the General Services (GS) scale. This is shown graphically in Figure 5.1.

Table 5.5. Average Annual Salary of Eight Top-Level Executives, 1989.

State	Salary	Rank
New England		
Connecticut	$ 72,341	18
Maine	54,559	45
Massachusetts	74,175	12
New Hampshire	62,128	32
Rhode Island	62,206	31
Vermont	57,223	38
Mid-Atlantic		
Delaware	$ 78,116	10
Maryland	77,883	11
New Jersey	82,970	5
New York	105,164	1
Pennsylvania	64,723	26
Great Lakes		
Illinois	$ 80,730	7
Indiana	65,493	25
Michigan	81,411	6
Ohio	59,733	35
Wisconsin	55,630	43
Plains		
Iowa	$ 57,805	36
Kansas	70,187	20
Minnesota	72,587	17
Missouri	64,508	28
Nebraska	50,684	48
North Dakota	54,201	46
South Dakota	57,398	37
Southeast		
Alabama	$ 72,833	16
Arkansas	49,602	49
Florida	78,829	8
Georgia	73,986	13
Kentucky	63,957	29
Louisiana	55,548	44
Mississippi	57,219	39
North Carolina	68,950	22
South Carolina	78,608	9
Tennessee	64,600	27
Virginia	87,812	3
West Virginia	53,198	47
Southwest		
Arizona	$ 56,706	40
New Mexico	60,533	34
Oklahoma	63,728	30
Texas	86,392	4
Rocky Mountain		
Colorado	$ 69,090	21
Idaho	56,056	42
Montana	47,489	50
Utah	68,641	23
Wyoming	56,624	41
Far West		
Alaska	$ 67,020	24
California	92,127	2

Table 5.5. Average Annual Salary of Eight Top-Level Executives, 1989, Cont'd.

State	Salary	Rank
Hawaii	73,875	14
Nevada	60,630	33
Oregon	72,301	19
Washington	73,580	15

Source: Council of State Governments, 1990.

Grade level	Average state compensation	Average private compensation	Ratio state/ private
3	$20,770	$20,060	1.04
4	23.161	23,848	.97
5	24,708	26,443	.93
6	26,516	29,262	.91
7	28,413	32,494	.87
9	31,925	39,239	.81
11	36,799	44,679	.82
12	41,607	51,889	.80
13	50,087	64,863	.77
14	57,836	76,769	.75
15	66,497	92,259	.72

A similar conclusion is reached in a recent National Bureau of Economic Research study by Lawrence Katz and Alan Krueger (1991). They found that less educated state-local workers tended to earn more than they would in the private sector, while the opposite was true for highly educated workers (Katz and Krueger, 1991).[7]

In reviewing particular job titles from the NASPE/CSG data with comparable private sector positions identified by the U.S. Bureau of the Census (1989b), two important findings emerge. First, among lower-level employment positions such as clerical, data entry, and manual labor jobs, the salary level in the public sector is usually at least as high as the private sector. However, as one considers upper-level positions and those requiring special training like engineering, medicine, and the like, a disparity emerges between private and state government payrolls. In other words, even though state and local salaries may compare favorably with private sector wages, this is not generally true for senior-level positions.[8]

The competitiveness of state government salaries is drastically reduced at the highest echelons of government service. The Hay Group analysis (1984) indicates that the compensation of state government executives does not approach salary levels of chief executives in the private sector. It shows that lower-paid corporate executives earned an average $230,000 per year and higher-paid executives earned approximately $600,000. Likewise, a survey

Figure 5.1. Comparison of State and Private Salaries.

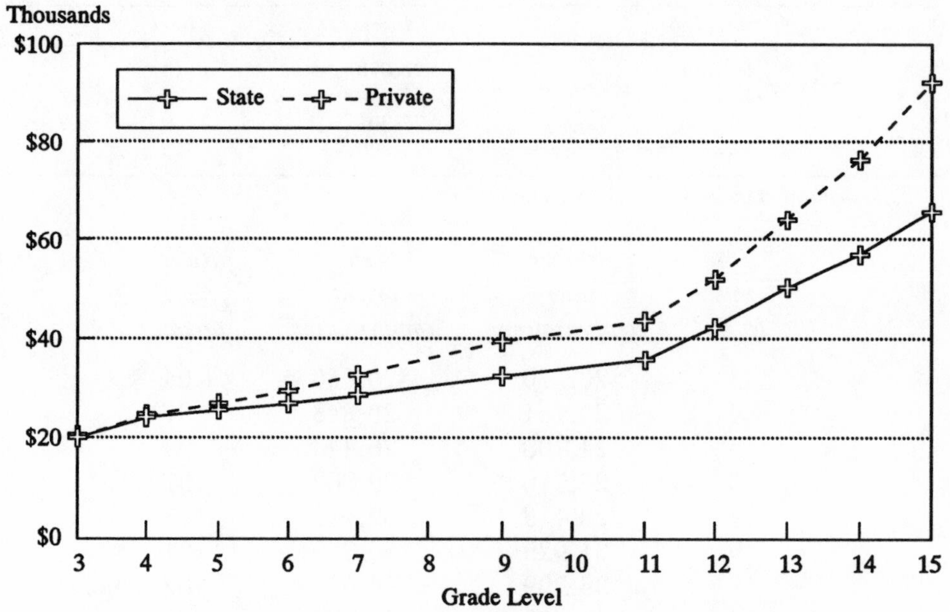

Source: Hay/Huggins Company and Hay Management Consultants, 1984.

of state government managers in Massachusetts (Commonwealth of Massachusetts, 1988) showed that salaries were 46 percent below comparable private sector positions. Earlier in this report it was reported that no state, except New York, has an average compensation level in excess of $100,000 for its executive cadre.

Most of the academic research comparing state and local government employees and private workers has focused on earnings rather than total compensation. It appears, however, that fringe benefit differences do not offset the finding that less educated state-local workers tend to fare better than private workers. Nor do differences in the probability of being laid off account for the salary differential (Ehrenberg and Schwartz, 1986).

The relationship between public and private wages varies among states. An interesting calculation, shown in Table 5.6, is the ratio of public to private earnings (not taking account of differences in the occupational mix). In nearly every state, the average earnings of state-local employees are higher than the average earnings of private sector employees. The only three states where the ratio is less than 1, indicating that average private earnings are higher, are Indiana, Louisiana, and West Virginia.

This indicator is a crude one because it makes no adjustment for differences in the kind of work and the skills needed in the private and public sectors. It is, however, of some value because the level of wages in the private sector has a major effect on wages in the public sector. Consider, for example, Connecticut and Michigan on one hand and Mississippi on the

Table 5.6. Ratio of Average Earnings of Public Sector
Employees to Average Earnings of Private Sector Employees, 1989.

State	Ratio	Rank
New England		
Connecticut	1.18	27
Maine	1.23	21
Massachusetts	1.20	24
New Hampshire	1.12	35
Rhode Island	1.35	9
Vermont	1.49	1
Mid-Atlantic		
Delaware	1.00	47
Maryland	1.25	19
New Jersey	1.08	43
New York	1.17	31
Pennsylvania	1.15	33
Great Lakes		
Illinois	1.17	28
Indiana	.98	49
Michigan	1.20	25
Ohio	1.13	34
Wisconsin	1.30	14
Plains		
Iowa	1.39	7
Kansas	1.17	30
Minnesota	1.33	11
Missouri	1.07	44
Nebraska	1.39	6
North Dakota	1.21	22
South Dakota	1.31	13
Southeast		
Alabama	1.11	39
Arkansas	1.09	42
Florida	1.27	18
Georgia	1.06	45
Kentucky	1.10	40
Louisiana	.99	48
Mississippi	1.11	38
North Carolina	1.17	29
South Carolina	1.12	36
Tennessee	1.16	32
Virginia	1.18	26
West Virginia	.87	50
Southwest		
Arizona	1.38	8
New Mexico	1.27	17
Oklahoma	1.09	41
Texas	1.05	46
Rocky Mountain		
Colorado	1.29	16
Idaho	1.21	23
Montana	1.24	20
Utah	1.33	12
Wyoming	1.12	37
Far West		
Alaska	1.44	3
California	1.43	4

Table 5.6. Ratio of Average Earnings of Public Sector
Employees to Average Earnings of Private Sector Employees, 1989, Cont'd.

State	Ratio	Rank
Hawaii	1.29	15
Nevada	1.42	5
Oregon	1.34	10
Washington	1.45	2
National Averages	1.21	NA

Sources: Private sector information is from U.S. Department of Labor, 1990a. Public sector data are taken from the U.S. Bureau of the Census, 1989a.

other. The first two states have particularly high public sector earnings compared to other states but not compared to their own private sector. Conversely, Mississippi's public sector earnings are lower than earnings in any other state, but public employees in a dozen states appear to fare worse compared to the private sector in their states. The dispersion among states of the ratio of public to private earnings is considerably less than the dispersion of public sector earnings itself.

An indicator that is sometimes used in studies of public versus private compensation is the relative rate at which workers quit their jobs. If public employees quit less frequently than private employees, it could be interpreted as evidence that public employees are relatively well compensated. Quit rates must be interpreted carefully. On first inspection, it appears that public quit rates are lower than private quit rates. As Ehrenberg and Schwartz (1986) point out, however, public agencies tend to be considerably larger than private agencies, and the quit rate is inversely related to the size of the employer's workforce because large organizations provide more opportunity to change job internally. If this is taken into account, it is not apparent that public quit rates are still higher than private quit rates (Ehrenberg and Schwartz, 1986). A recent study of federal employees (Ippolito, 1987) pointed out another problem with relying on quit rates as an indicator of relative compensation levels. It found that the reason why federal workers tended to quit so infrequently is not their pay rate but rather the manner in which their pensions are structured, imposing a large financial penalty for leaving government employment.

Fringe Benefit Comparisons

Fringe benefits are a large and growing component of employee compensation. According to a survey conducted by the Census Bureau every five years, in October 1987 selected fringe benefits cost states 23.7 percent and localities 22.4 percent as much as salaries and wages. Five years earlier, the corresponding figures were 21.9 percent and 22.2 percent, respectively. (The fringes included in this survey were retirement, health and life insurance,

Social Security, unemployment insurance, workers' compensation and disability insurance, uniform and equipment allowances, bonuses and cash awards, severance pay, and certain miscellaneous benefits.) If a broader definition of fringe benefits were used, their importance would appear even greater. Because of rapidly growing health insurance costs, the current cost of fringe benefits is considerably higher than it was in 1987.

When comparing compensation levels among states, it can be very misleading to ignore fringes because their range is very wide, as Table 5.7 shows. In 1987, fringe benefit levels for state employees varied from a low of 15.9 percent of salaries and wages in New Mexico to a high of 36 percent in West Virginia. For local workers, the range was from 14 percent of earnings in Louisiana to 31.3 percent in New York. On a regional basis, the percentages were highest in the Mid-Atlantic states for both state and local government workers.

An analysis published by the Public Affairs Research Institute of New Jersey (1991) provides some specific examples of differences between fringe benefits provided by New Jersey and typical private employers. State workers enjoy better fringes in terms of vacations, sick pay (and sick-leave buybacks), and pensions, but they have less generous opportunities to participate in supplemental retirement programs like 401(k) plans. In terms of health insurance, government and private workers have nearly the same coverage but state employees pay less for hospitalization and major medical insurance. For vision and eye care and prescriptions, benefits are about the same for both sectors.

Several points need to be considered in comparing fringe benefits. First, they may be viewed from at least three different perspectives, each of which is appropriate in answering certain questions:

- Current out-of-pocket cost to the employer (which is what the Census Bureau figures reflect)
- Accrual cost to the employer (which may differ from out-of-pocket cost because, for example, future pension commitments may be underfunded)
- Benefit perceived by the employee (which may be less than the cost to the employer if certain fringes provide benefits that the worker does not care about)

Current out-of-pocket costs to the employer reflect more than just the fringe benefits that are provided. For example, the health insurance costs of young workers tend to be lower than those for older workers, while certain benefits are used more by employees with children than by employees without children. Thus, two governments providing an identical fringe benefit package may have different costs, as reflected in Table 5.7.

Another way of looking at fringe benefits is to compare the average value for each employee. It appears that a positive relationship exists between salary and benefit levels. That is, states providing higher overall salaries

Table 5.7. Cost of Selected Employees
Fringe Benefits as Percentage of Payroll, October 1987.

	State	Rank	Local	Rank
New England				
Connecticut	31.3%	3	25.1%	8
Maine	22.3	32	23.7	11
Massachusetts	24.9	13	22.6	19
New Hampshire	17.9	46	19.8	28
Rhode Island	28.8	5	22.2	21
Vermont	23.8	26	17.2	40
Mid-Atlantic				
Delaware	29.2	4	23.5	12
Maryland	26.0	8	28.2	2
New Jersey	22.3	33	22.1	22
New York	24.2	17	31.3	1
Pennsylvania	32.7	2	28.0	3
Great Lakes				
Illinois	17.9	45	18.8	33
Indiana	19.9	38	15.9	43
Michigan	23.3	29	23.1	15
Ohio	23.4	28	22.9	16
Wisconsin	24.2	19	25.1	9
Plains				
Iowa	19.3	42	19.5	31
Kansas	23.8	25	15.6	46
Minnesota	22.7	30	19.6	30
Missouri	24.6	16	15.9	44
Nebraska	21.8	34	17.7	38
North Dakota	19.5	40	17.1	41
South Dakota	24.1	20	14.6	48
Southeast				
Alabama	24.8	14	19.7	29
Arkansas	19.0	43	19.2	32
Florida	25.1	12	22.0	23
Georgia	22.5	31	18.7	34
Kentucky	19.0	44	14.9	47
Louisiana	19.5	39	14.0	50
Mississippi	20.2	37	16.6	42
North Carolina	20.6	36	23.3	13
South Carolina	24.2	18	17.2	39
Tennessee	24.1	21	22.7	18
Virginia	19.5	41	23.2	14
West Virginia	36.0	1	14.5	49
Southwest				
Arizona	24.0	23	18.2	36
New Mexico	15.9	50	18.3	35
Oklahoma	23.9	24	20.5	26
Texas	23.6	27	15.8	45
Rocky Mountain				
Colorado	17.2	49	19.8	27
Idaho	17.6	47	20.5	25
Montana	24.7	15	18.1	37
Utah	26.0	9	27.5	4
Wyoming	27.0	6	21.4	24
Far West				
Alaska	24.0	22	22.4	20
California	26.7	7	22.8	17

Table 5.7. Cost of Selected Employees
Fringe Benefits as Percentage of Payroll, October 1987, Cont'd.

	State	Rank	Local	Rank
Hawaii	25.4	11	25.5	6
Nevada	17.6	48	26.0	5
Oregon	25.8	10	24.3	10
Washington	21.5	35	25.5	7

Note: Included in this survey were retirement, health and life insurance, Social Security, unemployment insurance, workers' compensation and disability insurance, uniform and equipment allowances, bonuses and cash awards, severance pay, and certain miscellaneous benefits.
Source: U.S. Bureau of the Census, 1987, pp. 4–13.

tend to provide more generous average benefits for their employees, according to a comprehensive 1985 survey (Central States Salary Conference, 1985). The survey ranked the following states highest in the provision of health, retirement, and life insurance benefits. One will note that a number of these states—including California, Connecticut, Michigan, Minnesota, Massachusetts, and New York—are among those with the highest salary levels, too.

Rank	Health insurance	Retirement benefits	Life insurance
1	Michigan	Hawaii	Washington
2	Iowa	California	Arkansas
3	Alaska	Pennsylvania	Tennessee
4	Delaware	Georgia	Connecticut
5	California	Oregon	Delaware
6	Massachusetts	New York	Minnesota
7	Maryland	Maine	Hawaii
8	Indiana	Delaware	Pennsylvania
9	Connecticut	Oklahoma	Oklahoma
10	Wisconsin	Ohio	Utah

State and local government benefits, overall, are apparently competitive with those in the private sector, according to Wiatrowski (1988). In terms of pensions, Lovejoy (1988) shows that the proportion of preretirement earnings gained in retirement is higher for state and local government employees than for private sector workers.

Cost-of-Living Adjustments

An important shortcoming of most of the data provided above is that it fails to take account of differences in price levels and living conditions. It is not a coincidence that employees in Alaska earn much more than their counterparts in other states. The cost of living is much higher there, and the hard winters are a disincentive to living and working in Alaska. On the other hand, the cost of living in southeastern states, where employees earn relatively

Table 5.8. Two Estimates of Cost
Differences Among States (100 = National Average).

State	ACIR	AFT
New England		
Connecticut	108.5	127.3
Maine	77.4	95.0
Massachusetts	95.6	126.6
New Hampshire	86.0	105.9
Rhode Island	92.6	110.5
Vermont	79.0	96.0
Mid-Atlantic		
Delaware	100.3	106.2
Maryland	105.7	111.5
New Jersey	108.1	129.3
New York	100.7	116.0
Pennsylvania	99.6	103.9
Great Lakes		
Illinois	109.7	95.8
Indiana	100.1	92.1
Michigan	111.9	93.7
Ohio	103.9	94.7
Wisconsin	98.4	93.1
Plains		
Iowa	94.3	91.5
Kansas	94.2	91.1
Minnesota	102.0	93.2
Missouri	95.6	91.6
Nebraska	89.1	90.8
North Dakota	86.4	89.5
South Dakota	77.1	89.1
Southeast		
Alabama	90.6	89.8
Arkansas	85.6	88.4
Florida	90.6	96.2
Georgia	93.7	91.8
Kentucky	97.2	89.1
Louisiana	102.1	91.3
Mississippi	83.7	88.1
North Carolina	86.6	91.2
South Carolina	86.8	90.1
Tennessee	91.6	90.3
Virginia	97.7	95.7
West Virginia	93.4	89.6
Southwest		
Arizona	96.8	100.6
New Mexico	88.4	92.8
Oklahoma	94.0	89.6
Texas	102.3	91.2
Rocky Mountain		
Colorado	99.6	98.0
Idaho	85.3	91.6
Montana	85.3	91.3
Utah	94.7	90.2
Wyoming	95.8	91.7
Far West		
Alaska	134.4	130.0
California	105.5	107.4

Table 5.8. Two Estimates of Cost
Differences Among States (100 = National Average), Cont'd.

State	ACIR	AFT
Hawaii	96.0	127.0
Nevada	97.6	95.4
Oregon	97.9	94.4
Washington	102.9	97.6

Note: Advisory Commission on Intergovernmental Relations (ACIR) measure is a unit labor cost index for 1987. The AFT measure is a cost-of-living index for 1989.
Sources: American Federation of Teachers, 1990; Rafuse, 1990.

low wages, is also relatively low. In other words, employees in Alaska are not as well off and employees in Mississippi are not as badly off as the figures on salaries suggest.

Unfortunately, there are no generally accepted data available to adjust for these factors. Two recent efforts—by Robert W. Rafuse, Jr. (1990) and the American Federation of Teachers (AFT) (1990)—produced inconsistent estimates that illustrate the problem of drawing definite conclusions about this issue. The figures they produced are shown in Table 5.8. There are some striking similarities between the two sets of estimates. For example, they agree that Alaska has the highest costs, and their adjustments for that state are similar (30 percent and 34.4 percent). Both also have Mississippi and South Dakota with relatively low costs. Their estimates for California are very similar as well. In fact, for twenty-four states the cost indexes are within five percentage points of each other, indicating a substantial agreement between the two approaches.

On the other hand, Rafuse says that unit labor costs in Michigan are the second highest (11.9 percent above average), while AFT has its cost of living 6.1 percent below average. They are also far apart on states like Connecticut and New York, with Rafuse showing Connecticut 8 percent above average and New York only 1 percent above average, while AFT describes them as 27 percent and 16 percent above average, respectively.[9]

There are some distinct regional differences between the two measures. Most notably, Rafuse's measures are lower in all eleven states in New England and the Mid-Atlantic region, while they are higher in all five Great Lakes states. These patterns are reasonable in view of the fact that Rafuse's measure is based on 1979, and labor costs in the Northeast rose considerably faster than the national average between 1979 and 1987 (Nelson, 1991, p. 105).[10]

Table 5.9 shows the average monthly earnings of state noneducation employees adjusted by the Rafuse and AFT indices. The earnings of noneducation workers are used for calculations because they are a more homogeneous group than all workers. These adjusted earnings measures have considerably less dispersion than unadjusted earnings (which were shown in Table 5.2). In other words, the adjustments for living costs reduce some of the wide differences in the unadjusted earnings figures.

Table 5.9. Average Monthly Earnings of State Noneducation Employees
Adjusted for Differences in Living Costs.

State	Unadjusted	Rank	ACIR Adjusted	Rank	AFT Adjusted	Rank
New England						
Connecticut	$2,867	3	$2,642	5	$2,252	18
Maine	2,038	25	2,633	6	2,145	21
Massachusetts	2,510	9	2,626	7	1,983	38
New Hampshire	1,984	30	2,307	17	1,873	47
Rhode Island	2,492	11	2,691	4	2,255	17
Vermont	2,649	6	3,353	1	2,759	4
Mid-Atlantic						
Delaware	$2,006	29	$2,000	40	$1,889	46
Maryland	2,340	14	2,214	22	2,099	26
New Jersey	2,535	8	2,345	15	1,961	39
New York	2,769	4	2,750	3	2,387	11
Pennsylvania	2,161	19	2,170	26	2,080	30
Great Lakes						
Illinois	$2,377	12	$2,167	27	$2,481	9
Indiana	1,933	33	1,931	44	2,099	25
Michigan	2,724	5	2,434	12	2,907	1
Ohio	2,226	18	2,142	31	2,351	13
Wisconsin	2,250	17	2,287	18	2,417	10
Plains						
Iowa	$2,339	15	$2,480	10	$2,556	5
Kansas	2,060	23	2,187	23	2,261	15
Minnesota	2,602	7	2,551	8	2,792	2
Missouri	1,786	43	1,868	47	1,950	40
Nebraska	1,888	36	2,119	32	2,079	32
North Dakota	1,868	40	2,162	29	2,087	28
South Dakota	1,721	46	2,232	21	1,932	42
Southeast						
Alabama	$1,873	39	$2,067	36	$2,086	29
Arkansas	1,684	48	1,967	43	1,905	45
Florida	1,972	31	2,177	25	2,050	36
Georgia	1,883	37	2,010	39	2,051	35
Kentucky	1,720	47	1,770	48	1,930	43
Louisiana	1,758	44	1,673	49	1,926	44
Mississippi	1,596	49	1,907	45	1,812	48
North Carolina	2,018	28	2,330	16	2,213	20
South Carolina	1,746	45	2,012	38	1,938	41
Tennessee	1,876	38	2,048	37	2,078	33
Virginia	2,039	24	2,087	34	2,131	23
West Virginia	1,490	50	1,595	50	1,663	49
Southwest						
Arizona	$2,113	21	$2,183	24	$2,100	24
New Mexico	1,843	42	2,085	35	1,986	37
Oklahoma	1,861	41	1,980	42	2,077	34
Texas	1,944	32	1,900	46	2,132	22
Rocky Mountain						
Colorado	$2,496	10	$2,506	9	$2,547	6
Idaho	2,106	22	2,469	11	2,299	14
Montana	1,916	34	2,246	20	2,099	27
Utah	2,038	26	2,152	30	2,259	16
Wyoming	1,907	35	1,991	41	2,080	31

Table 5.9. Average Monthly Earnings of State Noneducation Employees
Adjusted for Differences in Living Costs, Cont'd.

State	Unadjusted	Rank	ACIR Adjusted	Rank	AFT Adjusted	Rank
Far West						
Alaska	$3,271	1	$2,434	13	$2,516	7
California	2,984	2	2,828	2	2,778	3
Hawaii	2,033	27	2,118	33	1,601	50
Nevada	2,368	13	2,426	14	2,482	8
Oregon	2,121	20	2,166	28	2,247	19
Washington	2,327	16	2,261	19	2,384	12
National Totals	$2,142	NA	$2,234	NA	$2,179	NA
Standard Deviation	375.6		313.2		280.5	

Note: Supplemented by revised data for Vermont.
Sources: American Federation of Teachers, 1990; Rafuse, 1990; U.S. Bureau of the Census, 1989a.

Although both the Rafuse and AFT indices reduce the dispersion of earnings considerably, they offer inconsistent indications in numerous states. For example, Connecticut earnings are the third highest in unadjusted terms, fifth highest using Rafuse's adjustment and eighteenth highest according to AFT. Ohio's ranking is eighteenth unadjusted, thirty-first according to Rafuse, and thirteenth according to AFT. Illinois's adjustments are similar to Ohio's, moving up according to Rafuse and down according to AFT. These findings suggest strongly that adjusting for unit cost differences is important but that technical details in how the adjustments are constructed are extremely significant. Further research to refine the estimates should be a high priority.

Table 5.10 takes the analysis one step further by incorporating the data on fringe benefits in Table 5.7 with the cost adjustments in Tables 5.8 and 5.9. Note how states with relatively expensive fringe benefit packages, such as West Virginia, Pennsylvania, and Connecticut, rank relatively higher in total compensation than they do in earnings, while the opposite is true for states with inexpensive fringe benefits, such as Colorado and New Mexico.

This discussion has focused on cost variations among states, but it is also important to consider variations within states. For example, according to the American Chamber of Commerce Research Association (ACCRA) (1990), the price level is more than 50 percent higher on Long Island than in Syracuse, New York. Although that is probably an overestimate of the difference for the average worker (the ACCRA estimate is for a management executive), it does illustrate the fact that costs vary considerably within states.

Changes in Earnings over Time

In general, state employees' salaries at least kept pace with inflation during the 1980s. Between 1980 and 1989, average earnings adjusted for national-

Table 5.10. Average Monthly Compensation (Including Fringe Benefits)
of State Noneducation Employees Adjusted for Differences in Living Costs.

State	Adjusted according to			
	ACIR	Rank	AFT	Rank
New England				
Connecticut	$3,469	3	$2,957	10
Maine	3,220	7	2,624	25
Massachusetts	3,279	6	2,476	37
New Hampshire	2,720	25	2,209	48
Rhode Island	3,466	4	2,905	13
Vermont	4,151	1	3,416	4
Mid-Atlantic				
Delaware	$2,584	31	$2,440	38
Maryland	2,789	20	2,644	22
New Jersey	2,868	15	2,398	41
New York	3,415	5	2,965	9
Pennsylvania	2,879	14	2,760	19
Great Lakes				
Illinois	$2,555	35	$2,925	11
Indiana	2,315	46	2,516	34
Michigan	3,002	10	3,585	1
Ohio	2,644	30	2,901	14
Wisconsin	2,840	17	3,002	7
Plains				
Iowa	$2,959	11	$3,050	6
Kansas	2,707	27	2,799	18
Minnesota	3,130	8	3,426	3
Missouri	2,328	45	2,429	39
Nebraska	2,581	33	2,533	33
North Dakota	2,584	32	2,494	36
South Dakota	2,770	21	2,397	42
Southeast				
Alabama	$2,580	34	$2,603	28
Arkansas	2,341	44	2,267	46
Florida	2,723	24	2,564	31
Georgia	2,462	40	2,513	35
Kentucky	2,106	49	2,297	45
Louisiana	1,999	50	2,301	44
Mississippi	2,292	47	2,178	49
North Carolina	2,810	18	2,669	21
South Carolina	2,498	38	2,407	40
Tennessee	2,542	36	2,578	29
Virginia	2,494	39	2,546	32
West Virginia	2,170	48	2,262	47
Southwest				
Arizona	$2,707	28	$2,604	27
New Mexico	2,416	42	2,302	43
Oklahoma	2,453	41	2,573	30
Texas	2,349	43	2,635	24
Rocky Mountain				
Colorado	$2,937	12	$2,985	8
Idaho	2,903	13	2,704	20
Montana	2,801	19	2,617	26
Utah	2,712	26	2,847	16
Wyoming	2,528	37	2,641	23

Table 5.10. Average Monthly Compensation (Including Fringe Benefits)
of State Noneducation Employees Adjusted for Differences in Living Costs, Cont'd.

State	Adjusted according to			
	ACIR	Rank	AFT	Rank
Far West				
Alaska	$3,018	9	$3,120	5
California	3,584	2	3,520	2
Hawaii	2,656	29	2,007	50
Nevada	2,853	16	2,919	12
Oregon	2,725	23	2,827	17
Washington	2,748	22	2,897	15

Note: Supplemented by revised data for Vermont.

Sources: American Federation of Teachers, 1990, Rafuse, 1990, U.S. Bureau of the Census, 1989a.

average inflation, as measured by the Consumer Price Index, rose in every state except Nevada, Utah, Wisconsin, and Wyoming. The average real earnings increase during the 1980s was 11 percent (Maurer, 1990). As Table 5.11 shows, states with the highest growth in real earnings were concentrated in the New England and Mid-Atlantic regions.

The average earnings of state and local employees fared better than those of private sector employees in the 1980s. For example, Ehrenberg and Schwartz report (1986) that the average earnings of state-local employees rose from 121 percent of the earnings of private sector, nonfarm, nonsupervisory workers in 1980 to 141 percent in 1988. The 1988 margin was the highest at any time since 1956, as Table 5.12 shows. The previous high point was in 1970, when state-local earnings were 29 percent higher.

This finding is confirmed by other data. The Bureau of Labor Statistics reports that total compensation per state-local worker rose 73.2 percent between June 1981 and June 1990, while the comparable rise for private industry workers was 53.8 percent. This difference reflects both greater increases in wages and salaries (65.4 percent compared to 48.6 percent) and benefits (U.S. Bureau of Labor Statistics, 1990).

It does not necessarily follow that individual state-local workers fared much better than comparable private sector workers. According to Richard Schumann (1987, p. 18), "Much of the difference in the size of wage changes between the two sectors can be explained by differences in the industrial and occupational composition of their work forces." For example, wages rose at a particularly rapid rate for professional technical occupations during this period. Such occupations account for nearly two-fifths of state-local employment, compared with slightly more than one-tenth in private industry. By contrast, blue-collar workers, who represent a much bigger share of private employment, had relatively small wage gains (Schumann, 1987).

In fact, blue-collar workers who worked for state and local governments fared considerably better than those who were in the private sector

Table 5.11. Percentage Change of Average Earnings of Full-Time
State Employees, Adjusted for Inflation, October 1980 to October 1989.

State	Percent change	Rank
New England		
Connecticut	56.8	1
Maine	10.1	23
Massachusetts	39.5	2
New Hampshire	13.6	14
Rhode Island	26.4	6
Vermont	35.8	3
Mid-Atlantic		
Delaware	12.4	19
Maryland	26.4	5
New Jersey	26.4	7
New York	30.1	4
Pennsylvania	7.7	28
Great Lakes		
Illinois	12.9	15
Indiana	10.0	24
Michigan	12.7	16
Ohio	17.4	10
Wisconsin	- .3	47
Plains		
Iowa	26.0	8
Kansas	2.0	41
Minnesota	14.5	42
Missouri	2.2	11
Nebraska	16.0	40
North Dakota	1.6	43
South Dakota	0.4	46
Southeast		
Alabama	5.8	33
Arkansas	9.5	26
Florida	10.6	22
Georgia	11.7	20
Kentucky	13.7	13
Louisiana	6.5	30
Mississippi	12.4	18
North Carolina	14.3	12
South Carolina	1.41	44
Tennessee	12.7	17
Virginia	19.1	9
West Virginia	4.9	34
Southwest		
Arizona	6.7	29
New Mexico	3.8	36
Oklahoma	6.5	31
Texas	11.4	21
Rocky Mountain		
Colorado	9.1	27
Idaho	2.4	39
Montana	1.0	45
Utah	- 11.3	50
Wyoming	- 9.7	49

Table 5.11. Percentage Change of Average Earnings of Full-Time
State Employees, Adjusted for Inflation, October 1980 to October 1989, Cont'd.

State	Percent change	Rank
Far West		
Alaska	3.8	35
California	9.5	27
Hawaii	2.7	38
Nevada	− 1.0	48
Oregon	6.0	32
Washington	3.3	37

Sources: U.S. Bureau of the Census, 1980, 1989a.

Table 5.12. Ratio of Earnings for State-Local Government Employees
to Earnings for Private Sector Employees, 1956–1988.

	Private sector comparison group	
	Nonagricultural nonsupervisory workers[a]	Manufacturing production workers[b]
Year	(1)	(2)
1956	1.11	1.03
1958	1.12	1.04
1960	1.14	1.06
1962	1.19	1.10
1964	1.19	1.11
1966	1.21	1.14
1968	1.27	1.20
1970	1.29	1.24
1972	1.24	1.20
1974	1.27	1.21
1976	1.25	1.17
1978	1.19	1.10
1980	1.21	1.10
1982	1.24	1.12
1984	1.29	1.17
1986	1.38	1.24
1988	1.41	1.29

Notes: [a]Average annual earnings of state-local governmental workers divided by average annual earnings of private nonagricultural, nonsupervisory workers. [b]Average annual earnings of state-local government workers divided by average annual earnings of manufacturing workers.
Source: Ehrenberg and Smith, 1991.

in the 1980s. While the wages of less educated private workers increased much less than salaries of highly educated private workers, there was much less difference according to education in the public sector. According to Katz and Krueger (1986, p. 17), "Over the last decade, less educated workers fared extremely well in the government relative to the private sector. In the

Table 5.13. Percentage Change of Salaries for Eight
High-Level State Officials, Adjusted for Inflation, 1980–1989.

New England	
Connecticut	6.4
Maine	–5.0
Massachusetts	16.2
New Hampshire	–21.6
Rhode Island	9.0
Vermont	2.4
Mid-Atlantic	
Delaware	30.8
Maryland	3.6
New Jersey	9.3
New York	9.8
Pennsylvania	–6.2
Great Lakes	
Illinois	–2.4
Indiana	2.4
Michigan	1.6
Ohio	–22.9
Wisconsin	–20.2
Plains	
Iowa	–7.4
Kansas	20.1
Minnesota	0.1
Missouri	13.5
Nebraska	4.1
North Dakota	–11.5
South Dakota	17.7
Southeast	
Alabama	–11.9
Arkansas	–4.3
Florida	13.2
Georgia	14.6
Kentucky	1.5
Louisiana	7.9
Mississippi	–12.4
North Carolina	–4.6
South Carolina	1.5
Tennessee	–16.0
Virginia	24.6
West Virginia	1.9
Southwest	
Arizona	–19.0
New Mexico	3.0
Oklahoma	18.4
Texas	9.9
Rocky Mountain	
Colorado	–6.5
Idaho	9.2
Montana	–10.9
Utah	–7.5
Wyoming	–16.3
Far West	
Alaska	–18.0
California	29.2

Table 5.13. Percentage Change of Salaries for Eight
High-Level State Officials, Adjusted for Inflation, 1980–1989, Cont'd.

Hawaii	22.8
Nevada	5.7
Oregon	2.5
Washington	–0.4

Source: Council of State Governments, 1990.

state and local government sector, pay compression reflects improvements in wages for less educated workers relative to the private sector, rather than sharp declines in the wages of highly educated workers."

There were wide differences in the salary increases during the 1980s for the department heads and other high-level state officials discussed in the second section of this chapter, as Table 5.13 shows. Officials in the Northeast tended to have larger-than-average increases as the economy of that region boomed.[11]

Conclusion

State and local governments should pay close attention to how well they are compensating their employees because they must compete with each other and with the private sector to attract and retain a high-quality labor force. If compensation is inadequate, mobile employees will tend to leave government service. The government will continue to function, but the quality of service will diminish. On the other hand, if compensation is higher than for comparable jobs in the private sector, this is unfair and wasteful. As we have emphasized, drawing valid conclusions about public sector compensation is very complicated. If careful research methods are not followed, incorrect conclusions may be reached.

A recent report by the American Legislative Exchange Council (ALEC) illustrates many of the pitfalls highlighted earlier in this chapter (Cox and Brunelli, 1992). ALEC makes some serious research errors that lead to their conclusion that excessive state employee salaries are the main cause of the current fiscal stress in the American states. One problem with the report is that it compares *aggregate* compensation figures for all state workers and private sector employees; aggregating figures completely ignores how public and private sector occupational and industrial distributions differ. Instead, salaries for workers in similar jobs in the public and private sector should be compared. ALEC also does not take differences in the cost of living among regions into account. It is clear that actual levels of compensation vary greatly among states and localities. Much of this variation can be explained by differences in the cost of living and the nature of the private labor market, but a considerable amount of variation remains unaccounted for by those factors.

This report has uncovered information about the status of state-local employee compensation that is both positive and negative, from the viewpoint of employees. On a positive note are the following patterns:

• Salaries have been keeping up with inflation.
• Salaries are generally competitive with the private sector for jobs that do not require a high level of skill and specialized training.
• Fringe benefits tend to be at least as generous as those provided in the private sector.

On the other hand, there are several negative patterns:

• Some states have salaries that lag well behind those in other states, even when account is taken of differences in price levels.
• Jobs requiring a high degree of training tend to be less competitive with similar jobs in the private sector.
• Salaries at the highest level of state government—for the directors of agencies—appear relatively low considering the size of agency budgets and the importance of their missions.

One important reform that could improve compensation policies is to make pay scales more sensitive to market conditions.[12] Salary schedules often give too little weight to differences in supply and demand for particular jobs. This reform would be helpful in several ways. First, if private labor costs vary significantly among the geographic regions of a state, for example, due to price levels, state salaries should be adjusted accordingly. Such geographic salary differentials are not provided in most states, and they are often inadequate when they are employed.[13] Second, many states do not use the results of their own private market salary surveys to adjust their salary schedules because it would cost too much. Third, states should adjust salaries upward or downward depending on whether they are experiencing shortages or surpluses of qualified applicants.

As noted at the beginning of this chapter, adequate compensation is crucial to attracting and retaining high-quality state-local employees. This chapter should be helpful in focusing attention on how compensation can be analyzed. Because of the difficulties of comparing compensation and the fifty-state coverage of this report, it represents only a first step in studying this area, but there is no substitute for in-depth research on a state-by-state basis.

Notes

1. The U.S. Bureau of the Census (1990) provides the payroll and full-time employee average earnings data for the month of October. The figure for average monthly earnings was multiplied by twelve to esti-

mate average annual earnings. The data on fringe benefits are from the U.S. Bureau of the Census (1987, Vol. 3, No. 4, pp. 4–13).

2. The correlation coefficient between state and local earnings is .72 (excluding education workers, .79), and the correlation coefficient between earnings of all employees and noneducation employees is .61.

3. Employment areas include the following: office and allied services; custodian and food services; maintenance and construction trades; data processing; fiscal management and staff services; legal; education and library; agriculture inspection; engineering and allied services; medical and medical support; and law enforcement and fire prevention. Data for New Hampshire and South Dakota were not reported.

4. According to the data published by the Census Bureau, Vermont is similar to Maine. However, the published data for Vermont are inaccurate.

5. Fourteen states were covered by the Central States Salary Survey, and the analysis included information on thirty-one job titles. The research showed that Colorado, Minnesota, and Wisconsin tended to pay the highest wages. These states also had the lowest degree of variation among salaries (variances of 2.64, 1, and 4.26, respectively, for job title rankings). In addition, states paying lower salaries, including New Mexico and South Dakota, had more deviation in wage levels (variances of 11.76 and 18.8).

6. In a multivariate regression analysis, the variables for per capita income and state population were statistically significant. The R^2 value for the equation was .59.

7. This research covered the period through 1988. Most previous research, summarized by Ehrenberg and Schwartz (1986), dealt with periods prior to 1980 and focused heavily on less skilled workers. The authors emphasized the finding that state-local workers tended to be paid more than their private sector counterparts.

8. For instance, public/private pay comparisons were made using data from NASPE/CSG and the U.S. Department of Labor (1988). The ratio of public to private salaries in clerical or custodial jobs was 1.024. A similar comparison for technical jobs in computer science, engineering, medical, and legal fields yielded a ratio of .85.

9. The two measures are considerably different in methodology — one is based on wages, the other on consumer prices. The Rafuse measure is based on earnings controlling for age, sex, and educational attainment in 1979. The AFT measure [described in detail in Nelson (1991)] is derived from estimates of metropolitan cost-of-living differences produced by the American Chamber of Commerce Research Association. Another difference is that Rafuse's estimates are for all costs of government, with nonlabor costs assumed to be equal for all states. Thus, the figures reported understate the difference among states in labor costs.

10. Some of the data used by Nelson are for 1980, and he notes that they may be particularly problematic in the Northeast because of the high rate of housing inflation the area experienced between 1984 and 1987.

11. The correlation coefficient between the growth of per capita income and changes in high-level salaries was .25. Per capita income growth had a closer correlation with the growth of average earnings ($r = .46$).

12. A reform of this type recently occurred in the federal government under the Federal Employees Pay Comparability Act (FEPCA) adopted in November 1990. This legislation adopts the concept of "locality pay" for federal white collar employees paid under the General Schedule pay system. The FEPCA specifies that the GS rates will vary depending on prevailing nonfederal salary levels in each local area (U.S. General Accounting Office, 1991).

13. The U.S. Office of Personnel Management (1989) found that only two of fourteen states studied made such adjustments, so that salaries tended to be less competitive in metropolitan areas than in small cities or rural areas.

References

American Chamber of Commerce Research Association. *Cost of Living Index: Comparative Data for 293 Urban Areas: Fourth Quarter*. Washington, D.C.: American Chamber of Commerce Research Association, 1990.

American Federation of State, County, and Municipal Employees. *Fact Versus Fiction: Debunking the American Legislative Exchange Council's Report Blaming Public Employees for Government's Fiscal Problems*. Washington, D.C.: American Federation of State, County, and Municipal Employees, 1992.

American Federation of Teachers. *Salary Survey*. Washington, D.C.: American Federation of Teachers, 1990.

Central States Salary Conference. *Fringe Benefit Report*. Lincoln, Nebr.: Nebraska Personnel Department, 1985.

Commonwealth of Massachusetts, Department of Personnel Administration, Division of Technical Services. *Status Report on Massachusetts Management Compensation*. Boston, Mass.: Department of Personnel Administration, 1988.

Conlan, T. *New Federalism: Intergovernmental Reform from Nixon to Reagan*. Washington, D.C.: Brookings Institution, 1988.

Council of State Governments. *The Book of the States*. Iron Works Pike, Ky.: Council of State Governments, 1990.

Council of State Governments and National Association of State Personnel Employees. *1989 United States Governmental Wage and Salary Survey*. Sacramento, Calif.: California Department of Personnel Administration, 1990.

Cox, W., and Brunelli, S. A. *America's Protected Class: Why Excess Public Employee Compensation Is Bankrupting the States*. Washington, D.C.: American Legislative Exchange Council, 1992.

Dickson, E., and Peterson, G. E. *Public Sector Compensation: A Twelve City Comparison*. Washington, D.C.: Urban Institute, 1980.

Ehrenberg, R., and Schwartz, J. "Public-Sector Labor Markets." In O. Ashenfelter and R. Layard (eds.), *Handbook of Labor Economics*. New York: Elsevier, 1986.

Ehrenberg, R., and Smith, R. *Modern Labor Economics*. New York: Harper-Collins, 1991.

Gold, S. D. *The State Fiscal Agenda for the 1990s*. Denver, Colo.: National Conference of State Legislatures, 1990.

Hay/Huggins Company, and Hay Management Consultants. *Study of Total Compensation in the Federal, State and Private Sectors*. Washington, D.C.: Hay Company, 1984.

Henderson, Y. "Government Employment and Compensation." In A. Munnell and L. Brown (eds.), *Massachusetts in the 1990s: The Role of State Government*. Boston: Federal Reserve Bank of Boston, 1990.

Ippolito, R. A. "Why Federal Workers Don't Quit." *Journal of Human Resources*, 1987, *22*, 281–299.

Katz, L. F., and Krueger, A. B. "Changes in the Structure of Wages in the Public and Private Sectors." *National Bureau of Economic Research Working Paper Series*, 1991, *3667*, 1–36.

Lovejoy, L. M. "The Comparative Value of Pensions in the Public and Private Sectors." *Monthly Labor Review*, 1988, *93*, 18–26.

Maurer, G., Jr. *Public Sector Compensation Survey*. Detroit, Mich.: Maurer and Kalls, 1990.

Moulton, B. R. "A Reexamination of the Federal-Private Wage Differential in the United States." *Journal of Labor Economics*, 1990, *8*, 270–293.

Nathan, R. P., Doolittle, F. C., and Associates. *Reagan and the States*. Princeton, N.J.: Princeton University Press, 1987.

National Association of State Personnel Executives and the Council of State Governments. *United States Governmental Wage and Salary Survey*. Sacramento, Calif.: California Department of Personnel Administration, 1989.

Nelson, F. H. "An Interstate Cost-of-Living Index." *Education Evaluation and Policy*, 1991, *13*, 103–111.

Public Affairs Research Institute of New Jersey. *State Government Employee Compensation in Perspective*. Princeton, N.J.: Public Affairs Research Institute of New Jersey, 1991.

Rafuse, R. W., Jr. *Representative Expenditures: Addressing the Neglected Dimension of Fiscal Capacity*. Washington, D.C.: U.S. Advisory Commission on Intergovernmental Relations, 1990.

Schumann, R. R. "State and Local Government Pay Increases Outpace Five Year Rise in Private Industry." *Monthly Labor Review*, 1987, *92*, 18–20.

State of New York. *Temporary Commission on Executive, Legislative and Judicial Compensation*. Albany, N.Y.: Temporary Commission on Executive, Legislative and Judicial Compensation, 1988.

U.S. Bureau of the Census. *Public Employment in 1980.* Washington, D.C.: U.S. Government Printing Office, 1980.

U.S. Bureau of the Census. *Census of Governments, 1987, Public Employment, Government Costs for Employee Benefits.* Washington, D.C.: U.S. Government Printing Office, 1987.

U.S. Bureau of the Census. *Public Employment in 1989.* Washington, D.C.: U.S. Government Printing Office, 1989a.

U.S. Bureau of the Census. *White Collar Pay: Private Sector Service Producing Industries.* Washington, D.C.: U.S. Government Printing Office, 1989b.

U.S. Bureau of the Census. *Public Employment in 1990.* Washington, D.C.: U.S. Government Printing Office, 1991.

U.S. Department of Labor, Bureau of Labor Statistics. *National Survey of Professional, Administrative, Technical, and Clerical Pay.* Washington, D.C.: U.S. Government Printing Office, 1988.

U.S. Department of Labor, Bureau of Labor Statistics. *Employment and Earnings, May 1990.* Washington, D.C.: U.S. Government Printing Office, 1990a.

U.S. Department of Labor, Bureau of Labor Statistics. *Employment Cost Indexes and Levels, 1985–90.* Washington, D.C.: U.S. Government Printing Office, 1990b.

U.S. General Accounting Office. *Federal Pay: Comparisons with the Private Sector by Job and Locality.* Washington, D.C.: U.S. Government Printing Office, 1990.

U.S. General Accounting Office. *Federal Pay: Comparisons with the Private Sector by Job and Locality.* Washington, D.C.: U.S. Government Printing Office, 1991.

U.S. Office of Personnel Management. *Federal White Collar Pay System: Report on a Market Sensitive Study.* Washington, D.C.: U.S. Government Printing Office, 1989.

Wiatrowski, W. "Comparing Employee Benefits in the Public and Private Sectors." *Monthly Labor Review,* 1988, *93,* 3–8.

Witt, E. "Are Our Governments Paying What It Takes to Keep the Best and Brightest?" *Governing,* 1988, *2,* 30–39.

SIX

Diversity in the Public Workforce:

New Needs, New Approaches

Rita Mae Kelly

The current national emphasis on diversity stems from several demographic and economic trends that have altered the composition of the U.S. workforce. These trends, in turn, are affecting the means by which the public sector can facilitate leadership; help attract, retain, and develop talent; and maintain and enhance performance (National Commission on the Public Service, 1989).

By 1990 white males represented only one-third of the new entrants to the U.S. labor force. Women and minorities together composed the other two-thirds. By 2000 women will constitute 47 percent of the labor force. Minorities will constitute 26 percent (12 percent African American, 10 percent Hispanic, and 4 percent Asian and others), up from the current 22 percent. By the twenty-first century white males will be a definite minority in the workplace, representing fewer than 39 percent of all U.S. workers. In 1990, according to the U.S. Department of Labor, native white men represented only 45 percent of the 117.8 million U.S. workers (Johnston and Packer, 1987; Loden and Rosener, 1991). These workforce trends are reflected in state and local government employment data as well.

I wish to thank Kimberly Fisher, Kathleen Kelly, Becky Peterson, and Linda Williams for their assistance in gathering data and materials for this project and to acknowledge the support of Janet Soper of the Publications Assistance Center of Arizona State University's College of Public Programs in preparing the graphs.

This chapter documents the increasing gender, racial, and ethnic diversity of the state and local public service in 1990 and compares 1990 employment patterns with those of 1974. These data clearly show continuing occupational segregation and pay inequities. The second part of the chapter examines factors related to public service employers' demand and need for a more diverse workforce, the adequacy of current equal employment opportunity/affirmative action (EEO/AA) policies to address workplace diversity, and the potential of a multicultural synergistic approach to improve management. Finally, the chapter describes selected successful efforts to promote multicultural synergy in the state and local public service.

Increasing Diversity but Continuing Segregation

Data collected by the U.S. Equal Employment Opportunity Commission (EEOC)[1] permit comparing the gender, racial, and ethnic composition of the state and local government workforce. Using 1974 as the point of departure (which is the first year for which the EEOC reported these data), Figure 6.1 depicts this increasing diversity. From 1974 to 1990 the percentage of full-time employees who are women increased from 35.4 percent to 42.8 percent while the percentage who are minorities rose from 19.5 percent to 27.1 percent. The proportion of public service employees who are white males correspondingly declined from 53.5 percent to 43.3 percent. State and local government employees obviously became more diverse over this sixteen-year period.

Diversity and Occupational Segregation

The changing composition of the U.S. workforce plus the emphasis on affirmative action and equal employment opportunity (AA/EEO) since the 1960s have led to higher percentages of minority and female populations in many of the eight occupational categories documented by the EEOC. Figure 6.2 shows both the proportionate decrease in white males in each of the occupational groupings and the continuity of occupational segregation by gender, race, and ethnicity in state and local government. Figure 6.2a reveals that in 1990 white males were still considerably overrepresented (constituting over 60 percent) in the official/administrative, protective services, and skilled crafts personnel and considerably underrepresented (less than 18 percent) in the paraprofessional and office/clerical/administrative support categories. Females, although showing increases in all occupational categories but skilled crafts, remained in 1990 sharply overrepresented in the office/clerical and paraprofessional categories and underrepresented in skilled crafts, protective services, service/maintenance, official/administrative, and technical occupations. They approximated parity only in the professional and technical category, and even in this category women tended to work in different types of professions than men, for example, in nursing, public relations, and staff support positions.

Figure 6.1. Percentage of Labor Force in State and Local
Government: by Gender and Race/Ethnicity, 1974 and 1990.

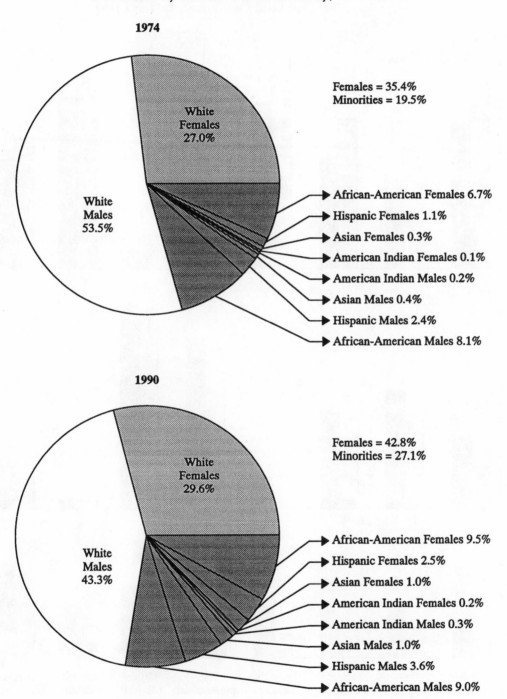

1974

Females = 35.4%
Minorities = 19.5%

White
Females
27.0%

White
Males
53.5%

African-American Females 6.7%
Hispanic Females 1.1%
Asian Females 0.3%
American Indian Females 0.1%
American Indian Males 0.2%
Asian Males 0.4%
Hispanic Males 2.4%
African-American Males 8.1%

1990

Females = 42.8%
Minorities = 27.1%

White
Females
29.6%

White
Males
43.3%

African-American Females 9.5%
Hispanic Females 2.5%
Asian Females 1.0%
American Indian Females 0.2%
American Indian Males 0.3%
Asian Males 1.0%
Hispanic Males 3.6%
African-American Males 9.0%

Note: Totals do not sum to 100 percent due to rounding.
Source: U.S. Equal Employment Opportunity Commission, 1975, 1991.

Figure 6.2. Percentage of White Males, All Females,
and All Minorities in Eight Major Occupational
Categories in State and Local Government, 1974 and 1990.

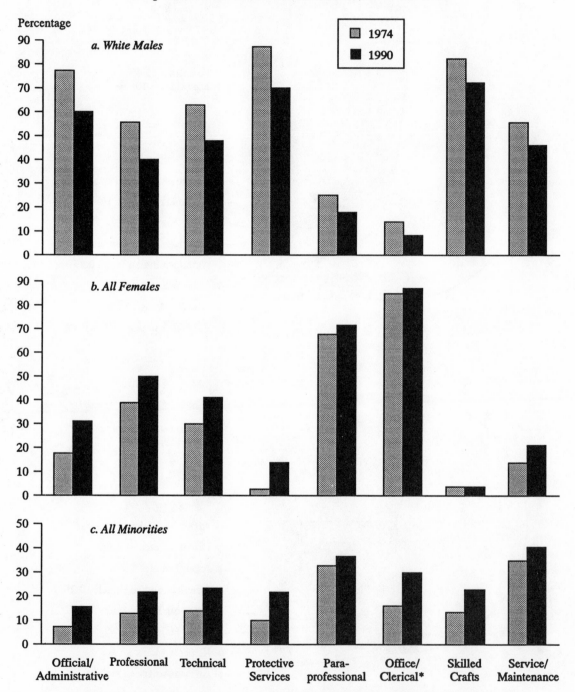

Note: *In 1990, the title for this category was changed to "Administrative Support." For
clarity this and the following charts retain the "Office/Clerical" label.
Source: U.S. Equal Employment Opportunity Commission, 1975, 1991.

Minorities increased substantially in each occupational category as well as shown in Figure 6.2c, but remained markedly overrepresented in the paraprofessional and service/maintenance categories. Overall, minorities would need to almost double their numbers in the official/administrative category to attain parity with their numbers in the state and local government workforce. Viewed in very broad terms, whites (females and males) dominated the official/administrative category in 1974, holding 92.5 percent of the positions, and in 1990, holding 84.9 percent of them. Over this sixteen-year period women increased their share of these occupations from 18 percent to 31.4 percent. Minorities increased their share from 7.5 percent to 15.1 percent. Although the percentage of white males holding these positions declined from the 76.6 percent they had in 1974, in 1990 they still dominated this occupational category, holding 60.4 percent of all official/administrative positions.

As Figures 6.3 and 6.4 show, work experience varies dramatically by racial/ethnic grouping for both males and females, but particularly for the males. Moreover, although some changes in the type of occupations in which the racial/ethnic group is employed have occurred since 1974, substantial occupational segregation remains, especially by sex.

These broad trends in occupational specialization of each grouping can be summarized briefly as follows:

- Four of every ten Asian males employed in the state and local workforce work in the professional category. About 5.5 percent work in official/administrative jobs. About 10 percent, significantly less than other male groups, work in the typically male occupations of protective services, skilled crafts, and service/maintenance. A slightly higher percent of Asian males work in the office/clerical category than other ethnic males.

- In 1990 about one of every four white males was in the protective service category, one of five was in the professional category, one of ten was in the technical category, one of twelve was in the administrative/official category, and about one of eight was in the skilled craft and service/maintenance categories.

- Among Hispanics, female as well as male, the participation rates in all governmental sectors were substantially less than they were in the private sector. In the entire United States in 1989, Hispanics accounted for 6.5 percent of the private sector workforce (U.S. Equal Employment Opportunity Commission, 1990, Table 1) but only 5.9 percent of state and local government employees (U.S. Equal Employment Opportunity Commission, 1990, Table 2). This percentage is above their 1988 federal rate of participation of 5.1 percent (U.S. Equal Employment Opportunity Commission, 1990, p. 12) and a substantial increase over the 3.8 percent of 1975 (U.S. Bureau of the Census, 1989b, Table 489) but still below parity for their percentage of the population. As Figure 6.3 indicates, in the last sixteen years Hispanic males have substantially

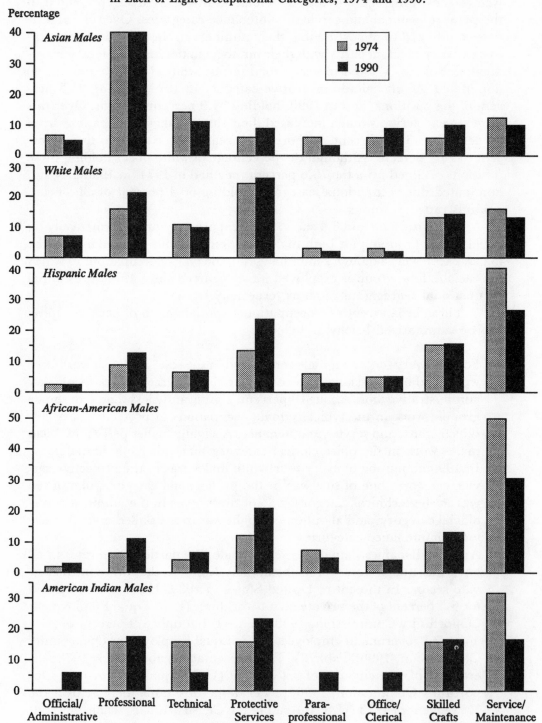

Figure 6.3. Percentage of Each Male Ethnic/Racial Grouping in Each of Eight Occupational Categories, 1974 and 1990.

Source: U.S. Equal Employment Opportunity Commission, 1975, 1991.

Figure 6.4. Percentage of Each Female Ethnic/Racial Grouping
in Each of Eight Occupational Categories, 1974 and 1990.

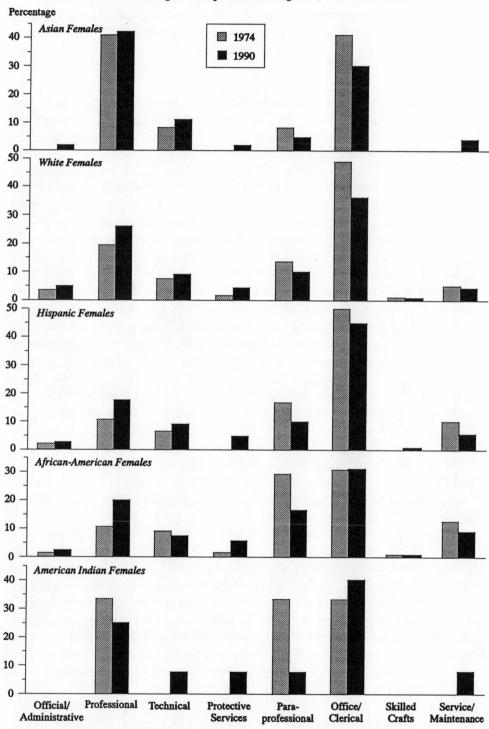

Source: U.S. Equal Employment Opportunity Commission, 1975, 1991.

decreased the proportion of their total who are employed in the service/maintenance category, declining from 40 percent to 27.1 percent. The biggest increases came in the protective services category (from 13.7 percent to 24 percent) and in the professional category (from 9.5 percent to 13 percent). No meaningful change in the percentage of Hispanic males holding official/administrative positions occurred: it remained at a low 3.1 percent.

- Fifty-four percent of all African-American males employed by state and local governments worked in 1990 in only two occupational categories: 32.4 percent in the service/maintenance category and 21 percent in the protective services category. Although these percentages are high, they reflect an improvement over 1974; in that year 51.2 percent worked in the service/maintenance category only, while 12.7 percent worked in the protective services category. During this same sixteen years the proportion of African-American males working as professionals increased from 6.5 to 11.6 percent. The increase in the official/administrative category was minimal, going from 2.5 to 3.1 percent.

- American Indian males showed progress between 1974 and 1990 in reducing the percentage of their total workers in the service/maintenance category from one-third to about one-sixth and in increasing the proportion of their group working as official/administrators, paraprofessionals, skilled craftsmen, and office/clerical workers. However, the proportion working as professionals and technicians declined, the latter by 10 percent.

Gender occupational segregation in the state and local public service is readily evident when comparing Figures 6.3 and 6.4. Typically fewer than 10 percent of the women in any racial/ethnic grouping work in the service/maintenance, technical, or protective services categories. Less than 5 percent of any female grouping work in the official/administrative category; and other than the white women, less than 3 percent of any other female racial/ethnic grouping work in this category. Barely 1 percent of any female grouping work in the skilled crafts area.

Assessments of position levels, salary, and type of functional tasks performed indicate women and minorities typically continue to work in stereotypical governmental agencies and departments as well as in occupational categories (Hale and Kelly, 1989). Women still are more likely to be in educational, health-related, and welfare services than in transportation, corrections, or law enforcement and to hold lower-level jobs within these agencies. Differentials in pay and fringe benefits within and across these agencies and departments reflect continued gender and racial/ethnic barriers.

The gender segregation is so substantial that fewer variations exist among the ethnic groups for women than for men.

- A higher proportion of white women are likely to be employed in the professional category than African-American, Hispanic, and American

Indian females are. In 1990, 65.5 percent of all white women were employed in the office/clerical and the professional categories. If the 10.9 percent working in the paraprofessional category are added, more than three of every four white women employed by state and local government work in these three of the eight occupational categories.

- Three of every four Asian women work in only two categories: the professional and the office/clerical.
- Hispanic women also typically work in these two categories, but a higher percentage, close to one of every two Hispanic women employed, do office/clerical work.
- In 1990 still over 70 percent of African-American female state and local employees were employed in only three categories: office/clerical, professional, and paraprofessional.
- American Indian women were concentrated in the office/clerical and professional categories (66.7 percent). In 1990 they had less than 0.5 percent representation in the official/administrative and skilled crafts categories. This is an improvement over 1974; in that year American Indian women were essentially employed in only three occupational categories.

Comparative data from the private sector reveal that, although the patterns are comparable, the figures for the private sector are worse than those for state and local governments. The U.S. Equal Employment Opportunity Commission (1990) reported the following data for 1985 on percentages of management jobs held by various gender and ethnic/racial groups in companies with 100 or more employees in 1988: 0.8 percent were held by Hispanic women; 1 percent were held by Hispanic men; 2 percent were held by African-American women; 2.9 percent were held by African-American men; 2.7 percent were held by Asian and American Indian men and women; 23.2 percent were held by white women; and 67.4 percent were held by white men (see also Alexander, 1990, p. B1, and Cox-Burton, 1988).

Occupational Segregation and Pay Equity

Concern exists not only regarding an increase in access to jobs in state and local government but also for pay equity. The pay one receives is obviously related to the skills one has and the occupation one holds. It also is correlated with one's gender and racial/ethnic status. Nationwide median annual earnings of full-time, year-round workers reaffirm the pay gap grounded on gender and racial/ethnic differences. Nationwide, women consistently earned less than the men in their respective racial/ethnic groupings. The median salary for white males in 1989 was $28,541; for African-American and Hispanic males it was 71.5 percent and 64.3 percent of that amount. Proportionally, white women earned 66.2 percent of the total earned by white males, African-American women earned 60.9 percent, and Hispanic women earned 54.8 percent (U.S. Bureau of the Census, 1990).

Recent Bureau of the Census labor statistics indicate that for African-American men these data reflect an increase in the pay gap with white men during the 1980s. In 1979, college-educated African-American men had median earnings ranging from 80 to 90 percent of white men; in 1989 the range was from 72 to 79 percent. The widening gap was worse for the twenty-five-to-thirty-four-year-old age group (Mesenheimer, 1990).

The data presented in Figure 6.5 show the median salaries for full-time state and local employees in 1974 and in 1990, presented by occupational grouping as well as by gender and minority status. The highest median occupational categories are the official/administrative and the professional. The medium pay level is for the technical, protective services and skilled crafts categories. The lowest pay levels are in the office/clerical, paraprofessional, and service/maintenance categories.

Figure 6.5 dramatically shows how occupational segregation in state and local employment affects pay. In 1974, white males dominated in both the high- and medium-salaried occupations. In 1990, they still constituted 45.1 percent of the high-salaried occupations and 64.3 percent of the medium-

Figure 6.5. Percentage of White Males, All Females, and All Minorities in Occupations with High, Middle, and Low Median Salaries, 1974 and 1990.

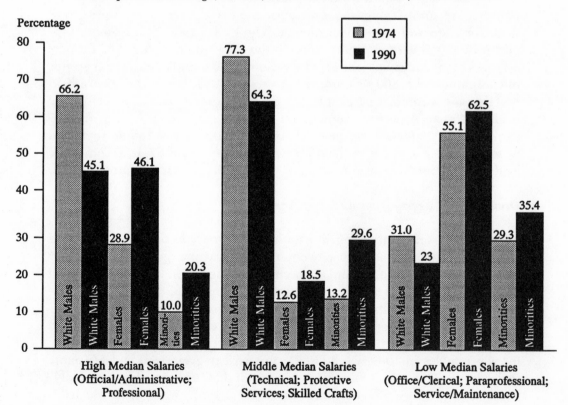

Source: U.S. Equal Employment Opportunity Commission, 1975, 1991.

salaried groups. In contrast, women composed 62.5 percent of those employed in the lowest-paying occupations in 1990, an increase over their share in 1974. Although these data show a decline in the proportion of white males and an increase in the proportion of women and minorities in all three categories between 1974 and 1990, they clearly reveal the substantial impact gender and racial/ethnic status still have on pay and occupational choice. It should be noted, however, that by 1990 about the same percentage of women held state and local government jobs with high median salaries as white men did. The higher percentages of women compared to men in professional jobs balanced the higher percentage of men in official/administrative positions.

Figures 6.6 and 6.7 depict the same data for each racial/ethnic grouping for each gender to examine the extent to which variations exist within each occupational category. Such variations do exist and in consistent patterns.

A common perception is that white males earn more than every other grouping. The data in Figure 7.6 show that Asian males, not white males, consistently earned more than all other groups in 1990 and that in 1974 only in one occupational category, that of office/clerical, did another male ethnic/racial group earn more: that was the African-American male group. (One factor contributing to these higher Asian salaries is that Asians tend to be concentrated in higher-income areas such as Los Angeles, San Francisco, California, and New York City.) The median salaries of white males consistently ranked second among the African-American, American Indian, Asian, and Hispanic government employees. Over the sixteen years, African-American males lost in the relative position of their median earnings. Whereas they earned the lowest or second lowest median salaries in three occupational categories in 1974 (professional, technical, and paraprofessional), in 1990 their median salaries were lowest or second lowest in six of the eight categories: official/administrative, professional, technical, protective services, paraprofessional, and service/maintenance. In other words, not only were African-American males predominantly employed in the lowest-paying occupations in state and local government, as shown in Figure 6.3, but they also were the lowest paid among all male groups in the middle- and highest-paying jobs. Moreover, in all job categories for African-American males but the official/administrative and professional categories, real wages in comparable dollars declined between 1974 and 1990, as shown in Figure 6.6. Over four of every five African-American males worked in the occupations with declining pay.

Over time the Hispanic males improved their relative standing in median earnings. The substantial decline of employment of Hispanic males in the service/maintenance occupations and rise in employment in protective services and the professions further increased the median salaries for Hispanic males as a whole. The median salaries of American Indian males generally remained below other ethnic/racial male groupings.

A comparison of Figures 6.6 and 6.7 shows clearly the consistently

Figure 6.6. Median Salaries Within Occupational
Categories for Males by Race/Ethnicity, 1974 and 1990.

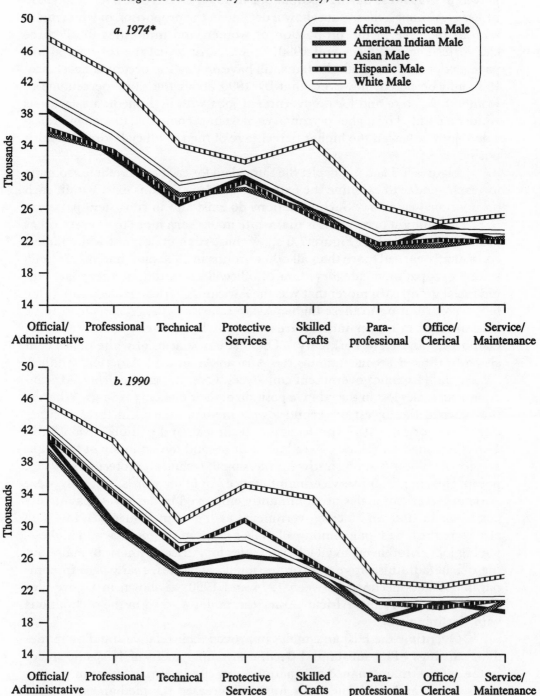

Note: *Calculated using a consumer price index multiplier. The 1974 index is 49.3; the
1990 index is 130.7. This produces the multiplier of 2.65 used here.
Source: U.S. Equal Employment Opportunity Commission, 1975, 1991.

Figure 6.7. Median Salaries Within Occupational
Categories for Females by Race/Ethnicity, 1974 and 1990.

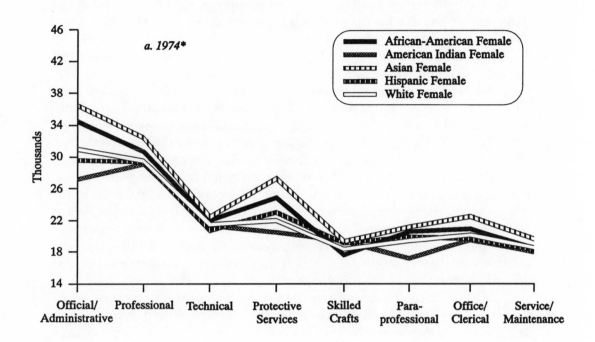

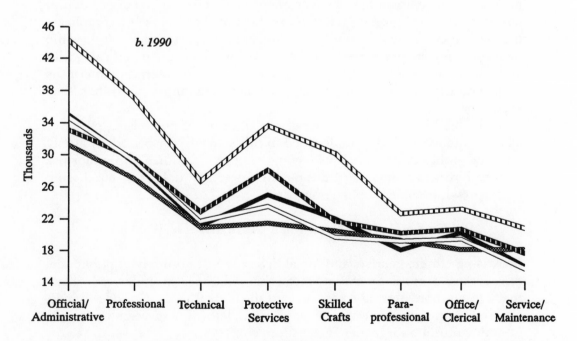

Note: Calculated using a consumer price index multiplier. The 1974 index is 49.3; the
1990 index is 130.7. This produces the multiplier of 2.65 used here.
Source: U.S. Equal Employment Opportunity Commission, 1975, 1991.

lower salaries earned by women compared to men in all occupational categories in state and local government. As with Asian men, Asian women have higher median salaries in all occupational groupings. In 1974 American Indian women had the lowest median salaries in six of the eight categories, the highest in category seven (skilled crafts). African-American women in 1974 earned the least in that category while Hispanic women earned the least in the technical category. Unlike white men, white women did not consistently earn the second highest median salary in each occupational category either in 1974 or in 1990. Frequently both African-American and Hispanic women as well as Asian women had higher median salaries.

In 1990, American Indian women had improved their median earnings so that they were no longer the lowest paid in the paraprofessional and service/maintenance categories. However, they fell from being the highest paid in the skilled crafts category to being the second lowest paid. In 1990, white women received the lowest median pay in two occupational categories: skilled craft and service/maintenance. In 1989, they were lowest in the protective services category as well. African-American females in 1990 also were relatively worse off than in 1974 in that they became the lowest paid on the average in the paraprofessional category.

These occupational and pay data suggest that in broad terms white females and African Americans in general have experienced some relative deprivation in the sixteen years between 1974 and 1990 in their employment status in state and local government. This relative loss of position in terms of pay and standing relative to others of their same sex complicate the data suggesting progress in access and equal opportunities. While white males see smaller percentages of themselves in all occupational categories and may perceive a relative loss of power, females and African Americans in general still can argue that their gains have been more token than they should be.

It should be noted that overall pay in terms of purchasing power of all state and local employees declined in this sixteen-year period. Not only are state and local governments paying less to hire women and minorities than to hire white men, they are paying fewer real dollars of purchasing power to white male employees as well.

Public Employers' Need for a More Diverse Workforce

Increasing ethnic, gender, and racial diversity in the supply of public service workers does not necessarily mean that public sector employers will actually foster more diversity, especially at the higher levels. Nor does it indicate that employers have the capacity to implement a successful program of multicultural and gender integration.

Several factors motivate public employers to foster greater and more effective cultural diversity in the 1990s. Among these factors three are critical: (1) the increasing political power of women and minorities, (2) the importance of co-production and representative bureaucracies in a democratic society, and (3) the increasing number of women and minorities obtaining advanced and technical degrees.

In the 1990s some employers might think they can escape being concerned with diversity because conservative courts are narrowing the possibilities for groups and classes of individuals to seek redress under the EEO/AA framework. However, data, consistent across gender, race, and ethnicity, indicate that the increasing diversity of elected and appointed officials are key factors promoting further diversity and the reduction of occupational segregation at the upper levels of state and local public service employment.

The women's movement and the gender gap have clearly spurred an increase in the numbers of women in upper-echelon positions. In 1974, Ella Grasso was the first woman elected governor in her own right. Since then eight other women have become governors, seven since 1983. In 1992, three states (Kansas, Oregon, and Texas) had female governors, and women held 18.1 percent of the 332 elected statewide executive offices in the fifty states (Center for the American Woman and Politics, 1992). By mid 1986, 18 percent of 845 state cabinet-level positions throughout the nation were held by women. Female heads of agencies increased from 70 in 1981 to 130 in 1987 (Carroll, 1988).

As at the state level, higher proportions of women and minorities are likely to be hired in local governmental agencies when women and minorities hold political power. A 1989 study of 136 police departments reported that cities with African-American mayors had higher numbers of African-American police officers as well. These cities were more likely to have institutionalized civilian control over the police department (Saltzstein, 1989). This political linkage has been found for the number of African Americans on school boards and African Americans as school administrators (Meier, Stewart, and England, 1989) and the percentage of African Americans elected to city councils and in city administrative positions (Dye and Renick, 1981; Eisinger, 1982). A 1989 study of barriers to Hispanic employment success in 1,200 cities reported similarly that Hispanic representation on city councils was a major determinant of Hispanic employment in city government, particularly at the upper levels and in administrative positions (Mladenka, 1989).

The notion that citizens themselves, particularly taxpayers in the workforce, must co-produce the public goods and services they receive is another factor promoting diversity, as is the ideal that governmental bureaucracies in a democracy ought to be representative of the people being served. By the year 2000 minorities are expected to constitute one-fourth of the U.S. population, and English is likely to be the second language of most of the residents of our nation's largest state, California. In 1991, one of every five Americans was either African American, Asian, or Hispanic. These demographics suggest that successful delivery of public goods and services will require increasing diversity in the public service, and at the higher levels as well as at the lower levels. Most simply, voters will demand such diversity.

Some larger cities illustrate the magnitude of the cultural diversity these demographic changes reveal. In 1991 in New York City about one-third of the residents were foreign born; about two-thirds of Miami's residents were Hispanic; two-thirds of Detroit's population were African American; and one-third of San Francisco's population were Asian (Dreyfuss, 1990). Particularly in those regions, states, and cities where demographics and politics unite, all employers, but especially public sector employers, will need to publicly and systematically address racial, ethnic, and gender diversity issues.

Given the historic persistence of employers to refuse to hire and promote those lowest in the labor queue (traditionally women and minorities), it is possible that at the higher levels of the public service an effort will be made to hire white male immigrants from Europe, especially Eastern Europe, or Latin America in order to avoid more diversity among the upper echelon. However, the state and local public service in the United States is sensitive to the U.S. voter. Political realities place very real constraints on this strategy, especially in America's largest cities and most populous states.

College education is a prerequisite for most leadership positions. A significant portion of the African-American and Hispanic occupational segregation stems from differential education and skill attainment than that achieved by white and Asian males. The 1980s saw significant changes in the percentages of women and minorities completing high school and college and penetrating traditional white male specialties. Between 1979 and 1989 blacks reduced the educational gap with whites, moving from a figure of only 9 percent of all blacks between the ages of twenty-five and sixty-four completing college in 1979 to that of 19 percent in 1989. The comparable figures for whites were 19 percent in 1979 and 24 percent in 1989 (Mesenheimer, 1990). Hispanics also have made progress. In 1987 about 10 percent of the men and 7.5 percent of the Hispanic women over the age of twenty-five had completed four or more years of college (U.S. Bureau of the Census, 1987). Women also have made dramatic progress. In 1965, about 5 percent of the law, medical, and architectural students in the United States were women (Tucker, 1985). By 1986, one-third of such students were. By 1988, women were 13 percent of the engineering graduates, and in 1990 women were about one-half of the students in MBA, law, and other professional programs (Kelly, 1991).

The extent to which these forces will push public service employers to promote greater diversity will clearly vary by political and regional jurisdictions as well as the racial/ethnic and gender group. Different approaches will be needed to deal with the changing location and nature of jobs and the concentration of minorities in certain geographic areas. By 1990, twenty-five of the major metropolitan area suburbs had 11 percent more jobs than central cities. In contrast, central cities had 13 percent more jobs than suburbs in 1975. This shift in the location of jobs reflects the abandonment of the central city by the middle and upper-middle class and, as often as not, by whites. It is estimated that in the year 2000 African Americans will be the majority in thirteen of these largest cities (Fosler, 1989). In twenty-five of the largest U.S. cities and metropolitan areas, a majority of the public school students will be from an African-American, Asian-American, Hispanic, or American Indian heritage. By the year 2000, more than four of every ten public school students will be either from these groups or from a family meeting federal guidelines for poverty. To reduce the number of dropouts and a loss of aspiration among these youths, policies promoting careers rather than just jobs in both the public and private sector will be needed. It is not probable that programs that will work for the Asian populations are likely to be equally effective for the African-American, American-Indian, and Hispanic populations.

Within many U.S. major cities, addressing racial and ethnic discrimination and providing equal opportunity in both the public and the private workplace might well require hiring ex-offenders and, hence, having special programs for them. Washington, D.C. provides a clear illustration of the compounded nature of employment discrimination. In the 1989–90 school year, less than 1,600 African-American males graduated from high school, whereas the district's Lorton Prison jailed over 6,000 African-American males during 1989. Nationally, although African-American males represented only 10 percent of the U.S. male population, they constituted close to 50 percent of U.S. prisoners (P. Thomas, 1990). Providing any job for those who do not graduate and those who have criminal and drug-usage records (regardless of race or ethnicity) is obviously important, but for broad progress to occur in ending the evident racial/ethnic occupational segregation remaining in the public service — and in the nation — new policies permitting career development in fields other than service/maintenance for these individuals will be needed.

Historically the paramilitary organizations, such as prisons, police, and other uniformed services, have been the worst offenders in discriminating against women and minorities, especially in terms of incorporating them into the managerial, administrative ranks. Given the demographic trends as well as the U.S. philosophy of government, it is difficult to see how these agencies of social control can persist for long in such exclusionary hiring and promotion practices.

Adequacy of Current EEO/AA Policies
to Meet Current Multicultural Needs

The current patterns of occupational segregation and success differ so considerably among women and minorities that neither traditional EEO/AA policies nor simple, global approaches are likely to be very effective. In the 1990s access issues compete with other goals: breaking through "glass ceilings" and ending more subtle forms of sex and racial/ethnic discrimination. Simply put, EEO/AA policies address the issues of entry and access much better than they address the issues of advancement, integrating, and developing an effective, highly productive, racially and ethnically mixed workforce consisting of women as well as of men.

Differences in types of occupational segregation for all women compared to minority males suggest that the problems of women and minority males need to be addressed with different policies. The gender stereotypes and gender culture biases undergirding the "pink ghetto" of office/clerical and paraprofessional work for two out of three employed women in state and local government cannot be eliminated by the same policies used to fight racial and ethnic discrimination. The "velvet ghetto" of staff and support rather than line administrative positions in which women typically find themselves working will not be dispersed by policies addressed to the inner-city male worker. At the minimum, recognition must exist that the monocultural domination associated with middle- and upper-middle-class white males within the workplace consists of more than just racial and ethnic stereotypes. It also has a very strong gender and sex role ideological base (see Kelly, 1991).

The inability of traditional notions of equal pay for equal work and EEO/AA guidelines to address gender and racial pay inequities, whether in the public or in the private sector, illustrate further the inadequacy of such policies to meet current diversity problems. These traditional policies were inadequate largely because they ignored the sharp occupational segregation by gender — and race and ethnicity. By 1990 three of every four states had a pay equity task force or commission. At least six states had instituted pay equity adjustments as part of a comprehensive plan to resolve sex- and race-based wage discrimination (National Committee on Pay Equity, 1990; see also National Committee on Pay Equity, 1989; Kelly and Bayes, 1988). To implement these pay adjustments, the notion of comparable pay for comparable worth had to replace the idea of equal pay for equal work. Given the occupational segregation, by gender in particular but also by race, no other approach could systematically reduce extant pay gaps with any due speed.

The comparable worth debates revealed two key points about the problem of managing diversity in the public service in the 1990s. Perhaps the most important is that the workforce is still so segregated by race, ethnicity, and gender that balancing equality claims requires new interpretations of what is being made equal. The very notion of comparable worth indicates deviation from the aspirations of equality understood as sameness. A second point is that in efforts to develop a neutral standard for assessing the appropriate salary for a job, the male job is seldom the basis for comparison. To have a chance of working, concepts such as skill level, decision-making responsibility, ability, and work environment have to be used to develop the salaries related to the job value.

In sum, EEO/AA policies alone are inadequate to meet the needs of the 1990s for several reasons. First, such policies do not draw attention to the monocultural organizational structure and the implied metaphor of a pipeline that is used to bring women and nonwhite males into the workplace. The pipeline notion suggests that the same track and pattern of recruitment and advancement is open and can be used by all individuals regardless of background or current circumstances. It also leads to placing great emphasis on the qualifications of the person recruited — and blaming the inadequacy of these qualifications for the failure of more women and minorities to be retained and promoted. The burden of failure, in other words, is placed on the nonconforming, unassimilated newcomers.

Second, EEO/AA in a monocultural organization stigmatizes women and minorities as "others." As long as they remain at the lower levels of the hierarchy and do not challenge or threaten the traditional dominant values, their presence is acceptable. A 1990 study of cultural diversity in the regional office of a federal agency concluded that "men, women, and minorities do not share a common culture of organizational life" (Fine, Johnson, and Ryan, 1990, p. 317). This study found that 46 percent of the women respondents perceived a "white male culture/network" as a major obstacle to women's promotion; only 2 percent of the men did (Fine, Johnson, and Ryan, 1990, p. 315). A comparable 47 percent of minorities perceived that this "white male culture/network" and stereotyping (37 percent) were obstacles to their promotion; only 26 percent of white males perceived a comparable obstacle for minorities; and only 11 percent believed stereotyping prevented minority promotions (Fine, Johnson, and Ryan, 1990). White males also placed substantial importance on being team players, having friends in the right places, and working hard. Women and minorities, who mostly talked to other women and other minorities on the job — even those who worked primarily with white men — placed considerably less emphasis on being a team player and having friends in the right places. Their "otherness," which excludes them from the team currently, apparently facilitates reducing their perception of its importance in promotion. These differential perceptions reinforce extant beliefs that extra care must be taken to find qualified women and minorities and that vigilance is needed not to promote anyone just because a quota exists. A major problem for women and minorities, however, is that no paper qualifications facilitate entrance onto the team. Quality workers find this second-class status to be unacceptable. EEO/AA within this setting does not work in part because women and minorities leave. The seeming arrogance, dominance, and tokenism become intolerable to them. The cycle of seeking the "truly well-qualified" minority male or woman and protecting the organization from "incompetents" then begins anew. By the 1990s this "other" category has increased so dramatically in size that the tremendous scope and nature of the U.S. workforce diversity can no longer be ignored.

In his book *Equality and Public Policy*, Vernon Van Dyke (1990) notes another reason why EEO/AA policies are inadequate: the only compelling public interests that the courts seem to approve are remedial ones; "that is, differentiation that is suspect and therefore subjected to 'strict scrutiny' is cleared only if it provides redress for earlier violations of the rule of equal treatment" (p. 238). This interpretation makes it very difficult for state and local governments to promote racial and gender differentiation in forward-looking rather than backward-looking ways. Proactive steps are easily turned into reverse discrimination matters. All too often steps to promote diversity need to be presented as remedial actions to alleviate past transgressions by white males or the old monocultural institutions. Critics of the courts' interpretation of EEO/AA policies note that the emphasis on race as a suspect and gender as a quasi-suspect classification encourages battles between racial and ethnic groups and between the sexes. MacKinnon (1987), Tribe (1988), and Van Dyke (1990) suggest that a positive approach to promoting diversity might require focusing more on "an antisubjugation principle, which aims to break down legally created or legally enforced systems of subordination that treat some people as second-class citizens" (Van Dyke, 1990, p. 241).

Promoting Multicultural Synergy

Multicultural synergy is a term used to convey the notion that a culturally diverse workforce can be positive, dynamic, and a contribution to the national well-being. Diversity need not be a burden, requiring only compliance with the law. The means of moving toward multicultural synergy in state and local governments are not terribly different from moving toward it in other organizations.

Although stressing equal opportunity and affirmative action alone are insufficient, continuing the use of goals and timetables for measuring progress in increasing diversity at all ranks within an agency or organization is important. Data from a 1983 study of 77,000 companies by the Office of Federal Contract Compliance Programs showed that, between 1974 and 1980, affirmative action requirements for federal contractors led to significantly more employment for females (15 percent versus 2 percent) and for minorities (20 percent versus 12 percent) in companies with federal contracts compared to those without such contracts (Simpson, 1986, p. 264).

Studies of hiring and promotions by state and local governments in the 1970s and 1980s indicate that a variety of factors are involved in promoting the inclusion of women and minorities. Having either racial or gender diversity at the upper levels of the bureaucracy facilitates attaining greater diversity in lower governmental positions. Kelly and others (1991), in studies of four state civil service systems completed between 1987 and 1990, found this to be the case for women. Lewis (1989) reported similarly for African Americans in city police organizations for the ten-year period from 1975 to 1985. Other factors identified include a positive attitude of personnel directors and co-workers; support of political leaders and higher-level administrators; competition among minority groups; a growing economy; and a large proportion of women and minorities in the population and in the available eligibility pool. Finally, newer agencies tend to hire women and minorities at the middle levels of management at higher rates than more entrenched bureaucracies where males control promotional opportunities more (Eribes, Cayer, Karnig, and Welch, 1989). The movement toward a multicultural synergistic organization requires other significant steps in addition to these more traditional efforts. Although a consensus seems to be developing that EEO/AA policies and programs need supplementing, no dominant alternative model has taken hold yet.

The successful promotion of diversity takes thought and skill. R. Roosevelt Thomas, Jr. (1990), executive director of the American Institute for Managing Diversity at Atlanta's Morehouse College, suggests ten basic guidelines for learning to manage diversity, including such practices as articulating a clear motivation and a clear vision. In other words, establish a picture of what diversity and respect for difference and individuality means for the agency. They also include expanding the management focus to encompass the objective of creating a dominant heterogeneous culture, not just assimilating minorities and women into a dominant white male culture. Establishing audits of an organization's culture will facilitate describing and periodically assessing the culture existing in an agency or department. Modifying organizational assumptions, metaphors, and systems also represents a useful guideline for promoting change; for example, do not think about the organization as a family if that means only sons are to be promoted. If you have a pipeline notion of how and who will be promoted, mentored, or sponsored to reach higher levels, change it to fit the multicultural synergistic model. Thomas also recommends modifying management models so that subordinates are the doers and the managers manage by supporting and empowering. Promoting a pioneering spirit in the organization also will lead to a more synergistic organization and workforce. Allow error and change performance standards to facilitate change efforts. Finally, Thomas recommends continuing affirmative action. As Thomas (1990, p. 117) explains,

> The ability to manage diversity is the ability to manage your company without unnatural advantage or disadvantage for any member of your diverse work force. The fact remains that you must first have a work force that is diverse at every level, and if you don't, you're going to need affirmative action to get from here to there.
>
> The reason you then want to move beyond affirmative action to managing diversity is because affirmative action fails to deal with the root causes of prejudice and inequality and does little to develop the full potential of every man and woman in the company. In a country seeking competitive advantage in a global economy, the goal of managing diversity is to develop our capacity to accept, incorporate, and empower the diverse human talents of the most diverse nation on earth. It's our reality. We need to make it our strength.

Successful efforts to move from a traditional affirmative action to a managing diversity perspective in the state and local public service are still relatively rare. The city of Monterey Park, California, population of 62,800, provides a recent positive case study (phone interview by Rita Mae Kelly with Judy Cheu, mayor of Monterey Park, California, January 10, 1991). In 1986, as in 1991, this city near Los Angeles had 51 percent Asians, 31 percent Hispanics, 16 percent whites, and about 2 percent African Americans living within its boundaries. The mid 1980s witnessed a tumultuous period where a backlash against Asian immigrants strengthened an English-only movement that successfully prevented Chinese language books from being held in the public library and Chinese signs being placed on its streets. In 1988, the all-white city council was penetrated by one person of color, Judy Cheu. In the next two years her presence and voice led to increased participation of the citizenry. In 1990, a considerably more ethnically balanced and forward-looking city council was elected and Judy Cheu was voted mayor. She appointed a new city manager committed to diversity in the public service and launched numerous multicultural programs. New departmental and agency heads were appointed, reflecting the diversity of the citizenry. An Asian Task Force was established to address local crime issues. By 1991, over 20 percent of the Monterey Park police force was Asian, compared to only 2 percent of the Los Angeles force. (About 10 percent of the Los Angeles population is Asian.) Citywide multicultural fairs, highlighting ethnic foods, crafts, and customs, were held. Harmony Week was declared, culminating in brainstorming sessions on how to link hands across cultures better. A Sister City program, a multicultural film series, and roundtables on future relations among the city's cultural groupings were developed. An essay contest around the theme "Living in a multiethnic culture is important to me because . . . " attracted about 500 responses and helped shape a positive citywide focus on the virtues of diversity. By 1991, the advantages of promoting and living diversity in Monterey Park were quite evident. In contrast, in nearby Alhambra, California, where an equally diverse citizenry still had not elected one Asian or Hispanic to the city council, law suit after law suit for lack of affirmative action was being filed. Monterey Park illustrates two vital aspects of the move to a diversity perspective in the state and local public service: elected officials must lead the way and it must be a communitywide effort.

The city of Aurora, Colorado (194,000 in 1989), launched several new efforts to incorporate their new Korean residents into city life. The city provided support for a Korean-language newspaper and contributed articles on city activities and policies to it. The city also sponsors special recruitment, targeting, and diversity training programs for women and all minorities, going to their local organizations and publishing advertisements and public notices in relevant newspapers and other media outlets. The municipal employees are given workshops and cultural training on the backgrounds, cultures, and languages of their new immigrants from Korea, Japan, Vietnam, Cambodia, Laos, and China. Usage of multilingual phrases pertinent to municipal dealings is taught. The Asian community is, in turn, provided with access to translation services, codes, and regulations, and a part-time staff person facilitates their private entrepreneurship and entrance into the business community (Shannon-Bannister, 1989). Other cities, such as Independence, Oregon, have established more limited programs directed toward Hispanics, seeking to entice them to apply for municipal jobs.

One nationwide study of efforts to recruit women and minorities to the fire service identified several innovative methods (Booth and Rohe, 1988). Fire departments have been strongly dominated by white males. Historically recruitment has been primarily through word-of-mouth, from friend to friend, and strenuous physical testing has been important in the hiring process. In fact, in order to match the percentage of women in the current labor force (45 percent), many, probably most, fire departments would need to hire a woman for every vacancy that occurs for the entire next decade. Some would need to follow this procedure well into the twenty-first century (Booth and Rohe, 1988). It is clear that steps need to be taken to alter current recruitment procedures. Among the steps this nationwide study recommended are the following: (1) make the physical ability tests pass or fail rather than taking those with the very highest scores; (2) encourage local community colleges, high schools, and even physical fitness centers to offer extensive physical development programs that will appeal to women and that also meet the fire department's test requirements; (3) for both testing and on-the-job activities, provide proper gear for women and smaller men so that the equipment does not cause failure; (4) facilitate practice tests; (5) provide in-house or local community college tutoring programs for the written examinations; (6) develop cadet/apprenticeship programs for interested high school and community college students; (7) develop a community task force consisting of established female and minority firefighters to recruit; (8) target recruiting efforts to groups, neighborhoods, communities, and media outlets linked to women and minorities; and (9) develop appropriate brochures and signs that will appeal to women and minorities.

Conclusion

Several changes in organizational goals are needed to successfully manage diversity in the 1990s. Replacing the emphasis on assimilation to white male-oriented monocultural organization must be a top priority. Instead of stressing tolerating differences, the focus must be on valuing differences. Tokenism and the meeting of either real or imaginary quotas are no longer acceptable. Focusing on the isolated outstandingly competent woman or minority needs to give way to systematic programs for leadership training, mentoring, and skill development for all eligible employees. The organizational goal of eliminating or denying individual and group differences needs to become a goal of understanding and directly addressing such differences. Finally, state and local governments as well as all other organizations must move from controlling and containing diversity from a white male perspective to promoting performance at the full potential of all individuals. The problem of diversity must be changed from one of what to do about or with women and minorities to how to collectively and collaboratively improve the interface, the interrelationship of men and women and of all subgroups with all other subgroups.

Note

1. The EEOC data presented here are based on data for full-time employees from all fifty states, political jurisdictions with one hundred or more employees, and an annual sample of jurisdictions with fifteen to ninety-nine employees. Jurisdictions with fourteen or fewer employees do not need to file. The EEOC data exclude state and local elected officials, certain appointed officials, and their immediate staffs, as Section 701(f) of the Equal Employment Opportunity Act of 1972 permits. These reporting requirements result in these EEOC data reflecting about one-half of all state and local employees, and excluding all part-time employees. Compare with the U.S. Bureau of the Census, *1987 Census of Governments,* Public Employment (Vol. 3), Compendium of Public Employment (Vol. 13, no. 2), February 1991. According to the census of governments, there were 14.1 million state and local government employees in October 1987, data that include elected and appointed officials and all jurisdictions. Unfortunately, the Census of Governments report does not provide data by sex and ethnic group. The EEOC data on race and ethnicity can be based on visual surveys of employees or self-identification by the employee.

References

Alexander, K. L. "Minority Women Feel Racism, Sexism, Are Blocking the Path to Management." *Wall Street Journal,* July 25, 1990, p. B1.

Booth, W. S., and Rohe, C. A. "Recruiting for Women and Minorities in the Fire Service: Solutions for Today's Challenges." *Public Personnel Management,* Spring 1988, *17*(1), 53–61.

Carroll, S. "Women in State Cabinets: Status and Prospects." *The Journal of State Government,* 1988, *60*(5), 204–208.

Center for the American Woman and Politics (CAWP). Fact Sheet. Women in Elective Office. National Information Bank on Women in Public Office, Eagleton Institute of Politics, Rutgers University, Apr. 1992.

Cox-Burton, J. "Leadership in the Future—A Quality Issue." *SAM Advanced Management Journal,* Autumn 1988, p. 41.

Dreyfuss, J. "Get Ready for the New Work Force." *Fortune,* Apr. 23, 1990, p. 167.

Dye, T. R., and Renick, J. "Political Power and City Jobs: Determinants of Minority Employment." *Social Science Quarterly,* Sept. 1981, *62,* 475–486.

Eisinger, P. K. "Black Employment in Municipal Jobs: The Impact of Black Political Power." *American Political Science Review,* June 1982, *76,* 330–392.

Eribes, R. A., Cayer, N. J., Karnig, A. K., and Welch, S. "Women in Municipal Bureaucracies of the Southwest." In M. M. Hale and R. M. Kelly (eds.), *Gender, Bureaucracy, and Democracy.* Westport, Conn.: Greenwood Press, 1989.

Fine, M. G., Johnson, F. L., and Ryan, M. S. "Cultural Diversity in the Workplace." *Public Personnel Management,* Fall 1990, *19*(3), 315–317.

Fosler, R. S. "Demographics of the 90s: The Issues and Implications for Public Policy." *Vital Speeches of the Day,* July 1, 1989, *55*(18), 575.

Hale, M. M., and Kelly, R. M. (eds.). *Gender, Bureaucracy, and Democracy.* Westport, Conn.: Greenwood Press, 1989.

Johnston, W. B., and Packer, A. H. *Workforce 2000: Work and Workers for the 21st Century.* Indianapolis, Ind.: Hudson Institute, 1987.

Kelly, R. M. *The Gendered Economy.* Newbury Park, Calif.: Sage, 1991.

Kelly, R. M., and Bayes, J. (eds.). *Comparable Worth, Pay Equity, and Public Policy.* Westport, Conn.: Greenwood Press, 1988.

Kelly, R. M., and others. "Men and Women of the States." *Public Administration Review,* Sept.-Oct., 1991, pp. 402–412.

Lewis, W. G. "Toward Representative Bureaucracy: Blacks in City Police Organizations, 1975–1985." *Public Administration Review,* 1989, *49*(3), 257–267.

Loden, M., and Rosener, J. B. *Workforce America: Managing Diversity as a Vital Resource.* Homewood, Ill.: Business One Irwin, 1991.

MacKinnon, C. A. *Feminism Unmodified.* Cambridge, Mass.: Harvard University Press, 1987.

Meier, K. J., Stewart, J., Jr., and England, R. E. *Race, Class, and Education: The Politics of Second Generation Discrimination.* Madison: University of Wisconsin Press, 1989.

Mesenheimer, J. R. II. "Black College Graduates in the Labor Market, 1979 and 1989." *Monthly Labor Review,* Nov. 1990, *113*(11), 13–21.

Mladenka, K. R. "Barriers to Hispanic Employment Success in 1,200 Cities." *Social Science Quarterly,* June 1989, *70,* 391–407.

National Commission on the Public Service. *Leadership for America: Rebuilding the Public Service.* Task Force Reports to the National Commission on the Public Service. Washington, D.C.: National Commission on the Public Service, 1989.

National Committee on Pay Equity. *Pay Equity Activity in the Public Sector, 1979–1989.* Washington, D.C.: National Committee on Pay Equity, 1989.

National Committee on Pay Equity. *1990 Press Kit Update.* Washington, D.C.: National Committee on Pay Equity, 1990.

Saltzstein, G. H. "Black Mayors and Police Policies." *Journal of Politics,* Aug. 1989, *51,* 140–164.

Shannon-Bannister, B. "Culture Program Increases Awareness." *The Guide to Management Improvements in Local Government. ICMA,* 1989, *13*(3).

Simpson, P. "Why the Big Backlash Is a Big Bust." *Working Woman,* Nov. 1986, *11*(11), 264.

Thomas, P. "Talking It Over Man to Man: Black Mentors Aid Youths 'on the Threshold.'" *Washington Post,* Dec. 31, 1990, p. A1.

Thomas, R. R. Jr. "From Affirmative Action to Affirming Diversity." *Harvard Business Review,* Mar.-Apr. 1990, pp. 107–117.

Tribe, L. H. *American Constitutional Law.* (2nd ed.) Mineola, N.Y.: Foundation Press, 1988.

Tucker, S. "Careers of Men and Women MBAs, 1950–1980." *Work and Occupations,* 1985, *12*(2), 166–185.

U.S. Bureau of the Census. *Educational Attainment in the United States, 1982–1985.* Series P-20. Current Population Reports, Population Characteristics Subseries, no. 415. Washington, D.C.: U.S. Government Printing Office, 1987.

U.S. Bureau of the Census. *Public Employment in 1989.* Washington, D.C.: U.S. Government Printing Office, 1989a.

U.S. Bureau of the Census. *Statistical Abstract of the United States.* Washington, D.C.: U.S. Government Printing Office, 1989b.

U.S. Bureau of the Census. *Money Income and Poverty Status in the United States: 1989.* Series P-60. Current Population Reports, Consumer Income Subseries, no. 168. Advanced data from the March 1990 Current Population Survey. Washington, D.C.: U.S. Government Printing Office, 1990.

U.S. Bureau of the Census. *The 1987 Census of Governments.* Public Employment (Vol. 3). Compendium of Public Employment (Vol. 13, no. 2). Washington, D.C.: U.S. Government Printing Office, 1991.

U.S. Equal Employment Opportunity Commission. *Indicators of Equal Employment Opportunity Status and Trends.* Washington, D.C.: U.S. Government Printing Office, 1990.

U.S. Equal Employment Opportunity Commission. *Job Patterns for Minorities and Women in State and Local Government, 1974.* Washington, D.C.: U.S. Government Printing Office, 1975.

U.S. Equal Employment Opportunity Commission. *Job Patterns for Minorities and Women in Private Industry, 1989.* Washington, D.C.: U.S. Government Printing Office, 1990.

U.S. Equal Employment Opportunity Commission. *Job Patterns for Minorities and Women in State and Local Government, 1990.* Washington, D.C.: U.S. Government Printing Office, 1991.

Van Dyke, V. *Equality and Public Policy.* Chicago: Nelson-Hall, 1990.

PART THREE

Special
Management
Challenges

SEVEN

The Implications
of Changing Technology

James L. Perry
Kenneth L. Kraemer

New technologies are frequently described as "transforming," or "having the potential to transform," state and local governments and society more generally. In fact, however, technology has rarely been shown to have such effects. Rather than transforming state and local governments, technology has been adapted by government leaders to fit their perceptions of the opportunities and threats of its application. For the most part, such adaptive application of technology has been incremental and evolutionary rather than dramatic and revolutionary. Taken together, however, incremental, evolutionary change can, and often does, affect the way in which state and local governments operate. And these effects have implications for the public service.

We examine three broad questions with respect to changing technology:

1. What will be the effects of technological developments on the state and local public service during the 1990s?
2. What are the implications of these technological effects for the recruitment, development, and retention of government personnel?
3. What are ways of dealing with these implications?

The authors gratefully acknowledge the helpful comments of Enid Beaumont, Walter Broadnax, Jim Danziger, Thomas Galvin, Thomas Kinney, Rob Kling, Eugene McGregor, Sally Marshall, Richard Nathan, John Ottensman, and Frank Thompson.

This chapter seeks to address these questions with respect to technology generally, and with respect to information technology in particular. We focus on information technology because it is pervasive in governments and will become more so during the next decade and beyond. Ninety percent or more of all state and local governments have adopted computing, and computing accounts for about 3 percent of state and local government operating budgets (Kraemer, King, Dunkle, and Lane, 1989; Caudle and Marchand, 1989). The ratio of computing devices to state and local government employees currently is about 1:200 and is expected to reach 1:1 by early in the twenty-first century. Most applications of computing in government currently are conventional and oriented toward business functions rather than service delivery. The productivity improvements from these applications are marginal for the most part, or confounded with other improvements and difficult to identify and measure. However, productivity gains are expected to be greater in the future as more emphasis is placed on applications that radically restructure service delivery. These developments will only increase the pervasiveness of information technology.

The Effects of Technological Change

Our review of research and practice indicates that the effects of information technology can be broadly classified into two general areas: (1) the activities performed by government and (2) the nature of work. These effects are generally well documented by individual studies, empirical surveys (both cross-sectional and longitudinal), and/or literature reviews. However, not all effects are equally well understood, as will become apparent below.

Activities Performed by Government

Over the last twenty years or more, it has become apparent that information technology is altering the activities performed by state and local governments. It has resulted in the creation of new government functions and institutions — the information systems function and the management information specialist (MIS) department, the telecommunications function and the Office of Telecommunications, the information resources management (IRM) function and the IRM Office (Andersen and Dawes, 1991). Information technology also is altering the social organization and distribution of activities in government and is changing the broad processes by which work is carried out within and between government institutions.

Social Organization and Distribution. Information technology facilitates more diverse forms of social organization and distribution of governmental activities. For example, it permits either centralized or decentralized organization and central or local distribution of the activities of government while also permitting greater central monitoring and control. Historically, mainframe computers have been viewed as facilitating greater centralization. The advent of microcomputers is viewed as facilitating greater decentralization. In fact, computing has always facilitated either approach, or a mix thereof, and still does today (Attewell and Rule, 1984; Robey, 1981).

It is also the case that particular advances in the technology seem to coincide with administrative reforms or trends and reinforce one another. This was true in the 1950s with the introduction of the computer and centralized accounting and budgeting, in the 1960s with time sharing and intergovernmental systems such as the National Crime Information Center/ Computerized Criminal History (NCIC/CCH), and in the 1970s with large-scale computer networks and service integration. Throughout the eighties, there has been a trend toward decentralization of federal government activities to the states and, in turn, from the states to local governments. This decentralization trend will continue and perhaps even accelerate during the nineties. It will be facilitated by the increasing availability of computer networks, databases, electronic mail systems, and microcomputers at each level of government and throughout the federal system.

It is important to recognize that information technology has not brought about the trend toward decentralization, just as it did not bring about the earlier centralizing trends. Rather, it has been brought about by changes in perceptions of what governments can and should do, and by political or managerial ideologies (King, 1984; Kraemer, Dickhoven, Tierney, and King, 1987). However, information technology does facilitate the trend toward decentralization and will do so even more in the future because of decreases in cost combined with increases in the processing power and storage capacity of newer computer systems.

Information technology also changes the terms on which small-scale information processing competes with mass processing. It permits rapid and frequent changes of products and services, and it permits frequent changes in processes themselves. A possible effect therefore is that government workplaces will be smaller and more distributed, more flexible and changeable, and closer to the clients they serve. This can be seen in various efforts over the years to create "little city halls" and distributed service centers with the aid of computerized information systems that allow central records to be directly accessed and changed locally (Kling, 1978; Kraemer and King, 1988).

A related change is the distribution of workers themselves. The bulk of government workers will continue to be located in central places like the statehouse, the county hall of administration, and city hall. Some will be decentralized to distributed workplaces such as regional offices, metropolitan subcenters, and little city halls. Still others will work at home with a link to the office via the computer and telecommunications; that is, they will "telecommute." The proportion of such workers is estimated to be around 10 million nationally by the year 2000. Whether it reaches such numbers or not, government workers are likely to be among such telecommuters because of the "services" nature of their jobs. The type of workers who will telecommute first and foremost are those who already work at home, such as computer professionals, writers and editors, handicapped workers, and "piece workers." For the most part, work at home will not replace work at the office but will supplement it. That is, workers will work certain days (or parts of days) at the office and the remainder at home (Vitalari and Venkatesh, forthcoming).

Changes in Work Processes. The foregoing changes in social organization and distribution of activities will be reflected in changes in the processes by which work is carried out within and between institutions. Although the possible changes are many, four are especially important: co-production, sophisticated coordination and optimization, automation of direct services to citizens, and electronic communication with citizens.

Co-production refers to the increasing mix of public, private, and voluntary institutions in the provision of services to citizens. Although there are more sophisticated examples of co-production, the simplest is found in the volunteer fire and emergency services found in many small communities. The municipal governments provide and maintain the equipment and train and insure the volunteers, but the actual services are carried out by citizens who are notified of emergencies by beepers and other special signaling devices and who can call a special number where a recording tells them the nature of the emergency and the response that is to be mounted. Information technology will enable such innovation in other services as well.

Coordination and optimization refers to the ability of government agencies in far-flung locations to coordinate their activities and to optimize them in terms of some overall interest. Although such systems seldom currently exist in state and local governments, the prototypes exist in the federal government and can be extended to state and local governments for purposes such as job matching and eligibility determination.

A modest example at the state level is Colorado's job bank, a system that exists in other states as well. Most of Colorado's major cities and counties are linked through a central computer to a system that keeps track of participants in job training programs and job openings and allows social service personnel to match job openings to clients' backgrounds and qualifications. A logical extension of this system is to provide terminals for both employers and employees so that they can enter job openings and resumes and do searches for a match on their own (Gurwitt, 1988).

Automation of service delivery refers to the completely computerized handling of requests for information or service. Many examples are already in operation around the country. Several cities have automated citizen access to public services such as building inspections and bibliographic retrieval (from public libraries) and to public records such as land records, tax records, vital records, business licenses, and other "public" information.

For example, Dallas, Texas, has a system for the scheduling of building permit inspections. Instead of calling a city office that is only open from eight to five to schedule an inspection, builders can now call the building inspection office at any time of the day or night. The phone is answered by a microcomputer with a voice response system, which asks them to key in information about the building on a push-button phone. It then gives them a time for an inspection. At the inspection office, that information is then fed automatically to a mainframe computer, which goes on to arrange inspectors' daily schedules and routes (Gurwitt, 1988).

Another example is provided by experiments in Ramsey County (St. Paul), Minnesota, the state of Washington, and Berks County, Pennsylvania, that involve rethinking the way in which public assistance payments are made to individuals. Instead of issuing checks, which the welfare recipients then have to take to the bank to get cashed, the county is issuing bank cards for welfare recipients who can then use them at ATMs around the county to draw out cash against their public assistance accounts. Like any other bank cards, these cards have an expiration date and so the individual's eligibility and assistance is reexamined before a new card is issued. In addition, the cards and/or the ATMs can be programmed with information that limits the amount of any one cash withdrawal, the number of cash withdrawals within any time period, or other user options to encourage cash management (Gurwitt, 1988).

Electronic communication with citizens can occur in a variety of ways, but most frequently it is occurring through the automated handling of citizen requests for information and complaints and through two-way, interactive electronic mail and dialogues. An example is provided by Santa Monica, California's Public Electronic Network (PEN). Anyone with access to a personal computer, once registered with the city, can use PEN to obtain information about city council hearings or city commission activities; to communicate with city staff, city council members, and other city officials; or to engage in a "public dialogue" on community issues such as rent control, the environment, the economy, women's issues, or senior citizens' issues. Computer terminals are located in city hall, public libraries, senior citizen centers, other public buildings, and shopping malls to facilitate access by people without computers (Richter, 1991).

The Nature of Work

As might be expected from the foregoing changes, the new information technologies are changing the nature of work in state and local governments. Empirical research conducted over the last twenty years shows that the increasing automation of work processes is producing several changes, including (1) a speed-up of work, (2) a tighter coupling of work, (3) greater independence for professional and staff workers and greater interdependence for operations workers, (4) greater control over people for managers and professionals and greater control over jobs for clerical and administrative workers, and (5) greater flexibility in work organization.

Speed-up. Computerization has produced a speed-up of work at all levels within government, ranging from street-level workers to office workers to professional workers to policymakers and managers. The speed-up has occurred because the technology allows individuals to work faster, shortens the cycles for processes such as billing, paying and collecting, and records information in real time, as events and actions occur, and thereby creates an expectation for fast response. An important effect of this speed-up is a general increase in time pressures felt by all types and levels of workers (Danziger and Kraemer, 1986).

Tighter Coupling. Information technology is also creating a tighter coupling of work, especially where individuals from several different governmental departments and functions are tied together in a single system such as a financial system, personnel system, geographic information system, or emergency dispatch system. A tighter coupling of work means that what a person does in one part of the organization triggers decisions or action by others, or that what people do in their own parts of the organization creates a picture of something happening that all must respond to in a coordinated fashion. The former is illustrated by the case of a building inspection that discovers serious health, safety, and environmental hazards and triggers the need for response by the fire department (hazardous materials), health department, and police department. The latter is illustrated when the independent actions of these departments result in determinations that taken together suggest that a building must be vacated, sealed off, and torn down because of the total set of hazards present and the improbability of their amelioration.

Greater Independence and Interdependence. There is growing interdependence among some work groups as a result of automation, but there is also a growing independence for others. Information technology appears to increase the independence of highly professional and specialized work groups such as engineers, planners, economists, statisticians, management analysts, and staff analysts. These groups have always been able to function relatively independently, and computing has only increased their independence at the margins. It has done so by providing them with direct hands-on access to the technology, to data, and to the power to manipulate data in order to produce information relevant to their jobs. This increased capability has tended to heighten their stature and their independence of action (Danziger and Kraemer, 1986).

In contrast, the extension of computing into government has increased the interdependence of office work groups at the operational level, especially when they rely upon one another for input of data (and its accuracy, timeliness, format), for processing cases and clients in a sequence of steps, or for manipulations of data that form the basis for action by others (for example, forecasts or work schedules). The groups most often affected are the clerical, administrative, and managerial in both operational and staff functions such as finance and personnel, planning and building, fire and police, and across these functions (for example, geographic information systems, financial systems, and personnel systems).

Control over People and Jobs. Information technology (IT) has been shown to increase potential for control of individuals and jobs while actually increasing the autonomy of particular roles. First, IT provides a higher level of organizational control and greater capacity for judging performance via computerized monitoring systems built into the operating systems of government. This capacity for work monitoring via the computer is now a reality for professionals as it has been for clerical and administrative workers (Bjorn-Anderson, Eason, and Robey, 1986).

Second, managers and professionals generally enjoy greater increases in control attributed to computing than do clerical and administrative workers (Danziger and Kraemer, 1986). However, computerized systems also can make the task of control more difficult, especially for those in superordinate roles who themselves become dependent on the technology. For example, a study of supervisors and customer service representatives in a large public utility (Kraut, Dumais, and Koch, 1989) found that as a result of installing a new customer inquiry system, the supervisors' work was made both more difficult and more technology-dependent. In the past, supervisors had known the jobs of their subordinates because they themselves had previously been customer service representatives. However, with the introduction of the new computerized system, supervisors' knowledge was suddenly obsolete, and they did not possess nor were they provided with training to develop the skills they needed to operate in the new computerized environment.

Third, computerization has increased workers' sense of control over certain aspects of the job, including mastery over relevant information and improved communications. This has especially been the case for clerical and administrative jobs, and it has been accompanied by an increase in time pressures (Kraemer and Danziger, 1990).

Greater Reliability. The most significant impact of IT on work organization is that the technology enables managers and policymakers to choose whatever structural arrangements they desire, including combinations of structural arrangements. IT does not determine work organization; it facilitates it. Although information technology may enhance employee skill and autonomy, thereby facilitating decentralization and distribution of work, it also facilitates hierarchical control and task fragmentation (Bjorn-Anderson, Eason, and Robey, 1986). For example, hierarchical control and task fragmentation are facilitated by information technology when efficiency is the primary goal, the organizational scope is limited, capital cost is low, equipment reliability is high, workforce interest is low, and computerized monitoring is effective (for example, in the mail room or central records department of a state or local government organization). This fact highlights the importance of recognizing that the organization of work is at least as much a matter of political/managerial choice as it is of function/task necessity. It is a matter of choice about the structure of governance in organizations (Kraemer, 1991).

Summary

As the foregoing suggests, the effects of information technology are being felt at all levels of state and local government. There are many areas where we do not yet know or have a completely clear idea of the effects, but we have been able to draw some conclusions. IT has generated opportunities to reconfigure relationships, including those between levels of government, among subunits of the same jurisdiction, and between levels within state and local governments. The effects of IT on the activities of state and local governments and the organization of work have had ramifications for the nature of work itself. State and local government employees are experiencing greater time pressures, tighter coupling of their work activities, and changes in dependence and autonomy. In toto, the effects of technological change on state and local governments require the greatest adjustments for public service since the reform movement of the early twentieth century.

Technology's Challenge for the State and Local Public Service

The processes of technological change will have substantial implications for the composition, skills, organization, and psychological disposition of the state and local public service. They pose substantial challenges for public service in five respects: (1) worker displacement; (2) the creation of new jobs; (3) skill transformation; (4) redefinition of the temporal, physical, and social meaning of public service; and (5) technology-induced stress. These challenges and their linkages to effects of technological change are discussed next.

Worker Displacement

The restructuring of work will displace large numbers of employees. For example, information technology has reduced, and will continue to reduce, the demand for middle managers through the creation of organizationwide information networks (Millman and Hartwick, 1987). These networks, through the capabilities they provide for messaging, broadcasting, scheduling, and so forth, eliminate or at least reduce the need for some middle manager functions related to the collection, reduction, transmission, and distribution of information. At the same time, middle managers will have increased requirements to help define and manage automation projects both within their own area and with others (Osterman, 1986).

Information technology will continue the long-standing automation of the less skilled workforce and the impact will be greater in the office than at the street level. IT will also result in greater automation of physical processes such as waste water treatment, flood control, and traffic signal control, and consequently it will reduce the number of blue-collar workers in state and local governments. For example, in waste water treatment the opening and closing of valves, the monitoring of flows, and the testing for water quality, which were previously done by people, are now done automatically by IT applications. Moreover, the use of IT in the planning and design of these facilities and processes has increased the ability of engineers and designers to simulate the systems in advance of their construction and to make changes that further reduce the need for people to operate them.

The shifts in the occupational structure of the state and local public service, however, are not likely to mirror those of the American economy as a whole. Worker displacement in the state and local government sector due to technological change is likely to differ radically from most other sectors of the American economy because of a variety of institutional factors. One of these is the nonmarket character of most state and local government activities, which is likely to affect displacement in several ways. First, relatively few workers will be displaced through ordinary processes of displacement — plant shutdowns, business failures, or relocations — because of the essential character of most public services and their restriction to a specific geographic area. Displacement in a traditional sense will be limited to workers whose jobs (in contrast to organizations) are eliminated or who may be placed on long-term or permanent layoff, although decisions to privatize certain public services could have more far-reaching consequences.

Another reason that the role of technological innovation in state and local government, particularly information technologies, is likely to differ from the economy as a whole is that the role of technological innovation is more ambiguous. Technological changes may be adopted as a means for enhancing efficiency, but other non-efficiency-inducing motivations might also influence their adoption. State and local officials may pursue an innovation as a means of enhancing the quality of services or their own professional or political standing and visibility. To the extent that technologies are adopted for nonefficiency reasons, worker displacement is less likely to be one of the human resource consequences of the decision.

Traditional sources of displacement are also likely to be attenuated by job security practices in state and local governments, which will direct policymakers toward other strategies, such as attrition, as adjustment mechanisms. Thus, to the extent that certain occupational groups suffer from technological change, the manifestations of the displacement are likely to be managed either through changes in in-flows (for example, recruitment) and out-flows (for example, attrition) or hidden within the internal labor markets of state and local government organizations. Given the probable processes of worker displacement in the state and local government sector, compositional shifts in skill levels (Spenner, 1988), that is, occupational changes, occurring as a result of worker displacement are likely to be dramatic only when viewed in the long term.

Creation of New Jobs

Another long-term consequence of technological change will be the creation of entirely new functions and jobs in government. Completely new categories of organizational activity, such as technology policy, technology development, information resources management, and telecommunications management, have already been recognized in many large state and local governments (Caudle and Marchand, 1989). New job titles and classifications, both in particular technologies such as information technology and in technology generally, also have been recognized. Positions such as network specialist, information analyst, information resources manager, technology policy analyst, technology transfer agent, and technology adviser will become more commonplace with regard to technology development in state and local governments (U.S. Advisory Commission on Intergovernmental Relations, 1990).

The growing use of information technology requires not only the introduction of more technical personnel into government but also new kinds of personnel, both in the functional areas of government and in the IT function itself. In the functional areas, IT is creating the need for new specialists who are knowledgeable and skilled in both their functional specialty and in IT, for example, police systems analysts.

In the IT function, several new developments are bringing about the need for new kinds of people. First, the introduction of telecommunications, computing, and office automation is creating the need for people who can work at the interface of these three technologies to bring about their integration. Second, the diffusion of personal computers (whether stand-alone, networked, handheld, or portable) is creating the need for end-user specialists who can act as trainers, consultants, troubleshooters, and planners. Third, the increasing accumulation of data is requiring computer specialists in data management. Finally, and most important, IT demands the creation of information analysts—people who know how to work with the technology in order to produce useful information for decision making.

Skill Transformation

The skill implications of new technologies, particularly information technologies, are likely to be highly variable, depending on the technology itself and arrangements of organizational and environmental variables (Spenner, 1988). At the risk of overgeneralizing, however, the long-run implications of the types of technological changes state and local governments are presently experiencing or are likely to experience will require enlargement and upgrading of employee skills. There already is and will continue to be an upgrading of skills as a result of computerization, and of automation more broadly (Attewell, 1987; Danziger and Kraemer, 1986).

The basis for arguing that skills will generally need to be upgraded is that the automation that underlies many information technologies tends to broaden responsibilities, increase the abstractness of tasks and goals, and increase and broaden forms of task interdependence (Adler, 1984; Zuboff, 1988). The skill requirements can be described broadly as falling into four categories. The first is user literacy, which refers to the ability to understand and to use the technology in one's work regardless of the type of work or the level in the organization. The second is information literacy, which refers to the ability to recognize, locate, evaluate, and use meaningful information (American Library Association, 1989). The third is technical literacy, which refers to the ability to create with the technology. And the fourth is managerial literacy, which refers to the ability to make intelligent and wise choices about the application of the technology to government.

Although state and local government organizations could choose to fractionate work to overcome changing skill requirements associated with automation, several factors are likely to militate against job simplification as a means for coping with the skill transformations inherent in many new technologies. Given the decline in the growth rate of the labor pool, narrow definition of the skill requirements of new jobs is not likely to be an optimal strategy. The need for state and local governments to maintain their attractiveness to job seekers in the face of increasingly tight labor markets (Johnston and Packer, 1987; Johnston, 1988) is likely to stimulate the enrichment of jobs rather than their simplification. Reported trends that employee preferences for satisfying work are increasing also diminish the viability of simplification as a strategy for adjustment. Thus, the dominant pressure on state and local governments will be to respond to needs for a workforce with enlarged and enhanced skills.

The implication of these developments for the public service is that electronic communication will increasingly be a complement to face-to-face communication with other officials, other governments, and the public. For the most part, it will not substitute for existing communication, but will reinforce and enhance such communication.

Temporal, Physical, and Social Meaning of Public Service

The transformation of the social organization of work accompanying the evolution of information technologies in state and local governments also will have far-reaching implications for public service. For example, office automation technologies have tended to redefine the social space in which work is conducted. Telecommunications and networking technologies widen the prospects for personal isolation by increasing the feasibility of work-at-home or remote-site activity. These technologies potentially expand opportunities for novel scheduling arrangements such as flextime and compressed work weeks.

The redefinition of physical, temporal, and social space will not be received in the same way by all employees, and its effects are likely to be both positive and negative. For example, Bair (1987), extrapolating from interviews with office workers that these employees experience strong needs for connectedness with each other as well as with organizational levels above and below, identified personal isolation as a secondary consequence of office automation. On the other hand, voluntary work-at-home arrangements have been reported to increase employee satisfaction. In addition to altering employee perceptions about the physical and social space in which they work, managers will be challenged to motivate employees they cannot physically supervise and to respond rapidly to changing demands for service. These by-products of changing information technologies must be monitored, diagnosed, and managed.

Technology-Induced Stress

Another threat to achieving the potential of new technologies is the failure of state and local governments to assist employees to adapt physically and emotionally to the demands of new technology. Only recently have some of the forms of physical and emotional stress associated with the revolution in information technologies become widely known. These adaptive problems have taken a variety of forms, creating an entirely new vocabulary in occupational medicine. Among the physical manifestations of technology-induced stress are repetitive-motion syndrome and VDT-related eye, back, and neck strains. Emotional manifestations of technology-induced stress are equally common. Some employees experience *technostress,* which results from an inability to adapt to the introduction and operation of new technology (Nykodym, Miners, Simonetti, and Christen, 1989). Others may experience even more intense phobias, called cyberphobia or computerphobia, which produce physical symptoms such as dizziness, shortness of breath, and sweating palms.

The consequence of these pathologies is reduced performance effectiveness. Furthermore, there is some evidence to indicate that technology-induced stress is not distributed randomly but is more prevalent among female and older workers (Elder, Gardner, and Ruth, 1987), demographic groups who will be even more vital components in the future workforce of state and local governments (Johnston and Packer, 1987; Johnston, 1988).

Responding to the Challenges Posed by Changing Technology

What types of responses have state and local governments made to the human resource consequences of changing technology? For the most part, few governments have responded explicitly. What responses would be necessary if state and local governments pursue the types and rate of technological changes that permit them to improve efficiency and effectiveness? What types of responses to technological change would give state and local governments an advantage in competing for employees in the environment predicted by *Workforce 2000* and *Civil Service 2000*? These questions are addressed in this concluding section.

Worker Adjustment Policies

The concept of worker adjustment is typically used to refer to labor market policies that assist displaced workers to find new jobs with reasonable earnings prospects (Cyert and Mowery, 1987). We believe the meaning of worker adjustment should be broadened to encompass not only public policies but also organizational policies that represent the social contract between employers and employees who may be affected by technological change. In order to expeditiously and effectively integrate new technologies into the workplace, state and local governments must be prepared to deal comprehensively with some of the negative side effects of technological change. Among the side effects most likely to be viewed negatively by employees are displacement and technology-induced stress. A comprehensive policy to deal with these problems is likely to have several components: a formal statement of policy, training, advance notice, job security, and career counseling and outplacement opportunities.

An Explicit Statement of Policy. This is one way of allaying employee fears about how new technology will affect them and building trust within the workforce. The policy statement should articulate the state or local government's vision about a range of human resource issues arising from the introduction of new technology, including the role of employee involvement, opportunities for advance notice, training commitments, and job security. The impetus for such policy statements may come from employee interests rather than management. For example, the International Association of Machinists and Aerospace Workers has developed a "Worker's Technology Bill of Rights," which articulates its approach to dealing with job security, retraining, and job protection (Deutsch, 1987). The bill of rights has been the basis for negotiated agreements in both the public and private sectors.

Training. Long-term ability to maximize the benefits of technological change and to minimize adverse consequences is crucially dependent on the provision of appropriate education and training. In a recent survey, local government officials identified computer literacy as the greatest training and education need confronting local governments (Slack, 1990). That local officials would identify computer literacy, an early stage in training for new information technologies, as the greatest need reflects both the breadth of impact of information technologies and the long road most state and local governments still have to travel to meet their needs.

An example of the magnitude of the commitment that state and local organizations must devote to training is provided by Long Beach, California's approach to implementing office automation, beginning in 1984 (McMillen, 1984). Several extraordinary steps were taken by the Information Services Department in fulfilling the city manager's directive to install office automation throughout the city. One was the creation of a training center that was used for group training sessions and hardware and software demonstrations. Another step was to assign full-time personnel to support tasks such as ordering supplies, ongoing training, and problem resolution. Training was provided at both the training center and the worksite. Backup personnel were provided to replace staff who were trained off site.

The Long Beach example illustrates some generalizable requirements for workforce training. For all but small cities, state and local governments will need to prepare in-house training programs to augment vendor or contractor training. They will also have to devise ways to train workers for new technology without interfering with current operations.

Formal training and education programs will probably not suffice to ensure adequate support for adoption and utilization of new technologies. State and local government organizations must recognize that user-to-user interaction may be important for overcoming employee fears about new technology and enhancing the utility of formal training. For example, based on his study of information technology in cities ranging in size from 5,000 to 55,000, Rocheleau (1988) recommended that cities should use the informal system to train personnel and should seek to encourage the informal sharing of information. Among the examples he provides is the location of a microcomputer in the police department lunch room to encourage sharing about the new technology. Support services provided by an information center are another means of informally training personnel.

The training needed simply to keep pace with the operation of new information technologies per se is vast, but secondary training needs associated with changing technological/organizational interrelationships are likely to be even more substantial and far reaching (Helfgott, 1988). For example, managers and supervisors will require training in job design to improve their ability to structure jobs mediated by technology.

Advance Notice. Although the concept of advance notice is controversial, it may become an essential component of human resource practices in future labor markets. We noted earlier that certain features of the state and local government sector make outright displacement of employees less likely, but state and local governments may reap substantial benefits from full and early disclosure of their plans for technological changes regardless of the disemployment effects associated with a particular change. One example of a broad disclosure policy is that of Boeing Aircraft, which annually briefs members of the International Association of Machinists about company plans for the introduction of new technology that may affect employees (Deutsch, 1987). The adoption of similar policies by state and local governments would help to alleviate anxieties associated with the introduction of new technologies, build employee commitment, and speed workforce adaptations. Research indicates that advance notice policies have widely favorable effects, with few adverse effects either to organizations or to employees (Addison and Portugal, 1987; Ehrenberg and Jakubson, 1989).

Job Security. In an earlier time, guarantees of job security would have been viewed with alarm, but in the future, assurances of continued employment may pay big dividends (O'Brien and Kroggel, 1989). Job security can be an effective device to convince employees that technological progress is not threatening to their well-being. It is one way of diminishing resistance to technological change in state and local workforces. Given the shrinking rate of growth in the size of the labor pool, job security is also a means for ensuring that an organization retains potentially scarce employees. An organization's promise of job security may be made contingent on an employee's willingness to retrain for a new job at comparable pay.

Career Counseling and Outplacement Assistance. As jobs in state and local organizations increase in complexity and historical patterns of job ladders and job families change, state and local governments will have to become more proactive in career counseling for their employees. This will probably require a series of changes in the ways that state and local governments presently manage employee careers. One of the changes will be essentially managerial — to vest line managers with more responsibility to counsel their subordinates about career opportunities and to prepare them to undertake new jobs.

Not all employees will be ready or able to adjust to newly defined jobs and therefore will need job search assistance. For employees who prefer to leave the organization rather than adapt, some form of outplacement assistance policies for displaced employees would be appropriate. AC Transit (Oakland, California) used outplacement as part of a seven-point downsizing plan to humanize the layoff for fourteen nonunionized and management employees for whom there was no other alternative (Settles, 1988). Similarly, Anaheim Memorial Hospital used an outplacement service together with workshops on resume preparation, interviewing skills, action planning, and emotional adjustment to soften the hardships for employees when it closed Fullerton Community Hospital (Newman, 1987). In situations where relatively large numbers of employees face loss of their jobs, state and local government organizations may choose to provide job search workshops either directly or in conjunction with employee representatives.

Restructuring Human Resource Management Systems

The sweeping changes attendant to information technology not only require adjustments in work itself but also in the management and control systems that support state and local government activities. Most of the changes will occur in personnel systems, but other management and control systems will also need to be modified; among them the governmental unit's planning, procurement, and budgeting systems. Planning systems will have to be modified so that they take better account of potential strategic constraints imposed by human resource flows. Similar advances are needed in the procurement of information technologies and in managing the complex, long-term, large-scale, and inherently risky projects these systems entail. Capital and operating budgets will need to more completely reflect training and other human-resource-related costs.

It is difficult to predict precisely how state and local government recruitment practices will be altered by technological change. To the extent that government becomes a player in high-technology labor markets, it will probably have to recruit more from regional and national markets. Although this may require few adjustments for state governments, local governments will have to reassess traditional residency requirements that may limit their attractiveness. High demand in many technology specialties will necessitate rapid assessment and hiring of applicants. This is likely to require streamlining government hiring practices and shifting merit system controls from input practices (for example, testing) to post audit.

Career ladders will need to be altered to fit new distributions in occupations and transitions between occupations and to facilitate movement between jobs (Debons, King, Mansfield, and Shirey, 1981). Narrowly defined job categories will have to be replaced by broader job classifications to provide incentives to workers in the form of on-the-job learning opportunities.

State and local government organizations will have to reassess their relationships with organized labor. Adjusting successfully to technological change will demand large doses of cooperation between labor and management. Management and labor will increasingly need to approach negotiations as a problem-solving rather than adversarial process. Issues such as advance notice and job security will be of central importance to labor organizations, but labor can also help to forge innovative solutions for training and career development.

Incentives

State and local government organizations can encourage employees to voluntarily respond to technological change and future workforce needs by providing appropriate incentives. Previous experience indicates, however, that such incentives will not occur without explicit attention from state and local government managers and policymakers. For example, Iacono and Kling (1987, p. 75) note that the introduction of new technologies has not altered organizational incentive systems for clerical workers: "A new generation of integrated computer-based office systems will not automatically alter the pay, status, and careers of clerks without explicit special attention."

A starting point for restructuring incentives must be organizational pay systems. The shifting occupational and skill requirements associated with changing technology will require state and local governments to adopt pay systems that are congruent with the new technologies and consistent with a government's goals. Pay systems will increasingly need to be structured to reward the acquisition, modification, and development of individual competencies. Such a pay system will encourage workers to acquire new skills and thus facilitate redeployment and job redesign. One pay philosophy that seeks to increase organizational flexibility in these ways is pay for knowledge or skills-based pay. Pay for knowledge developed as a support system for team development in quality of working life programs. It typically includes three design features: (1) an employee's rate of pay is adjusted as new skills are mastered and demonstrated in performing job duties; (2) an employee will perform several assignments requiring different kinds and levels of knowledge and skills; and (3) employees will be involved in planning, setting standards, and measuring results from their work (Henderson, 1989).

A reassessment of existing educational incentives would also be a move in the right direction. Many governments presently provide for some type of tuition reimbursement, but such reimbursements are often restricted to job-related or job-specific courses. These programs will have to be liberalized to accommodate the need for retraining.

To the extent that employees affected by technology resist its adoption or implementation, state and local government organizations will be unable to realize technology's promise. The likelihood of resistance increases the importance of the process governments use to introduce new technologies. State and local government managers must seek out a variety of means to reduce resistance to appropriate technological changes. One means is to involve employees in the design and implementation of new technologies (O'Brien and Kroggel, 1989). User involvement in information systems development and implementation increases both systems usage and user satisfaction. Another step is to build employee trust and to avoid threats by adopting the type of worker protection policies discussed at the beginning of this section. These steps could be augmented by programs designed to reduce stress associated with a technology's use. For example, New York City has passed an ordinance that provides employees with extra breaks to diminish possible effects of prolonged exposure to VDTs (Halachmi, 1991).

Executive Leadership

As information technology becomes an integral part of service delivery, the education and training of public servants in the future must convey this state of the practice and instill habits of thinking about the role of technology in services innovation. The need for such thinking is important for all managers and professionals in the public service, but it is particularly critical for senior executives where the authority and resources exist to make bold decisions about services innovation. The need is not for senior executives to generate the innovations. Rather, it is for them to evaluate innovations presented to them by subordinates and staff professionals and to sift the effective from the ineffective and the marginal. The need is also for senior executives to take the lead in developing relationships with the private sector as well as with other public agencies to mobilize the technical and social support required for these innovations and to create the conditions for successful implementation and use.

    Perhaps the single factor that most limits the executive's ability to exercise leadership in the application of technology will be the continuing serious fiscal shortfalls of state and local governments. This suggests that governments might be encouraged to use information technology to help reduce costs, but that executives will have much less money to do so effectively, and it will cost more to innovate in the 1990s than in the 1980s. For example, while the costs of hardware of given capability are declining, modern systems require wider distribution of hardware than their predecessors, and the costs of skilled computer staff and user training are increasing. As a result, executives will have to make much more careful decisions about the innovations in which to invest. Moreover, they will have to focus attention on getting the most from the information systems in which they do invest, as well as those in which they have already invested. Careful investment analysis and continuous user training will be critical tools for senior executives to ensure payoffs from information systems investments.

Conclusion

Technological change is transforming public service in state and local governments. The transformation is an evolutionary process, still probably in its early to middle stages, judging by its effects across all state and local governments. Despite the early stage, many of the implications of technological change for the state and local public service have become apparent, such as worker displacement; creation of entirely new job classifications; skill transformation; redefinition of the temporal, physical, and social meaning of public service; and technology-induced stress.

    These consequences of technological change will require vigorous and thoughtful responses from state and local governments if they hope to achieve their productivity and service improvement objectives. The cornerstone of a vigorous response is a comprehensive worker adjustment policy that represents a state or local government's commitment to its employees as reflected in a vision statement, training programs, guarantees of advance notice and job security, and other provisions designed to diminish anxiety and displacement. State and local government organizations will also have to reassess their management and control systems to ensure that they are aligned with the new organizational realities. Appropriate incentives will be needed to reinforce organizational objectives.

    Finally, it is important to consider a comment by Erich Bloch (1986), former director of the National Science Foundation, in the *Journal of State Government*. He pointed out that "technological strength results from a chain of events that *ends* with new products competing successfully on international markets" (p. 144). The key to technological strength is skilled people and knowledge, both of which are created and fostered in universities. What public servants need more than anything is the transfer of knowledge and skill to understand and deal with technology. That knowledge and skill exists in universities, and the universities should be challenged to provide them through degree programs, executive education, and continuing education aimed at ensuring that there is a competent public service for today's technological society.

References

Addison, J. I., and Portugal, P. "The Effect of Advance Notification of Plant Closings on Unemployment." *Industrial and Labor Relations Review,* Oct. 1987, *41,* 3–16.

Adler, P. *Rethinking the Skill Requirements of New Technologies.* Cambridge, Mass.: Harvard Business School, 1984.

American Library Association, Presidential Committee on Information Literacy. *Report of the American Library Association Presidential Committee on Information Literacy.* Chicago: American Library Association, 1989.

Andersen, D. F., and Dawes, S. S. *Government Information Management.* Englewood Cliffs, N.J.: Prentice-Hall, 1991.

Attewell, P. "The Deskilling Controversy." *Work and Occupations,* 1987, *14*(3), 323–346.

Attewell, P., and Rule, J. "Computing and Organizations: What We Know and What We Don't Know." *Communications of the ACM,* Dec. 1984, *27,* 1184–1192.

Bair, J. H. "User Needs for Office Systems Solutions." In R. E. Kraut (ed.), *Technology and the Transformation of White-Collar Work.* Hillsdale, N.J.: Erlbaum, 1987.

Bjorn-Anderson, N., Eason, K., and Robey, D. *Managing Computer Impact: An International Study of Management and Organization.* Norwood, N.J.: Ablex, 1986.

Bloch, E. "The Challenge of Science and Technology in the States." *Journal of State Government,* 1986, *59*(4), 144–145.

Caudle, S. L., and Marchand, D. *Managing Information Resources: New Directions in State Government.* Syracuse, N.Y.: Syracuse University, School of Information Studies, Center for Science and Technology, 1989.

Cyert, R. M., and Mowery, D. C. (eds.). *Technology and Employment: Innovation and Growth in the U.S. Economy.* Washington, D.C.: National Academy Press, 1987.

Danziger, J. N., and Kraemer, K. L. *People and Computers.* New York: Columbia University Press, 1986.

Debons, A., King, D., Mansfield, U., and Shirey, D. *The Information Professional: Survey of an Emerging Field.* New York: Marcel Dekker, 1981.

Deutsch, S. "Successful Worker Training Programs Help Ease Impact of Technology." *Monthly Labor Review,* Nov. 1987, *110,* 14–20.

Ehrenberg, R. G., and Jakubson, G. H. "Advance Notification of Plant Closings: Does It Matter?" *Industrial Relations,* Winter 1989, *28,* 60–71.

Elder, V. B., Gardner, E. P., and Ruth, S. R. "Gender and Age in Technostress: Effects on White Collar Productivity." *Government Finance Review,* Dec. 1987, *17,* 17–21.

Gurwitt, R. "The Computer Revolution: Microchipping Away at the Limits of Government." *Governing,* 1988, *1*(8), 35–42.

Halachmi, A. "Productivity and Information Technology: Emerging Issues and Considerations." *Public Productivity and Management Review,* Summer 1991, *14,* 327–350.

Helfgott, R. B. "Can Training Catch Up with Technology?" *Personnel Journal,* Feb. 1988, *67,* 67–72.

Henderson, R. *Compensation Management.* (5th Ed.) Englewood Cliffs, N.J.: Prentice-Hall, 1989.

Iacono, S., and Kling, R. "Changing Office Technologies and Transformation of Clerical Jobs: A Historical Perspective." In R. E. Kraut (ed.), *Technology and the Transformation of White-Collar Work.* Hillsdale, N.J.: Erlbaum, 1987.

Johnston, W. B., and Packer, A. H. *Workforce 2000: Work and Workers for the 21st Century.* Indianapolis, Ind.: Hudson Institute, 1987.

Johnston, W., and others. *Civil Service 2000.* Indianapolis, Ind.: Hudson Institute, 1988.

King, J. L. "Ideology and Use of Large-Scale Decision Support Systems in U.S. Economic Policy Making." *Systems, Objectives, Solutions,* Apr. 1984, 81–104.

Kling, R. "Automated Welfare Client Tracking and Service Integration." *Communications of the ACM,* June 1978, *21, 484*–493.

Kraemer, K. L. "Strategic Computing and Administrative Reform." In C. Dunlop and R. Kling (eds.), *Computerization and Controversy: Value Conflicts and Social Choices.* Orlando, Fla.: Academic Press, 1991.

Kraemer, K. L., and Danziger, J. N. "The Impacts of Computer Technology on the Worklife of Information Workers." *Social Science Computer Review,* 1990, *8*(4), 592–613.

Kraemer, K. L., Dickhoven, S., Tierney, S. F., and King, J. L. *Datawars: The Politics of Modeling in Federal Policymaking.* New York: Columbia University Press, 1987.

Kraemer, K. L., and King, J. L. "Computing and Public Organizations." *Public Administration Review,* Nov. 1986, *46,* 488–496.

Kraemer, K. L., and King, J. L. "Centralization, Decentralization and the Role of Information Technology in Managing the Metropolis." *Local Government Studies,* 1988, *14*(2), 23–47.

Kraemer, K. L., King, J. L., Dunkle, D. E., and Lane, J. P. *Managing Information Systems: Change and Control in Organizational Computing.* San Francisco: Jossey-Bass, 1989.

Kraut, R., Dumais, S., and Koch, S. "Computerization, Productivity, and Quality of Work-Life." *Communications of the ACM,* 1989, *32*(2), 220–238.

McMillen, S. "Office Automation: A Local Government Perspective." *Public Administration Review,* Jan.-Feb. 1984, *44,* 64–67.

Millman, Z., and Hartwick, J. "The Impact of Automated Office Systems on Middle Managers and Their Work." *MIS Quarterly,* 1987, *11*(4), 479–491.

Newman, L. "Hospital Closure: Managing the Pain of Going Out of Business." *Healthcare Forum,* July-Aug. 1987, *30,* 35–37.

Nykodym, N., Miners, I., Simonetti, J. L., and Christen, J. C. "Computer Phobia." *Personnel Journal,* Aug. 1989, *68,* 54–56.

O'Brien, J. P., and Kroggel, L. P., Jr. "Technology: Training, Not Trauma." *Personnel Journal,* Aug. 1989, *68,* 32–41.

Osterman, P. "The Impact of Computers on the Employment of Clerks and Managers." *Industrial and Labor Relations Review,* 1986, *39,* 175–186.

Richter, M. L. "The Real Advantages of Putting Government on Line." *Governing,* 1991, *4*(8), 60.

Robey, D. "Computer Information Systems and Organization Structure." *Communications of the ACM,* Oct. 1981, *24,* 679–686.

Rocheleau, B. "New Information Technology and Organizational Context: Nine Lessons." *Public Productivity Review,* Winter 1988, *12,* 165–177.

Settles, M. F. "Humane Downsizing: Can It Be Done?" *Journal of Business Ethics,* 1988, *7,* 961–963.

Slack, J. D. "Local Government Training and Education Needs for the Twenty-First Century." *Public Productivity and Management Review,* Summer 1990, *13,* 397–404.

Spenner, R. In R. M. Cyert and D. C. Mowery (eds.), *The Impact of Technological Change on Employment and Economic Growth.* Cambridge, Mass.: Ballinger, 1988.

U.S. Advisory Commission on Intergovernmental Relations. *State and Local Initiatives on Productivity, Technology, and Innovation: Enhancing a National Resource for International Competitiveness.* Washington, D.C.: U.S. Advisory Commission on Intergovernmental Relations, 1990.

Vitalari, N., and Venkatesh, A., "An Emerging Distributed Work Arrangement: An Investigation of Computer-Based Supplemental Work at Home." *Management Science,* 1992, *38*(12), 1687–1706.

Zuboff, S. *In the Age of the Smart Machine: The Future of Work and Power.* New York: Basic Books, 1988.

EIGHT

The Myths, Realities, and Challenges of Privatization

Donald F. Kettl

Privatization has been sold, especially since the late 1970s, like the snake oil of old. It is based on a simple diagnosis of what ails government: because government does not operate under the discipline of market competition, government can never be as efficient or responsive as the private sector. It is a simple nostrum: Turn as much of government over to the private sector as possible; for those programs that must remain in public hands, encourage as much competition as possible, especially by contracting out the programs. Privatization promises smaller, cheaper, more efficient, and more responsive government.

The reality, of course, is considerably more subtle. The evidence is that privatization does save money, although many of the savings come from the lower wages and less generous fringe benefits paid by private contractors. In fact, what seems to matter most is not turning work over to the private sector but inducing competition in whatever government has done. Most important, privatization does not so much reduce government as *transform* it—it leads to a sharing instead of a division of responsibilities. Privatization muddies the lines between the public and private sectors more than it defines them. It fundamentally transforms the demands on the public service (Coleman, 1989).

The privatization debate dates principally from the tax revolts of the late 1970s. Proposition 13 focused the key issues: government was too big and must be shrunk; government was too lazy and must be made more efficient; government size and inefficiency were rooted in the lack of competition; replacing government monopolies with private competition would improve everything about government. The *practice* of privatization, however, is far older, and that focuses the central problem of state and local privatization: the rhetoric about shrinking government has hidden far deeper, more lasting, critical problems about making privatization work. The rhetoric suggests that privatization will be self-administering, but in practice, it is not.

In this chapter, I will lay out what we know about privatization; then I will examine the application of privatization in an important policy area, social services; finally, I will discuss the implications of privatization for the public service. The research in the field is voluminous, but it is most thin in this last area. That, as it turns out, is the most important issue, because without effective public management the promises of privatization can never be fulfilled.

The debate over privatization has often been confusing because advocates and opponents alike have used similar terms interchangeably. "Privatization" actually refers to a whole range of activities designed to reduce government's role. These activities include sales, the selling of government-owned operations to the private sector; franchises, the selling of the right to conduct business to the private sector; vouchers, the distribution of government subsidies to recipients, which allow them to decide for themselves what goods and services to buy; grants, the distribution of money to recipients, usually with more governmental controls than with vouchers; and contracts, an agreement between the government as buyer and a private organization as seller for the provision of some good or service (Savas, 1987). Some analysts include volunteerism, self-help, regulation, user charges, "demarketing" to reduce demand, and taxing authority under the privatization banner as well (Hatry, 1983).

Of all of the privatization strategies that state and local governments have tried, contracting out is by far the most used and the most important. While some states and communities have experimented with the other strategies, contracting out has become part of the mainstream of public management. Its implications are also the most far reaching.

What We Know About Contracting Out

The debate over contracting out has been feverishly ideological. Conservatives have argued that government has grown too fat and must be reduced (Savas, 1982; Lauder Commission, 1992). Liberals have contended that in the conservatives' campaign for efficiency is an implicit campaign to unravel the welfare state (Kammerman and Kahn, 1989). Government employee unions have sensed a campaign to eliminate their jobs (American Federation of State, County, and Municipal Employees, 1984, 1987). Neoliberals have embraced the case for competition as a way of improving government operations (Osborne and Gaebler, 1992).

The often passionate debate has then proceeded with the assumption that the privatization prescription is a new way of doing business. In fact, American governments have long contracted out supplies and equipment. When Progressive reformers at the turn of the twentieth century worried that corruption was undermining the efficiency and integrity of government, they developed formal procedures for government contracts: careful specification of what was to be contracted out and a bidding process to eliminate favoritism. In the early years of the twentieth century, the focus of reform was to *decrease* private competition and *increase* government power, to reduce the pernicious effects of the market on public services. At the close of the century, the debate over public-private relations is proceeding in reverse.

During the 1950s, state and local contracting expanded in response to new federal programs. State governments built the interstate highway system mostly with federal money through private contractors. Local governments managed urban renewal programs the same way. In both cases, the planning was governmental for the most part, but the actual work was done primarily by private contractors. Federal social programs of the 1960s and 1970s spurred yet another increase in contracting out, this time with nonprofit organizations. First Model Cities and then the Community Development Block Grant Program and the Comprehensive Employment and Training Act stimulated a new breed of public-private partnerships. The programs set as a primary goal the empowerment of citizens and neighborhood organizations. Local governments thus quickly found themselves trying to sort out and manage complicated new relationships, founded on a presumption of their own incompetence and/or unrepresentativeness. At the state level, the trend started a bit later and moved a bit more slowly. The Title XX amendments to the Social Security Act provided social service grants to the states. These grants promoted uncontrollable spending and the creation of parallel managerial and political problems at the state level (Derthick, 1975). All of these programs stimulated the growth of substantial new partnerships with nonprofit organizations.

As the tax revolts of the late 1970s sparked new demands for privatization, state and local governments had ironically already developed substantial public-private partnerships. From 1972 to 1982, local government contracts with private organizations tripled, from $22 billion to $65 billion. Some experts estimate, in fact, that contracting out has been growing at the rate of 16 percent per year (National Commission for Employment Policy, 1988). These new partnerships, in another irony, were the product of *expanding* governmental ambition, not the shrinking of governmental power that privatization's advocates recommended.

The Consensus on Contracting

Despite the often contentious debate over contracting out, however, there are some points on which a consensus has developed.

1.   Almost everything can be — and has been — contracted out. Contracting-out enthusiasts argue: "Virtually every service provided or function performed by local government conceivably could be farmed out" (Mercer, 1983, p. 178). Scottsdale, Arizona, for example, contracted out its fire service. Some state and local governments have contracted out prisons, libraries, police service, and parole programs. For many privatization advocates, in fact, this has suggested the ideal form of government: a mayor to administer contracts, a bookkeeper to pay contractors, and a network of contractors to do the work. Some communities are not far from this target. In La Mirada, California, a city of 41,000, the local government has contracted out for more than sixty services, managed by just fifty-five government employees. Another California community with a population of 60,000, Lakewood, had just eight city workers. One Dallas suburb came close to the ultimate in privatization: it had just one secretary to manage the paperwork needed for its fully contracted-out service system (Donahue, 1989).

Although almost everything has been contracted out at one time or another, local governments tend to contract out some activities far more than others, as Table 8.1 shows. (Similar figures for state governments are not available. The scarcity of data about contracting, in fact, is a telling sign of how much its administrative implications have been ignored.) A separate

Table 8.1. Who Contracts Out What?

Most frequent		Least frequent	
Percentage of local governments contracting out the function	*Function*	*Percentage of local governments contracting out the function*	*Function*
80	Vehicle towing and storage	1	Operation of libraries
55	Legal services	1	Prisons and jails
46	Street light operation	1	Police/fire communication
44	Hazardous materials disposal	1	Fire
43	Operation of homeless shelters	1	Traffic control and parking enforcement
41	Fleet management and vehicle maintenance	3	Parole programs
38	Commercial solid-waste collection	3	Water treatment
		3	Sanitary inspection
36	Residential solid-waste collection	4	Water distribution
		4	Crime prevention and control
36	Street repair	6	Sewage collection and treatment
36	Tree trimming and planting		
35	Operation of mental health facilities	7	Payroll
		7	Secretarial services
34	Drug and alcohol treatment programs	8	Personnel services
		8	Operation of museums
34	Day care facility operation	8	Recreation services
33	Labor relations		
32	Utility billing		

Source: International City Management Association, 1989, pp. xii–xiii.

survey, conducted in 1990, showed that local governments were most likely to contract out engineering, management consulting, major construction, food services, and legal and architectural services. More than one-fourth of the communities surveyed contracted out janitorial services, solid waste collection, building maintenance, security services, towing services, management and maintenance of parking garages, landscaping and grounds maintenance, human resources, food and medical services, services for the aging, consulting, landfill, data processing, and wastewater services (Mercer Group, 1990).

Sifting through these long catalogues of programs for patterns is daunting. They simultaneously confirm the vast richness of the services local governments provide and the fact that virtually everything can be contracted out. There are, however, important patterns buried in the long lists. First, the programs most likely to be contracted out are those for which the services are already available in the private market. Towing services work the same whether the drivers are towing cars for the city or for a private garage. Tree trimmers and street repairers, planners and data processors do not differentiate according to whether their customers are in the public or private sector. An important exception to this first generalization are social service programs, for which there is no significant market apart from government programs; I will return to that point a bit later.

Second, local governments are least likely to contract out programs at the core of their missions. Prisons, police, fire, water and sewage treatment, and emergency communications—all are fundamental programs that protect the public health and safety. Although some government somewhere has contracted out each of these programs at some time, local governments in general have not aggressively done so. For both programmatic and political reasons, local officials have been reluctant to turn such basic responsibilities over to the private sector. The costs of service disruptions could be high, and the political fallout from problems on services such as police and fire would be fatal. Thus, while everything can be contracted out, local governments' contracting activities tend to concentrate on support programs for which there are private analogues. There is also substantial contracting for social service programs mandated and/or funded by other levels of government, for which contracting out makes pragmatic and political sense.

2. Almost everyone contracts out something. "Virtually all local governments surveyed contracted out at least one service to a private company," the Mercer Group found (1990). Contracting out has become a near-universal phenomenon, with more than three-fourths of the government in one survey contracting out at least some local functions (Touche Ross, 1987). The gospel of privatization's efficiencies has many converts, and cost reductions and administrative flexibility lure both large and small governments to contracting out.

3. Everyone contracts out different things. Even though almost everyone contracts out something, and almost everything can be contracted out,

there is little consensus among local governments about what services to contract out. Among the 1,681 local governments that the International City Management Association (ICMA) surveyed, only two services—vehicle towing and storage and legal services—were contracted out by more than half of the governments. Of the nearly seventy-five local government goods and services identified by ICMA, most were not contracted out by more than a third of all the governments surveyed. Contracting out has become a norm, but what to contract out has not.

4. Contracting out often does save money. Almost every local government that has tried contracting out reports having saved money, both the ICMA and Mercer Group surveys report. The ICMA survey revealed that 40 percent of local governments saved 10 to 19 percent from previous outlays. An additional 40 percent of the governments saved more than 20 percent. The much advertised savings available through contracting out appear, in fact, to be real—although savings are never guaranteed and some contracting-out efforts are aborted because of performance problems (Mercer Group, 1990; International City Management Association, 1989; see also Hatry, 1983; Berenyi and Stevens, 1988; Lauder Commission, 1992; National Commission for Employment Policy, 1988). Moreover, local government officials generally find that contracting out produces good-quality service. A 1989 survey showed that 72 percent of the local officials said that the quality of services they had contracted out was "very favorable" (Osborne and Gaebler, 1992, p. 89). According to a 1987 survey by Touche Ross, cost savings ranked as the top advantage, by far, of contracting out, as shown in Table 8.2.

Assessing the cost-saving arguments requires caution (Kettl, 1991). First, because contractors are free of government rules and civil service requirements, they have more flexibility than public agencies. They use incentives pay systems; they have greater freedom to hire and fire workers; they employ more part-time workers, have less absenteeism, and use employees for more than one task. The absence of civil service requirements provides more flexibility, but it also removes valuable protections that the civil service system provides both government and its workers. Contracting

Table 8.2. Advantages Seen In Contracting Out.

Advantages	Percentage of respondents
Cost savings	74
Solving labor problems	50
Sharing risk	34
Higher-quality service	33
Providing services not otherwise available	32
Shorter implementation time	30
Solving local political problems	21

Source: Touche Ross, 1987, p. 5.

out, in fact, has sometimes been little more than a thinly veiled strategy to reduce the power and size of public employee unions. Second, contractors tend to pay lower wages than government agencies; in some services, wages paid to contractors' employees were only half of those paid government workers. In other areas, however, contractors' employees were paid higher wages. Third and most important, contractors tend to pay their workers substantially lower fringe benefits, especially retirement benefits. The difference in fringe benefits is "the largest difference between the government and the private contractor" (National Commission for Employment Policy, 1988, pp. 2–3).

Thus, cost savings are certainly not the only reason why government officials have used contracting out — even when they have used the cost-savings rhetoric. Moreover, when contractors produce lower costs, it is often not because they have better workers who are working harder. It is typically because contractors pay their employees less generously; provide them with less extensive fringe benefits, including health and retirement programs; and give them fewer protections on the job. Sometimes contractors are cheaper because they sacrifice values about the public service that government, for better or worse, has established as important over the last century. And sometimes contractors are more expensive precisely because they are able to pay higher wages than government would allow.

The cost-savings argument, in fact, masks a genuine anti-government-worker sentiment underlying the privatization prescription. Compared with just 14 percent of the federal government's outlays, labor costs account for more than half of state and local government spending. With so much of state and local spending concentrated on personnel costs, any argument to reduce that spending inevitably is an argument to reduce the number of state and local government employees as well (Donahue, 1989; Rehfuss, 1989).

5.   Competition for contracts is not always easy to develop or promote. The Mercer Group survey reported that local governments nearly always use competitive bids in awarding contracts. The survey also found that the governments can usually, but not always, rely on sufficient competition among contractors to have confidence in the process. Sometimes there are not enough potential contractors available to create a truly competitive bidding process. For some services, such as code enforcement, it is almost impossible to find private suppliers. For other services, private concerns might not be interested in bidding on jobs in small jurisdictions, where the size of the contract and potential profits would also be small. Many contractors, furthermore, are often concerned about red tape and the slow pace at which governments pay vendors. Nearly 10 percent of all jurisdictions surveyed said that they had difficulty finding sufficient contractors, and the number rose to 30 percent among special district governments. The problem was most serious for governments of small jurisdictions, where there often were few contractors for some services (Mercer Group, 1990; International City Management Association, 1989).

Competition, moreover, is costly to create and sustain (Donahue, 1989). To manage a contract competition, government officials first must precisely define what they want to buy, and contract solicitations must be detailed and specific, for they shape the transaction that is to occur. Government officials must advertise the solicitation and review the bids; they must resolve technical disputes among bidders and between government officials and potential contractors; they must oversee the contract once it is awarded to ensure both the cost and quality of the services provided. Perhaps most important, they must ensure that the winning contractor does not grow into a monopolist, to which the government would find itself captive and from which the promised efficiencies might soon evaporate. Privately managed mass transit systems are frequently monopolies, and without competition they share the limited incentives to control costs that governments allegedly have (Perry and Babitsky, 1986).

6. Contracting out creates risks as well as advantages. Market competition, of course, poses significant problems as well as potential benefits (Donahue, 1989). Corruption can occur throughout the contracting process. A principal reason for the bureaucratization of state and local governments at the turn of the twentieth century was to insulate government from private corruption. Since then, bid rigging, bribery, and kickbacks certainly have not been eliminated. Privatization's opponents suggest that such problems are rampant (American Federation of State, County, and Municipal Employees, 1984, 1987). It is impossible, of course, to determine just how widespread such problems are, but they are undoubtedly real and will continue—at least to some degree.

Conflicts of interest can multiply. San Francisco, for example, hired a private consulting firm to manage its public works programs. The city also hired from this firm a new manager to oversee its budget and personnel policies. The manager awarded contracts to his own firm—and the city soon decided to cancel the contract (Donahue, 1989).

Services provided by private contractors can also be disrupted if the contractor does not perform well, if equipment breaks down, if the contractor suffers its own labor problems, or if the contractor goes bankrupt. "Shifting to contracting for at least some major activities is a major move and is not easy to reverse," Hatry points out (1983, p. 27). Services contracted out are far less resilient than services provided directly by governments. New York City switches its garbage trucks to snow plow duty when bad weather threatens; such an option might not be available if a community becomes dependent on private snow removal contractors who turn out to be poor performers. Transferring responsibility to the private sector can also reduce a government's own capacity, not only to provide but also to manage services. It can lose an important source of information about what works how, and that can undercut its ability to manage contractors effectively. How have jurisdictions responded to this problem? Often by hiring other contractors to supply what the government has lost.

Finally, governments that contract out risk becoming subject once again to monopoly power. Contractors in fields as far ranging as day care and garbage collection have often lobbied aggressively to restrict competition (Osborne and Gaebler, 1992). Not all market forces are self-policing.

7. *How* matters more than *who*. The evidence over all is not that the private sector is inherently better than the public sector. It is, rather, that what matters most is not *who* performs government services but *how* they are done. Donahue finds, "*Public versus private* matters, but *competitive versus noncompetitive* usually matters more" (1989, p. 78; see also Osborne and Gaebler, 1992). It is competition, not private sector methods, that produce the savings. One study, for example, examined the provision of electric service. In communities where there was competition, costs were reduced by about 11 percent, regardless of whether the service provider was government or a private concern (Primeaux, 1977). Private monopolies are just as subject to inefficiencies as is the government monopoly. It is the presence of competition, not the locus of power, that matters.

Some state and local governments, in fact, have introduced competition into their own operations. Phoenix requires its municipal workers to bid against private contractors for selected local services. In Rochester, New York, the city was ready to sign a contract with a private garbage collection firm when its employees proposed to reduce the crew size from four to three, which the city found significantly cheaper (Hatry, 1983). Workers at a Los Angeles county health clinic formed a private company and bid successfully for a county contract (Savas, 1992). In Newark, New Jersey, information the city gained from the bidding process for a refuse collection contract helped improve the productivity of city refuse workers (International City Management Association, 1989). Analysts contend that such competition might produce the biggest benefits of all in local education (Chubb and Moe, 1990).

What is important here is the concept that government will not permit monopoly power over resources, including manpower and expertise, that it needs. It is the introduction of the notion that suppliers of needed goods and services, whether inside government or out, can and will be replaced if they prove inadequate. The concept of competition is thus a very basic one, and it does not extend to a full-fledged marketplace full of free and open competition among buyers and sellers operating at arm's length. In his study of government procurement, Kelman points out that "if by 'competition' one means the principles of 'free and open competition' in government procurement, government shows more competition than private-sector purchasing does. In the private sector, companies have learned the advantages of developing informal long-term relationships to get the most value from vendors. Such relationships increase the incentive for vendors to perform well and to provide technical assistance. Free and open competition is likely to diminish the value created by these relationships" (1990, p. 62). The solution to the problems of government procurement, Kelman believes, is not more competition but "to increase dramatically the freedom we give public officials to use their judgment in the procurement process" (p. 90).

It is tempting to embrace simple-minded notions about the virtues of competition without examining the reality that lies behind the rhetoric. In practice, private industry rarely operates in markets characterized by a pure, survival-of-the-fittest competitive shootout. Industries, rather, must struggle with the many uncertainties that surround everything they do, uncertainties that impose transaction costs, which often are substantial. Industries seek to minimize these costs by developing stable, predictable relationships with the other firms on which they depend (Williamson, 1985). The privatization debate has tended to make a fetish out of competition instead of looking more deeply to the fundamental but often far more subtle issues. Competition is important because it raises the possibility that buyers can find new sellers if they are dissatisfied with the product. Competition thus is a valuable approach to breaking down the self-satisfaction that monopolies can develop — even the self-satisfaction that government employees can generate. It is not, however, an all-purpose remedy for government's problems and, if pursued too vigorously, can upset the stability that helps government deal with its own collection of uncertainties.

8.   Contracting out merges, not separates, the public and private sectors. One of the lures of contracting out is its implicit promise to reduce government, but the dirty secret of contracting out is that it increases, not decreases, government's penetration into the private sector. Government's contractors must provide services according to the government's goals; they must keep their books according to government-prescribed standards; they must file frequent reports about their activities; in some areas, they must pay government-set wages. They can find themselves exposed to substantially greater legal liability. They operate in a political, not a private, environment, where elected officials and private citizens alike can and will complain about their services.

Thus, contracting out does not so much separate as blur the lines between the public and private sectors. For some routine services, such as running a cafeteria or cleaning floors, the government need not operate any differently than any private concern. Much of what government buys is very specialized, however. Many of the programs on the "most" and "least" contracted-out lists in Table 8.1 are government-specific. Without government, many of the services would not exist, and competition among private providers for the government's business is limited for some of them. Government contractors are frequently not so much agents as partners of the government, and nothing illustrates the important implications of this fact better than contracting out for social services.

9.   Contracting out requires effective but different management. What this really suggests is that contracting out does not so much *reduce* as *change* the management responsibilities of state and local governments. If the government's direct role in service delivery is less, its managerial responsibilities can actually increase: the information demands of contracting out are substantially greater; the oversight responsibilities are larger. Governments, and their top officials, must be smarter. With services managed directly by govern-

ment the costs of a lack of intelligence are sloppy services that might be more costly than necessary. With services managed by private contractors, however, the costs and risks are far greater.

Contracting Out for Social Services

Public debates over contracting out have swirled around state and local managers since the late 1970s. Arguments for more contracting out provide a diagnosis for what is wrong with government — not enough competition — and what ought to be done — turn more of government over to the private sector. While the debate has raged, however, contracting out has expanded rapidly. This expansion, moreover, has had far more to do with the pragmatic realities of state and local management and with the interconnection among programs at all levels of government. Nothing makes this point more clearly than the case of state and local government contracting out for social services. In 1971, a national survey showed that 25 percent of social services provided by governments were contracted out. By 1979, the figure had climbed to 55 percent (Chi, Devlin, and Masterman, 1989). What has happened to the figures since then analysts can only guess, but the impressionistic evidence is that the share has continued to grow. Most public money spent on social services is spent through private and nonprofit contractors; governments directly manage relatively few programs (Savas, 1987).

Massachusetts has contracted out day care services to more than 600 providers. Other state governments have contracted out the management of hospitals, employment programs, mental health programs, adoption services, child care support enforcement, and Medicaid (Chi, Devlin, and Masterman, 1989; Lauder Commission, 1992). A 1984 survey of fifty-seven welfare agencies in the San Francisco Bay area showed that over 70 percent of them contracted out at least one social service. The scholars who conducted the survey wrote, "Contracting today is far more than an anomaly on the periphery of the welfare state; it is a core feature of ground-level social welfare administration in many service areas." They concluded, in fact, that "the mingling of public and private funds and functions pervades the welfare state" (National Commission for Employment Policy, 1988, p. 9).

The ICMA survey revealed a wide range in the contracting practices of local governments for social service programs, as shown in Table 8.3. Although contracting is widespread, different governments tend to contract out different programs. Human service programs like homeless shelters, mental health, drug treatment, day care, and programs for the elderly are contracted out most often. Just as important, though, contracting out is not the exclusive management strategy. For social services, most governments rely on a mixed strategy, with considerable contracting out accompanied by delivery of some services in part by local government employees. There is, in fact, no direct relationship between a local government's reliance upon contractors and its use of its own employees.

Table 8.3. Contracting Out for Social Services.

Employees	Provided by contractors	Provided by local government contract	
		In part	Completely
Operation of homeless shelters	43	32	4
Operation of mental health/retardation programs	35	40	14
Drug/alcohol treatment programs	34	41	14
Day care facility operation	34	27	25
Food programs for the homeless	26	43	5
Operation/management of hospitals	24	19	36
Programs for elderly	19	57	22
Public health programs	19	37	32
Child welfare programs	17	44	33
Operation/management of public/elderly housing	14	28	22

Percentage of cities and counties relying on given administrative strategy

Source: International City Management Association, 1989, p. 96.

Contracting out, furthermore, is most common in the largest jurisdictions, as Table 8.4 shows. Although the evidence on why is unclear, it is unlikely that smaller jurisdictions provide more services themselves. Rather, larger local governments tend to provide more social services — and many social services are contracted out. The underlying message is that when local governments provide social services, they usually rely on a mixed public-private-nonprofit system. The government's rising role in social services has been accompanied by steady erosion in the boundaries among the sectors and more interdependence among them in providing the services.

The reasons for this trend are complex. The federal government itself has fueled much of it, by providing state and local governments with grants and then mandating that much of the money be funneled through nonprofit community organizations (Smith and Lipsky, 1993). The first generation of programs, during the 1960s, was based on the federal government's fundamental distrust of state and local governments. The federal government directly funded community organizations as a strategy to enfranchise them. In the second generation of programs, during the 1970s, the federal government gave grants to state and local governments with the expectation that they would build upon and strengthen the community organizations that had been created the decade before. In job training and community development programs, much of the money was spent through neighborhood organizations (Kettl, 1980; Nathan, 1977, 1981). Federal grants to state governments for social services, such as through the Title XX amendments to the Social Security Act, encouraged many states to expand their purchase of services from nonprofit organizations (Derthick, 1975). Programs like the Title IV-A amendments to the Social Security Act also encouraged the use of contractors by allowing local welfare agencies to receive

Table 8.4. The Relationships Between Size and Contracting.

Population	Percentage of cities and counties contracting with a private firm for the given service		
	Food programs for the homeless	Programs for the elderly	Day care facility operation
Under 10,000	0	14	20
10,000–49,000	15	12	22
50,000–249,000	31	27	42
250,000 and over	46	46	59
All cities and counties	26	19	34

Source: International City Management Association, 1989, p. 97.

$3 for every $1 a state or local government contributed for social services provided by a contract. Such matching proved irresistible (Fisk, Kiesling, and Muller, 1978).

By the third generation of programs, in the 1980s, the federal-state-local-private-nonprofit partnership had been firmly established. The Job Training Partnership Act, as its title suggested, relied explicitly on public-private ties to prepare workers for employment. Even though federal funding for such programs decreased, the administrative patterns for the programs that remained became increasingly intertwined (Allen and others, 1989). They challenged managers to develop innovative tactics for coordinating and effectively managing community-based programs (Hatry, Morley, Barbour, and Pajunen, 1991).

The federal government's Medicaid program also contributed to state governments' reliance on private contractors. For many states it proved to be one of the fastest-growing areas of expenditure for the decade. To rein in cost growth, some states turned to private contractors, like H. Ross Perot's Electronic Data Systems (EDS), to improve their claims management. Kentucky state officials estimated that they saved more than $1 million per year through its EDS contract. EDS, they said, managed a 99 percent accuracy rate while processing claims in an average of three to four days, compared with more than two weeks before EDS was hired (Chi, Devlin, and Masterman, 1989). Other states have turned to private contractors to provide home health care and managed care to reduce the program's costs (Rubenstein, 1992). State-local relations have also played a heavy role in stimulating the nonprofit sector. Many states mandate local governments to provide social services — from child welfare to health programs — sometimes without financing the mandates. Faced with expanding state programs, local governments unsurprisingly have turned to nonprofits.

The growing role of nonprofit organizations in state and local social service contracting builds on several important features. First, nonprofit organizations are widely viewed to be altruistic and to have their clients' — not voters' or stockholders'—interests in mind. Second, because nonprofit organizations tend to be community based, it is often argued that they are "closer to the people" and hence more responsive. Third, because nonprofit organizations rely heavily on volunteers and tend to minimize their overhead, their costs are lower. Fourth, because nonprofits pool different sources of funds, from government contractors to United Way contributions, government officials often believe that they can stretch their money further (International City Management Association, 1989; O'Neill, 1989).

Nonprofits have grown rapidly over the last few decades. One study of the nonprofit sector in New York state discovered that, between 1981 and 1987, nonprofit employment increased twice as fast as employment in the for-profit world and three times as fast as government employment. Most nonprofits providing social services tend to be relatively small. They get a large share of their budgets—about 40 percent—from government, but they receive most of their revenue from other sources. Most of their money comes for programs they manage (Ben-Ner and Van Hoomissen, 1989).

What kind of system does this produce? From the point of view of service providers, it is a system dominated by nonprofit organizations. These organizations receive much but not most of their funding from government, which means that they must serve the needs of multiple funding sources, from voluntary contributors to other organizations like the United Way. Their financial footing is often uneasy, and their goals are diverse. They find they must meet the stringent financial and managerial standards of government programs even though government provides less than half of their funding. Serving public goals is an important part but not the only part of their mission.

From the point of view of governments, the system is extremely complicated and only partially under their control. They seek control of the programs they fund, but there are multiple constituencies simultaneously vying for control as well. They want to ensure that the money is spent well, but they must struggle with the sometimes bare-bones competence of nonprofit organizations. They seek coordination of their programs, but they struggle to link with other programs they do not control. Their very operation, in fact, is increasingly "hollow," with government responsible for programs but actually little more than an outside shell (Milward, Provan, and Else, 1993). For many social service programs, state and local governments have become little more than a holding company, providing public funding for a loosely knit conglomerate of programs whose behavior ultimately determines the effectiveness of social services.

From the point of view of analysts, finally, social services present special problems of privatization. Privatization advocates preach the benefits of competition, but competitive contracting is relatively rare in social services. Most social service contracts, in fact, tend to be negotiated, not put into competition (Savas, 1987). Social services are notoriously hard to define, which makes drafting precise contracts defining service goals difficult. Because they are hard to define, furthermore, results are hard to measure.

Government agencies tend to drift back into input measures (for example, how much money is spent or how many clients are "served") instead of outcome measures (for example, how much the client's life is improved by the service). This is the equivalent of judging how good a car or a restaurant meal is by how much one paid for it.

Finally, government has only loose control over the service. Contracting out for social services, in fact, might wander as far from market-based relationships as any in the public-private-nonprofit world. Social service contracting is far less supported by the cost-saving rhetoric of the privatization prescription and far more undergirded by the pragmatic and complex demands of service delivery.

The Case of Dane County

The management of social services by Dane County, Wisconsin, presents an interesting illustration of these issues. There can be no claim that the county is typical. Indeed, the level of research into contracting out at the state and local levels, let alone for social services at the state and local levels, makes it impossible to argue that *any* administrative pattern is typical. The problems experienced by Dane County social service managers, however, resonate through the academic literature. If the county is not typical, its problems are.

Dane County is a mixed rural-urban county, with a population of 367,000 most remarkable for its diversity. Madison, the county seat, has a microcosm of typical urban problems. During the late 1980s, the drug trade gradually seeped into this college town from Chicago, bringing the enduring problems of the urban underclass. Not far from the city limits, the rolling countryside turns into some of the county's most productive farm land. Agriculture and, of course, milk production abound, but the problems of rural poverty have crept into the county as well. The state government has been progressive in mandating that local governments provide a wide array of social services. Wisconsin has been home to some of the nation's most interesting welfare reform experiments (such as "workfare" and "bridefare") and experiments in school choice (notably the Milwaukee demonstration). No county dominated by Madison is "typical," but few counties offer a greater range of programs or population.

Most social services — about 80 percent of the county social services budget — are mandated by the state (such as homes for the elderly and youth) and the federal government (such as Aid to Families with Dependent Children (AFDC) and Medicaid, in which the counties play a major administrative role). The primary feature of the service delivery system is the sharp break between services contracted out and those performed directly by county employees. The staff of the Dane County Department of Human Services is 570 employees. Nearly all of these employees, however, were hired to manage just one-third of the budget. More than two-thirds of the $86 million budget (in fiscal 1991) was managed through contractors, mostly nonprofit organizations, as shown in Table 8.5. There were 143 contractors managing 360 contracts; nearly all of the contractors were nonprofit organizations. Supervising these contractors were just 11.3 employees. These are the most telling statistics of all in describing the county's social service system.

The central features of Dane County's social service program thus have been the following: little discretion in which programs to fund, since nearly all of the budget goes to mandate programs; a complex, labor-intensive set of programs; a small assortment of programs managed directly by the county; and a large group of contractors with very little oversight. The county, moreover, tended to rely far more on contractors for some activities—especially mental health, job training, and family services—than for others—such as program administration, public health programs provided outside the Madison city limits, and the county's nursing home. Most of the new era of social service programs, those prompted by state and federal policy initiatives of the 1970s and 1980s, tended to be contracted out, while more traditional programs tended to be managed in-house. For the newer programs, contracting out offered "a flexibility—you didn't have the civil service system to go through and you had some economies of scale," department director Carol Lobes explained.[1] The contractors often had lower wage levels and fewer fringe benefits. "There was a sense," Lobes said, "that if contractors could do it, then government shouldn't."

In managing this network of contractors, the county has struggled with five basic problems: choosing contractors; defining what the contractors ought

Table 8.5. Contracting Out for Social Services,
Dane County, Wisconsin, Department of Human Services.

Division	Percentage of division budget managed through contracts
Administration	3.9
Children, youth, and families (family social services)	66.7
Economic assistance and work services (job training)	68.8
Adult community services (long-term care, mental health)	91.4
Badger Prairie Health Care Center (nursing-home care)	20.0
Public health (programs outside city)	3.2
Total department budget	$86 million
Total department budget: Managed through contracts	68.5%

Source: Fiscal 1991 Budget, Dane County, Wisconsin, Department of Human Services.

to do; monitoring the contractors' performance; coordinating disparate services; and ensuring accountability. These problems are mirrored in other studies that have examined social service administration around the country.

Choosing Contractors

The case for privatization is built on the foundation of competition. It argues that contracting out is more efficient because it assumes that contractors competing for a government contract will produce the lowest costs at the highest quality. "In some services," Lobes pointed out, however, "we needed to develop our own contractors because there was no one out there." In several programs, there were no bidders: a program for developmentally disabled children under the age of three; a residential program for older developmentally disabled persons; and a program for homeless shelters. The county had to work closely with potential contractors to develop an interest in the programs and a capacity to perform them. In a different program, a home for minority boys, there were four bidders, which for the county was a lot of competition.

Dane County's problems in finding qualified contractors to deliver its social services is scarcely unusual. A survey of mental health contracting in Massachusetts found that each request-for-proposals issued by the state mental health department received just 1.7 responses. Two-thirds of the competitively bid contracts had responses from just one vendor, and only 15 percent had responses from two vendors. When state managers encountered problems in finding enough interested contractors, they obtained a waiver of the requirement for competitive bids. The easy way was to declare that a given contract required "unique capabilities" that only one vendor could meet. The state auditor found in 1982 that such "unique capabilities were a common feature; 75 percent of the state's contract administrators said that the lack of qualified providers inhibited competition" (Schlesinger, Dorwart, and Pulice, 1986, pp. 251–252). A study of mental health contracting in Arizona found a similar pattern. The level of contractor competition was so low that the authors described it as a "provider-dominated system" (Milward, Provan, and Else, 1993). In North Carolina, the "availability of suppliers" was a big problem for 42 percent of county officials (Cigler, 1990). Because of the small number of contractors in Michigan social service programs, "officials were often forced to give contracts to the only available providers, even though they did not always conform to the government's priorities" (DeHoog, 1984, p. 130).

What competition does exist tends to spring up in direct response to the presence of state and local contracts (Schlesinger, Dorwart, and Pulice, 1986). The other side of this issue is that government funds represent most of the revenue for many contractors. Lobes said, "For most contractors, we are the big player" in their budgets. The result is less a competitive market than a negotiated network. There are relatively few suppliers and often only one buyer. Information about what contractors can do is often meager, and social service technology—how to achieve the goals that the programs envision—is highly imperfect (DeHoog, 1990).

Neither side in the transaction, in fact, *wants* competition for many of the reasons that Kelman suggested. For the contractors, competition is a threat to their operations and thus to be avoided. In fact, social service contractors frequently become important political forces. As Lobes explained, "They present a real power. They've organized themselves into consortia and are very politically active." When budget cuts have threatened the department's programs, the consortia of contractors have frequently been the most active in the battle to save the programs.

For the local government, competition and the potential for replacing contractors threatens the consistency of the programs. In dealing with troubled persons, as is the case by definition in most social service programs, continuity of care is important. "You might compete at the front end to get in," Lobes said, "but once you get in, it tends to be a network. There has to be a stability in the system." Massachusetts scholars found the same thing. "Many programs may, therefore, to protect what they perceive as quality care, act to discourage competition" (Schlesinger, Dorwart, and Pulice, 1986, p. 252). That promotes a tendency to develop long-term relationships with contractors that social service managers know and trust, and dependence becomes mutual (Milward, Provan, and Else, 1993).

Competition is by its very nature disruptive to social services. It imposes high transaction costs on both the buyer—the government—and the seller—the contractor (DeHoog, 1990). If social service contracting is the child of the privatization movement, with its reverence for competition, it is a prodigal child. Virtually no one directly involved in the social service system—government, contractor, or client—has any incentive to disrupt the system once it is established. To the degree that social service contracting produces lower costs, it is by replacing government workers with contractors' workers, who often receive lower wages and less attractive fringe benefits.

Because wage and fringe benefit rates are open to competition, moreover, Dane County often had a difficult time judging the relative bids of contractors. The work was labor-intensive, so most differences between competing bids—when there were competing bids—rested on differences in wage and, especially, fringe benefit rates. County officials worried about whether they wanted to reward low bidders with contracts when the bids were lower because of a thin fringe benefit package. They struggled over whether they ought to find a way to make the playing field more level.

In the process, reliance on contractors has created an important new political force that works hard to keep the business coming. The monopolistic behavior of government, which lay at the core of the privatization arguments, has been replaced by monopolistic behavior on the part of its contractors.

Defining Goals

Both the nature of social services, with imprecise goals and uncertain technologies, and the nature of the social service system, with complex public-private partnerships, combine to make defining goals difficult. Contractors naturally resist goals that are too specific or that hold them to standards they cannot achieve. Governments cannot prescribe in advance exactly what outcomes they want or, if they know the outcomes, they cannot explain how to get there. This is a difficult enough problem for direct service provision. For a system of contracting, where precise definition of work is the keystone, the problem is far more difficult. In fact, in a survey of North Carolina counties, respondents rated the problem of what should be written into contracts as the top information problem they had to solve (Cigler, 1990).

Dane County has attempted to solve the problem in two ways. First, instead of defining in the contract what goals are to be achieved, contracts define units of service to be performed. A contract might specify, for example, the number of hours of consultant time to be provided, or the number of persons to be served. Contracts thus have tended to define input or process measures, not outcome measures. Second, these process measures have not been defined by the county but are negotiated with the contractor. With only eleven workers supervising the entire system, there is no way for any of them to know precisely what level of service is reasonable under a given budget. Setting the standards in consultation with the contractor who will have to meet them is the natural response.

These two steps predictably create two problems. First, because the goals are defined in terms of inputs, not outputs, it is difficult if not impossible to determine what Dane County's programs are truly accomplishing. It is a maxim in the social service business that activity alone cannot guarantee results. Given the nature of the activity, the contract mechanism, and the workforce devoted to contract management, definition of inputs is about the most the county can do. Second, because the relationship between buyer and seller is not at arm's length—that is, because goals are negotiated and not set in a competitive market—the government loses leverage and undercuts its oversight. In a competitive market, other suppliers are free to offer the same services at a lower cost, or better services for the same cost. In a negotiated market, the exchange is what the buyer and seller make of it. Without the information a market generates, it is difficult to determine what the goals ought to be.

Monitoring Performance

Because defining the goals is difficult, so too is judging results. In Dane County, there has been little real oversight of the system. Just eleven workers can scarcely do much more than quickly check the contractor-supplied paperwork on $60 million in programs. The county provides little automation to back up contract supervision, so it is difficult for contract managers even to know what what is happening with the money. Most of the oversight consists of self-reporting by contractors and constant demands by contractors for more money.

In meetings of the elected county board, the contractors frequently point to long waiting lists as a measure of the success of their services. Because their services are so good, they reason, demand grows and their waiting lists lengthen. With people in need, shouldn't more money be allocated to shorten the waiting lists? There is, of course, no methodology for compiling the waiting lists, and it is easy to manufacture lengthy ones. For some services, moreover, the waiting lists are meaningless. If a person walks in the door with drug or alcohol problems and cannot be treated, the opportunity is lost. A waiting list for such a program provides no information about the program's effectiveness; it does, however, increase the political power of the contractors. "Because we haven't been automated" to get good information on contractors' performance, Lobes noted, "we've been dogmeat" in the political battles over increasing funding for some programs. Without that information, "it becomes hard to manage a private provider with lots of clout."

With little oversight possible, Dane County social service managers have worked to keep the system stable. There is little reason to change vendors if the effects of the change cannot be measured. Any change, moreover, would disrupt the lives of the people the services are designed to help. Thus, not only does Dane County know relatively little about how well its contracted-out social service programs are working, but it also has strong incentives to reduce the system's volatility. The results are even more steps away from the assumptions of competition underlying the privatization prescription.

In fact, if there is any overriding consensus on social service contracting in state and local governments, it is that oversight is virtually nonexistent. "Actually, most agencies do not know what their costs are, and others do not consider it worth the cost to find out," John Rehfuss reports. Because most contracts do not have clear standards and state and local governments devote few resources to measuring results, most governments do not know what they are buying (1990, pp. 45–46). In Arizona, it is reported: "The degree of performance evaluation is very low. It is close to nonexistent. There was no attempt by the state department of health services to monitor the performance of the local providers. The department of health services stated that they did not have the administrative capacity to engage in performance evaluation" (Milward, Provan, and Else, 1993). Nearly two-thirds of North Carolina county administrators reported that "difficulty in managing the performance of contracts" was the "greatest disadvantage" in contracting out (Cigler, 1990, p. 293).

Two Michigan state departments charged with managing social service programs generally failed to conduct on-site inspections and relied instead on self-reporting by the contractors (DeHoog, 1984). In Massachusetts, the level of oversight was so low that the state embarrassed itself by paying contractors who delivered no service at all. In fact, without effective monitoring, contracts "may degenerate into what are effective monopolies for the private vendors" (Schlesinger, Dorwart, and Pulice, 1986, pp. 248, 254).

Thus it is no exaggeration to say that state and local governments tend not to know what they are buying through their social service contracts. Because competition is low, they have little opportunity to test the market to see what alternatives they have, few resources are spent to look past what the contractors themselves report, and there is little interest in the political system for digging deeper. The problems with oversight underline earlier observations: whatever advantages contracting out for social services might produce, greater efficiency through market-tested competition is not one of them. State and local governments are engaging in the equivalent of a shopping trip while blindfolded, with little effort spent to squeeze the tomatoes or thump the watermelons.

Service Coordination

Because of the complexity of the service networks, service coordination has become more difficult. At the core of many social service problems is a complex of issues: children, for example, who are developmentally disabled, in ill health, from poor and sometimes single-parent households where the parent needs job training to secure a better career. Coordination of services for such problems has always been daunting within the public sector, but for contractor-based services, the problem is even worse. The job of the contractor is to meet the terms of the contract; accountability—to the degree to which there is accountability—is to the narrow terms of the work defined within the agreement. Service coordination, on the other hand, demands great flexibility and attention not to activity levels (with the service as the focus) but to the client (with the person's needs as the focus).

Dane County executive Rick Phelps, for example, proposed to coordinate social service programs for children at the county's schools: "Families should not have to navigate their way through a bewildering array of unconnected services where no one is responsible for their overall condition. And we can't expect families to use services if they are offered far from home, in inaccessible, inconvenient settings, removed from easy public transportation connections. Coherent programs of services must be offered close to where people live and they must be oriented toward helping children succeed in school" (Phelps, 1992). He reasoned that the schools were the one place where children in need regularly encountered the government. If education and the social services to support that education were combined in one place, the local school, the services would be more effective and the children would be better off. The strategy, Phelps believed, would also draw parents into the building, which could not help but strengthen both the social service and education program.

The plan embodied some of the principal themes that Lisbeth B. Schorr championed in *Within Our Reach* (1988). Phelps's plan, however, soon encountered two major problems. First, the administrative apparatus itself was incredibly complex. The county managed most social services, although within Madison the city government had responsibility for most programs. Each town had its own school system, independent of the county, so each town's school district was a separate player with whom Phelps would have to negotiate to make the plan work. The county's own social services workers resisted the plan because it was so different from their usual work procedures. The nearly forty contractors working just on children and youth services had no incentive to cooperate, because their contracts specified units of work and not collaborative processes.

The fragmentation of the system was both immense and obvious. The underlying issue was the consequence for the recipients of the services. The most important observation underlying Phelps's proposal was that Dane County's social service system, like those nearly everywhere, was organized for the providers and not for the recipients. The primary advantage of contracting out is alleged to be responsiveness to the customer, in price and quality. In the system of contracting out social service, just who *is* the customer? In Dane County, the county "buys" the service, but on behalf of citizens in need. These citizens are the ultimate customer, but the market is not structured to register their satisfaction.

The county's Department of Human Services, in fact, is moving toward a quality management scheme to get its own employees to begin thinking of service recipients as "customers" instead of the time-worn word "clients." The hope of county social service managers is to encourage workers to behave more responsively to citizens. How can state and local governments do the same through a system of contractors? The customer, the one the contractor must satisfy, is the government, not the citizen. The government in turn must represent the citizens' needs to the contractor and ensure that the contractor responds. At best, the system is more complex than direct service provision by the government. At worst, it is not only more complex but also less responsive, as citizens lose the direct link to the organizations serving them.

Accountability

As John Johnston has pointed out, the increasing use of contractors has created a mixed service delivery system. In traditional administration, the basic players were elected officials, administrators, and citizens. With the addition of contractors, the players increase to four. "The number of relationships has doubled and the complexity has increased exponentially," he argues (1986, p. 550). As Figure 8.1 illustrates, contractors assume a critical new position as intermediaries in the governmental system.[2] They stand between the governmental apparatus — elected officials and administrators — and citizens. Because they stand on the front lines of service delivery, they

Figure 8.1. Accountability in the Social Service Network.

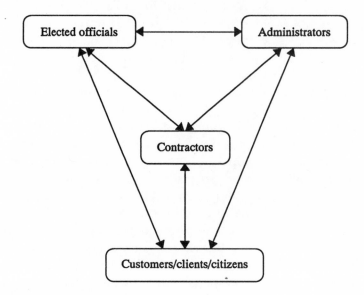

Source: Johnston, 1986, p. 550.

have direct relationships with citizens, independent of the officials. Administrators are charged with supervising them, while their considerable political power gives them a direct linkage with elected officials that transcends their administrative role.

For Dane County social service managers, the independent political clout of the contractors coupled with the managers' relative lack of knowledge about their performance make it hard to crack down—even if the managers were inclined to do so, which because of the drive to ensure continuity of service they are not. The contractors have constructed a direct, independent, and powerful line to the county board, which makes basic policy. In case of trouble, they can appeal over the heads of the administrators charged with supervising their contracts and make their cases directly with the board. Far less clear is how the customer/client/citizen fits into this scheme.

The philosophy of contracting out presumes that the basic relationship between government and contractor will be that of principal and agent. The contractor's job is to act as agent of the government's policy. The government-as-principal, however, is fractured, because the contractors have created independent links with the board and the Human Services Department. The contractor, moreover, is less agent than partner, helping to shape the very design of the program, left with relatively little oversight, and benefiting from the county's dependence on its performance.

Network Management and the Public Service

As federal and state mandates and opportunities have increased, most state and local governments have followed a conscious strategy to rely on contractors instead of increasing their own civil service employment. This pragmatic strategy met a happy match in the theories supporting privatization, particularly in the alleged advantages of the market over government. Especially in social service programs, however, the assumptions underlying the privatization movement have provided more political cover than supporting logic. Competition for government contracts has often been minimal. Both the goals of the services and the prices to be charged are set by negotiation rather than by the market. Government has developed little independent expertise to judge what the market has provided it. In the end, the relationship has been less one between buyer and seller and more one between mutually dependent parties. The relationships, in fact, have been far less market-based than a complex of networks, intricately woven together in ways that pose important new problems of accountability for government and its programs.[3]

What is required of state and local public servants to manage such networks effectively? For such programs to work well, government and its officials must first know what they want to buy. Second, they must know where to shop, and, as I have pointed out earlier, in government programs in general and social services in particular, this is easier said than done. Finally, they must know what they have bought when they have bought it.

The middle piece of this chain is troublesome. Competition for government contracts often is slight, and the government's options for shopping around frequently are few. The more troublesome the middle of the chain, the more important are the links on either end—and these links are where state and local governments have experienced the most difficulty. It is on these links that they have most chronically underinvested; they have tended to rely instead on contractors themselves to tell them what to buy. Cigler, in fact, points out that 61 percent of the counties she surveyed in North Carolina contracted out the development of background studies for new projects, 23 percent contracted out program evaluation, and 19 percent contracted out benefit cost analysis (1990). The contracting out of such studies, coupled with heavy reliance on service contractors to define what performance terms ought to be in their contracts, lessen government's ability to define what to buy.

If the government has had a hard time identifying what to buy, it has experienced even greater problems in knowing what it has bought. Program monitoring is almost always the weakest link in the chain. State and local governments tend to presume—or to behave as if they do—that hiring a contractor consistently produces high-quality services, but even a cursory glance at social services in any jurisdiction demonstrates that good performance is not automatic. Without at least minimal oversight, however, governments have no way of knowing which of their programs are working well and which are not. They have no way of fine-tuning their service-delivery systems to improve programs. And with citizens placed in a far more complex chain, the ability of governments to ensure that their citizens are treated well diminishes. "Contracting out doesn't solve our problems," Dane County's Carol Lobes pointed out. "It just brings new ones."

As state and local governments come to rely more on contractors for a wide range of activities, especially for social services, they can ensure quality performance at the lowest possible price only if they can act as smart buyers. The evidence is that state and local governments now are not investing nearly enough in program oversight. These activities, moreover, require a new breed of state and local government managers who can act as smart buyers. The level of dedication of state and local workers is undoubtedly high, but their training is all too often not up to the level demanded by the emerging contracting networks.

The difference between traditional social service delivery, with front-line social workers seeking to put clients together with the services they need, and a contracting network, with a handful of managers responsible for over-seeing a vast array of contractors, could scarcely be greater. All too often, social service contract managers rise through the direct-service ranks to take on the broad management tasks without adequate training. State and local governments must find new ways to develop four skills in particular: strategic management; customer focus; negotiating skills; and monitoring, oversight, and information management.

Strategic Management. Two basic facts muddle state and local management of their contractors. First, there usually are far more contractors than there are administrators charged with supervising them. Second, these administrators frequently rise to these positions not because of their skills in contract oversight but because of their technical skills in the functional area to which the agency is assigned. Case workers become social service contract managers, for example. Although such experience is useful in providing background for what happens in the field, it can hurt oversight. A front-lines perspective can focus the manager's attention on the minutiae of administrative activities and blind him or her to the broader policy issues at play. Training in strategic management—in how to focus on a sense of the big picture from the details swirling around the manager—is the first step in building effective contract management.

Customer Focus. The old language, which called recipients of government help "clients," especially in social service programs, raises a pair of problems. It signals a paternalism that does not match recent government programs. It also misses the need to tailor the system to serve the citizens' problems, instead of developing a system that provides services. The distinction between a service-dispensing system and a customer-focused system is a sharp one. Given the complexity of the government's service system, only an emphasis on the citizen-as-customer can help government solve the immense problems of coordinating a vast array of services.

Negotiating Skills. State and local contract administrators are, in fact, less managers than negotiators. They have often few choices of contractors, little clear guidance on what goals they ought to accomplish, uncertain technology for translating goals into action, and only a vague sense of what they are buying. Furthermore, they are in charge of a system where consistency in service delivery is often more important than low cost. In such a system, full of information gaps and uncertainties, their job is often one of problem solver. That demands skills in conflict resolution and negotiation, which often are not skills developed within the contracting bureaucracy—and in social service agencies in particular.

Monitoring, Oversight, and Information Management. Oversight is often both the critical link in the smart-buyer chain and the weakest link in state and local management. Beefing up the capacity of state and local governments—and of their managers—to monitor program effectively is the most important requirement for improved management of government-through-contract. This, in turn, demands not only basic skills in program monitoring and evaluation but also sound training in information management. The very fact that a handful of Dane County administrators must supervise 360 contracts suggests that only great facility in manipulating large quantities of data, and considerable skill in uncovering problems in such volumes of information, can promote effective management.

A mixed service network has evolved under cover of the privatization rhetoric, but its operation is very different than theorists would have predicted. The conclusion is not that this is bad, or that privatization is dysfunctional. The rise of contracting is a product of citizens' demands that government be made more flexible, more responsive, and less costly, and there is considerable evidence that contracting out helps accomplish each of these objectives. At the same time, however, it creates a very different set of relationships among administrators, elected officials, and citizens. The challenges for effective public services in such a system are enormous. Only a vigorous public service, invigorated by training that is up to the new challenges it faces, is likely to ensure that government meets those challenges.

Conclusion

The rhetoric of privatization has developed a life of its own quite apart from the realities of managing complex and interdependent state and local programs. State and local governments have been relying on contracts far longer than the privatization debate has been going on, so debating whether or not state and local governments ought to engage in contracting out is the wrong place to start. They already do, and they have come to depend on contractors for producing a remarkable range of their services. Thus, the question is how to make the mixed public-private-nonprofit contracting system work effectively and responsively.

State and local governments are unlikely to be able to make the markets for the goods and services they purchase more competitive. Significant imperfections, especially limited bidders for specialized contracts in social services, are inevitable because of the very nature of the services. More competition, and the instability that competition brings, is not the answer. Rather, state and local governments must become far better at defining what they want to buy. Even more important, state and local governments must develop much greater capacity to know what they have bought. The two ends of the contracting-out chain — defining the service and measuring the results — are the critical links.

Some of this fresh capacity has to come from a recognition by political leaders that investment in management capacity is the only way to ensure effective and efficient services. The markets in which state and local governments contract will not regulate themselves. Building this capacity, in turn, requires new skills in a new breed of public managers, trained in strategic management, a customer-based focus, negotiating techniques, and evaluation research.

Even greater political leadership and management capacity, however, will not be enough unless we all recognize that the growth of contracting out has fundamentally changed the face of government. The biggest failing of the privatization rhetoric is that it attempts to reassert and redefine the boundaries between the public and private sectors. The lesson that state and local governments teach is that contracting out blurs, not defines, these boundaries. Government-by-contract is less a buyer-seller relationship than a network in which government is only one, although perhaps the most important, player. Such networks bring great problems of service coordination as well as continuity in care for service recipients.

As governments come to operate more in such networks, their officials and citizens must redefine government's role. It is not to control programs or even to deliver services. Government cannot control programs to which it is only a partial contributor but instead must develop a new role: to integrate the different pieces of the network so that citizens-as-customers are served most effectively. Contracts, whether shaped by the lure of government dollars or by the market dynamics of supply and demand, cannot look on the broader issues of the public interest. That is the job of government and its officials, and it is a job made more challenging yet also more important by the government's growing reliance on contractors.

Notes

1. Unless otherwise noted, information about Dane County and all quotations come from an interview conducted on June 11, 1992, with Dane County Department of Human Services director Carol Lobes.
2. This figure is derived from a figure introduced by Johnston (1986, p. 550).
3. On the role of such networks in government programs, see Milward, Provan, and Else (1993); Chisholm (1989); and Landau (1991).

References

Allen, J. W., and others. *The Private Sector in State Service Delivery*. Washington, D.C.: Urban Institute Press, 1989.

American Federation of State, County, and Municipal Employees (AFSCME). *Passing the Bucks: The Contracting Out of Public Services*. Washington, D.C.: American Federation of State, County, and Municipal Employees, 1984.

American Federation of State, County, and Municipal Employees (AFSCME). *When Public Services Go Private: Not Always Better, Not Always Honest, There May Be a Better Way*. Washington, D.C.: American Federation of State, County, and Municipal Employees, 1987.

Ben-Ner, A., and Van Hoomissen, T. "A Study of the Nonprofit Sector in New York State: Its Size, Nature, and Economic Impact." Albany: Nelson A. Rockefeller Institute of Government, State University of New York, 1989.

Berenyi, D. B., and Stevens, B. J. "Does Privatization Work? A Study of the Delivery of Eight Local Services." *State and Local Government Review*, 1988, *20*, 11–20.

Chi, K. S., Devlin, K. M., and Masterman, W. "Use of the Private Sector in Delivery of Human Services." In J. W. Allen and others, *The Private Sector in State Service Delivery*. Washington, D.C.: Urban Institute Press, 1989.

Chisholm, D. *Coordination Without Authority*. Berkeley: University of California Press, 1989.

Chubb, J. E., and Moe, T. M. *Politics, Markets, and America's Schools*. Washington, D.C.: Brookings Institution, 1990.

Cigler, B. A. "County Contracting: Reconciling the Accountability and Information Paradoxes." *Public Administration Quarterly*, 1990, *14*, 285–301.

Coleman, W. G. *State and Local Government and Public-Private Partnerships: A Policy Issues Handbook*. New York: Greenwood Press, 1989.

DeHoog, R. H. *Contracting Out for Human Services: Economic, Political, and Organizational Perspectives*. Albany: State University of New York Press, 1984.

DeHoog, R. H. "Competition, Negotiation, or Cooperation: Three Models for Service Contracting." *Administration and Society*, 1990, *22*, 317–540.

Derthick, M. *Uncontrollable Spending for Social Services Grants*. Washington, D.C.: Brookings Institution, 1975.

Donahue, J. D. *The Privatization Decision: Public Ends, Private Means*. New York: Basic Books, 1989.

Fisk, D., Kiesling, H., and Muller, T. *Private Provision of Public Services: An Overview*. Washington, D.C.: Urban Institute Press, 1978.

Hatry, H. P. *A Review of Private Approaches for Delivery of Public Services*. Washington, D.C.: Urban Institute Press, 1983.

Hatry, H. P., Morley, E., Barbour, G. P., Jr., and Pajunen, S. M. *Excellence in Managing: Practical Experiences from Community Development Agencies*. Washington, D.C.: Urban Institute Press, 1991.

International City Management Association (ICMA). *Service Delivery in the 90s: Alternative Approaches for Local Governments.* Washington, D.C.: International City Management Association, 1989.

Johnston, J. "Public Servant and Private Contractors: Managing the Mixed Service Delivery Systems." *Canadian Public Administration,* 1986, *29,* 549–553.

Kammerman, S. B., and Kahn, A. J. (eds.). *Privatization and the Welfare State.* Princeton, N.J.: Princeton University Press, 1989.

Kelman, S. *Procurement and Public Management: The Fear of Discretion and the Quality of Government Performance.* Washington, D.C.: American Enterprise Institute, 1990.

Kettl, D. F. *Managing Community Development in the New Federalism.* New York: Praeger, 1980.

Kettl, D. F. "Privatization: Implications for the Public Work Force." In C. Ban and N. Riccucci (eds.), *Public Personnel Management: Current Concerns — Future Challenges.* New York: Longman, 1991.

Landau, M. "Multiorganizational Systems in Public Administration." *Journal of Public Administration Research and Theory,* 1991, *1,* 5–18.

Lauder Commission (New York State Senate Advisory Committee on Privatization). *Privatization for New York: Competing for a Better Future.* Albany: New York State Senate Advisory Committee on Privatization, 1992.

Mercer Group. "The 1990 Privatization Survey." Atlanta, Ga.: Mercer Group, 1990.

Mercer, J. L. "Growing Opportunities in Public Service Contracting." *Harvard Business Review,* 1983, *83,* 178, 186, 188.

Milward, H. B., Provan, K. G., and Else, B. "What Does the Hollow State Look Like?" In B. Bozeman (ed.), *Public Management Theory.* San Francisco: Jossey-Bass, 1993.

Nathan, R. P., and Associates. *Block Grants for Community Development.* Washington, D.C.: U.S. Government Printing Office, 1977.

Nathan, R. P., and Associates. *Public Service Employment: A Field Evaluation.* Washington, D.C.: Brookings Institution, 1981.

National Commission for Employment Policy. *Privatization and Public Employees: The Impact of City and County Contracting Out on Government Workers.* Washington, D.C.: U.S. Government Printing Office, 1988.

O'Neill, M. *The Third America: The Emergence of the Nonprofit Sector in the United States.* San Francisco: Jossey-Bass, 1989.

Osborne, D., and Gaebler, T. *Reinventing Government.* Reading, Mass.: Addison-Wesley, 1992.

Perry, J. L., and Babitsky, T. T. "Comparative Performance in Urban Bus Transit: Assessing Privatization Strategies." *Public Administration Review,* 1986, *46,* 57–66.

Phelps, R. J. "Joining Forces for Families: Reaffirming Dane County's Commitment to Children." Address to the Downtown Rotary, Madison, May 1992.

Primeaux, W. "An Assessment of X-Efficiency Gained Through Competition." *Review of Economics and Statistics,* 1977, *59,* 105–108.

Rehfuss, J. A. *Contracting Out in Government.* San Francisco: Jossey-Bass, 1989.

Rehfuss, J. A. "Contracting Out and Accountability in State and Local Governments—The Importance of Contracting Monitoring." *State and Local Government Review,* 1990, *22,* 44–48.

Rubenstein, E. S. "Medicaid." In Lauder Commission (New York State Senate Advisory Committee on Privatization), *Privatization for New York: Competing for a Better Future.* Albany: New York State Senate Advisory Committee on Privatization, 1992.

Savas, E. S. *Privatizing the Public Sector: How to Shrink Government.* Chatham, N.J.: Chatham House, 1982.

Savas, E. S. *Privatization: The Key to Better Government.* Chatham, N.J.: Chatham House, 1987.

Savas, E. S. "Introduction." In Lauder Commission (New York State Senate Advisory Committee on Privatization), *Privatization for New York: Competing for a Better Future.* Albany: New York State Senate Advisory Committee on Privatization, 1992.

Schlesinger, M., Dorwart, R. A., and Pulice, R. T. "Competitive Bidding and States' Purchase of Services: The Case of Mental Health Care in Massachusetts." *Journal of Policy Analysis and Management,* 1986, *5,* 245–263.

Schorr, L. B. *Within Our Reach: Breaking the Cycle of Disadvantage.* New York: Anchor Press, 1988.

Smith, S. R., and Lipsky, M. *Nonprofit for Hire: The Welfare State and the Age of Contracting.* Cambridge, Mass.: Harvard University Press, 1993.

Touche Ross. *Privatization in America.* Washington, D.C.: Touche Ross, 1987.

Williamson, O. E. *The Economic Institutions of Capitalism: Firms, Markets, and Relational Contracting.* New York: Free Press, 1985.

PART FOUR

The
Health Care
Challenge

NINE

Between a Rock and a Hard Place:
How Public Managers Manage Medicaid

Michael Sparer
Lawrence D. Brown

Once upon a time "public management" was understood to mean "public administration," which in turn connoted the faithful fulfillment by civil servants of policy (the ends and means set by political leaders). Today everyone recognizes that the ends of policy are too complex, and the means too ambiguous, to permit such managerial passivity. Public sector managers take up policies that are often incomplete and internally contradictory and refine and recast them so that they make sense in the real world. Managers innovate as they implement. They must balance the interests and intentions of policymakers with the concerns and constraints of those affected by particular policies. The more problematic the policy and the more dense (or recalcitrant) the universe of affected actors, the more difficult the managerial balancing act.

Medicaid surely ranks near the top of any list of programs posing the toughest managerial challenges. Not only is Medicaid policy extraordinarily problematic (as is health care policy more generally), but the universe of affected actors is both dense and difficult. Medicaid is a joint federal-state program with all the inherent tensions between federal desires for uniformity and equity and state concerns for diversity and flexibility. It is a program whose costs have soared lately — on average about 30 percent annually — but that cannot easily generate savings through eligibility cuts (only about 45 percent of the poor are covered by Medicaid now), benefit reductions (supposedly "easy" cuts in, for example, podiatry and chiropractic tend to save little but generate intense political heat), and lower provider payments (already so tight in many states as to jeopardize access to enrollees). It is a program whose size and explosive growth stimulate persistent efforts to contain costs but whose small, difficult "victories" on that score are often swamped by economic trends (recession means more unemployment and eligibility for welfare and Medicaid), social conditions (treatments for AIDS, mental illness, and drug abuse more often end up on the Medicaid budget), demographics (immigration), and national policy (for example, the recent series of federal mandates requiring the states to cover new groups). It is a federal-state enterprise in which federal frameworks and requirements tie the hands of state officials who, very much on the political and fiscal firing line, feel a constant need to improvise and innovate.

Medicaid is an entitlement program but one whose explicit links to welfare eligibility and the attendant stigmas complicate its political defense. It is, moreover, a welfare program of high political and economic salience to legions of providers (hospitals, physicians, nursing homes, mental health agencies). It is a program designed for such vulnerable populations as poor mothers and children but one that spends about half its funds on nursing home bills of the indigent elderly. And it is a program whose eligibility, benefit, and payment rules raise equity questions of a complexity rivaled only by those posed by every proposal to reform them.

If Medicaid appears to be virtually "uncontrollable," it is not hard to see why. Its numerous oddities make it a hard nettle to grasp, yet — given its rapidly growing costs — politicians have no choice but to try. Because Medicaid policy is perforce high on political leaders' agendas, it stands high on the agendas of managers who are often expected to devise acceptable answers to questions political leaders would prefer not to face forthrightly. As one observer in California put it: "Our state wants to be very generous. It wants the poor to have equal care, wants eligibility to be broad, wants to provide lots of services. But we don't fulfill the promise, and we maintain tight reimbursement. So the bureaucracy is given a broad mandate and little money and told to go make it work." Moreover, Medicaid managers must tackle this task despite federal rules that limit their discretion, opposition from savvy and influential interest groups, and a shrinking and often dispirited staff.

In this context, we present a study of what management means in Medicaid, and of how Medicaid managers cope with the complex balancing act they are asked to perform. We looked at four states: New York, California, Minnesota, and Mississippi. Aside from their obvious geographic diversity, each state offers a different political culture, policymaking environment, and administrative structure. We did extensive interviews and reviewed many documents. Here we try to distill both general patterns and important differences among them. We do not know how generalizable our findings are to the other forty-six states; in any case, we hope they are suggestive.

Who Manages Medicaid: The Four States Compared

The federal Medicaid law (enacted in 1965) provides federal funds to assist states to provide health insurance for poor people. Federal law also establishes both broad guidelines and specific regulations that all state Medicaid programs must follow. State officials retain significant discretion, however, to determine who in their state receives Medicaid coverage, what medical services are covered, and how much medical providers are paid for delivering care. State officials manage their Medicaid programs, under the intermittently watchful eye of the Health Care Financing Administration of the United States Department of Health and Human Services. Although states are required to designate a "single state agency" as their primary Medicaid manager, the federal government is uninvolved in the selection process. Who manages Medicaid is therefore a political issue resolved differently in different states.

The locus of Medicaid management emerged early on as a battleground for Medicaid policymakers. In some states (like California) the battle was between those who favored an expansive program and those who wanted to emphasize cost containment. In other states (like Mississippi) the battle reflected a continuing power struggle between the governor and the legislature. With such struggles commonplace, the nation never developed a model Medicaid management system. Different agencies with different skills and different bureaucratic missions manage different Medicaid programs.

Who and where are these Medicaid managers? They appear in complex institutional settings that generally include both departments of social services (welfare) and of health. Other agencies and actors often join the act as well: state offices of management and budget are often prominent players, as may be human services superagencies, state (and county) offices of aging and of mental health, and more. And the feds are never far from the action: many innovations require federal waivers that consume considerable managerial time and effort. Much management lies of course in the hands of civil servants in the lower and middle ranks of the agencies that handle the program. Our main concern here, however, is not with these but rather with the upper-level managers, at and near the rank of director of the Medicaid program, who oversee the civil servants. In other words, we address not routine administrative tasks but rather tasks in the larger context of enfolding strategies for managing (which may mean transforming) the Medicaid program.

Our high-level Medicaid managers are for the most part people who took (and keep) their jobs because of a purposive commitment to the program's goals. Most would like to expand benefits to a deserving clientele; they recognize, however, that the fiscal and political realities of the early 1990s make significant expansion difficult if not impossible. Their central and immediate objective, therefore, is to protect the program, to introduce into it defensible changes that preserve its benefits and other positive features while holding the line on costs. This quest requires new strategies to promote efficiency and productivity, to get more bang from the Medicaid buck. The managerial challenge today is increasingly one of cost-effectiveness. Fiscal necessity is the mother of policy invention, and Medicaid managers are key players in the new benefit-cost balancing act that protection and enhancement of the program now demand. But before describing these balancing strategies, and the barriers that they confront, we first review who manages Medicaid in the four states under review, and we provide a brief overview of the Medicaid programs that they manage.

New York

New York's Medicaid program is the nation's most expensive: in 1991, the program spent nearly $16 billion on approximately 2.4 million residents (New York State Department of Social Services, 1991a). There are many reasons for the high costs, including the unusually high reimbursement to nursing home providers, the state's generous benefit package (particularly its expansive home health care program), and a relatively liberal set of eligibility guidelines. The result is that New York accounts for approximately 17.5 percent of the nation's Medicaid bill, though it has less than 10 percent of the nation's Medicaid clients (National Governors' Association, 1991).

The size of New York's program makes the managers' task particularly challenging. The task is complicated, however, by the state's decision to divide management responsibility among several government agencies. This fragmentation began in the mid 1960s, as the state sought to designate the "single state agency" responsible for program administration. Governor Nelson Rockefeller and other Republican leaders proposed that the state's department of social welfare get the assignment. This proposal was opposed by legislative Democrats, who did not view Medicaid as a welfare program, and therefore they suggested instead the state's health department. With both sides anxious to claim credit for a bold new social program, a compromise was hastily drafted: the welfare department would be the "single state agency," but it was required to delegate administration of "medical" issues (facility certification, provider reimbursement, quality control, and more) to the health department. To complicate matters further, the state then delegated to the fifty-seven local social services districts the jobs of processing applications for Medicaid eligibility and (until the early 1980s) paying provider bills. In short, management of New York's Medicaid program is fragmented horizontally and decentralized vertically.

The welfare department (now called the department of social services) and the health department have occasionally lobbied for more centralized management authority, and county officials often propose an increased state role in Medicaid administration, but these efforts have invariably failed. Indeed, the state legislature has generally adopted the opposite approach, choosing greater decentralization whenever possible. A case in point is New York's ambitious Medicaid managed care initiative, adopted in 1991, which seeks to enroll 50 percent of the state's Medicaid clients in managed care plans in the next five years. The local social services districts oversee this managed care initiative.

Over the years, the fragmentation of Medicaid management encouraged an expansive and expensive program: cost containment was a low priority for many Medicaid managers, particularly those in the various social services agencies. Now, however, with the state's perpetual fiscal crisis, Medicaid managers tend to seek a common goal: a more cost-effective and efficient program.

California

California's Medicaid program (called Medi-Cal) covers 1.3 million more people than does New York's but spends around $8 billion fewer dollars doing so (California Department of Finance, 1991). What explains this curious outcome? One answer is that Medi-Cal managers enjoy unusual discretion over reimbursement policy and have used that discretion to keep provider reimbursement relatively low. The average California nursing home, for example, receives approximately $65 per day for each Medi-Cal patient; a similar facility in New York gets over $120 per day (California Department of Health Services, 1991; New York State Department of Social Services, 1991b).

The managerial focus on cost containment is rooted in the mid 1960s political battle to control the Medi-Cal bureaucracy. The early favorite to be named Medi-Cal manager was the California Department of Social Welfare (DSW), an arm of the state's health and welfare umbrella agency (HWA), which then administered a range of other indigent health care programs. But that choice was strongly opposed by governor-elect Ronald Reagan, who was critical of the liberal DSW director and who wanted Medi-Cal managers with more cost-containment commitment. Reagan won this political battle when he persuaded the legislature to require HWA to create a new "health" division to administer Medi-Cal. This victory enabled Reagan to install a Medi-Cal management team that implemented his policy preferences with a minimum of organizational conflict.

Today Medi-Cal cost-containment efforts cannot focus on reducing provider reimbursement rates that are already quite low. Indeed, officials face significant pressure to increase provider payments. Medi-Cal officials come by a different route to the same challenge facing their New York counterparts: how to get more bang for the Medicaid buck.

Mississippi

When Congress enacted Medicaid, it feared that several poorer and more conservative states would elect not to participate. To encourage these states

Congress varied the percentage of the Medicaid dollar financed by federal funds by state wealth: the poorer the state, the higher the federal percentage. An obvious target of this provision was Mississippi, the nation's poorest state and (particularly in the mid 1960s) one of the most conservative. Under the federal financing system, Mississippi could charge nearly 80 percent of each Medicaid dollar to Washington. With such easy financing, even the arch-conservative governor, John Bell Williams, became a (reluctant) Medicaid supporter.

There was, however, a fierce dispute over who would manage the controversial new program. Governor Williams proposed the state health department, but the legislature, which dominated Mississippi politics, was unwilling to delegate such authority to an executive agency. The legislature instead created a special Medicaid commission, composed of four legislators and three members of the public. Mississippi thus became one of only four states to establish a separate agency to run their Medicaid program (the others are Alabama, Georgia, and Virginia) (United States Congress, 1988). Because Mississippi's new Medicaid commission, and the staff it hired, answered primarily to the legislature, the governor was (once again) deprived of executive power.

The legislature suffered a significant blow in 1983 when Governor William Winter successfully challenged the constitutionality of the legislative commission model, on the grounds that it unlawfully usurped executive authority. In response to this judicial decision, the legislature delegated the ministerial tasks of Medicaid management to a newly created agency located in the governor's office. Nonetheless, the legislature retained for itself key managerial functions, including the authority to set reimbursement rates (a task delegated to Medicaid bureaucrats in most other states). Medicaid management in Mississippi is, as a result, unusually complicated and difficult.

Minnesota

By all accounts, the Minnesota Medicaid program has experienced less bureaucratic infighting than its counterparts elsewhere. The explanation for this anomaly seems to be twofold. First, neither the state legislature nor the state's health department expressed organizational interest in managing Medicaid: by unanimous consent, the state's Department of Welfare (now the Department of Human Services, or DHS) thus became the agency in charge. Second, the Medicaid managers employed by DHS stayed on the job for many years (in sharp contrast to the high turnover that plagued most other states). Bob Baird, for example, was the state's Medicaid director from 1972 until he retired in mid 1992, and many senior DHS officials worked with Baird for most of his tenure.

Over the years, the state's Medicaid managers earned the trust of their political supervisors, and the program itself earned a reputation as innovative and responsive. In this context, it is hardly surprising that when Minnesota recently enacted legislation to ease its health care crisis, it delegated to Medicaid officials the responsibility of administering the centerpiece of that legislation, the MinnesotaCare program, which provides state-funded assistance to the uninsured.

But administrative stability cannot by itself cure the raging price inflation that today burdens Minnesota's Medicaid program. Between 1984 and 1989, for example, Medicaid expenditures in Minnesota increased slowly: from approximately $920 million to $1.2 billion. Since 1989, however, costs have exploded and are now well over $2 billion. Although there are explanations for the rising costs (ranging from program enrollment growth to general medical inflation to federally mandated provider reimbursement increases), the bottom line is clear: Medicaid managers in Minnesota face the same challenge now befuddling their counterparts around the country — how to do more with less.

How Medicaid Managers Manage: Six Strategies for the 1990s

Medicaid managers run very different programs, and they do so in very different bureaucracies, as our review of New York, California, Mississippi, and Minnesota suggests. But Medicaid managers today face a common problem (rising costs) and share a common goal (reducing costs without undermining program integrity). At least in these four states, they have adopted strikingly similar strategies for meeting this goal. In this section, we describe and illustrate these strategies.

Reorganize the Health Care Delivery System

According to JoAnn Costantino, a high-ranking manager of New York's Medicaid program, the best way to cut Medicaid costs, while preserving program integrity, is to promote more cost-effective health care. Most Medicaid managers agree and are devising means to improve the health care delivery system. This strategy is illustrated by the effort (in nearly every state) to develop and implement managed care initiatives, the attempt in New York to change the home care delivery system, and the battle in Mississippi to close inefficient and unnecessary public hospitals.

Consider, first, the increased emphasis on managed care, which many state policymakers take to be a promising answer to the health care crisis. This perception is particularly strong among Medicaid program officials, who believe that managed care systems can provide recipients with better health care and save money while doing so. The reasoning is that managed care systems will steer Medicaid clients away from expensive and often inappropriate hospital emergency rooms and toward inexpensive and more appropriate primary care physicians. Moreover, primary care physicians are expected to act as "gatekeepers," channeling client access to the health care system.

Two of the more instructive managed care initiatives are found in New York and California. In New York, a state with a relatively small managed care industry, state officials have handed local social services districts an ambitious task: to increase the number of Medicaid recipients in managed care from 100,000 to 1.2 million over the next five years (New York State Department of Social Services, 1991c). By contrast, in California, a state with a relatively strong managed care industry, state officials are implementing a more modest plan: to increase the number of Medicaid recipients in managed care from 530,000 to 1.25 million over the next five years (California Department of Health Services, 1992).

The managed care initiatives pose several challenges for Medicaid managers, chief among them to develop a sufficiently large network of managed care providers, adequately endowed with primary care physicians for poor people. Efforts to persuade large numbers of private physicians to participate have been hindered by the low fees Medicaid pays physicians and by the frequent unwillingness of physicians to accept Medicaid clients. A second option is to convince the health maintenance organization (HMO) industry (which now serves a primarily middle-class population) to expand its Medicaid clientele. A third strategy is to encourage hospitals (particularly large inner-city hospitals) to become major players in the managed care industry. The hospital-based HMO presumably would collect much of the revenue that the hospital emergency room loses in a managed care world. It is not easy, however, to persuade large hospitals to revise their internal operations, or to convince doctors and traditional HMOs to enroll Medicaid clients.

Medicaid directors also are working to change their state's long-term-care system. One example is New York's effort to shift its Medicaid-funded home care system, from one in which home care clients have their own home attendant, who spends an average of eight hours per day tending to their needs (Crystal, Flemming, Beck, and Smolka, 1987), to one in which attendants spend less time with particular clients and clients spend more time in social settings. One approach, adopted by most other states, sets strict limits on the number of covered home care hours. But New York's Medicaid managers prefer a different strategy, in which a small number of home attendants care for fifty or so clients, all of whom reside in the same building (or in the same neighborhood). Officials believe that this system of "shared aides" will both save money and encourage recipients to spend more time at local senior citizen centers and other supportive social environments. Not surprisingly, many clients and their advocates are skeptical and the plan is off to a slow start. But state officials continue to push the program, and their efforts may yet pay off.

Medicaid managers in some states even take the lead to close substandard hospitals. The most dramatic illustration of state-imposed hospital closures occurred in New York in the late 1970s, but the issue persists, given the nation's sizable excess capacity. Dr. Clinton Smith, Mississippi's former Medicaid director, led a recent effort to close the state's three public charity hospitals, which by all accounts provided poor care to a shrinking pool of patients. Dr. Smith linked the closure campaign with an expansion of Medicaid eligibility for pregnant women and children. He even persuaded the governor, Ray Mabus, that the initiatives would not only improve Mississippi's health care system (by shifting money out of expensive, inadequate hospital care toward cheaper, better primary care) but also bring political rewards. Unfortunately, Smith's political predictions proved wrong—the hospital closures were unpopular, Smith was forced out of office, and Mabus lost his bid for reelection. But the effort illustrates a key strategy of today's Medicaid manager: wherever possible, couple Medicaid expansions with a more rational and cost-efficient health care delivery system.

Maximize Federal Reimbursement

Medicaid managers (and their lawyers) place a high priority on maximizing the federal contribution to state Medicaid programs. The explanation is obvious: with state budgets stretched to the limit, increased federal funding brings fiscal relief.

The most popular and controversial maximization effort involves a creative financing scheme, in which providers contribute funds to state Medicaid programs (either voluntarily or pursuant to provider-specific taxes) and these funds are then used to obtain federal matching monies. Consider, for example, the state of Mississippi, in which the federal government provides approximately 80 percent of each Medicaid dollar. If a Mississippi provider submits a bill for $1,000, the federal government should pay $800 and the state $200. But if the provider donates $200 to the state, then the state pays nothing. From the federal perspective, of course, if the provider donates $200, then the bill is really $800, and Washington should pay only $640. Nonetheless, in 1991 Mississippi "saved" $65 million by means of voluntary donations and provider-specific taxes.

By mid 1991, thirty-eight states were using donations and taxes to generate several billion dollars in federal funding. Finally, under significant White House pressure, Congress limited the availability of such financing arrangements: voluntary donations were prohibited and provider-specific taxes restricted ("Legislative Update . . . ," 1992). Of course, this setback simply accelerated state efforts to seek out and implement other maximization efforts.

Review Medical Use to Assure That Services Reflect Need

The Medicaid cost crisis offers an opportunity for program critics to complain about providers and recipients who overuse and abuse the system. Those comparatively few providers who accept Medicaid clients are sometimes alleged to multiply procedures inappropriately in order to gain through volume income that state payers deny them by setting penurious rates. In the free-wheeling, undisciplined Medicaid delivery system, clients can resort to emergency rooms and self-referral to specialists as often as they please. Even allowing for disadvantaged health status of poor people, whose needs have often gone neglected, few observers of the program doubt that its delivery patterns encourage significant waste. Therefore, to protect the program and save some money, Medicaid managers institute a range of utilization review procedures.

The most common of these procedures requires clients to get prior authorization before receiving in-patient hospital care. Medi-Cal officials are particularly committed to this approach. As far back as 1970, Medi-Cal required recipients to get prior authorization for all nonemergency hospitalizations. By 1981, prior authorization was required even for emergency admissions (though weekend admissions could be authorized on Monday). And although client advocates complained that the system discouraged some necessary care, state officials disagreed, arguing that the program eliminated unnecessary hospitalizations and saved money.

Not all states are as zealous as California, but the current fiscal crisis has prompted many to experiment with tough new utilization programs. In 1989, for example, Medicaid officials in New York adopted a "utilization threshold" program, in which recipients were generally limited to fourteen physician visits per year, along with three dental visits and eighteen laboratory procedures. When a state court invalidated the regulations as unauthorized by law, the state legislature itself established the program, thereby answering judicial objections. New York thus joined many other states that impose explicit restrictions on the "amount, scope, and duration" of Medicaid benefits.

Utilization review of a different type began in Mississippi, shortly after the federal government mandated expanded coverage for poor women and children. To be sure, Mississippi applauded both the beneficient intent of the provisions and the new federal dollars they entailed, but it feared that its own modest share would strain a state budget that was (as one legislator put it) "broke as a goat." Officials in the Medicaid agency sought to achieve a defensible expansion with a variation of case management: physicians drew up "plans of care" for eligible clients and sent them to the agency. The managers then reviewed them with a physician brought on as a consultant, scrutinizing them for medical necessity, authorizing those that passed muster, and returning for clarification and amendment those that did not. The manager in charge of the review opined that it deterred providers from seeking "things that are way out," thus averting constant nay-saying and saving more for the state (and the feds).

Neither benefit restrictions nor utilization review programs alone can have much impact on Medicaid costs, but Medicaid managers in every state are spending more and more time developing them. These programs at once permit managerial oversight of client behavior and generate good public relations for those guarding the fiscal gates.

Improve Computer and Data Systems

Medicaid programs were notoriously slow to enter the computer age. New York calculated and recorded hospital and nursing home payments in large ledger books until the early 1980s, and other states were equally reliant on pen and paper. In recent years, however, Medicaid managers have tried hard to modernize their operations, and the computer has replaced the ledgers. The advantages are obvious: states can keep better track of the care clients receive, they can authorize payments to providers more quickly, and they can use reliable data for planning. Indeed, Medicaid managers yearn for ever better and more accurate data, and when the Robert Wood Johnson Foundation announced a program to improve state health data systems, nearly every state applied.

Improved data, however, do not come without complications. In most states separate divisions develop and implement the latest computer technology, and these divisions must work with Medicaid managers who often lack strong computer skills. Communication may falter as a result. For example, when Minnesota's computer experts designed their new client eligibility system in the mid 1980s, they built in an automatic cutoff if clients failed to update their paperwork within a specified time. This system was too efficient for eligibility managers who previously had granted informal extensions for clients who needed them. The software was eventually changed to accommodate prior practices, and the lesson is clear: computer improvements can be no stronger than the clarity and collaboration managers bring to the definition of the ends they are to serve.

Given this history, when Minnesota contemplated modernization of its Medicaid data system, in the late 1980s, agency officials resolved to reject business as usual, namely "systems devised without listening to the users and that don't do what the users want done." They therefore insisted that any new format answer their needs as present and future managers and planners. Determined that new system builders would have user participation, like it or not, they convened meetings engaging "many hundreds of people" and debated at length the properties of a first-rate data system. They then spelled out their specifications and issued a request-for-proposals from contractors. When their choice offered up boilerplate successfully sold to other states, the Minnesota managers rebelled and settled down to long and sometimes angry negotiations to make the contractor customize the system. "We said we'd look at each piece on its merits and change what we pleased." They ended up with a state-of-the-art system that (they contend) is as flexible and powerful for supporting a single payer system or other major reforms as it is for managing the current Medicaid program.

Revise Payment Processes and Systems

In many states, Medicaid managers have broad discretion to develop and implement Medicaid reimbursement policy. New York's legislature, for example, delegates to the state health department the task of developing a reasonable nursing home payment system. And even where state politicians retain ratemaking authority (as in Minnesota and Mississippi), they often rely on Medicaid bureaucrats to guide their decisions.

In exercising this discretion, many Medicaid managers have moved away from retrospective systems (which reimburse providers for what they actually spend) and per-diem systems (which reimburse providers a fixed amount per day of care). They have favored more technically precise systems that pay providers an amount deemed appropriate for particular patients with particular problems. The most prominent example is the use of diagnosis-related groups (DRGs), by New York and others, to estimate what hospitals should spend when treating clients with various illnesses. Another instance is the use of resource utilization groups (RUGs), by Minnesota and others, to calculate what nursing homes should spend in serving residents with different needs.

These systems have gained popularity, mainly because their prospective budgeting breaks with the additive, retrospective payment norms of the past and promises a modicum of predictability and fiscal control. Their popularity also illustrates the growing power of the government bureaucrat as behind-the-scenes technocrat. In James Morone's words: "[these systems] appear (and in politics, appearance is crucial) to operate automatically, scientifically — without visible decisions by politicians or bureaucrats. . . . They are complicated to describe, hard to understand, not easily transformed into symbolic issues (like 'socialized medicine') and offer the illusion of precision. The American political system more easily produces incremental reforms of this kind than the broader, more visible, far riskier changes required for, say, national health insurance" (1992, p. 11).

Improve Provider Relations

The provider community is often at odds with the Medicaid bureaucracy: not only is Medicaid reimbursement considered to be too low, but it takes too much time and paperwork to get paid at all. The frustration is especially acute for physicians who are under growing pressure to provide primary care for Medicaid clients but think themselves underpaid and overregulated.

Because provider participation is obviously essential to a successful program, most Medicaid managers rank improving relations with providers as a high priority. To be sure, the cost crisis means that relations can never be smooth: Medicaid cannot pay what providers think they deserve. Managers, therefore, work all the harder to keep lines of communication open. In many states (including New York and Minnesota), program officials have created "advisory councils," in which providers air grievances and Medicaid officials propose solutions (or explain why solutions are unlikely). These councils are particularly important when Medicaid officials plan major changes in program operations: providers can ventilate their concerns and occasionally persuade managers to change course. And whether formal advisory councils exist or not, Medicaid managers spend considerable time talking informally to providers, schmoozing, cajoling, and networking. A Medicaid manager in Mississippi, for example, noted with pride that her efforts to cultivate the state's physicians had helped double the number who would see Medicaid children. "I went out on the road and sat down with them one to one. It's the only way, especially when payment is so low."

Talk, however, is no durable substitute for improvements in the authorization and payment process. California offers a useful case in point. A legislative staffer well versed in the program remarked, "Given the money limits, the way to make Medi-Cal work better day to day is to do a better job as fiscal intermediary and in the field offices handling authorization. That's where Medi-Cal meets the providers and can really influence care." He then recounted the state's recent efforts to improve these processes. The fiscal intermediary, hired to process and pay provider bills, took too long to do so, and Medi-Cal clients, who needed prior authorization for medical services, found it difficult to reach the right person in the bureaucracy. In response to the first problem, Medi-Cal officials took a political risk: when the fiscal intermediary's contract was rebid, they rejected the low bid submitted by the previous contractor and accepted a higher bid from a new contractor, justifying the choice by pointing to efficiency incentives in the winning bid. By most accounts, this boldness has been rewarded, with a much improved payment system. At the same time, however, Medi-Cal officials responded to recent budget cuts by closing four field offices, which makes it even harder for clients (and their doctors) to get prior authorization for care, and further strains relations between the program and its providers.

Making the Strategies Work: Four Managerial Resources

Management strategies are easier to list than to implement. Managers adopt these initiatives precisely because times are tough, and balancing cannot avoid causing stress and aggravation on all sides. The next question then, is on what resources and support do they draw in their managerial balancing? Four factors stand out.

Formal Administrative Authority

Medicaid managers write the rules and regulations that govern their programs. One would presumably expect this, the traditional formal administrative source of power, to be the most salient source of authority. Surprisingly, however, the Medicaid managers we met rarely mentioned their formal regulatory power. The explanation for this puzzle is twofold. First, many rules and regulations, especially those governing eligibility criteria and benefit coverage, simply echo legislative commands. Legislators seldom delegate to Medicaid managers the authority to decide who gets coverage or specific benefits. Indeed, as New York's unsuccessful attempt to impose a utilization threshold program administratively shows, the courts will examine carefully benefit restrictions not specifically authorized by the legislature. Second, the strategies described above generally require persuasion and persistence more than command and control. Managers cannot demand improved relations with providers by administrative fiat; they will not (though they probably could) require doctors to accept Medicaid patients; and they cannot rely on federal rulings, not state rules, to maximize federal funding.

Formal authority is most potent as a managerial resource in matters of ratemaking. Medicaid managers rely on their formal powers to determine the payment that providers receive, and, in some states, to revise the systems that govern such decisions. Medicaid managers may also use their formal powers to encourage changes they want in the delivery system. New York officials, for example, are now invoking their rate-setting powers over health maintenance organizations to persuade them to participate in the state's Medicaid managed care initiative. And, of course, Medicaid managers cite their formal powers whenever their actions are challenged in court.

In meeting the managers' central challenge—to generate the political support needed to implement their strategies—formal regulatory authority can be helpful but is rarely decisive. What more, then, do Medicaid managers require?

Political Demand for Change

Because Medicaid has become an intense, chronic budgetary headache in most states, reforming it stands high on the agenda of most top state policymakers, who turn to program managers (among other sources) for bright ideas. A health entitlement program growing at nearly 30 percent per year naturally drains scarce resources from other worthy and well-defended arenas (education, for example). Policymakers inclined to decry Medicaid as the monster that ate the state urgently seek correctives but quickly find that few are feasible and none is painless. Eligibility, benefits, and payments to providers are hard to cut. No one wants to seek higher taxes for this "welfare" program, but it is scarcely less difficult politically to continue to divert funds from other programs. Meanwhile, business and the middle class cry out for relief from rising private insurance costs and petition state leaders in the absence of (or preference to) federal leadership.

In responding to these pressures, state leaders tend to investigate two options. One (macro) is to pursue reforms in the larger health system that enfolds Medicaid. The other (micro) tries to redistribute funds within the Medicaid program itself.

Minnesota, for example, recently enacted the MinnesotaCare program which, among other things, subsidizes health insurance for otherwise uninsured residents with income below 275 percent of the federal poverty level. Oregon, famous for its proposal to ration medical services for Medicaid clients, also seeks to implement an employer mandate program by 1995. Vermont and Florida have proclaimed that they will guarantee health insurance for all state residents by 1995, though neither state has specified how they intend to meet the goal. And other states are busy developing more incremental reforms—high-risk pools for the uninsured, requirements that insurers community rate, special programs for pregnant women and children, Medicaid managed care, and much more.

Whether pressing large reforms or smaller ones, state policymakers often look to program managers for a menu of realistic ideas and for help close to home in focusing on the most promising options. Describing the aggressive efforts of himself and his staff to launch a new program of cost-effective child care, a top Medi-Cal manager in California explained that the energy flowed because "the governor and Molly Coye (director of DHS) said 'Go ahead.' That's what makes for progress. I'm a good technician and make government work, but to get that far you need that larger vision." The sharper the sense of crisis, the greater the demand for policy vision. The stronger the determination of pressured politicians to supply vision, the greater their call for program managers' insights on how to make vision bear programmatic fruit in the short run.

Expertise (in a Program Few Understand)

President Bill Clinton has promised to present proposals for a major overhaul of the health care system within the first 100 days of his administration. But even if national health insurance is enacted, state and local governments are sure to retain significant policy discretion, and Medicaid managers are sure to be significant players in state reform efforts. The nature of the managers' role, however, depends largely on the administrators' expertise in a policy arena that few generalists understand well. Successful Medicaid managers derive influence from their knowledge of this complex program, their experience in implementing it, and their ability to expand and explain options for action.

Bureaucratic expertise generates policy influence for program managers when it helps political generalists address pressing problems of their own. Managers extend such help in several ways; for example, they mediate between politicians and interested groups. (Legislators want to suppress nursing home rates, but the powerful lobby complains. Political figures turn to the agency for "technical" justification for their inclinations.) They help draft innovative legislation that by nature upsets precedent and settled expectations embodied in existing laws and rules. They tutor political generalists in the effects of change (or of persistence in the status quo) for counties and localities. They may prepare agency heads for testimony before legislative overseers, playing out worst-case scenarios and supplying credible answers to hard questions. They handle the hairsplitting and nitpicking required to mount a credible quest for federal waivers in support of proposed reforms. As a Medicaid manager in California put it, the manager's role is to define options for political leaders, who then decide what they want to do. These political decisions can seldom be made with confidence in the absence of the agencies' distinctive expertise.

We heard of the workings and results of agency expertise repeatedly in our four states; two examples must suffice here. The first is New York's effort to reorganize the state's home care system by developing and expanding a "shared aide" program, in which a handful of home attendants care for fifty or so clients, all of whom live in the same building or neighborhood. The proposal is controversial because it means a retreat from the principle that aged and disabled Medicaid clients have a right to their own home attendant, and few legislators care to spend much political capital to promote it.

In New York, however, a team of Medicaid managers, led by JoAnn Costantino, is pushing hard for a new direction in home care. Costantino's credibility with the legislature is unusually strong because she worked for years as chief of staff for Jim Tallon, the majority leader of the state assembly. Her staff is highly experienced and knowledgeable. Barry Berberich, the head of long-term care, previously worked for the state's budget office and has maintained good relations with that agency. Ann Hallock, Berberich's deputy, has worked for state DSS for more than twenty-five years and has high standing not only with the legislature but also with the home care providers. These three managers are the "quarterbacks" (as one of them put it) for the proposal, acting as intermediaries among elected officials, industry representatives, and client advocates; drafting legislation; testifying before legislative committees; and generally pushing for action in a contentious arena.

The political uses of agency expertise are illustrated too in the story of MinnesotaCare, that state's innovative effort to deal with the health care crisis. MinnesotaCare is the culmination of a strategy of incremental reform, launched by Bob Baird and others in the state's Department of Human Services. The story began in the early 1980s, when advocates at the Children's Defense Fund, working with neonatalogists at the University of Minnesota, argued convincingly that rising neonatal costs could be controlled, and health outcomes improved, if the state put more emphasis on prenatal care. Although the managers were persuaded, the state legislature needed education, so Baird assembled a task force to study and report on the issue. Not surprisingly, the task force report stressed the benefits of prenatal care. Report in hand, DHS staff helped draft a prenatal care initiative, lobbied for it in the statehouse, and "quarterbacked" it into law.

With the prenatal care initiative in place, Minnesota Medicaid managers worked to enact the Children's Health Plan (1988) and then the MinnesotaCare Plan (1991). In the Children's Health Plan, the state pays for a range of out-patient health services for children in uninsured families with income below 185 percent of the federal poverty level. Over time the Children's Health Plan will assimilate with the newer and more expansive MinnesotaCare Plan, in which the state pays for various out-patient and in-patient health services for residents with income below 275 percent of the federal poverty level (recipients pay a monthly fee, set by a sliding fee scale, to the state).

Why do Minnesota's Medicaid managers have such influence? The answer, according to nearly every Minnesota official we met, is their experience and expertise. The senior staff at DHS has been remarkably stable since the program's inception in 1966. These officials have mastered the complexities of Medicaid as law and program and have earned the trust of their political supervisors, who feel moved to change the program but understand it (and the reform options) more superficially than do the managers.

Other People's Money

Since even cost-effective programs require spending more money, Medicaid managers often point out that at least half (and sometimes much more) of all the program's expenditures are funded by the federal government. This argument can be very powerful in poor states, like Mississippi, that contribute relatively little to the federal treasury and get handsome Medicaid largess from Washington. As former Medicaid director Dr. Clinton Smith recalled: "I would always tell those public meetings that these dollars from New York and California are brought down here and help turn around our economy. It's a hard argument to defeat!"

In wealthy states, too, the lure of federal dollars is a major bulwark for managers anxious to protect the program against conservative attack. A Medicaid official in New York described the state's attitude as "schizophrenic"—relieved by the federal dollars, alarmed by the burgeoning state commitment.

Will the Strategies Succeed?
Three Barriers to Effective Management

Medicaid managers are increasingly influential, but their ability to rationalize and repair Medicaid faces important constraints and barriers. Three such obstacles to effective management are especially salient. *Internal* barriers arise from the structure and dynamics of the Medicaid agencies themselves. *Environmental* barriers emerge from the state-governmental context within which these agencies operate. *Intergovernmental* barriers derive from the federal government's vast say in Medicaid decisions.

Internal Barriers

Medicaid agencies need a capable and committed staff. Eligibility workers must sometimes apply four sets of complicated rules when reviewing the application of a four-person family. Rate setters need the skills of sophisticated technocrats to devise and implement the latest reimbursement methods. High-level managers must respond quickly to the latest federal mandate, helpfully to legislative demands for innovation, and sympathetically to provider pleas for relief. All in all, Medicaid workers at every level tackle a stressful, demanding, and frustrating set of tasks.

Often, moreover, internal agency dynamics add insult to the (probably inescapable) injuries of roles and tasks. Three factors stand out: staff cutbacks, civil service restrictions, and the eternal crisis atmosphere. In nearly every state, budget cuts have forced Medicaid managers to reduce their workforce, by attrition, transfer to other agencies, or dismissals. In New York, for example, the size of the state DSS workforce has shrunk by about 10 percent (about 500 employees) over the last five years. In California, the state DHS workforce has been cut even more dramatically over the same years (about 30 percent, or 500 employees). These cuts have ironic consequences: handed more to do, Medicaid managers have fewer staff with which to do it, and the staffers who remain worry increasingly about their own job security and their disrupted workplace routines.

The restrictive civil service rules that govern most state and local employees aggravate the strains that staff cutbacks inflict. Medicaid managers everywhere complain regularly about civil service requirements that prevent them from firing "deadwood" in their agencies, preclude them from attracting bright outsiders and offering them lateral entry into agency ranks, and inhibit them from transferring workers among jobs to enhance productivity. The impact is especially noticeable in states like Mississippi, where the state's Medicaid director is the only person in the agency who is not on a civil service line. But in larger states, too, like New York and California, Medicaid is enmeshed in large and often inflexible bureaucracies. In short, civil service laws not only limit managerial discretion but they also can encourage a workforce that is resistant to change and innovation.

Staff cutbacks and the inflexibility of civil service rules contribute to a crisis atmosphere that dominates many Medicaid agencies. Every day (or so it may seem to the Medicaid manager) a new federal mandate arrives to implement, a new waiver request to process, a new budget reduction target to meet. Medicaid managers tend to grope along from crisis to crisis without the time or the staff for long-term research and planning. Medicaid management is thus too often reactive to suit the tastes of managers who would like to think that their energy, insights, and expertise entitle them to a modicum of control over events.

Environmental Barriers

Although political demands for change may lead elected officials to turn to knowledgeable health care bureaucrats for solutions, thereby increasing the power of Medicaid managers, the bureaucracy is seldom the dominant force in health care politics, or even in the politics of Medicaid. Agency influence unfolds within a populous political environment and responds to the constraints and preferences of external actors. Four environmental forces are of special importance: the governor's priorities, especially his or her emphasis on, and agenda for, change in health care policy; the details by the legislature; the resources and skill of groups with a stake in change; and managerial fragmentation among the several agencies that take a hand in formulating and implementing policy innovations.

Executive Leadership. The importance of executive leadership is illustrated vividly in California, where agency influence has waxed and waned depending on the attitudes of the state's governor. Governor George Deukmejian (1982–1990), for example, set as his chief priorities expansion of the state's prison system and protection of its educational programs. With little interest in or knowledge of health and welfare issues, and with a clear commitment to reducing health and welfare expenditures as much as possible, Deukmejian was content to entrust Medi-Cal policy primarily to the state's finance department, staffed by officials interested in little more than bottom-line savings. The political environment changed significantly with the election of Governor Pete Wilson, in 1990. A conservative Republican, Wilson is certainly eager to cut Medi-Cal spending. But he has also underscored the need to provide all children with quality health care and to improve the state's primary health care system. In January 1992, Governor Wilson not only directed his Medi-Cal managers to make plans to increase the number of recipients enrolled in managed care programs but also promised to support the agency's initiatives. A green light from the governor's office is probably the single most powerful impetus to agency innovation; by the same token, although executive indifference or opposition may not always defeat innovation, it greatly increases the scope of legislative, group, and public support required to make it happen.

Legislative Control. State legislatures are rarely content to delegate broad authority to Medicaid agencies, and some write into law highly detailed specifications of program details. In Mississippi, for example, Medicaid was managed for years by a legislative commission and even today a few legislators dominate Medicaid policy. In this context, the state's official Medicaid managers, now housed in the governor's office, lack the influence and the authority sometimes granted to their counterparts in other states. For example, Mississippi's Medicaid managers want to implement an innovative RUGs reimbursement system, but the Mississippi legislature (influenced by the powerful nursing home industry) refuses to authorize it.

Ironically, tight legislative specification can augment agency influence in the very process of constraining it. Minnesota managers described a recurrent dynamic that is evident in many other states too. In the wake of nursing home scandals and billing abuses by providers, worried legislators advertise their indignation to the public by writing new regulatory and pay-ment procedures into law. Implementing the restrictions creates headaches for broad classes of institutions and providers (including those untainted by scandal) and generates cries for clarification and relief. Legislators turn to agency experts for ideas on reconciling the new safeguards with due operat-ing flexibility, and the managers have a new mandate for administrative improvisation.

Group Influence. Spending in Medicaid, as in the larger health care system, means earnings and income for providers defended by well-organized, well-heeled groups that do not hesitate to state their preferences and grievances or to reinforce their positions with campaign contributions, media appeals, and other potent political resources. The Medicaid manager who wants to save money on provider payments risks losing participation, thereby jeopar-dizing timely access for public clients. A quest to cut drug costs means a fight with the pharmaceutical industry. Policy analysis may recommend a strong state tilt toward home- and community-based care, but the nursing home lobby may have other ideas. Political capital is scarce and program managers—not to mention their elected superiors—must pick their fights carefully.

Medicaid managers recognize the omnipresence of group politics (thus the continuing emphasis on improving provider relations), but they also know that some groups are more influential and some states are more susceptible to group influence than others. The variability of group politics is illustrated by a comparison of nursing home payment policy in New York and Califor-nia. Why does a nursing home in New York receive, on average, $120 per day per Medicaid client, while a similarly situated home in California gets about $65 per day? One explanation is the salaries of nonprofessional nurs-ing home workers in the two states: New York's workers earn nearly twice as much as their counterparts in California (New York State Comptroller's Office, 1989). What explains the difference? New York's powerful health care unions have consistently persuaded Medicaid officials to fund wage increases, while California's weak union movement has little influence with Medi-Cal officials and little leverage over nursing home owners.

It is of course difficult to generalize about when, why, or where in-terest groups succeed in having their way in the health policy process or about the conditions that permit policymakers to overrule them. One vari-able that stands out in our four Medicaid programs, however, is the per-ception of fiscal crisis. New York tends to offer a broad stage for the play of group influence, but even there budgetary aggravations have produced consolidations of administrative authority.

Following the fiscal crisis of the mid 1970s, for example, the state legis-lature delegated to Richard Berman and his staff in the Office of Health Sys-tems Management (within the state Department of Health) increased au-thority to regulate hospital capital expansion programs. Despite loud hospital protests, the state continues strictly to enforce certificate of need procedures.

And the fiscal crisis of the early 1990s, much influenced by Medicaid costs, produced an ambitious new mandate for Medicaid managers in Albany — to seek enrollment of half the program's clients in managed care plans by 1996.

The perception of crisis is also essential in explaining Minnesota's willingness to impose new taxes on providers and cigarettes to fund the MinnesotaCare program. New taxes were obviously controversial, and the provider community waged a bitter campaign against the new program. Nevertheless, the legislature, working closely with the state's Medicaid managers, rejected the providers' pleas and enacted the law. The explanation lies partly in political culture, the state's strong progressive tradition, and partly in strong legislative leadership. But equally important was the perception that the health care system was spinning out of control, and the state had to do something. In times of crisis, provider influence often wanes.

Managerial Fragmentation. State Medicaid programs are not vested in a single agency. Typically, a department of social services sets eligibility policy, a department of health makes payment rules, and other entities addressing aging, mental health, substance abuse, and other arenas take a hand in service delivery. And, as noted earlier, overarching supervisory units — human services superagencies, offices of management and budget, and more — may also shape Medicaid decisions. This fragmentation derives partly from the intrinsic split nature of a health care program rooted in the welfare system and partly from legislative-executive tugs-of-war over power and accountability (Mississippi, for instance, initially ran Medicaid by a legislative commission to constrain executive power and then put it in the governor's office to avoid further strengthening the influential head of the Department of Health [DOH].) Whatever its source, fragmentation can work against managerial coherence and may enhance the leverage of interest groups on policymakers.

The importance of managerial fragmentation is illustrated by New York's decision to divide authority over its Medicaid-funded home care programs. Under the current division of labor, state DSS generally oversees the state's personal care program, which provides long-term home care to the chronically ill, but it delegates administration of the program (including rate setting) to the county welfare agencies. Meanwhile, yet another agency, state DOH, regulates and sets rates for the state's Home Health Care program, which provides short-term home care to people recently discharged from hospitals. With the task of setting home care reimbursement rates divided among so many agencies, home care providers can use settlements with one agency to leverage settlements with others. In 1987, for example, the health care unions in New York City mounted a vigorous campaign to increase the compensation received by home care workers. The effort was so successful that the city increased wages and benefits by 42 percent. Although state DOH neither participated in such negotiations, nor approved of the outcome, its officials felt bound to offer a similar package to home care workers employed by its programs.

Intergovernmental Barriers

The most significant barrier to effective Medicaid management, according to nearly every Medicaid manager with whom we spoke, is the federal government. The two most common complaints deplore the recent rash of federal mandates (which require states to liberalize their Medicaid eligibility criteria) and the bureaucratic hoops through which states must jump to secure a waiver from a federal requirement. But state officials voice other concerns too, ranging from a belief that Medicaid is burdened with a disproportionate share of the nation's nursing home bill to allegations that the Employee Retirement Income Security Act (ERISA) inappropriately restricts state solutions to the health care crisis. A Minnesota legislator who had played a major role in passing MinnesotaCare acknowledged the justifiable celebration over the state's innovations but cautioned that the rules governing four federal programs—Medicare, Medicaid, ERISA, and the tax code (which works strongly toward an employer-based and against a single payer system)— inherently condemn state achievements to be incremental and marginal at best. These challenges that federal policy poses to state management can only be understood in the context of the history of the Medicaid program and the inherited intergovernmental anomalies that derive from that history.

Medicaid is a prominent but only partly coherent compromise in America's long and unresolved debate over national health insurance. That debate first emerged in the early twentieth century, as part of the Progressive agenda. For many reasons, neither the Progressives, the New Dealers, nor the Fair Dealers made significant headway. And after Harry Truman's universal insurance proposal was defeated in 1949, it would be twenty-five years before national health insurance would again seem possible.

As the prospects for universal health insurance declined, the seeds of the Medicaid program took root (Marmor, 1970). In 1950, Congress enacted an amendment to the Social Security Act that provided federal matching funds to states willing to fund medical services for certain welfare recipients. Liberals endorsed an acceptable, if inadequate, first step: at least some poor people could now receive previously unavailable medical care. Conservatives acquiesced in hopes that a "welfare medicine" approach would undermine demands for a more comprehensive program. With most workers covered by private health insurance plans, only the truly needy warranted the safety net of public support.

The adoption of a "safety net" program to undermine a more comprehensive approach recurred again a decade later, in 1960. The Kerr-Mills program provided federal assistance to states willing to fund medical services for the aged poor, even if such recipients were not receiving cash assistance. This expansion was adopted, however, only after Congress rejected proposals to provide hospital insurance for all of the aged, regardless of income. A compromise "welfare medicine" expansion, which delegated key policymaking authority to the states, was again an antidote to a more comprehensive social insurance approach.

The political equation changed, in 1964, with Lyndon Johnson's landslide election. In the House Ways and Means Committee, dominated by the previously recalcitrant Wilbur Mills, Johnson now had the votes to pass a health care reform bill. Perhaps national health insurance was now at hand. But President Johnson, unwilling to sponsor too bold an initiative, proposed instead a program to cover the hospital costs of the aged. The American Medical Association countered with an expanded version of Kerr-Mills (hoping that a welfare medicine compromise would again kill a more expansive program). Congressman John Byrnes (the senior Republican on the House Ways and Means Committee) proposed a voluntary program to cover physician costs incurred by the aged. These then were the choices before the Congress, and these were the programs that Wilbur Mills fashioned into law (as Medicare Parts A and B and Medicaid).

Medicare and Medicaid were, of course, significant advances for a nation unaccustomed to public health insurance. But the decision to let the states administer and help pay for Medicaid, while leaving Medicare federally funded and administered, contributed greatly to the intergovernmental battles of today.

Consider, for example, nursing home care. Medicare covers short-term nursing home stays (of up to 100 days) that are preceded by and related to a hospital visit. Thus limited, Medicare pays for less than 5 percent of the nation's nursing home bill. Medicaid, in contrast, provides unlimited nursing home coverage to all recipients. For this reason, middle-class senior citizens may "spend down" to become Medicaid recipients when (or shortly after) they enter a nursing home. As a result, Medicaid now pays approximately 45 percent of the nation's nursing home bill, and long-term care is the fastest-growing portion of Medicaid spending.

This outcome seems unfair to most state officials: in their view, Medicare (and thus the federal government) should fund long-term care for the middle class, and Medicaid should concentrate its resources on the truly poor. Such a division of labor would clarify the program's mission and encourage more effective management. But with long-term-care reform low on the federal agenda, state Medicaid programs are likely to remain the biggest third-party payers of nursing home bills, spending nearly 70 percent of their money on the 30 percent of their clients that are aged and disabled. And Medicaid managers will continue to administer two very different programs: a health insurance program for the poor and a long-term-care insurance program for the middle class.

The dispute over long-term care illustrates an important and enduring problem for the Medicaid manager: there is no durable consensus on which governmental level should be responsible for what. This problem was less obvious in the late 1960s, when state officials were given broad discretion to fashion distinctive Medicaid programs. That delegation of authority produced the wide interstate variations we see today: in California, for example, a family of three with income below $11,208 may be eligible for Medicaid, while in Alabama that same family must earn less than $1,488 to qualify (Prospective Payment Assessment Commission, 1991). In recent years, however, the federal government has tried to reduce the variation in Medicaid programs, imposed more national standards, and required many Medicaid programs to expand their social safety net. But many Medicaid managers complain that these federal departures are detrimental to their efforts to manage and innovate.

The most common state complaints address mandates and waivers, which we take up here in turn. In the mid 1980s, the health care crisis again came onto the national agenda. There was increased recognition of the problems of the uninsured; voices again called for national health insurance; fierce opposition greeted such proposals. And, as in 1950, 1960, and 1965, compromise focused on expanding the state-based welfare medicine system. This time the beneficiaries of the expansions were pregnant women and young children. In 1988, for example, Congress required states to phase in Medicaid benefits for all children below age seven in families with income under the federal poverty line. In 1989, Congress required them to cover pregnant women and children below age seven in families with income less than 133 percent of the federal poverty line. In 1990, it required states to phase in Medicaid coverage for all children up to age eighteen in families with income below 100 percent of the federal poverty line.

The explanation for these expansions is threefold. First, most Americans have sympathy for pregnant women (or at least the children they are carrying) and children. Second, expanded prenatal care and primary care are considered cost effective. Third, liberals and conservatives who could agree on little else could endorse Medicaid expansions for these groups. The rationales are familiar. For liberals, here was an acceptable, if limited, first step: some additional poor people could now get medical care. Conservatives hoped that the "welfare medicine" approach would again derail a more comprehensive program. The Medicaid mandates were the latest improvement in the public "safety net" that undergirds the broader health insurance system.

Support for expansion was also encouraged by the initial positive response of most state officials. States in the mid 1980s had money to spend, and spending it on prenatal care, which could reduce infant mortality rates and low-birth-weight babies, was often a high priority. By the early 1990s, however, the recession was driving most state budgets into deficits, and state officials began to complain about the new mandates. Encouraging indigent pregnant women to receive prenatal care was doubtless a good policy, but if the federal government wanted to mandate such coverage then it should cover the costs.

The mandate "millstone" (to quote Ed Koch) is not, moreover, limited to eligibility criteria (Koch, 1980). In 1987, for example, Congress enacted a series of reforms in nursing home quality of care that took effect on October 1, 1990. The reforms require nursing homes throughout the country to meet minimal standards on several counts, including staff-patient ratios, patient rights, and staff training. The law also obliges states to include the cost of complying with the new standards in Medicaid reimbursement rates. In some states, the cost of implementing the reforms is staggering: California Medi-Cal officials predict that implementation will cost approximately $500 million a year, and the state's nursing homes view that figure as far too low. Medi-Cal officials battled vigorously (but unsuccessfully) to avoid compliance.

Medicaid mandates are hardly new: from the beginning, federal law has imposed rules and regulations that all state programs must follow. The new and troubling elements are the increased volume of mandates, their tighter specificity, and the reluctance of federal officials to grant waivers to them. Many Medicaid managers contend that federal constraints frustrate innovation and boldness precisely when the system needs more of both. They complain that the federal government takes too long to review waiver applications, that it too often rejects applications for trivial reasons, and that when waivers are granted they may be undermined by conditions and caveats set by HCFA.

State officials also decry ERISA, which precludes state requirements that employers provide health insurance to their employees and thereby restricts state flexibility in responding comprehensively to the health care crisis. In short, state managers (in and out of the Medicaid bureaucracy) argue that they have been put in an untenable position: federal officials tell states that they must administer and help pay for the health care of the poor, but federal rules simultaneously restrict the states' ability to plan and innovate. There is no easy out; the Medicaid manager is condemned to micromanage a program that desperately needs macro policy repair.

Conclusion: Can Medicaid Be Managed?

The mission of today's Medicaid manager is to control costs without cutting eligibility, benefits, or reimbursement, and despite numerous internal, environmental, and intergovernmental constraints. As a job description, this assignment leads inevitably to frustration. To be sure, Medicaid managers are generally talented and resourceful, and they work hard to implement various balancing strategies. Moreover, many of these strategies seem to be working: Medicaid bureaucracies have better computer systems, reimbursement methods are increasingly refined, and utilization review procedures grow more sophisticated daily. But despite individual victories, the managers are losing the war: Medicaid costs continue to escalate dramatically, the rising costs thrust enormous burdens on state budgets, and the vision of a decent yet cost-effective program slips further away.

What is to be done? The first step is to acknowledge that the Medicaid program needs macro policy repair and that micromanagerial fixes, while useful in their fashion, will inevitably disappoint. Medicaid managers have no magic that cuts costs while maintaining an expanding eligibility criteria, benefit coverage, and provider reimbursement. The Medicaid crisis is embedded in the larger health care crisis and cannot be solved in isolation from it. And it is doubtful that the best state efforts can supplant the need for federal leadership and national solutions.

In the meantime, several reforms would help. Internal reforms — the public administrator's forte — can do some good. Civil service laws should be amended to give Medicaid managers more flexibility in deploying their agencies' workforce; public managers at least should have more flexibility to move employees to new positions to address new needs. Environmental reforms too can make their contribution. Managerial fragmentation should be reduced. A state like New York should not run a $16 billion dollar Medicaid program without the clear chain of command that California's experience suggests can reduce interest group influence and enhance that of the bureaucracy. Finally, if the federal government is not willing to lead, it should get out of the way and grant the states more flexibility. Federal mandates should come backed by federal dollars, the waiver process should be simplified, and the ERISA preemptions should be amended or scrapped.

In the end, however, incremental adjustments by managers can go only so far. Policymakers alone can create the coherent and purposive framework of law and regulation that will permit Medicaid managers to do more than struggle to keep their programs afloat.

References

California Department of Finance. *Medicaid Expenditures, 1991*. Sacramento: California Department of Finance, 1991.

California Department of Health Services. *Nursing Home Data, 1991*. Sacramento: California Department of Health Services, 1991.

California Department of Health Services. *California's Managed Care Initiative*. Sacramento: California Department of Health Services, 1992.

Congressional Budget Office. *Economic Implications of Rising Health Care Costs*. Washington, D.C.: U.S. Government Printing Office, 1992.

Crystal, S., Flemming, C., Beck, P., and Smolka, G. *The Management of Home Care Services*. New York: Springer, 1987.

Koch, Edward. "The Mandate Millstone." *The Public Interest*, 1980, *61*, 42–57.

"Legislative Update: Medicaid Voluntary Contribution and Provider-Specific Tax Amendments of 1991." *Health Care Financing Review*, 1992, *13*, 131–135.

Levit, R. L., Lazenby, H. C., Cowan, C. A., and Letsch, S. W. "National Health Expenditures, 1990." *Health Care Financing Review*, 1991, *13*, 29–54.

Marmor, T. *The Politics of Medicare*. New York: Aldine, 1970.

Morone, J. "Implementing National Health Insurance: Administrative Snares." Paper presented at the eighty-eighth annual meeting of the American Political Science Association, Chicago, Sept. 1992.

National Governors' Association. *A Healthy America: The Challenge for the States*. Washington, D.C.: National Governors' Association, 1991.

New York State Comptroller's Office. *Staff Study on New York State's Medicaid Program*. New York: New York State Comptroller's Office, 1989.

New York State Department of Social Services. *Medicaid Expenditures, 1991*. New York: New York State Department of Social Services, 1991a.

New York State Department of Social Services. *Nursing Home Data, 1991*. New York: New York State Department of Social Services, 1991b.

New York State Department of Social Services. *New York State Managed Care Plan*. New York: New York State Department of Social Services, 1991c.

Prospective Payment Assessment Commission. *Medicaid Hospital Payment Congressional Report C-91-02*. Washington, D.C.: U.S. Government Printing Office, 1991.

United States Congress, House Committee on Ways and Means. *Overview of Entitlement Programs: 1991 Green Book*. Washington, D.C.: U.S. Government Printing Office, 1991.

United States Congress, House Committee on Ways and Means. *Medicaid Source Book: Background Data and Analysis*. Washington, D.C.: U.S. Government Printing Office, 1988.

List of Interviews

Barry, Anne, Minnesota Department of Finance, May 26, 1992.

Bergelin, Linda, member of the Minnesota legislature, May 27, 1992.

Beulow, Ed, member of the Mississippi legislature, Apr. 28, 1992.

Block, Rachel, on the staff of James Tallon, Majority Leader of the New York State Assembly, Feb. 12, 1992.

Cobb, Alton, Mississippi Department of Health, January 17, 1992.

Colliander, Barb, Minnesota Department of Human Services, May 26, 1992.

Cooke, Rick, New York State Office of the Governor, Feb. 14, 1992.

Costantino, JoAnn, New York State Department of Social Services, Feb. 14, 1992.

Foster, Dexter, Mississippi Office of the Governor, Apr. 28, 1992.

Greenley, Bob, Mississippi Legislative Budget Office, Jan. 17, 1992.

Gruenes, Dave, member of the Minnesota legislature, May 27, 1992.

Hallock, Ann, New York State Department of Social Services, Feb. 14, 1992.

Johnson, Kathleen, Commission on California State Government Organization and Economy (the "Little Hoover Commission"), Mar. 13, 1992.

Kelley, Joe, California Department of Health Services, Mar. 13, 1992.

Kennedy, Mary, Minnesota Department of Human Services, May 26, 1992.

Maxwell-Jolley, David, California Legislative Analyst Office, Mar. 12, 1992.

Meyer, Bob, Minnesota Department of Human Services, May 27, 1992.

Moore, Kristin, Minnesota Department of Health, May 27, 1992.

Mulligan, Rosinna, New York State Department of the Budget, Feb. 14, 1992.

Parker, Pam, Minnesota Department of Human Services, May 26, 1992.

Parker, Terri, California Health and Welfare Agency, Mar. 12, 1992.

Parks, Jim, California Health and Welfare Agency, Mar. 12, 1992.

Prokup, Mary, New York State Department of the Budget, Feb. 14, 1992.

Riley, David, Mississippi Legislative Budget Office, Jan. 18, 1992.

Ringrose, Jim, California Medical Assistance Commission, Mar. 12, 1992.

Rodriguez, John, California Department of Health Services, Mar. 13, 1992.

Sack, Jeanette, Mississippi Department of Health, Apr. 28, 1992.

Schroeder, Nan, Minnesota Department of Health, May 27, 1992.

Schuler, Kathleen, Minnesota Department of Human Services, May 27, 1992.

Smith, Clinton, former Medicaid director for the state of Mississippi, Apr. 28, 1992.

Stewart, Kirk, California Department of Finance, Mar. 13, 1992.

Stibbs, David, Minnesota Department of Human Services, May 26, 1992.

Stolmark, Allen, California Department of Health Services, Mar. 13, 1992.

Sweeney, Ray, New York State Department of Health, Feb. 12, 1992.

Weatherbee, Helen, Mississippi Medicaid Department, Jan. 17, 1992.

Winter, William, former governor of the state of Mississippi, Jan. 18, 1992.

Woods, Larry, Minnesota Department of Human Services, May 27, 1992.

PART FIVE

Toward
Revitalization

TEN

The Challenges
Revisited

Frank J. Thompson

Revitalization is not the same as resuscitation. The chapters in this book show that state and local governance is in many respects a story of achievement. By and large, revitalization is more akin to encouraging better health habits (lose weight and don't smoke!) than to treating the sorely afflicted, but nonetheless, it is important. The demands facing the United States will probably require higher performance levels by both public and private organizations than in the past: "good enough" practices will no longer suffice. The new game requires superbly conditioned players. Efforts to enhance the efficiency and effectiveness of state and local governments, while at the same time assuring their accountability and bolstering citizen confidence, should be front and center. As the introductory chapter emphasized, the American political system and its culture do not make revitalization easy, nor does the fiscal stress so pervasive in the 1990s. Progress can be made, however, in meeting the challenges described in this book: leadership, workforce, information, privatization, health care.

This chapter returns to some of the central themes that emerge from the book, from other papers prepared for the National Commission on the State and Local Public Service, and from the commission's hearings around the country. I focus on (1) leadership that shuns micromanagement; (2) an approach to the workforce challenge rooted in deregulating the public sector, customer orientation, the involvement of front-line workers, and a performance or bottom-line emphasis; (3) the quest not only to attract and retain the talented but to engage them in life-long learning; (4) a balanced approach to information technology issues; and (5) understanding the private delivery of government programs, especially by nonprofits, as a partnership.

These propositions all target activities that state and local officials can substantially undertake themselves. But we should not get so wrapped up in self-help thinking that we ignore the federal government's role. Federal policies intersect (at times collide) with virtually all of these challenges. Nowhere does this loom larger than in health care. As Michael Sparer and Lawrence D. Brown emphasize in Chapter Nine, states and localities cannot cope with the conundrums of cost containment, access, and quality without significant changes in federal policy. Failure to meet the health care challenge ensures that fiscal stress will become more acute, even crippling, for many jurisdictions. Floundering at health care reform will vitiate efforts to cope with the other challenges.

Executive Leadership Without Micromanagement

The commission's research and hearings attest that revitalization requires strong and enlightened leadership by chief executives and their top appointees. In a "sloppy governmental system" designed to prevent tyranny rather than to promote efficiency or centralized accountability, chief executives face many challenges (Aberbach, 1990, p. 201). They must above all contend with the massive fragmentation that, as one observer notes, makes American politics more of a "barroom brawl" than a "prizefight" (Wilson, 1989, pp. 299–300). In a barroom brawl, "anybody can join in, the combatants fight all comers, and sometimes change sides, no referee is in charge, and the fight lasts not for a fixed number of rounds but indefinitely or until everybody drops from exhaustion." Executives in the United States need to provide vision and bring order to political conflict; otherwise, the cacophony of voices of unfettered pluralism can quickly give way to gridlock. Problems of formulating and implementing coherent, plausible policies intensify in a fragmented political system.

Leadership can, of course, come from many quarters, but that provided by chief executives seems particularly critical. In contrast, for instance, legislative bodies provide less fertile soil; legislators face more barriers to attracting media and public attention—hence to the bully pulpit. They look at policy through lenses shaped by a desire to represent interests of a specific territory within a broader jurisdiction. Moreover, their fortunes at the ballot box tend to be divorced from the product of their institutions. Their constituencies usually hold them accountable for their own individual behavior rather than for the performance of the legislative body as a whole (Aberbach, 1990). Governors, mayors, city managers, and county executives, on the other hand, are more visible to the public, represent broader constituencies, and shoulder more responsibility for the functioning of the entire government. They cannot so readily pass the buck.

Of course, vigorous chief executives do not necessarily abet the forces of revitalization — some play to those strands in the political culture that hold public administration in low esteem. Such executives take cheap shots at the bureaucracy, ignore implementation issues, and pay minimal attention to the implications of their actions for the long-term capacity and performance of government. Or they at times espouse reform but do little to galvanize it. In testimony before the commission in Philadelphia, Stan Lundine, lieutenant governor of New York, captured one dimension of this behavior when he observed: "You've all heard of NIMBY — not in my backyard; a lot of politicians are now honoring the NIMTO — not in my term of office." They endorse tough choices and reform but seek to postpone action or its consequences until far into the future.

Of course, the NIMTO syndrome often reflects an accurate reading of the difficulties of forging coalitions for reform. As Kathy Whitmire, former mayor of Houston, told the commission at its Austin hearing: "As one who has tried to campaign on civil service reform, let me tell you it doesn't sell. It's just not one of the issues that sells out on the campaign trail. I got a lot of criticism for campaigning on that issue through the years, but it is one of the issues that motivated me into public service in the first place because I felt that the reform was so important." These problems notwithstanding, the prospects for revitalization seem greater if chief executives acquire additional authority to counter the powerful centrifugal forces present in the American political system.

Among the array of institutionalized powers, both Chapter One by Deborah D. Roberts on the governor as leader and the commission's hearings indicate the priority top executives place on having the authority to put together their own management teams. Kathy Whitmire was not alone in fighting for this right (see my introductory chapter). At the commission's Philadelphia hearing, for example, Theodore Hershberg, director of the Center for Greater Philadelphia, noted that due to concerns about patronage, the Philadelphia city charter allowed every commissioner to have just two deputies and a secretary exempt from civil service. "It's incredible — can you imagine you've got 500 to 600 people in a department and you bring in your new team and it's two deputies? And when you sit down with your senior managers . . . they're all union."

Ensuring that executives can fashion their top management team could well be the linchpin to a leadership style more conducive to revitalization. The opportunity to work with "their" people encourages executives to delegate authority; it inclines them toward acceptance of loose control rather than micromanagement. Roberts reminds us that an effective leadership system implies responsibility and discretion spread deep throughout the bureaucracy. Otherwise, executives risk drowning in a sea of detail; they risk becoming barriers to innovation. Chief executives can do much to provide vision, mission, broad direction, and tone to state and local governance — they can appropriately insist on results and manage the budget gates — but effective leadership seldom rests on a command-and-control model. Strong leadership can coexist with the substantial deregulation of public administration and the involvement of front-line employees in problem solving.

Of course, either God or the devil may reside in the details. Exactly how many top employees (or what proportion of all workers) should chief executives and agency heads be able to hire, transfer, or fire? What kinds of senior executive systems, if any, ought to mediate relationships between the political and career strata of state and local governments? Should career administrators who accept political appointments be able to retreat back to other administrative positions when political leaders change? These and countless other questions require more systematic investigation. But meanwhile, the available evidence cautions against assuming that greater personnel authority for chief executives is the fast train to amateur government dominated by highly partisan appointees. Instead, it can be the provenance of a constructive leadership style that avoids the impulse to layer the bureaucracy with more and more controls.

Aside from personnel authority, other institutional changes that can bolster prospects for executive leadership and counter the excesses of fragmentation deserve attention. One of the more imaginative options draws on the military base closing model of the federal government, a model that seeks to overcome gridlock and the political system's inability to target and set priorities. Under it, the defense department makes recommendations concerning specific base closures to an independent commission appointed by the president with the approval of the Senate. The commission then forwards its recommendations to the president, who has the choice of accepting the entire list or sending it back to the commission for revision. Once the president accepts the list, it automatically goes into effect unless Congress passes a joint resolution rejecting it within forty-five working days.

This model has two compelling characteristics. First, it gives the executive branch substantial leeway to prepare a policy package that the legislative branch must accept or reject in its entirety. It helps buffer the proposal from special interest politics that can yield internally contradictory, implausible policies. Second, it has a bias toward action, because change will occur unless the legislative branch rejects the proposal. Obviously, this model will be inappropriate in many spheres, but its potential applicability to various aspects of state and local governance should be considered. For instance, one analysis suggests that such a mechanism may help the states make difficult choices concerning health care cost containment. State health authorities could forge plans and policies to fulfill budget targets for health care expenditures in a state. Both the governor and legislature could reject the plan — send it back to the authority for more work — but they could not amend it (Tallon and Nathan, 1992).

Toward High-Performance Agencies

Revitalization also requires meeting that aspect of the workforce challenge that develops organizational and management strategies conducive to quality and productivity. Four key concepts spring from the contributions to this book, the research of other experts, and the commission's hearings: public sector deregulation, customer focus, front-line involvement, and a bottom-line orientation.

Public Sector Deregulation

At its heart, deregulating the public sector involves granting managers and others within state and local agencies more discretion and flexibility, countering tendencies to proliferate rules that reduce opportunities for managers and others to respond sensibly, creatively, and responsibly. Of course, many of government's rules serve important purposes; others, however, do little other than to contribute to a mindset that undermines revitalization. They reinforce the incentive for public managers to worry more about constraints than tasks, more about processes than outcomes, more about rules than mission (Wilson, 1989; Barzelay, 1992). Recent federal initiatives have echoed this theme. In directing Vice President Gore to conduct a review aimed at streamlining and modernizing the operations of federal agencies, President Clinton emphasized the need to place "a premium on speed and function and service, not rules and regulations" (Vernon, 1993, p. 513).

Much of the focus on deregulating the public sector targets staff agencies (Barzelay, 1992), which control the vital inputs a manager needs to operate — personnel, office space, money, procurement, information systems, training, travel, and more. Often these agencies see managers as the targets of regulation rather than as customers deserving service. They style themselves as the guardians of massive, finely detailed codes of rules that erode managerial discretion. Top elected officials layer on some of these rules through law; the staff agencies in turn develop others. Frequently, these agencies specialize in finding fault, sometimes publicly, rather than in reaching out to provide a helping hand. It is no accident that resigned humor mingled with frustration often marks discussions of staff agencies. In this vein, a commission member with ample government experience only half facetiously observed at one of the commission's meetings that the definition of an auditor is "someone who shows up after the battle is over and shoots the wounded."

Many who testified before the commission expressed support for one form of deregulation or another. The message can be quite pointed. At its Philadelphia hearing, Theodore Hershberg described how that city's charter had in the wake of response to earlier scandals "eliminated virtually all management prerogatives. Up until last year, you could not buy anything that cost more than $2,000 without formal competitive bidding. You couldn't buy a PC and a printer until you went through a six-month, 180-step process, to procure something." Other rules make it hard to transfer monies among detailed line-item budgets, or they penalize agencies for not spending all funds by the end of the fiscal year.

Civil service systems and the personnel offices that administer them often rank in the forefront of the agencies that irritate managers — that seem to represent the triumph of technique over purpose. Frustration with these systems ran strong at many of the commission hearings. Consider promotion processes, for example. Compared to many state and local agencies, the federal government is a model of flexibility in its promotion practices, allowing managers to emphasize past performance and experience in deciding whom to interview and advance. In contrast, many states and localities continue to rely heavily on written tests for promotion. In this regard, Stan Lundine observed at the commission's Philadelphia hearing:

> Everybody knows that the way to promote policemen isn't based on their ability to take a test. We get some of the worst officers promoted simply because they are the better test takers, but there's no reward in that system for merit, for quality performance. Now clearly there's something wrong with that system. I know I'm suspect as an elected official, that they'll think we are trying to get our hands on it. But I really believe that we're beyond that narrow limitation and that we can come up with a performance-based system for promotion that would be more like the private sector but with some public-sector and nonpolitical basis built into it.

Others at the hearings voiced comparable concerns.

Of course, not all civil service systems are so rule bound. In Chapter Two, Carolyn Ban and Norma Riccucci document the wide variation that exists across the country, pointing to the substantial flexibility achieved in such states as Minnesota and California. For their part, James K. Conant and Dennis L. Dresang, in Chapter Three, demonstrate that the waiting time to fill certain positions in Wisconsin is far shorter than many critics of civil service systems suggest. Our commission hearings also yielded evidence of highly innovative human resource management. In California's decentralized civil service system, for instance, the state Franchise Tax Board has established links with several educational institutions to assist its recruitment efforts.

Recognizing and learning from the variation that exists at the state and local levels, Ban and Riccucci as well as others suggest several important steps that could add flexibility to human resource management. Four deserve particular note. First, state and local governments should move away from the extensive use of written tests for screening purposes, especially for promotions. It is expensive to develop, sustain, and administer valid and reliable exams. Instead, criteria such as the careful review of experience, educational achievement (or skill acquisition), and past performance can narrow the pool of applicants for managers to consider.

Second, state and local governments should abandon the "rule of three" for selection and give managers the discretion to pick from longer lists of qualified applicants. Written tests and other selection devices are not finely honed predictors of subsequent performance on the job. Limiting managers to the top three on a list of eligibles hardly ensures a more merit-based approach than presenting them with a somewhat larger number of qualified job hunters.

Third, state and local agencies should increase opportunities for lateral entry by outsiders into civil service positions. Even Conant and Dresang, who paint a sanguine picture of recruitment to Wisconsin state government, note that limited lateral entry to higher-level positions erodes the quality of the recruitment pool. With more discretion to pick from the outside, executives would still have an incentive not to ignore those already working for the agency: most executives want to reward subordinates who have performed well for them; insiders often enjoy a competitive edge over outsiders because of the knowledge and skills acquired in working for the agency. Greater opportunities for lateral entry often function mainly as a fail-safe mechanism for executives just in case no suitable insider emerges.

Fourth, state and local agencies should consolidate job titles into broad bands, reducing the substantial overhead costs of administering a highly differentiated classification system. This facilitates flexibility in deploying personnel to different assignments and in setting their salaries. Morever, as James L. Perry and Kenneth L. Kraemer show in Chapter Seven, in the case of information specialists, movement away from narrowly defined job categories to broader classifications opens the door to more on-the-job opportunities to learn and acquire new skills.

Customer Focus

Wherever it went for hearings — literally East, West, North, and South — the commission heard testimony that assigned great importance to treating clients or citizens as "customers." In Vicksburg, Mississippi, for instance, the mayor, Robert Walker, told the commission: "More and more, we have been pushing the idea that the 30,000 to 35,000 people in the City of Vicksburg are our customers. . . . We work for them. And we are going to have to improve the quality of service delivered to our customers." At the commission's Texas hearing, Camille Barnett, Austin city manager, described an initiative called BASIC (Building Austin's Standards in Customer Service) that emphasized "leadership, teamwork, and service improvement to achieve customer satisfaction." In Philadelphia, Louis J. Gambaccini, the chief operations officer of the Southeastern Pennsylvania Transportation Authority, described the practice of using "rider report cards to find out from our customers what they believe are the important things." He described special initiatives "where we have senior managers meet at different station locations to hear directly the personal complaints of passengers, complaints and suggestions — and to a surprising degree, increasingly, compliments."

Some contributors to this book have reinforced this emphasis on the customer. Jorge Chapa, for instance, in Chapter Four, speaks of the need to make organizations more customer sensitive. Donald F. Kettl in Chapter

Eight, calls for a new breed of public manager with a "customer-based" focus, rejecting an emphasis on the citizen as client for one that sees the citizen as customer.

However, not everyone finds the customer concept a powerful orienting device (for example, Nathan, 1993; Swiss, 1992). They note that (1) many of government's products and services target involuntary recipients or compliers (for example, individual taxpayers, prisoners)—groups that hardly resemble customers in the private sector; (2) agencies have many customers with conflicting desires; (3) the quest to serve the general public may at times call on agencies to offend their immediate clients; and, given these complexities, (4) the principle of satisfying customers begs too many questions to be very useful. Moreover, as Ernesto Cortes, Jr., southwest regional director of the Industrial Areas Foundation, told the commission in Austin, the concept of customer loses its appeal if citizens lack the capacity to judge the services and products of state and local governments. "To learn to make judgments, the people have got to have institutions which cultivate those habits of thinking that mentor and guide them." At its worst, rhetoric about being "customer driven" can become an expression of symbolic politics where officials posture as progressive, innovative managers while doing little to improve the performance of state and local agencies.

For all these problems, however, careful use of the customer concept may help, at least on the margins. To designate groups of individuals as customers implies learning about and respecting their tastes and preferences; it implies being vigilant in searching for new ways to serve them. To the degree that the concept becomes part of the mindset of state and local officials, it can (though it need not) motivate them to become more service oriented and helpful. It can help counteract the rule-driven, control-oriented approach that often dominates public agencies.

Those attracted to the concept of customer need to keep certain caveats in mind (Barzelay, 1992). To be useful, it cannot apply to everyone who cares about the agency's performance. The agency needs to define its *primary* service target—its customer. The concept also fits more easily with public bureaucracies that provide a service (health clinics) or subsidies (unemployment checks) than those that regulate (prisons) or otherwise provide involuntary services. Moreover, as in the private sector, the customer is not always right but may want services that the agency cannot lawfully or ethically provide. Finally, agencies cannot resolve all issues of accountability exclusively in terms of customer satisfaction. Obviously, the informed preferences of the more general citizenry and top elected officials, as well as legal requirements, factor heavily into the accountability equation.

Ultimately, the motivational impact of the term *customer* needs more study. Do officials who think in these terms behave any differently than those who do not? In the absence of evidence on this question, we should not automatically dismiss the possibility that the concept has a positive motivational effect.

Front-Line Involvement

The research and hearings of the commission also support the notion that revitalization requires involvement of front-line employees in defining and remedying problems. This conclusion not only springs from the sensible view that these employees often know more about the nature of their tasks than those further up the hierarchy but also parallels a growing concern about private sector practices. Many worry that the competitive position of the United States has declined in part because of organizational forms and educational practices that leave our front-line workers much less prepared to be problem solvers than those in such countries as Germany and Japan (Marshall and Tucker, 1992).

In this book, Chapa in particular has stressed the rejuvenating effects of involving these workers. He approvingly notes arguments for delayering organizations to bring those at the top levels of management closer to those at the bottom of the hierarchy. He also sees considerable value in quality circles, which, among other things, bring front-line employees together to analyze and discuss problems of service delivery. Chapa's endorsement of this technique received a resounding second at the commission's Sacramento hearing, where Mary Grogan, director of parks and recreation in the city of Modesto, California, described her department's use of quality circles. Spurred to employ the technique by the widening gap between the demands of a growing population and the dwindling resources available to her agency, she asserted that quality circles had fueled significant improvements in the performance of park maintenance workers. "We have gone from an average maintenance per acre of 3.2 acres per employee to 5.7 per employee. This is significant, ladies and gentlemen, because it practically doubles our efficiency." Although they did not necessarily endorse quality circles, others who appeared before the commission also stressed the importance of involving employees, especially in agencies facing fiscal stress.

But how much staying power do efforts to involve front-line employees in problem solving have in public agencies? Middle managers and even executives often resist this development. Union leaders express skepticism that a meaningful employee contribution to problem solving can occur without their participation. Speaking of this issue in the context of total quality management (TQM), union leader Mark Neimeiser observed at the commission's Tallahassee hearing: "TQM speaks to worker empowerment and long-term team building and not short-term hoop diving. Unions can get managers to see the need to empower workers and not feel threatened. We think we provide a balance." Moreover, some empirical evidence supports the view that union participation bolsters employee involvement in constructive ways (Kelley and Harrison, 1993). The greater security of employment in unionized settings may enable workers to speak more confidently and freely about organizational problems. In this vein, Perry and Kraemer suggest that the key to involving front-line workers in implementing new information technologies may well depend on providing them with job security.

A Bottom-Line Orientation

The need for governments to develop better performance measures also permeates discussion of revitalization. As Camille Barnett, city manager of Austin, Texas, told the commission at its hearing in that city: "We in government need to quit the emphasis on input measures and focus on what we get with the resources that we have. If we are to do this, we have to find new ways to measure results. I would love to see a *Consumer Reports* for cities where there is a way to measure ourselves against other cities' services. Benchmarking is a concept we could really use in government." If agencies can develop more bottom-line indicators, the deregulation of public administration becomes easier. Managers and employees can have more discretion yet ultimately be held accountable for their performance relative to a commonly understood scorecard. Representative Ric Williamson, vice chair of the Appropriations Committee in the Texas legislature, described the evolution of his thinking on this subject at the commission's Austin hearing. "I spent from 1985 to 1987 trying to learn as much about the Texas budget cycle and trying to promote command and control concepts that I felt were lacking in state government." Increasingly concerned about the limits to this approach, however, Williamson had become convinced by 1989 of the need "to move away from so much micromanagement toward goal setting and measurement."

Developing good performance measures is, of course, extremely difficult. Coming up with valid indicators of an agency's performance (for example, police enforcement) is hard; linking these to outcomes (for example, less crime) is even harder. Nagging questions about performance measurement persist. Do the improvements resulting from this information outweigh the costs of acquiring, analyzing, and communicating it? Will the emphasis on quantifiable standards cause employees to let other important but less measurable components of their jobs slide? How can top policymakers hold employees accountable for failure to score well on performance measures, if these employees can point to forces beyond their control that produced defeat?

Perhaps a paraphrase of the adage about democracy sums matters up best: The quest to develop performance measures is the worst approach except for all the alternatives. In fact, many states and localities have made considerable headway in developing these indicators, and more progress seems possible at reasonable cost. Smart managers can monitor and correct some of the distortions in employee behavior spawned by these measures. The advent of new information technologies, described by Perry and Kraemer, brightens prospects for developing performance indicators. Ultimately, movement away from excessively rule-oriented management requires a continued search for more satisfying bottom lines in states and localities.

Barriers to High-Performance Agencies

Deregulated, customer-driven, results-oriented management that reaches out to front-line employees will not flourish easily, as some skeptics say. In this book, for instance, Ban and Riccucci have reservations about the ability of the quality movement, especially TQM, to spark revitalization. Others dismiss many aspects of the quality movement as the latest fad.

But even fads can have a positive side. They can focus attention on important management issues, lead to the reappraisal of goals and technologies, spur new thinking, or reaffirm the importance of proven paths to success. As Louis Gambaccini told the commission in Philadelphia when asked about the quality management movement, "I tend to think that certainly the focus on TQM and the 'Osborne' approach are healthy because they really stimulate a lot of innovative thinking. But I'm afraid I've been around too long and I think about all the other fads that have passed in review. . . . So I think it's very useful to have the fad to force the innovative thinking, but I think when you get down to the basics, there are some very elemental themes."

Fad or not, deregulating the public sector rests uneasily in the American context. It requires considerable trust in administrative discretion, which runs against the grain of a political culture built on the suspicion of public power. Moreover, mistrust within agencies can also make deregulation and other change difficult. In many public agencies, front-line and lower-level employees harbor doubts that their supervisors would use greater discretion wisely. This point came home to the commission at its Tallahassee hearing when Mark Neimeiser of the American Federation of State, County, and Municipal Employees justified the union's opposition to the Florida civil service reform effort: "Not that we like the existing rules and their absurdity, but the solution to do away with the rules or give management flexibility lacked credibility to us. It is not the worker manipulating the system—it is the managers. We just want to know what the rules are and hold people accountable to them." In a similar vein, Frank Sherwood of Florida State University told the commission that any benefits of greater managerial discretion hinge on whether agencies succeed in acquiring, utilizing, developing, and retaining capable leaders and managers.

For all the difficulties, many state and local governments have scaled the barricades to reform. Change does not necessarily rest on highly visible campaigns launched by top elected officials; in fact, these campaigns often carry symbolic overtones that cause stakeholders to dig in and resist (Walters, 1992; Wechsler, 1992). In many cases, quiet diplomacy and problem solving better lubricate the wheels of reform. In this regard, Gloria Harmon, executive officer of the California State Personnel Board, testified at the commission's Sacramento hearing about "a number of systemic changes" in California's personnel practices that "promoted diversity and which have also put more flexibility and accountability in the hands of departmental managers. Key among these was the total decentralization of the selection process." Of particular relevance here, she noted that "the changes have been evolutionary and incremental rather than a cataclysm of reform."

Toward High-Performance Personnel

Meeting the workforce challenge demands more than well-crafted organizations and sound management strategies; it also requires the recruitment, development, and retention of high-quality people. State and local governments need committed, talented, and diverse employees.

Some evidence in this book bodes well for efforts to tackle this aspect of the workforce challenge. Conant and Dresang suggest that at least some state governments succeed in promptly hiring able people for entry-level and other positions. Steven D. Gold and Sarah Ritchie, in Chapter Five, find that for lower- and mid-level jobs many states and localities have competitive compensation packages. Rita Mae Kelly, in Chapter Six, traces progress in placing women and minorities in higher-level positions in state and local government. But the commission hearings and other research caution against complacency. Kelly underscores that we are far from achieving a state and local workforce demographically representative of the populace at all hierarchical levels. Nor do we know enough about how to manage a workforce marked by greater ethnic and gender diversity.

Furthermore, it is often hard for state and local governments to recruit and retain certain personnel, such as health professionals and information specialists. As Gold and Ritchie observe, state and local salary schedules frequently add to the problem by giving too little weight to issues of supply and demand. These and other forces have generated concern even among agencies with good track records of attracting highly qualified employees. In testimony before the commission in Sacramento, for instance, Gerald Goldberg, executive officer of the California Franchise Tax Board (FTB), asserted:

> In previous years California was seen as a place to be for highly skilled civil servants. Now we are at best in a holding mode if not into survival drills. In the short term the FTB may be in a position to recruit highly skilled workers looking for work because of current economic conditions. The longer term prognosis isn't as bright. The demands for efficiencies in revenue production will be higher than they have ever been. This will require that we continue to retain and recruit skilled workers. At the same time, the competition level for some of our most critical skills will increase.

Sustaining a pool of talent at the top may prove particularly perplexing. As Gold and Ritchie note, pay at these levels tends to be the least competitive with the private sector. The lack of privacy in executive searches in the public sector can make matters worse. At the commission's Austin hearing, Kathy

Whitmire described her frustration with top-level searches where "everybody wants to do a public airing of the search process." She recalled how many of the talented individuals she wanted to recruit refused to become candidates under these circumstances. "People who are in critical public positions cannot afford to go through that public process where everyone in town expresses their opinion of them and you ultimately pick one after they have been hashed over in the newspaper. This turns off a lot of good people from government."

Among the strategies for recruiting the talented to state and local governments, Ban and Riccucci note the particular value of intern and apprentice programs. Research prepared for the commission documents that many states and localities show great ingenuity in developing these programs (Edwards, 1992), including cities such as Long Beach (California), Dallas, and Phoenix and states such as New York. But fiscal stress has taken its toll. Internship initiatives throughout the country need rejuvenation if they are to be a significant vehicle for bringing the best students into state and local public service.

Getting talented and committed citizens to work for states and localities will, of course, be a very modest victory if little is done subsequently to train, educate, and develop them. Human resource capitalism depends on a workforce that constantly learns and acts on the basis of the new knowledge and skills it has acquired (Marshall and Tucker, 1992).

Training and education needs extend from the bottom to the top of state and local governments. Chapa's emphasis on the needs of lower-level workers also surfaced in testimony before the commission. Some expressed concern that these workers would be unable to keep pace with rapid changes in information technology. For instance, at the commission's Sacramento hearing, Gerald Goldberg described his agency's efforts to develop "a new Taxpayer Information System . . . which will fully modernize all of our systems implemented in the seventies and eighties." The demands of the new system "must be addressed through a significant amount of employee re-training which goes beyond just the technical changes. The new system will require increased functional skill levels in reading, mathematics, computer literacy, and basic problem solving" (see also Perry and Kraemer). These demands seem like a tall order given the basic skills deficiencies of many entry-level employees at the Franchise Tax Board. In Goldberg's words, these include

- Employees in our files unit who do not know how to alphabetize
- Employees who cannot compute simple percentages or even know if an answer generated by the computer is in the ballpark
- Employees who . . . cannot write a single complete sentence
- Employees opening envelopes in our receiving unit who cannot count the number of envelopes opened for their production slips
- Employees who must have someone else fill out their application for a promotional examination

Educational needs do not stop at the front lines. Questions also persist as to whether state and local governments invest enough in high-quality education for executives and middle managers. In a paper prepared for the commission, Robert Behn of Duke University (1992, p. 1) asserts: "In state and local government . . . too little thought is given to the education of key managers or the development of future leaders. There is little commitment to executive education. A few states (and a few agencies) do conduct their own internal programs, and other jurisdictions and organizations do send some of their people to universities for special programs. But the executive-education ethic, which so permeates the business world, is almost completely absent in government." This training deficit may be even more acute for middle managers, who are critically important to the success of most programs and often resist change. As Chapa indicates, middle managers can all too easily define themselves as the guardians of the rules rather than as service providers. A study of leadership in a Massachusetts social service agency found that middle managers were "inherently risk averse." They saw themselves "as criticized and penalized for their mistakes while rarely benefiting from their successes." Rather than being results oriented, these managers kept "their heads down, trying to avoid mistakes" (Behn, 1991, p. 74).

Education and training for middle managers becomes more important to the degree that state and local governments involve front-line employees in efforts to diagnose problems and bolster performance. Middle managers are among those most threatened by this initiative. For instance, in describing her program to draw on the insights of front-line employees through quality circles, Mary Grogan told the commission in Sacramento: "One of the things that happened initially, which we had to overcome, was that some of our greatest and most reluctant participants were the supervisors; those first- and second-level supervisors felt that if employees came up with ideas to be more productive and improve job efficiencies, then management would perceive the situation as though supervisors weren't doing their jobs and would be critical of them. We had to find a way to make them buy into the program because if they didn't they would become the obstructionists."

Training middle managers to become a positive force for the involvement of front-line employees may also allay the concerns of union leaders, who complain that all the talk about quality management is seldom accompanied by the training dollars needed to make it work. To be sure, some states and localities have invested in training and education for middle managers (for example, Faerman, Quinn, and Thompson, 1987), but few, if any, would argue that the investment achieves the level needed to meet the workforce challenge.

How much do state and local governments spend on training and education? Precise data are difficult to obtain. In part this uncertainty reflects the tendency of officials to hide training monies in other line items to avoid seeing these dollars chopped at the first sign of fiscal stress. Although these hidden training investments occur, however, few believe that employers in either the public or private sector pour sufficient dollars into developing their personnel for the country to remain competitive in the global economy. One analysis suggests that employer expenditures for continued education and training should be 3 to 5 percent of salaries and wages, a significant increase over the 1.4 percent average currently spent (Marshall and Tucker, 1992).

Providing adequate incentives for state and local government to make investments of this magnitude may appear to be work for Sisyphus. Policy-makers often view training and education as an amenity, even a frill, without immediate or tangible benefits. Hence, we need to search for creative ways to stimulate and protect training and educational spending. In some jurisdictions, collective bargaining processes provide a partial answer. In New York state, for instance, the Governor's Office of Employee Relations and public sector unions negotiate continuing education support as part of their contract. Once stipulated in the three- or four-year contracts, these dollars cannot so readily be sacrificed at the first sign of fiscal storm clouds.

Of course, dollar targets for life-long learning should not obfuscate thorny questions of how to maximize the learning bang for the training and educational buck. Frank Sherwood told the commission in Tallahassee: "We probably do not spend enough money on training, but my guess is that we are wasting about half that which we do spend. Recently, the police chief of Kansas City said that about 95 percent of police training went to activities which occupy police about 3 percent of the time . . . . We typically do such a miserable job of needs assessment that it is almost impossible to say how much training is directed toward the real priorities of the system."

Education and training do not differ from other administrative activities in their means-ends uncertainty. Fog often shrouds how best to maximize the learning that will contribute most to revitalized governance. Calibrating and evaluating the outcomes of education and training remain difficult at best, especially since some of the most important benefits are long term. No doubt some education and training initiatives will flop. Whatever the limits, however, failure to strive for more and better modes of facilitating life-long learning among employees will almost certainly erode the quality of performance achieved by state and local governments.

Information Technology

The challenges of information technology also intersect with efforts to ensure revitalization. As Perry and Kraemer show, its proliferation can be a force for efficiency and effectiveness, accountability, and citizen outreach. It can, for instance, facilitate results-oriented management that gives higher-level officials better feedback on performance and thereby mute tendencies to seek higher-level control through endless rule promulgation and micromanagement. But, as Perry and Kraemer also indicate, information technology can serve many less desirable ends. More is not always better; costs can exceed benefits; simply throwing information technology at a problem seldom works. The effective use of this technology requires good judgment by executives and managers—judgment that is sensitive to its human resource implications.

Testimony to the commission showed that officials understand many of the benefits of information technology; as indicated in the introductory chapter, this technology can even help them overcome the debilitating effects of fragmentation. But it would be a mistake to see this technology as a quick fix for problems rooted in the American institutional framework. At the commission's Austin hearing, for instance, DeAnn Friedholm of the Texas lieutenant governor's office described an abortive initiative undertaken by the March of Dimes to use information technology to surmount the complexities of determining eligibility for Medicaid benefits. The March of Dimes

> funded a single intake computer system for maternal and child health services. What they found was that 70 percent of the questions an individual gets asked across about fifteen programs—state, federal, city programs in Houston—is the same. They have put together a very sophisticated software program, where an intake worker doesn't have to memorize the Medicaid manuals, which are miles long. But instead the computer has all the information, and that person can focus on the family—what does it need, what are its problems. They can tell the family, after one hour or so at the most, about the vast array of any of the services that they might be able to use to solve the problems they have.

But fragmentation of authority and federal regulations have stymied use of the software. As Friedholm observed, "the county hospital district is the group using the software, and they cannot certify a family for Medicaid. . . . For two years, we have struggled to find a way around the barriers and regulations to say that this software is so accurate that we can use it to determine who can qualify for what within the error rate levels that the federal government requires. We are still nowhere on that."

Private Nonprofits as Partners

As Kettl shows, the use of private agents to deliver state and local services also poses a special challenge to revitalization. Those who testified before the commission took a hard-headed view of the potential and limits of privatized service delivery, and no one saw it as a panacea. Moreover, they tended to share Kettl's view that such relationships are best seen as partnerships rather than as principal-agent, or master-servant, relationships.

The concept of partnership took on particular weight in the case of relations between government and private nonprofit entities. For instance, in his remarks before the commission in Philadelphia, Stan Lundine heaped praise on the private nonprofit groups for playing a major role in delivering social services for New York state. He advocated "strengthening the partnerships between state and local government and not-for-profit community-based organizations, which are proactive, tend to have ingenious managers and workers who have spirit and energy that comes from believing in what they do." Lundine's observations and Kettl's analysis of nonprofits in Dane County, Wisconsin, suggest that nonprofits as a category pose special issues for those wrestling with privatization issues. As distinct from proprietary contractors (or, for that matter, government bureaucracies), nonprofit groups are presumed to have special symbolic and instrumental properties. They evoke the image of "community" and can help forge a greater sense of community identity and responsibility, summoning visions of "neighbor-helping-neighbor." Through their emphasis on voluntarism, they become an outlet for the altruistic, public service impulses of the citizenry. They allegedly attract salaried employees who nurture strong commitments to the nonprofits' goals of helping others (Lipsky and Smith, 1989–1990).

Kettl shows that relationships between governments and nonprofit groups depart markedly from the idealized model of private organizations vigorously competing for contracts. Moreover, these relationships raise genuine issues of accountability. A handful of public employees who supervise large numbers of contracts in Dane County tend to be in the dark about what these organizations accomplish. Vigorous efforts to impose conditions or elaborate controls on nonprofits may, however, backfire, leading to some of the same excessive regulation and micromanagement that at times bedevils state and local agencies. Any special qualities that private nonprofits bring to the implementation of social programs may get lost in the aftermath (Lipsky and Smith, 1989–1990). The best hope for avoiding this quandary is for government to get more and better data on what nonprofits actually accomplish. Developments in information technology can ease (although surely not solve) problems of obtaining output and outcome data.

An ongoing issue for states and localities is how private nonprofits (and for that matter, proprietary) contractors achieve cost savings. To the degree that the competitive advantage of contractors springs from providing less generous compensation packages, major issues surface. If contractor pay rates and fringe benefits become too penurious, other problems state and local governments face may be compounded, such as the number of citizens without adequate health insurance. In this regard, meeting the health care challenge by guaranteeing every citizen access to a basic health insurance policy would be a plus. It could help level the playing field between "responsible" employers (which, in this sense, nearly all state and local governments are) and less socially conscious ones, which do not provide minimally acceptable compensation packages.

Ultimately, the role of nonprofits as partners of government requires much more research. Do the nonprofits in fact have more motivated, responsive, and effective employees than state and local agencies performing the same service? Can state agencies become as inventive in tapping community voluntarism? In general, how do nonprofits and government social agencies differ in their service delivery? The analytic spotlight should focus on these and related questions.

Conclusion

The research and hearings conducted for the National Commission on the State and Local Public Service helped build the knowledge base for its final report (see the appendix). Although this inquiry yielded insights, it was also an exercise in humility. Greater knowledge of these levels of the federal system also brings greater awareness of their enormous complexity and the limits to current understanding.

Many refer to states and localities as the laboratories of democracy. However, they are often laboratories without a systematic observer to record and analyze the results of the many natural experiments under way. To be sure, some aspects of state and local governance have been put under the microscope — schools, police departments, and finance, for instance — but in many areas of direct relevance to the commission, we have not in the past seized opportunities to learn from state and local experience.

Procedures and systems vary widely; one or another jurisdiction has tried almost every procedure or structure currently being discussed and advocated by proponents of revitalization. Seldom, however, can we find careful comparative studies of how these innovative practices work in the settings where they exist. For instance, those who believe that centralized rule-bound civil service systems function poorly can profit from examining how decentralized flexible arrangements actually work in certain states and localities. Do managers in these systems have an easier time achieving effectiveness than their counterparts in more centralized, rule-driven structures?

Researchers should also target other topics suggested by this book. We need comparative analyses of executive leadership at the state and local levels — the institutions that buttress it, its qualities, and its effects. Public organizations that in varying degrees feature deregulation, a customer orientation, the involvement of frontline employees, and a bottom-line focus also deserve study. So do recruitment, retention, and training strategies as well as a host of topics associated with information technology and the use of privatized agents (especially nonprofits) to deliver programs. Additional inquiry into state and local health agencies — especially as they grapple with the institutional, capacity, and management implications of health care reform — is also desirable.

The commission will have accomplished much if it stimulates more systematic, rigorous efforts to learn from the great variation present in the federal system. Those of us committed to a revitalized public service must combine our fascination with the marvelous diversity of state and local governments and the need for action in the face of uncertainty with a renewed focus on opportunities to find patterns and learn lessons.

References

Aberbach, J. D. *Keeping a Watchful Eye.* Washington, D.C.: Brookings Institution, 1990.

Barzelay, M. *Breaking Through Bureaucracy.* Berkeley: University of California Press, 1992.

Behn, R. *Leadership Counts.* Cambridge, Mass.: Harvard University Press, 1991.

Behn, R. "Thinking About Executive Education in State and Local Government." Paper prepared for the National Commission on the State and Local Public Service, Albany, New York, 1992.

Edwards, A. "Professional Internships in State and Local Public Service: Transcending the Traditional." Paper prepared for the National Commission on the State and Local Public Service, Albany, New York, 1992.

Faerman, S. R., Quinn, R. E., and Thompson, M. P. "Bridging Management Practice and Theory: New York State's Public Service Training Program." *Public Administration Review,* 1987, *47,* 310–319.

Kelley, M. R., and Harrison, B. "Unions, Technology, and Labor-Management Cooperation." In L. Mishel and P. Voos (eds.), *Unions and Economic Competitiveness.* Armonk, N.Y.: M. E. Sharpe, 1993.

Lipsky, M., and Smith, S. R. "Nonprofit Organizations, Government, and the Welfare State." *Political Science Quarterly,* 1989–1990, *104,* 625–648.

Marshall, R., and Tucker, M. *Thinking for a Living.* New York: Basic Books, 1992.

Nathan, R. P. *Turning Promises into Performance.* New York: Columbia University Press, 1993.

Swiss, J. E. "Adapting Total Quality Management (TQM) to Government." *Public Administration Review,* 1992, *52,* 356–362.

Tallon, J. D., Jr., and Nathan, R. P. "Federal/State Partnership for Health System Reform." *Health Affairs,* 1992, *11*(4), 7–16.

Vernon, I. J. "Citizens to Partake in Cutting Waste." *Congressional Quarterly Weekly Report,* 1993, *51,* 513.

Walters, J. "The Many Lives of Civil Service." *Governing,* November 1992, *6,* 30–35.

Wechsler, B. "Restructuring Florida's Career Service System: The Chiles-MacKay Reform Initiative." Paper prepared for the National Commission on the State and Local Public Service, Albany, New York, 1992.

Wilson, J. Q. *Bureaucracy: What Government Agencies Do and Why They Do It.* New York: Basic Books, 1989.

APPENDIX

Report of the National Commission on the State and Local Public Service: *Hard Truths/Tough Choices: An Agenda for State and Local Reform*

HARD TRUTHS / TOUGH CHOICES

An Agenda for State and Local Reform

THE FIRST REPORT OF THE NATIONAL COMMISSION
ON THE STATE AND LOCAL PUBLIC SERVICE

THE HONORABLE WILLIAM F. WINTER
CHAIRMAN

PRESENTED AT A WHITE HOUSE MEETING
WITH PRESIDENT BILL CLINTON

Sponsored by

The Nelson A. Rockefeller
Institute of Government
State University of New York
411 State Street
Albany, New York 12203-1003
(518) 443-5825

1993

Address inquiries to:
The National Commission on the State and Local Public Service
The Nelson A. Rockefeller Institute of Government
411 State Street
Albany, New York 12203-1003
(518) 443-5825
(518) 443-5788 (Fax)

Manufactured in the United States of America

ISBN: 0-914341-26-X

MEMBERS OF THE COMMISSION

William F. Winter, *Chair,* Watkins Ludlam & Stennis

Meg Armstrong, Leadership Group, Inc.

Reubin O'D. Askew, Florida Atlantic University, Broward

Mary Jo Bane, U.S. Department of Health and Human Services

Barbara B. Blum, Foundation for Child Development

Walter D. Broadnax, U.S. Department of Health and Human Services

Yvonne Brathwaite Burke, Los Angeles County Board of Supervisors

Karen S. Burstein, New York State Family Court Judge

Henry G. Cisneros, U.S. Department of Housing and Urban Development

John J. DiIulio, Jr., Princeton University

R. Scott Fosler, National Academy of Public Administration

Robert Fulton, Public Policy Analyst

John Herbers, Governing magazine

Elizabeth L. Hollander, Illinois Commission on the Future of the Public Service

Robert A. Kipp, Hallmark Cards, Inc.

L. Bruce Laingen, American Academy of Diplomacy

Ray Marshall, University of Texas at Austin

Ruth W. Massinga, The Casey Family Program

William G. Milliken, Chrysler Corporation Board of Directors

Richard P. Nathan, State University of New York

Neal R. Peirce, Writer

Nelson W. Polsby, University of California, Berkeley

Michael B. Preston, University of Southern California

Charles T. Royer, Institute of Politics, Harvard University

Lisbeth B. Schorr, Harvard University

Max Sherman, University of Texas at Austin

Eddie N. Williams, Joint Center for Political and Economic Studies

STAFF AND ADVISORS

Frank J. Thompson
Executive Director

Paul C. Light
Senior Advisor

Miriam Trementozzi
Project Manager

Enid Beaumont
Special Advisor

Barbara C. Guinn
Research Assistant

Steven D. Gold
Advisor

Echo D. Cartwright
Project Assistant

Michael S. Sparer
Senior Health Advisor

Michael Cooper
Publication Advisor

Lawrence D. Brown
Senior Health Advisor

Mary Mathews
Former Project Assistant

SPONSORS

The Commission acknowledges with gratitude the following foundations for providing financial assistance:

The Florence and John Schumann Foundation

The Ford Foundation

The Henry J. Kaiser Family Foundation

Carnegie Corporation of New York

The Commission is solely responsible for the content of this report.

CONTENTS

CHAIRMAN'S FOREWORD

At no time in recent American history has there been a more searching concern about the performance of our political institutions than at the present.

This state of mind in the body politic is amply demonstrated by the flood of remedies that are now being proposed to improve the system.

All of this has to be put into perspective. In the first place, there are no silver bullets. Our political system is a reflection of our individual values and priorities. It will function properly only when it is led by those for whom leadership means more than the inclination to read public opinion polls and when it is sustained by a citizenry who understand that it cannot always opt for the easy choice. Anyone who has seriously worked at it will acknowledge that making democracy function properly has never been simple. But today it is harder than ever.

Making democracy work is what the state and local public service must be about. It is here that the actual delivery of the most basic and essential services takes place. Since people have the most direct contact with their public officials in county seats, city halls, and state capitols, it is here that most citizens form their opinions of how well government is performing.

An obvious part of the process of addressing the problems that face us as a society is examining the structure of government and determining how it can be better organized to do its job more efficiently. This must be a continuous activity, and one sufficiently dynamic and broadly based to resist those defenders of political turf who would argue for maintaining the status quo. But there is another measure of governmental performance that is even more important: the human dimensions of public service.

The process has to start with executive leadership. Certainly the chief executive has the benefit of the bully pulpit. But, as important as that is, it is still only a platform for oratory. It is the act of leading by example that more often makes the difference. It is this quality that is at the heart of public leadership, and it is this element that in too many cases is lacking, thereby contributing to a rising cynicism both within and outside government.

The concept that public service, especially public service at the state and local level, is a noble and worthy calling must somehow be revitalized in this country. Those of us who have had the good fortune to serve in state and local government know how many genuinely dedicated and committed people work there. In most cases their efforts are unsung and their contributions to society are unrecognized and inadequately rewarded.

Most people with whom I have been associated in government take added pride in their work and produce infinitely more satisfactory results when they are kept informed of the larger mission in which they play a supporting role. It is an elementary fact of life that most of us like to be involved in a meaningful process that is larger than ourselves. The key to more successful and efficient performance by the various elements of state and local government lies in sharing the vision of together building and serving a better society.

In the final analysis, the quality of our lives in the future will depend on how well we come to grips with our concerns about the capacity of our political system to handle the issues of the moment. That capacity will be determined in large measure by the commitment of the men and women who make up the state and local public service, sustained and supported by a citizenry intent on forging a better future.

The National Commission on the State and Local Public Service follows in distinguished footsteps. Our work is the logical sequel to the important work of the National Commission on the Public Service, which primarily focused on the national government. This commission was chaired by Paul A. Volcker, who has been helpful and supportive in our work. L. Bruce Laingen, who was Executive Director of the Volcker Commission, ably serves as a member of our Commission.

I wish to thank my colleagues on the National Commission on the State and Local Public Service as well as the staff for working so effectively together over the past two years as we start down a road that we hope will lead to real governmental reform in America.

William F. Winter
Chairman

1

THE CHALLENGE

---

*. . . One of the great failings of democracy is its tendency
to take the path of least resistance and to avoid controversy wherever possible, and above all, to silence debate
because it is not fashionable.*

Eugene Patterson
Editor Emeritus, The *St. Petersburg Times*
Tallahassee Hearing, May 1992

There are over 15 million state and local public employees, making
up 13 percent of the nation's total work force. These employees
do much of the real work of domestic governance. We literally could
not live without them. They provide our water, collect our trash,
vaccinate our children, police our communities, and administer traffic
safety, airports, and the vital systems we need to communicate with
each other and with other nations. They do much of the teaching,
training, and counseling in our public schools, universities, and community colleges to prepare our children for fulfilling careers. They are
responsible for environmental clean-up and protection programs.
They design and carry out programs to lift our most needy out of
poverty and into jobs and housing. They operate the hospitals that are
the last hope of the uninsured. They staff most of our prisons, as well
as our court system. Not a day passes during which their work does
not touch and shape our lives (see Table 1).

Yet there is a growing consensus among both citizens and
public officials that state and local institutions of government need to
drastically improve their capacity and performance if we are to meet
the challenges of our rapidly changing economic and social systems.
This report contains a series of proposals that taken together would
constitute a significant change in how our more than 15 million state
and local public employees perform their duties. These proposals, we

believe, would move us away from an encrusted and outmoded system of command and control and its rule-bound management that emphasizes constraints and process at the expense of mission and results. They would move us to a new way of operating, which is to build trust and then lead. This approach, which we call *trust and lead*, requires strong and positive relationships between the leaders of state and local government, public employees, citizens, and the many diverse groups essential to the governmental process.

TABLE 1: STATE AND LOCAL GOVERNMENT EMPLOYMENT (FULL- AND PART-TIME), 1991	
TYPE OF GOVERNMENT	
TOTAL	**15,451,772**
State	**4,521,385**
Local	**10,930,387**
County	2,196,263
Municipalities	2,661,823
Townships	414,717
School Districts	5,045,433
Special Districts	612,151

Source: U.S. Bureau of the Census, *Public Employment: 1991*, Series GE-91-1. Washington, D.C.: U.S. Government Printing Office, 1992.

Ours is a frank and urgent call for change in the nature of these relationships. How they evolve in the years to come will offer America a choice between two quite different futures. The first is mired in the hidebound, outmoded ways of doing business that too often get encrusted in our governmental institutions. The second emphasizes leadership and trust on a basis that we believe is fully appropriate to a strong democracy.

One future would result from a stand-pat approach that allows elected officials, public servants, and citizens to hide from the kinds of tough choices that would infuse new energy and purpose into public service and that would force nonresponsive bureaucracies into the forefront of change. That approach would surely lead to a future in which our nation would be poorer—in economic strength, in global influence, and in the ability of all the nation's citizens to lead satisfying, productive, and prosperous lives.

But America's state and local governments can work toward an alternate future. Achieving it would call for courageous leadership, not politics as usual—for empowered public servants, an engaged citizenry, and new ideas. It is a future in which schools are more effective, families stronger, the environment cleaner, and the economy more productive. It is a future that allows us to continue that remarkable historical legacy of passing on a more vibrant nation and a higher standard of living to each subsequent generation.

Unfortunately, too many of America's state and local governments appear to muddle along, deceiving themselves and ducking decisions. Just as discouraging—and more to the point of this report— those who are willing to face reality confront a host of obstacles to action. Imagine a governmental system that embodied all of the often-caricatured problems that prevent governmental systems from making tough choices and effecting change. This system would have many debilitating features:

➤ It would deny chief executives the authority to act, by fragmenting and diffusing authority over the programs and agencies those chief executives are supposed to lead.

➤ It would put those executives in charge of unyielding bureaucracies, clogged with layers of management and supervision, driven by antiquated personnel, procurement, and budget systems that seek to regulate even the smallest decisions.

➤ It would foster a "knowledge gap" inside those public agencies, preventing employees from acquiring the skills and information they need to do their jobs better and enjoy them more.

➤ It would encourage public distrust by blocking access to information about who influences the system, including information on campaign finance and lobbying. At the same time it would bring citizens into the policy-making process at the latest possible moment, so that their ideas would really have no bearing on final outcomes. It would be a system that keeps the public off balance and uninformed, thus fueling their anger, apathy, and cynicism.

➤ Finally, that system would saddle itself with an overwhelming fiscal burden, guaranteeing that it would operate in a state of recurring budget crisis, further dampening the willingness of potential executives to serve, hampering the ability of rank and file employees to muster the resources to do their jobs right, and confirming public suspicions that state and local government cannot do the job.

Unfortunately, these conditions are realities for many state and local governments. Governments hamstring their chief executives by diffusing their power. They operate with antiquated and obsolete personnel, procurement, and budget systems. They fail to invest in the most critical resource they have: their rank and file personnel. They isolate and frustrate their citizenry. And, finally, they find themselves struggling to cope under the weight of a crushing crisis in health care funding. In many ways it could be described as a system undergoing death by a thousand paper cuts, while states are losing their fiscal life blood to Medicaid costs.

Of course, many are coping—even prospering—through remarkable energy and innovation, an energy and innovation that helped inspire this report. But the fact is that many are far from able to play a role in assuring the alternative American future. And if state and local governments are not ready to lead an American renewal, it will not happen. Washington has its own budget problems, and while it may offer some financial relief to states and localities, the federal government cannot provide a quick fix. Furthermore, the economic recovery is likely to be slow and will be unable to lift states and localities out of their fiscal difficulties. That means that governments will have to make tough choices if they are to realize their alternative future. In fact, even if fiscal stress is much less than we expect, they must pursue this future if only to keep faith with the American people.

The Commission does not believe that the roughly 87,000 state and local governments and the people who work for them are failing America. Surveys show that citizens mostly like what they get from their 50 states, 3,000 counties, 36,000 cities and towns, 15,000 school districts, and 33,000 special districts.

Yet there is a growing sense that our state and local governments—and the citizenry that supports them—are missing the wake-up call. At a time when standing pat has become a recipe for decline, even dismantlement, the Commission believes that too many states and localities and their citizens are doing just that. Consider the warning signs:

➤ The number of citizens who want government to spend more in virtually every category is up—more on education, child care, AIDS, homelessness, the environment, the elderly, parks, and transportation. At the same time, the state and local tax revolt movement appears alive and well.

➤ The number of citizens who expressed a great deal or a fair amount of confidence in local government fell from 73 percent in 1987 to 60 percent in 1991, while the number who expressed confidence in state government fell from 73 percent to 51 percent. "If we could get the public as involved and as informed about politics as they are about Monday Night Football," one Florida legislator told *The New York Times*, "we wouldn't have as many problems. People have to get off their duffs and participate."

➤ A recent survey of college honor society students by the National Commission on the Public Service (the Volcker Commission) showed that only 1.8 percent and 0.9 percent of them, respectively, ranked state and local government as their "most preferred employer." The federal government ranked at 3 percent, large corporations at 34 percent.

➤ The number of states and localities in fiscal distress has never been higher—for example, 29 states cut spending below original appropriations in 1991; 23 froze across-the-board salary increases; 17 cut the absolute value of welfare benefits; 12 laid off employees; 34 raised taxes.

Ironically, we did this to ourselves, usually with the best of intentions. We want strong leadership, but in the name of democracy we often fragment and temper authority. We want to hire the best employees, but to keep the process fair and patronage-free we have designed a system so complex that good people turn away out of frustration.

We want to use money efficiently but in the name of fiscal responsibility we have papered the procurement process with so many rules and procedures that many of our best companies refuse to bid on contracts, and the simplest and cheapest of purchases are treated as equal to the most complex and expensive. We want our bureaucracies to be fiscally accountable, but in that quest we have created enormous incentives to "spend it or lose it" at the end of each fiscal year.

There is, of course, no statute that says we have to frustrate our leadership; that we have to pile rule upon rule or manager upon manager until decision-making becomes the exception rather than the rule. There is no law that says we have to preclude front-line staff from having a say in how services are delivered or how government does its job. There is no rule that says government has to maintain an aloof relationship with citizens. There is no provision that says we cannot change. It all starts with putting away the smoke and mirrors and the chewing gum and baling wire that too many states and localities have been using to get by over the past few years. It starts by recognizing that business as usual is a guarantee that this generation of leaders will fail the next generation of Americans. Owning up to reality is at the heart of the Commission's agenda.

The Commission is based at the Nelson A. Rockefeller Institute of Government at the State University of New York in Albany, a national center for the study of American state and local government. Two years ago the 27-member Commission embarked on a journey of study and debate leading to this report. The Commission includes three former governors, two former big-city mayors, one former big-city manager, a member of the Los Angeles County Board of Supervisors and a former county council member, seven former state and local agency heads, a former U.S. Secretary of Labor, nine scholar/experts, and two journalists who made careers in covering state and local government. (Member biographies can be found starting on page 67 of this report, and lists of Commission hearing witnesses and research papers begin on pages 75 and 81, respectively.)

Launched with a generous grant from the Florence and John Schumann Foundation, and additional support from the Ford Foundation, the Henry J. Kaiser Family Foundation, and the Carnegie Corporation of New York, the Commission held six hearings, starting in Jackson, Mississippi, in January 1992, and moving to Austin the following March, Tallahassee and Sacramento in May, and Chicago and Philadelphia in June. The Commission solicited over two dozen papers from leading scholars in the field, and sought input from a host of local, state, and national organizations.

In the course of its travels, the Commission was strengthened in its conviction that state and local governments need to change, that too many are waiting for miracles that will not happen. At the same time, the Commission was heartened by the reports it heard of hard-won successes:

➤ Two of the four largest cities in Jackson County, Mississippi, have saved hundreds of thousands of dollars by letting the county government collect their taxes, thereby eliminating needless duplication of services.

➤ The city of San Francisco implemented a labor-management committee recommendation to free paramedic ambulances for emergencies by contracting out routine medical transport tasks.

➤ Bellevue Hospital, the largest public hospital in New York City, has undertaken a series of management initiatives that save money, assure accurate billing, and require less time in the waiting room. These changes and others have generated the needed revenue for a new ambulatory care program.

➤ The state of California has decentralized its personnel process, reduced the reliance on written test scores to give managers more hiring discretion, and established an aggressive program for increasing the diversity of the public work force.

➤ The Neighborhood Capital Budget Group, a nonprofit organization in Chicago, helped the city find a way to retire and refinance public debt, lowering interest costs and enabling it to take on new obligations to rebuild inner-city neighborhoods.

➤ The state of Florida has moved 500 of its health care workers into "outposts" to make them more accessible to people. It has streamlined its regulations and computerized the eligibility process so that its health care workers no longer have to memorize reams of complex eligibility requirements.

➤ Contra Costa County, California, has established a $100,000 "Productivity Investment Fund" to loan departments money for new projects. The fund is a revolving one; the departments repay the money through budget savings from their projects.

➤ The city of Orlando, Florida, now provides citizens with a *City Owners Manual* and computer access to information on city resources, thus giving citizens a clear stake in their government.

> ➤ With help from the Clark Foundation and the founders of Homebuilders (a program that allows children headed for out-of-home placement to remain safely with their families), 13 states, including Michigan, Missouri, New York, and Tennessee, have adapted their child welfare systems to incorporate this innovative family preservation initiative. With 80 percent of families staying together successfully, many states have been able to finance at least part of these intensive services by redirecting dollars that otherwise would have been used for out-of-home placement.

These states and localities knew they were at the watershed, and that they would some day look back on these years as a time when they had the chance to choose a better future. In large or small measure they made the tough choices. Whether working with their local nonprofit organizations, with other governments, or on their own, they changed direction; they tried something new. And in their efforts the Commission sees great hope for America. That is why the Commission does not intend to stop its work after the release of this report. The Commission will continue as a resource to states, localities, and the federal government in helping set and fulfill a national agenda for change.

The National Commission on the State and Local Public Service is a new kind of commission. This first report indicates the direction our work is taking based on the six hearings held in cities throughout the country and the book of research papers, to be published in the fall of 1993, described in the appendix to this report. But we intend to be a working commission. Plans have been made to conduct state conferences on the ideas put forward in this report with matching contributions from sponsoring groups. We also will be issuing further reports—including one on health care policy. Other Commission products will include reports in videocassette form that can be used by students and television stations, as well as instructional materials for interactive teleconferences using network facilities. The Commission also plans to undertake a field research program on the leadership systems and managerial capacity of states and localities. The chairman, staff, and members of the Commission intend to make theirs a continuing commitment to educate and motivate people and to make our work part of the "new movement" to improve the capacity of state and local governments so that they can lead and manage effectively.

2

SUMMARY: STEPS TO HIGH-PERFORMANCE GOVERNMENT

The Commission believes that the path to high-performance government based on the *trust and lead* strategy is clear: Give leaders the authority to act. Put them in charge of lean, responsive agencies. Hire and nurture knowledgeable, motivated employees, and give them the freedom to innovate in accomplishing the agencies' missions. Engage citizens in the business of government, while at the same time encouraging them to be partners in problem-solving. Finally—and a key to further progress—solve the health care funding crisis.

The changes called for by the recommendations that follow will hardly be easy or painless. Reforms may require constitutional amendments, new legislation, changes in rules and regulations, and restructuring many agencies and departments. Accomplishment of many of the changes may require political leaders and civic groups to mount aggressive public campaigns.

In the next five chapters, we make ten major recommendations organized under five themes:

➤ Removing the Barriers to Stronger Executive Leadership
➤ Removing the Barriers to Lean, Responsive Government
➤ Removing the Barriers to a High-Performance Work Force
➤ Removing the Barriers to Citizen Involvement
➤ Reducing Fiscal Uncertainty

This program challenges those who say that America can somehow stumble to recovery through the coming decade by tinkering here and there. It also calls into question the idea that a financial bail-out from Washington or rapid economic growth will be our governmental cure-all.

One size cannot fit all. Still, the Commission believes that all states and localities can benefit from a close look at how they frustrate high performance. They will find that piecemeal change will not produce the kind of reform that is now necessary to get states and localities back on track. What is needed—and needed now—is concerted action from chief executives, the agencies they run, the employees they lead, and the citizens they serve. Finally, action is needed from the federal government on what remains a crippling budgetary problem: health care financing.

If anyone in state or local government has any doubt about whether his or her government should seriously consider any of the following recommendations, the Commission suggests that he or she now take a moment to complete the State and Local Public Service Stress Test offered on page 85 of this report.

REMOVING THE BARRIERS TO STRONGER EXECUTIVE LEADERSHIP

Chief executives need the authority to forge their own leadership teams. Too many governments, especially state governments, have scattered that authority among too many elected cabinet-level officials, boards, and authorities. Legislative bodies—whether legislatures, county commissions, or city councils—need to set broad policy in concert with chief elected officers and then let the executive branch go to work. That means avoiding the tendency on the part of legislatures to parcel out executive-level proposals to a patchwork of committees with varying jurisdictions.

Recommendations for Stronger Executive Leadership

1. Strengthen executive authority to act by reducing the number of independently elected cabinet-level officials.

2. Temper the fragmentation of government by consolidating or eliminating as many overlapping or underperforming units as possible through a "base-closure" approach.

3. Use the executive budget approach and give state and local executives more opportunity to have their program considered as a whole in the legislative process.

REMOVING THE BARRIERS TO LEAN, RESPONSIVE GOVERNMENT

Here the Commission echoes and reinforces what many observers of state and local government have been saying for some time now: To effect *real* change, the structures and systems that underpin state and local governments must change. Bureaucracies need to be de-layered so that the front line is in touch with upper-level management. Personnel, procurement, and budget systems need to be amended so that hiring, purchasing, and spending are not filtered through myriad layers of management or subverted by reams of rules.

Recommendations for Lean, Responsive Government

4. Flatten the bureaucracy by reducing the number of management layers between the top and bottom of agencies and thinning the ranks of the managers who remain.

5. Deregulate government by (1) reforming the civil service, including reduced use of veterans preference and seniority; (2) streamlining the procurement process; and (3) making the budgeting process more flexible.

REMOVING THE BARRIERS TO A HIGH-PERFORMANCE WORK FORCE

The role of public employees in pursuing an alternative future cannot be overstated. They need to be both encouraged and challenged. Those public employees who no longer care about challenging work or accomplishing something worthwhile should leave; those who still want to make a difference must develop and broaden their skills. Far too many of our front-line employees have spent their careers learning narrow specialties that no longer serve the public well. Far too many of their managers are still stuck in the micromanagement mindset that substitutes for the mentoring, coaching, and team-building that our front-line employees need. Given a chance to participate, those front-line employees have to be ready to take risks and share their ideas. In turn, their managers need to listen to them—to *trust* them to accomplish their agreed-upon goals in the way they think best, and to *lead* them by coaching and championing, not by dictating and disciplining.

Recommendation for a
High-Performance Work Force

6. **Create a learning government by (1) restoring employee training and education budgets; (2) creating a new skills package for all employees; (3) basing pay increases on skills, not time in position; (4) insisting on a new kind of problem-solving public manager, not merely a paper passer; and (5) encouraging a new style of labor-management communication.**

REMOVING THE BARRIERS TO CITIZEN INVOLVEMENT

All too often, governments become islands unto themselves, with their own languages, calendars, goals, and internal measures of success. They lose touch with the citizenry. Citizens must be able to play their vital role in solving society's most pressing problems, whether the problem is how to make schools better, streets safer, or neighborhoods stronger.

Opening the door to constructive citizen involvement will require responsible political leadership. Too many politicians encourage citizens to think that they can have more of everything from government without having to pay the necessary taxes. Too many engage in election-year bidding wars for votes. Too many manipulate and play to public opinion rather than create the conditions needed for informed citizen judgment in facing the hard choices. Too many seek to build voter rapport by such superficial means as bureaucrat-bashing.

State and local governments should provide clear avenues and greater support for citizen involvement. Absolutely vital to such a partnership between governments and citizens is the restoration of trust. Government needs to open up the books on campaign finance practices and on lobbying activity, two areas that currently play a significant part in fueling citizen cynicism.

Recommendations for Greater
Citizen Involvement

7. Open the books on government by providing detailed information on campaign financing and lobbying.

8. Limit the political fundraising season to the six months before an election and limit the use of carry-over campaign funds.

9. Encourage citizen problem-solving by experimenting with citizen liaison offices and setting up a national service corps.

REDUCING FISCAL UNCERTAINTY

Finally, the federal government must act on national health care reform. States and localities should not expect that a decade of cuts in aid will suddenly be reversed, but they ought to expect Washington to take the lead on what has clearly become a national crisis: health care funding, in particular, Medicaid funding. The federal government has failed to carry out its fundamental responsibility in this area. If it continues in this failure, then it ought to at least unleash state and local governments to deal with the problem themselves.

Recommendation for Reducing
Fiscal Uncertainty

10. Begin to deal with the financing crisis in health care, with the federal government leading, following, or getting out of the way.

The Commission does not pretend that the reforms it suggests will pay for themselves. Creating a government that emphasizes skills training, for example, will mean restoring cuts made over the years in training and education budgets. Encouraging greater mobility through earlier vesting of pensions will also have a fiscal impact. The Commission did pay attention to the bottom line in drafting its proposals, dropping a number of ideas as unrealistic in today's budgetary climate. But ultimately the Commission believes that whatever reform does cost, state and local governments can no longer afford to avoid it.

In the final analysis, money is not the key obstacle to implementation of this report's recommendations. Pervasive cynicism about government is. It is a cynicism based on some widespread and crippling beliefs: That candidates will say anything to get elected and then will only play it safe until the next election. That public employees only care about job security and bigger paychecks. That public employee unions will not cooperate in implementing change. That citizens are apathetic and uninformed. That government is simply too big, taxes too high, and spending too loose, and that our fiscal problems could be solved with just a little belt-tightening.

The realities are that many elected officials want to do the right thing, but have not been given the authority to do so. Many of our agencies were created to solve tough problems, but are now too rule-bound and slow-footed to move with the times. Many of our public employees are motivated by undertaking challenging work and accomplishing something worthwhile, but are not offered the skills to do either or the decision-making authority to make it worth their while. Many of the unions that represent those employees want to share in constructive change, but feel that they have been shut out because of a management-knows-best mentality that pervades government. Many citizens have the potential to participate in solving their own problems, but have been discouraged and frustrated by government and government systems.

More to the point, the complaining and finger-pointing have to stop and the difficult job of reform has to begin. None of this is simple, and it would be naive to think that a handful of even the most thoughtful and sophisticated recommendations will offer a fail-safe formula for progress. But governments can change, and citizen action is possible.

3

REMOVING THE BARRIERS TO STRONGER EXECUTIVE LEADERSHIP

One of the biggest problems in getting good executive leaders is their concern about being able to manage their departments. In other words, if you have a city council that wants to micromanage the department, are you going to be able to attract good leadership? Strong leaders are going to want to make decisions, carry them out, and be held accountable—not have someone else do it.

Kathy Whitmire
Former Mayor, Houston, Texas
Austin Hearing, March 1992

The Commission believes that the place to begin building high-performance state and local government is at the top, with stronger executive leadership. Obviously, there is no way to legislate strong leadership. Our elected and appointed chief executives either have the courage to effect change or they do not. But the Commission feels strongly that effecting certain government reforms will make it easier to lead.

Once in office, executives face one obstacle after another in any quest for change. They are denied the chance to appoint their own teams, shape their agencies, and hold their key legislative proposals together. It should not be a surprise that so many of the best and the brightest refuse public service, and that so many of those who make the commitment end up quitting in frustration. Far more difficult to understand is why so many good people still try.

Ultimately, this report is largely about stronger leadership, whether in giving executives more responsive agencies, more knowledgeable employees, more connection with citizens, or a degree of fiscal breathing space. But other steps have to be taken to increase the odds that leaders will be able to act and act effectively.

At a minimum, states and localities can start by giving their chief executives the opportunity to shape governments. Making clear who is in charge is part of assuring constituents that their votes matter and establishes a clearer picture of who is accountable for what goes wrong or right in government. Toward that end, the Commission makes three proposals.

RECOMMENDATION ONE: STRENGTHEN EXECUTIVE AUTHORITY

Strengthen executive authority to act by reducing the number of independently elected cabinet-level officials.

One aftermath of Reconstruction was that we constructed a [state] government with a weak governor, a strong legislature, and a system of boards and commissions to run agencies. That was fine in 1879 . . . now we have 250 agencies that are basically islands unto themselves.

Billy Hamilton
Deputy Comptroller of Public Accounts
State of Texas
Austin Hearing, March 1992

Many state and local governments limit their executives from the very beginning through the direct election of key executive department heads. However well intended this practice may be, direct election of cabinet-level officials undermines accountability and dilutes a chief executive's ability to direct key elements of the government. Yet, of the nearly 2,000 major administrative officers serving in American state government, almost 300 were elected directly by the public, while another 750 were appointed by somebody other than the governor. Over half the officers of state government are independent in one way or another from the chief executive. Consider the following figures:

➤ 36 states elect a separate secretary of state
➤ 38 elect a treasurer

➤ 25 elect an auditor

➤ 16 elect a comptroller

➤ 12 elect an agriculture commissioner

➤ 11 elect public utility boards or commissioners

➤ 10 elect an insurance commissioner

➤ 5 elect a land commissioner

➤ 15 elect a superintendent of education

Even though states have been moving in the direction of greater consolidation of executive authority, more needs to be done. Governors should be given full authority to select their cabinet-level officials. The Commission believes that the public is best served when they can identify a single elected or appointed executive at the top of government who is responsible for what government does. Where states continue to elect independent cabinet-level officials, the Commission strongly urges that those officials run as a ticket under the chief executive's banner, thereby providing a measure of unity and accountability.

At the local level, we still have too many outmoded and highly dispersed forms of government. This is a particularly serious problem at the county level. Among county governments, commissions or boards that divide executive authority among several officials are still the most common form. Counties must establish more efficient arrangements to combat fragmentation of public services and cut costs. Mayors too need the executive authority to select and deploy managers in order to replace the old command and control approach with a *trust and lead* approach.

RECOMMENDATION TWO:
TEMPER THE FRAGMENTATION OF GOVERNMENT

Temper the fragmentation of government by consolidating or eliminating as many overlapping or underperforming units as possible through a "base-closure" approach.

Government directories are filled with agencies that no longer serve a public need or with agencies and departments with overlapping, competing, and/or conflicting missions. Unfortunately, once created, many government agencies prove immortal. It is obviously far easier to create an agency than to kill one. Many states have tried automatic sunsetting of agencies and commissions as a way to ensure regular review, only to find that it is renewal—rather than dismantlement—that becomes automatic. Agencies develop special niches in the budget process, cultivate strong allies in the legislature and among lobbying groups, and invariably find a way to wait out the latest blue-ribbon reform group.

In the transportation sector, we had five or six agencies doing transportation-related planning [so] that we had a turnpike authority that was building turnpikes that didn't connect with any feeder roads from nonturnpike areas . . . we have a Texas Water Commission, Texas Water Development Board, Texas Air Commission, Texas Low-Level Radioactive Waste Commission. I can't even name them all. They do good work, but frequently they don't do it together.

Billy Hamilton
Deputy Comptroller of Public Accounts
State of Texas
Austin Hearing, March 1992

If chief executives are to cull the ranks of outmoded, defunct agencies and reorganize governments, they need a mechanism with which to do so. The Commission recommends a device such as the one used by the federal government to close outmoded military bases. Facing enormous resistance from individual members, Congress passed a law in 1988 to require the President to appoint a commission to recommend a list of bases to be closed. The base-closing commission presents an "all-or-nothing" plan: Congress can either approve closing all the bases on the list—thereby spreading the pain across a number of districts in one bold move—or reject the entire package and be left with no closures at all. Congress has a fixed period of time in which it can act; otherwise the base-closing plan goes into effect automatically.

Given the resistance to eliminating and consolidating agencies on a case-by-case basis, the Commission urges establishment of similar reform commissions in state and local governments. Although we recognize that setting up the Congressional base-closing process was in and of itself a highly political exercise—one that took leadership and courage—it did ultimately achieve its goal.

RECOMMENDATION THREE:
KEEP THE EXECUTIVE AGENDA INTACT

Use the executive budget approach and give state and local executives more opportunity to have their program considered as a whole in the legislative process.

> *Instead of seeing the issues debated, . . . we see . . . finger-pointing, blame-assessing, petty partisan politics, name-calling, and personality attacks. The citizenry is frustrated and I don't blame them. I am frustrated too, and I am part of the system. More and more people are becoming dissatisfied. I am convinced that we are not going to want the harvest we are now sowing for our future.*
>
> The Honorable Dick Molpus
> Secretary of State, State of Mississippi
> Jackson Hearing, January 1992

Executive leadership is further hampered by highly fragmented legislative procedures. State legislative processes sift statutes through a confusing committee structure, splitting what should be comprehensive bills into hundreds of pieces, occasionally allowing endless amendment on the floor of the legislature, and increasingly requiring "super-majorities" of three-fifths or two-thirds for certain bills to win final passage. The Commission believes that states and localities need to give chief executives a greater chance to hold their agendas together through the legislative gauntlet.

Consider the rules governing amendments. Many states and localities allow the executive's agenda to move through the legislative process under "open rules," which allow individual members of the legislature or council to introduce what are sometimes extraneous and unrelated amendments. The Commission believes that accountability is fostered by giving executives clear votes of approval or disapproval on their priorities. We therefore believe that legislatures should limit the use of open rules.

The executive budget is a second example. Twenty-nine states currently split the budget into pieces en route to passage. Oregon and Pennsylvania both consider roughly 100 spending bills each year; Illinois, 150 to 200; Mississippi, over 200; and Arkansas, 450. Alabama splits the budget into 2 major and over 600 minor bills. This fragmentation may weaken the legislature's ability to keep track of the bottom line, and increases the chance that pieces of the budget will be isolated and captured by special interest groups, again weakening executive authority and diffusing accountability.

Bills to reorganize or improve the overall organization of government are a third example. Because such bills involve comprehensive reform, crossing many committee jurisdictions, they may present yet another opportunity for extraneous amendments, becoming either Christmas trees or freight trains for special projects that have nowhere else to go.

Thus, where possible the Commission urges legislatures to keep the executive agenda whole, first by using temporary, cross-jurisdictional committees to consider large-scale reform, and second, when bills must be divided, by setting clear deadlines for action and reassembling bills into omnibus measures before final consideration. And, at all points in the process, super-majorities should be abandoned. Hard choices are tough enough to make at 50 percent plus one.

A small minority—27 of the 80 Assembly members or 14 of the 40 Senators—can block action. A very tiny minority—14 members of a 27-member Assembly minority party caucus, or 8 members of a 14-member Senate minority party caucus—can bind the rest of their caucus to a "no" vote and block action.

The Honorable Barry Keene
Majority Leader
California State Senate
Sacramento Hearing, May 1992

4

REMOVING THE BARRIERS TO
LEAN, RESPONSIVE GOVERNMENT

*At one point I was asked, on behalf of the county, to
implement . . . nutrition feeding programs for senior
citizens. It took me two and a half hours a day to fill out
the paperwork on 57 meals.*

The Honorable Sunne Wright McPeak
Supervisor, Contra Costa County, California
Sacramento Hearing, May 1992

Giving chief executives greater authority to pick their cabinets,
reorganize their agencies, and hold their programs together
will help make clear who is in charge. The question then becomes
"In charge of what?" Being able to pick cabinet-level officers does not
count for much if the agencies they run will not respond to the new
leadership, or if the rules and regulations by which they operate
inhibit innovation and action at every turn.

In reality, many of our state and local agencies stand as great
monuments to themselves, sustained and protected by their internal
rules and hierarchies. They often stifle the creativity that is so
desperately needed, putting one obstacle after another in the way of
new ideas and energetic leaders. Innovation tends to become an
accident when it could so easily be the natural result of reconnecting
chief executives, employees, and concerned citizens. That is how
Illinois initiated a program to recruit minority adoptive parents
through a network of churches; how Tupelo, Mississippi, invented a
public-private partnership in education; and how Massachusetts
designed a unique antipollution program that worked with manu-
facturers to prevent pollution at the source. Their experiences, and
those of other winners of the Ford Foundation's innovations program

---

Table 2: 1992 Winners of the Ford Foundation's
Innovations in State and Local Government Award

Automated Traffic Surveillance and Control (ATSAC), City of Los Angeles, California

Los Angeles cuts congestion, improves air quality, and reduces travel time for
millions with ATSAC, a state-of-the-art computerized signal management system.

Environmental Cleanup Project, City of Wichita, Kansas

The Environmental Cleanup Project balances environmental recovery and economic health. By
assuming responsibility for a costly environmental cleanup, Wichita avoids federal Superfund
regulations, which invite excessive cost and time delays.

Bilingual Outreach, Arlington County, Virginia

Bilingual Outreach stabilizes immigrant communities and helps immigrant families adjust to
American lifestyles through easily accessible acculturation services.

Humanitas, Los Angeles Unified School District, California

Humanitas returns relevance to urban education through writing-based learning and
interdisciplinary team teaching that puts teachers in control of curriculum and students in control
of learning.

CityWorks, City of Cambridge, Massachusetts

CityWorks prepares ninth graders for jobs in the twenty-first century by re-integrating vocational
and academic learning and by marrying the classroom to the community at the Rindge School
of Technical Arts.

Fleet Improvement R&D Network, City of New York, New York

New York City's Fleet Improvement R&D Network provides low-cost, quality maintenance for
6,000 sanitation vehicles by tapping the creativity of front-line mechanics.

Workers' Compensation System, State of Washington

Washington's Workers' Compensation System that compensates workers for on-the-job
injuries was rescued through sound financial investment and management programs, updated
information technology, and worker safety campaigns.

Quincy Court Model Domestic Abuse Program, Quincy District Court, Massachusetts

Quincy Court's Model Domestic Abuse Program protects battered women and children through
court-based services that encourage victims to seek justice and safety by effectively controlling
and punishing batterers.

Child Assistance Program (CAP), State of New York

CAP builds on the premise that parents want to work to help their children out of poverty, by
reforming welfare to encourage employment, savings, and child support.

Elderly Services Program, Spokane County, Washington

Spokane County's Elderly Services Program helps isolated elders remain independent through
referrals by public and private service workers who link elders with at-home support services.

(administered by Harvard University), teach us that there are things state and local governments can do to assure that innovation will emerge and endure (see Table 2).

All organizations—from the smallest businesses to the largest corporations, from the tiniest public agencies to the largest bureaucracies—grow thicker and more rule-bound over time. This does not really happen by choice. No agency wants to be fat and sluggish. Rather, it occurs through the steady buildup of layers over time.

The need to flatten and thin out these agencies goes to the heart of high-performance government. Chief executives must be connected with front-line employees in order to gauge how well an agency or department is doing its job—indeed, to gauge what job, exactly, should be done. At the same time front-line employees should not be the last to know when a decision comes down from on high, or kept in the dark about why the decision was made. In fact, they should be included in the decision-making process from the start.

Chief executives may believe that adding layers of management will somehow improve communication—or control—but the result is often exactly the opposite. They often find themselves more isolated and more unable to shape the roles and performance of their organizations.

There are other reasons for cutting layers of management, not the least of which is the reduced salary and administrative costs made possible by a low manager-to-employee ratio. Heavily layered organizations are also slow to respond, limiting executive and legislative options for changing directions to meet new problems. Finally, holding an agency responsible for outcomes is nearly impossible when no one is quite sure who is responsible for a given objective. Government has to be as fast off the mark as possible. Toward that end, the Commission makes one proposal.

RECOMMENDATION FOUR: FLATTEN THE BUREAUCRACY

Flatten the bureaucracy by reducing the number of management layers between the top and bottom of agencies and thinning the ranks of the managers who remain.

There is no magic number of layers between the top and bottom of government, no proven ratio of managers to employees, no maximum number of units a chief executive should supervise. The appropriate number of layers depends on mission and goals.

The fragmented, balkanized arrangements characteristic of many governments today evolved for a variety of reasons: Executives added layers to foster command and control; managers, to promote employees into better-paying positions; legislators, to run new programs. Whatever the reason, it is time to cut the hierarchies. The Commission believes that most agencies can cut their management layers significantly, without any decline in efficiency. Just the opposite. The cuts should improve accountability and save money, while allowing most agencies to shift personnel dollars to the front line.

In this regard, we believe that in many areas demands on front-line workers—for example, job counselors, social service case workers, public health nurses—are excessive and unrealistic and inhibit quality performance. On occasion more, not fewer, personnel are needed.

RECOMMENDATION FIVE: DEREGULATE GOVERNMENT

Deregulate government by (1) reforming the civil service, including reduced use of veterans preference and seniority; (2) streamlining the procurement process; and (3) making the budgeting process more flexible.

Creating flat, responsive agencies also involves freeing chief executives, managers, and front-line employees from the thicket of outmoded laws, internal regulations, and controls that has grown up around them over the years. Deregulation is virtually required by de-layering—there will be fewer managers and supervisors available to enforce the rules.

Even without de-layering, however, a reduction in rules is long overdue. Hiring, purchasing, and budgeting systems now often frustrate the goals they were enacted to achieve.

In order to create more responsive agencies, the Commission makes the following proposals for an overhaul.

END CIVIL SERVICE PARALYSIS

America's civil service was invented 100 years ago to guarantee merit in the hiring process. Sadly, many state and local governments have created such rule-bound and complicated systems that merit is often the last value served. How can merit be served, for example, when supervisors are only allowed three choices from among hundreds of possible candidates for a job? How can merit be served when pay is determined mainly on the basis of time on the job? How is merit served when top performers can be "bumped" from their jobs by poor performers during downsizings?

I do think government needs more flexible personnel systems. I strongly believe in collective bargaining. I strongly believe that public employees' rights have to be protected. But I think we could come up with a more rational structure and a better structure for public employees to work in; I envision an era of higher quality public service, better skilled and motivated workers, and as a result of that, more satisfied taxpayers.

The Honorable Stan Lundine
Lieutenant Governor, State of New York
Philadelphia Hearing, June 1992

Over the years, the basic purpose of the civil service system has been forgotten: To recruit the most talented among our citizens into government, not to employ legions of classification experts and personnel administrators who spend their days tracing bumping routes and rewriting job descriptions. State and local governments have a hard enough time as it is recruiting the best and the brightest without actively discouraging them. We must not be so hidebound in order to protect against failure that we quash the spirit of innovation.

The Commission believes that states and localities are best served by a decentralized merit system that helps agencies and departments address issues of hiring and mobility, pay, diversity, firing, and the operation of the personnel system. Obviously public sector unions have worked hard in these areas over the years and care deeply about safeguarding workers against management actions they feel are arbitrary. In many jurisdictions it will be pivotal to develop a full partnership with unions to achieve the reforms needed to create a high-performance work force.

The task for government is to find a suitable balance or accommodation in its civil service processes for these often conflicting interests and values. . . . One person's perceived "red tape" is another person's preferred accountability system. In California we believe we have approached a reasonable balance between these competing values. However, the changes have been evolutionary and incremental rather than a cataclysm of reform.

Gloria Harmon
Executive Officer
California State Personnel Board
Sacramento Hearing, May 1992

On Hiring and Mobility

Many civil service systems sharply limit freedom to hire in two ways: (1) They rely heavily on written tests that may be biased, out-of-date, poor in predicting performance, and expensive to construct. (2) They sharply limit the number of candidates who are forwarded for interviews, through a "rule of three" or other limiting provision. Under such a rule, only the top three individuals on a list of eligibles are certified for hiring. Placement on the list often depends heavily on performance on a written test, downplaying other important characteristics such as interpersonal skills.

These constraints on managerial discretion were put in place to ensure the primacy of merit, and cannot be dropped without instituting clear protections for those who might face discrimination. Nevertheless, the Commission recommends that states and localities reconsider these requirements in light of today's needs. Many governments are finding that using selection criteria other than written tests is critical to finding and promoting good people. In addition, expanding the list of candidates who can be forwarded for interviews can allow more aggressive recruitment in order to achieve diversity.

The Commission further recommends that effective pipelines for recruiting the best and the brightest into public service be fully exploited. Fortunately, there appears to be a renewed interest in public service as a career. Good intern programs, of which there are many, help make for good government, often serving as fast-track vehicles for outstanding students to enter government service. They should be sustained and expanded.

The Commission also urges that states and localities pay greater attention to seniority and veterans preference rules and recommends that, when they present a problem, limits be placed on their use in determining who gets hired, promoted, and protected during downsizing. Seniority rules, which protect longtime workers, can present a fairness issue, especially for women and minorities. A special advantage in the personnel selection process should only be extended once to any one individual who has served in the military, and then only in order to break a tie between otherwise equally qualified applicants.

The Commission proposes reducing the number of job families into which all employees fit, instead of continuing to wrestle with the hundreds or even thousands of classifications that currently characterize most state and local systems. In states, for example, the number of classifications ranges from as high as 7,300 in New York to as low as 551 in South Dakota (see Table 3). The Commission believes that no more than a few dozen are needed, with some provision for distinctions between positions within job families to reflect different levels of expertise or "bands." Under such a system—which has been recommended by the National Academy of Public Administration for the federal government—the number of job classifications in most jurisdictions would drop significantly. Such a system would allow much greater flexibility in staffing government according to shifting needs and would also permit greater flow of staff among agencies and departments.

The Commission believes that keeping good people once government finds them is equally important. At the same time, employees should not be handcuffed to a lifetime of government service, nor should talented candidates be locked out of lateral entry at midcareer by antiquated, nonportable pension systems. The Commission therefore recommends that states and localities at the least honor the same five-year vesting minimum required of private firms under federal law. After five years employees could take both their contribution and the government's when they leave and roll the money over into a new pension fund, if they wish. As of 1991, an estimated 40 percent of all state and local employees had to work ten years before becoming vested.

Table 3: State Government Job Classifications, 1991	
State	Number of Classifications
Alabama	1,600
Alaska	1,050
Arizona	1,500
Arkansas	1,900
California	4,324
Colorado	1,348
Connecticut	2,600
Delaware	1,434
Florida	1,596
Georgia	1,570
Hawaii	1,660
Idaho	1,550
Illinois	1,680
Indiana	1,500
Iowa	1,250
Kansas	1,142
Kentucky	1,614
Louisiana	3,800
Maine	1,500
Maryland	3,000
Massachusetts	1,150
Michigan	2,700
Minnesota	2,140
Mississippi	2,053
Missouri	1,100
Montana	1,350
Nebraska	1,300
Nevada	1,300
New Hampshire	1,490
New Jersey	6,400
New Mexico	1,200
New York	7,300
North Carolina	3.500
North Dakota	1,075
Ohio	1,804
Oklahoma	1,418
Oregon	1,100
Pennsylvania	2,782
Rhode Island	1,500
South Carolina	2,318
South Dakota	551
Tennessee	2,258
Texas	1,339
Utah	2,500
Vermont	1,280
Virginia	1,888
Washington	2,100
West Virginia	2,000
Wisconsin	2,000
Wyoming	774

Note: The numbers of classifications for some states are approximations.

Source: National Association of State Personnel Executives and the Council of State Governments. *State Personnel Office: Roles and Functions* (2nd ed.). Lexington, KY: Council of State Governments, 1992.

One aim of such mobility reform should be to encourage free movement between the public and private sectors. Many of the skills they require are interchangeable, and it is in the nation's long-term best interest to have its workers understand both worlds.

On Pay

In HRS [Health and Rehabilitative Services] there was high turnover, with people making less than a metro zookeeper. When they had ten open positions, I suggested they hire five people and pay them more, but regulations didn't let us do that.

Janet Reno
Florida State Attorney
Eleventh Judicial Circuit, Dade County
Tallahassee Hearing, May 1992

The Commission advocates a simple pay and promotion structure that would allow much greater flexibility in rewarding good employees and also encourage greater movement of employees across agencies and easier reassignment on an as-needed basis. Such a system uses a small number of broad pay bands, usually three, to replace the complicated grade-and-step system currently in place. Under that system, employee pay is based on a set number of grades—usually 15 or so—and on various steps based on seniority within those grades—usually 10 or so. Not surprisingly, a system with as many as 150 different pay levels can create an enormous amount of conflict within the workplace. Besides being less complex, broad-banding of pay allows managers to reward employees without having to give them a new job title. It allows managers to reassign personnel more easily to meet shifts in demand and priorities.

The Commission proposes that state and local governments reevaluate their pay-for-performance plans. Almost half of all states, and a majority of counties and cities, now have at least some of their employees in pay-for-performance plans. Unfortunately, many of those plans promise far more than they deliver. Some of the systems are unbelievably complicated and paper-intensive. Others are simply poorly administered. Still others are launched without adequate funding. The best available research suggests that pay-for-performance in the public sector has been a disappointment, and that states and localities should be exceedingly cautious about overselling what are likely to be small performance bonuses allocated through a cumbersome and potentially political process. The Commission recommends that such plans be dropped if they are not perceived by employees as fair or if they are underfunded.

The Commission further encourages pay-setting approaches and bonus systems that make it every employee's business to assure the overall success of the organization. For example, team-based pay-for-performance systems—whether the team is several employees, a small unit, or an agency—send the right signal, that employees rise or fall on the basis of outcomes. Gainsharing is a viable step toward such a system. Under a gainsharing formula, workers on a given team split the savings from higher productivity equally with taxpayers, whether through a one-time bonus or an innovation investment fund for the team's future productivity improvements.

On Diversity

In the public sector, we have a special responsibility to try to make sure that the people who take care of our patients reflect the diversity of those patients. I cannot imagine providing appropriate psychiatric services to largely Spanish- and Chinese-speaking patients if you cannot speak the language.

Pamela S. Brier
Chief Executive Officer
Bellevue Hospital Center, New York City
Philadelphia Hearing, June 1992

The pattern and the problem are clear. The face of America outside government is changing faster than the face of the work force inside. Consider the situation in Los Angeles. According to the report of the Independent Commission on the Los Angeles Police Department in the wake of the Los Angeles riots, 63 percent of the city's population is nonwhite compared to approximately 31 percent of the city's police officers. In spite of aggressive recruiting of

African-American and Latino officers, the city still has a long way to go in assuring that the force both is representative and allows minority officers the opportunity to rise to the highest-level positions.

The disconnection between those whom government serves and those who serve government can only create tensions. There is a very legitimate question as to whether a government that does not reflect the demographic makeup of the governed can operate effectively over the long haul, or in the face of widespread hostility or resentment on the part of disenfranchised groups.

Remedying this disconnection is going to take more than aggressive recruitment of women and minorities. In some communities government agencies may have to take a leading role in ensuring a diverse work force. The Commission strongly recommends that government not only actively recruit workers to reflect the diversity of the community served, but that it also actively promote investment in all young people, encouraging everyone to stay in school so that more women and minorities will qualify to work in public service.

States and localities have made progress in the area of recruiting women and minorities in the past two decades—the proportion of female full-time employees increased from 35 percent in 1974 to 42 percent in 1989, while the proportion of minorities rose from 20 percent to 27 percent. But women and minorities still staff the front lines and not the front office. The vast majority of the lowest-paid positions in state and local government are held by women and minorities. Although the imbalance has been substantially redressed since the mid-1970s, states and localities have a long way to go (see Figure 1).

The Commission endorses efforts to find innovative ways for women and minorities to break through the ceiling to higher-level jobs. State and local governments should initiate educational opportunities for their current work forces that will better prepare underrepresented groups for top management positions. Introducing more flexible hiring and promotional practices can also help these groups move into the middle- and upper-ranks of government.

But money and titles are not the only issues. The Commission believes that part of government's effort to create a work force that mirrors the population it represents also ought to include elimination of barriers that keep women out of mid- and upper-level jobs in many departments. Women are still far more likely to be found in education, health, aging,

Figure 1: Percentage of women (A) and all minorities (B) in eight major occupational categories in state and local government, 1974 and 1990

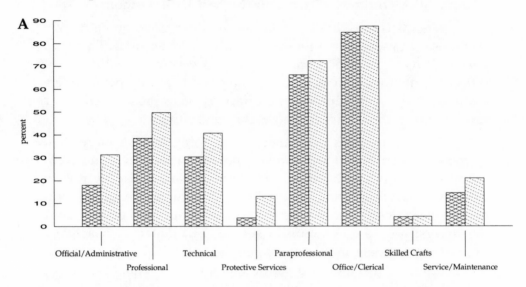

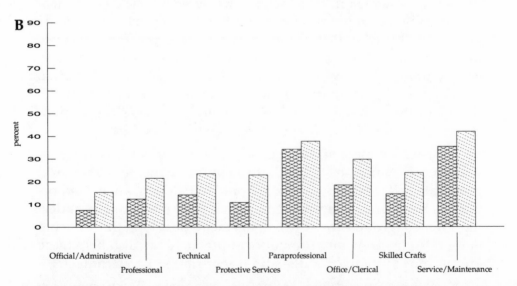

Note: In 1990, the title for "Office/Clerical" changed to "Administrative Support." For clarity these charts retain the "Office/Clerical" label. Source: Adapted from Rita Mae Kelly, "Diversity in the Public Workforce: New Needs, New Approaches," in Frank J. Thompson (ed.), *Revitalizing State and Local Public Service* (San Francisco, CA: Jossey-Bass Inc., forthcoming). Data adapted from U.S. Equal Employment Opportunity Commission, *Job Patterns for Minorities and Women in State and Local Governments*, 1974 and 1990 (Washington, D.C.: U.S. Government Printing Office).

library, and welfare agencies than in transportation, corrections, agriculture, or law enforcement, yet women have time and again proved themselves to be capable contributors in these and other fields.

... We began to take a closer look at what the demographic changes . . . mean in terms of the future work force. By weaving the demographic pieces together, the emerging picture for employers, especially public employers, can be particularly grim. . . . the Franchise Tax Board . . . will continue to administer an increasingly complex body of tax law. We will need to inform an increasingly diverse public about their tax obligations. . . . The challenge for the FTB is to become a desirable buyer in a sellers' market for skilled workers, or, failing in that effort, [to implement] strategies to grow our own skilled employees from those people who are willing to work for us.

Gerald Goldberg
Executive Officer
Franchise Tax Board, State of California
Sacramento Hearing, May 1992

On Firing

Many of the current systems demonstrate the worst of two worlds: The hiring process can be ponderous, frustrating both managers and highly qualified candidates for government jobs, and at the same time the mechanism for releasing poor performers can be even more daunting. Many managers are so stymied by the process that they would rather promote a poor performer into a new, useless job than initiate termination proceedings. Firing should always be a last resort, but once the decision has been made, the Commission recommends that there be mechanisms in place to move it to resolution, preferably through binding arbitration that brings both sides to the table within days.

On Operating the Personnel System

Most state and local governments rely on highly centralized personnel systems that exert a good deal of control over all personnel decisions government-wide. In California, however, the central board gives the responsibility to the departments under clearly written guidelines, then gets out of the way—thus saving time, money, and frustration. The Commission strongly recommends that states and large local governments consider turning more authority for staffing decisions over to agencies and departments, then acting as a consultant to ensure that such decisions are fair and conform to all applicable state, local, and federal laws.

The fairness of the civil service hiring and promotional process can best be measured by the quality of the people hired and the work they perform, not by the number of steps in the process, the amount of paperwork involved, or the rigidity of the policies.

ACCELERATE THE PROCUREMENT PROCESS

We treat buying a police car and buying psychiatric services for children in almost the same way. . . . We treat a $1 million bid the same way we treat a $5,000 bid. . . . That is a system, much like the civil service system, that we have been trying to overhaul for a hundred years. . . .

Elizabeth C. Reveal
Former Director of Finance
City of Philadelphia
Philadelphia Hearing, June 1992

By far the greatest impediment to fast, sensible government contracting and procurement practices is the multiple layers of approval through which requisitions must pass. The process has become so complex and so expensive that many of our best companies refuse to bid on government contracts because it is simply not worth the time and effort. Government managers and employees, meanwhile, cannot obtain the supplies or equipment they need or cannot get them when they need them. Worst of all, cost, rather than quality, is often the overriding criterion for purchasing and contracting decisions.

In the end, the process really only serves to subvert the goals it was intended to achieve. Competition is reduced, unrealistically low bidding becomes commonplace, and neither the government nor the taxpayers get their money's worth. As a step toward fixing the system, the Commission recommends that any state and local procurement process possess four key characteristics:

➤ *An emphasis on quality and results over cost*, with clear incentives for high performance and strong penalties for poor work. The low bid cannot be the only or the overriding criterion in selecting a contractor, whether it is a road builder or a foster care provider.

➤ *A process streamlined enough to keep pace with new technology and procedures*. State and local governments cannot afford to wait two years to procure new computer systems, nor should employees have to wait six months for basic supplies and services. Government must seek devices for speeding up its timetable to provide quick access to supplies and services, perhaps by raising the threshold for noncompetitive bidding, by allowing managers the flexibility to make faster decisions on their own, or by the awarding of multiple open-ended contracts to suppliers who would then have an incentive to provide fast service.

➤ *A minimum of paperwork*. Multiple reviews and justifications not only slow the process, they add needless costs to the final contract—costs that must ultimately be paid by the taxpayers.

➤ *A single-signature policy on small purchases*. It makes no sense to force front-line employees to seek multiple signature approval on every small purchase. It makes no sense to require that every piece of equipment or office supply come from the agency or department's central supply department. If an employee needs some relatively inexpensive item and can get it quickly and at competitive cost at a nearby store, management should provide for that sort of quick decision. Adherence to the *trust and lead* strategy implies that our employees have to be trusted to do the right thing.

In sum, governments need to put in place contracting and procurement systems that emphasize quality, efficiency, and accountability for outcomes.

ELIMINATE SPEND-IT-OR-LOSE-IT BUDGET SYSTEMS

Almost all state and local budget systems create enormous incentives toward waste by requiring managers either to spend the money in their budgets by the end of the fiscal year or to send it back to the general fund, and probably suffer a cut in next year's appropriation on top of that. In other words, frugality is punished, not rewarded.

Think about line-item budget systems. First of all, you are a manager and all your money is trapped within these line items, which may or may not have made sense five and ten years ago when they originated, but may not be where you need to spend the money today. . . . Second, if you don't spend every penny of every line item in every fiscal year, you lose it. You have to give it back; you get less next year and the budget director yells at you because you asked for too much last year. So if you are not a total idiot, you spend every penny of every line item every year. . . .

David Osborne
Coauthor of *Reinventing Government*
Jackson Hearing, January 1992

Spend-it-or-lose-it budgets are more onerous still in concert with highly detailed line-item budgets, with specific accounts for virtually every activity imaginable, so that funds cannot be transferred to areas of more serious need. Instead of being able to reprogram funds quickly to meet an emerging problem, managers are locked into strict categories by budget lines. The Commission believes that every budget system should have four simple features:

➤ *As few budget lines as possible to give chief executives more flexibility to reprogram funds to meet unforeseen problems and emerging needs.* While the Commission recognizes legitimate legislative responsibilities in both raising and spending funds, chief executives must have considerably more freedom to move funds quickly than they do now. The Commission recommends that states and localities experiment with complete "de-lining" of an agency's budget, guided by clear performance goals set in consultation with the legislature, council, or other legislative body.

➤ *The ability to carry over unspent funds from fiscal year to fiscal year.* If agencies cannot, managers and employees are being punished for thinking carefully about how to spend money, and rewarded for spending money in an end-of-the-fiscal-year frenzy. Allowing carry-over of a quarter of a given budget line into the next fiscal year is a good first step toward reducing the spend-it-or-lose-it incentives that currently exist.

> *It occurred to me that I was making the same mistake that a lot of people in elected office make: that is, thinking that the best way to control spending was to get your hands around—and control—your budget. It is a mistake that virtually all governments make. We don't fashion a cohesive strategic plan that identifies statewide goals, and then cuts people loose to achieve those goals, with rewards and consequences for success or failure.*
>
> The Honorable Ric Williamson
> Vice Chairman, Appropriations Committee
> Texas State House of Representatives
> Austin Hearing, March 1992

➤ *The ability to depreciate capital investments.* Without depreciation, the budget shows long-term maintenance as a luxury, actually encouraging states and localities to wait until our roads, bridges, water systems, and other public works seriously deteriorate before thinking about the future. Such a practice is costly because it discourages the much more sound financial practice of maintaining our infrastructure rather than having to overhaul or replace it—a process, incidentally, that assures that citizens bear the full brunt and aggravation of disrepair. The Commission encourages states and localities to experiment with ways of depreciating physical capital, and, in doing so, to show that the failure to maintain assets is an expensive illusion.

> *The Governmental Accounting Standards Board is currently working on finding a good public-sector equivalent to depreciation so that politicians cannot pretend they are saving money when they don't maintain assets.*
>
> David Osborne
> Coauthor of *Reinventing Government*
> Jackson Hearing, January 1992

➤ *A link between spending inputs and program outcomes.* Although performance budgeting is tough to implement, it does get states and local workers thinking about the right thing: *performance*. Instead of asking how many state troopers or city patrolmen have been hired, performance goals ask whether the roads are safer because accident rates are reduced or whether cities are safer because crime rates are down. Instead of asking how many workers there are in our welfare agencies, performance goals ask whether case loads are dropping, family heads are finding jobs, or at-risk children are graduating from high school. The key idea is that program goals should be clear from the start and should then be ratcheted up as a way to motivate workers and give the public a sense of progress and accomplishment.

Thus striving for lean, responsive government will require making many tough choices—about civil service provisions, hiring and other personnel practices, pay, vesting requirements, procurement processes, and budgeting. It also means being open to rethinking relationships and defining new opportunities between government and the private sector. This may take the form of innovative partnerships such as those that the California Franchise Tax Board has developed in working with businesses and educational institutions at all levels; the purpose is to be an active partner in addressing community concerns and to help prepare its work force for the future.

In some cases, privatizing services may make sense. Although privatization is far from a cure-all and can actually increase fragmentation of responsibilities as well as long-term costs, it can bring freshness and energy into government. Actually, state and local governments have done more than most people realize to privatize program delivery. Nonprofit groups especially have grown in competence and sophistication, and are frequently worthy of consideration to shoulder responsibilities. These groups already play a major role in delivering the social service programs of state and local governments.

5

REMOVING THE BARRIERS TO A HIGH-PERFORMANCE WORK FORCE

If training is so obvious a need, then why do we do it so badly?

Frank P. Sherwood
Jerry Collins Eminent Scholar
in Public Administration
Florida State University
Tallahassee Hearing, May 1992

The flat, lean agencies of tomorrow can only work if staffed by a new kind of employee. Public employees need the training to broaden their skills and horizons, and they need to be strongly encouraged to abandon the play-it-safe style of working in favor of taking risks.

If they are going to be asked to accept this new role, though, they need to be involved in all aspects of organizational decision-making. For work to be fulfilling—for risk-taking to be worth it—employees need to know that their opinion and judgment count.

The first step is changing how employees are viewed. Rather than seeing them as "personnel" to be micromanaged, managers prepared to make the commitment to the *trust and lead* approach to managing would benefit greatly by recognizing them as problem solvers and innovators—as a source of institutional savvy about what works and what does not. Instead of being placed at the bottom of every organizational chart, they should be elevated to the front line. As part of their new role, public employees need the freedom to take risks and to act quickly to solve problems themselves, even if that means they may make some mistakes.

*Public worker demoralization is now rampant—in part
because employees are being asked to do a job with far
too few resources, and in part because of negative attitudes toward them. But the morale problem is due in
large measure to a work culture which utterly denigrates
the people at the bottom who are in many instances the
very people who are actually delivering the service, who
are actually in direct contact with the public. And I would
argue that when you hear talk of incentives—and people
often think of pay as what we mean when we talk about
incentives—in fact one of the most powerful incentives to
people being able to do a better job is having more control
over the job that they're doing.*

Roberta Lynch
Director of Public Policy
American Federation of State, County and
  Municipal Employees, Council 31
Chicago Hearing, June 1992

The problem is not a lack of challenging work or chances to
accomplish something worthwhile at all, but a "knowledge gap"
created by a decade of cuts and narrow thinking about government's
human capital. Too many of our state and local employees simply are
not ready to take on the jobs of tomorrow.

RECOMMENDATION SIX:
CREATE A LEARNING GOVERNMENT

*Create a learning government by (1) restoring employee training and
education budgets; (2) creating a new skills package for all employees;
(3) basing pay increases on skills, not time in position; (4) insisting on a
new kind of problem-solving public manager, not merely a paper passer;
and (5) encouraging a new style of labor-management communication.*

It is clear by now that when asked to take on such a new role,
employees do not just respond, they get excited. That energy needs to
be captured and magnified by ensuring that state and local governments become learning centers. It is utterly self-defeating to that goal
for governments to cut training money the instant that budgets get
tight, or to make spending so restrictive that employees are only able

to get training in narrow career areas. It makes no sense to limit access to new skills and valuable information by restricting scarce travel and conference budgets to mid- and upper-level managers. Surveys, such as that carried out by the National Commission on the Public Service, have shown that employees are motivated primarily by challenging work and the opportunity to learn (see Table 4). Denying them in these areas is a sure way to discourage them. By recognizing this fact,

---

Table 4: Rankings of What the Best and Brightest Value Most in a Job

1.	Challenging work
2.	Personal growth
3.	Pleasant working conditions
4.	Good social relations
5.	Job autonomy
6.	Service to society
7.	Job security
8.	Professional recognition
9.	Opportunity for advancement
10.	Pay and other financial rewards
11.	Prestige

Source: National Commission on the Public Service, 1988 survey of college honor society members-- Phi Beta Kappa, Sigma Xi (science and engineering), and Phi Alpha Alpha (public affairs).

---

governments can compete for top talent with the private sector in key ways other than level of pay.

We will never be able to compete in a salary war with the private sector in the skilled job market. . . . We must also be prepared to offer those things that are as important as money to the new worker—a workplace culture that recognizes that today's worker wants more out of life than just a job.

Gerald Goldberg
Executive Officer
Franchise Tax Board, State of California
Sacramento Hearing, May 1992

Creating learning organizations means that government training units are going to have to change their views on who knows best about what employees need. They will also have to think in broader career terms, and allow employees to pick up a variety of skills, whether in the area of basic computer use, in communications, or in customer service. Toward this end, the Commission makes five proposals.

REBUILD GOVERNMENT'S HUMAN CAPITAL

Ultimately, learning involves access to education, which, in turn, requires funding. While the quality of the learning is far more important than the number of hours purchased, the Commission believes that states and localities should aim for a stable learning budget set at at least *three percent of total personnel costs.*

Once a figure is set, the Commission urges states and localities to protect those budgets by making learning an earned right—that is, a part of basic compensation agreements and labor contracts. Thus, instead of giving the learning budget to a training department to be doled out, money is assigned to employees as individual accounts to be spent under general guidelines consistent with the mission of the organization. If those employees want to purchase courses from their government training units, fine; if they want to purchase courses from local colleges and universities, that is fine, too. These training accounts would create incentives for every employee to continue learning, while fostering healthy competition both inside and outside government for the learning dollar.

CREATE A NEW SKILLS PACKAGE

Get good people around you and give them considerable latitude to do their thing and you get a radiating effect. . . . I'm a deep believer that you've got to build an incentive, attract the best people with potential, give them lots of incentive and encouragement, develop an élan of not having any problems that can't be overcome.

Louis Gambaccini
Chief Operations Officer/General Manager
Southeastern Pennsylvania Transportation Authority
Philadelphia Hearing, June 1992

Complementing its endorsement of government as a learning or-ganization, the Commission believes that there are certain skills every public employee should have. Just as our education and training units ought to, as a rule, emphasize broad, outcome-related learning over narrow specialization, so too should the courses reflect a new set of competencies essential for performance:

> ➤ *Competency in team building.* The Commission believes that much of government's future work will be carried out by small teams, some of them led by executives and managers, some by front-line employees. To succeed, managers and employees alike need to know how team-building works and should be trained in the dynamics of goal-setting and conflict resolution.

> ➤ *Competency in communication.* One of government's greatest challenges is to communicate with constituents, whether to advertise services to potential users, or solicit public input on or build support for proposed programs and projects. Good marketing in government calls for two kinds of skills often missing in the public sector: (1) the ability to shape a per-suasive message for a particular audience and (2) the ability to understand what that audience thinks and wants. If govern-ment is to articulate a clear vision of the future—and build support for it—it must learn to listen and respond.

The thing I like about quality circles is that we go to the people who do the work every day and ask: "How can it be done better?" Whether or not you call it a quality circle . . . doesn't really matter. The point is that employees get a say in what they do and how they do it.

Mary E. Grogan
Director, Parks and Recreation Department
Modesto, California
Sacramento Hearing, May 1992

> ➤ *Competency in involving employees.* A recurring theme of this report is the need to get front-line employees more involved in the day-to-day work of government. However, such invol-vement requires a new style and level of communication be-

tween the front line and management. It requires that managers learn how to create a receptive environment for participation. At the same time, employees have to learn how to shape their ideas into persuasive proposals.

➤ *Commitment to cultural awareness.* As our society becomes more multicultural, every public employee should learn to communicate across cultures. This learning goes well beyond traditional sensitivity training to involve real-world learning about different cultures that public servants will be encountering every day, as either service providers or co-workers. This new learning is not a frill. In localities and states where the population is becoming increasingly diverse, government will be both the glue that binds the diverse cultures together and a source for jobs and upward mobility.

➤ *Commitment to quality.* While the Commission does not endorse any specific philosophy of management, such as Total Quality Management, it does see value in an emphasis on quality and in a new view of constituents as customers, where that is appropriate to the service being provided by government. Certainly, departments of motor vehicles are obvious examples of places where a consumer focus would be appropriate. But such an orientation is equally appropriate in many of government's other dealings with its citizens, not only those that take place across a counter. A commitment to quality is not exactly a "skill." Nevertheless, the Commission endorses any training that challenges labor and management to higher levels of achievement and service.

CREATE FINANCIAL INCENTIVES FOR LEARNING

Pay increases based on skill acquisition are clearly a powerful way to encourage learning and to improve performance. Such a system may be difficult to design at the outset. However, skill-based acquisition pay gives employees a better incentive to stretch and develop their abilities than do automatic annual pay raises. Another year spent on the job does not necessarily make for a better employee. But a skill acquired adds new capabilities to an organization and thus can make an employee more valuable. Ultimately, of course, the most powerful incentive for learning is to assure that employees can use their skills in meaningful, challenging work.

ENCOURAGE A NEW TYPE OF PUBLIC MANAGER

Managers are going to have to relearn their jobs, too, in some cases applying the new skills package outlined earlier. More broadly, however, managers have to accept a new role. They must forego the supervising, disciplining, second-guessing and double-checking that have for so long passed for leadership and begin the coaching, benchmarking, listening, mentoring, and championing that new times and a new type of job-motivated employee demand. It is to them that the challenge of implementing the *trust and lead* strategy on a day-in, day-out basis falls.

➤ As *coaches*, their role is in teaching and encouraging workers to do what comes naturally—innovate and achieve. A manager's role is not to prescribe in detail how to get the job done, but to help workers pick up the skills and confidence to decide the best way to get it done themselves.

➤ As *benchmarkers*, their role is to search out "best practices" for getting things done and then work with employees on investigating whether similar practices would improve efficiency in their own offices and shops. Their job is not to quash new ideas, but to borrow and fine-tune any idea they can find, or that an employee brings to them, that will help their operation run more smoothly.

➤ As *listeners*, their role includes taking employees' suggestions and treating them seriously. The best way to discourage employee involvement in any organization is to invite ideas from the front line and then ignore the input. Once employees recognize that managers are ready to listen *and* act, they will start sharing their ideas.

➤ As *mentors*, their role is to share authority and knowledge with their employees. In the flat, flexible agencies of the future, managers will no longer solely be directors. They will be creating self-managed teams in which all employees share responsibility for performance, and in which many perform duties once reserved for managers.

➤ As *champions*, their role is to support employee ideas. Their job is to say "yes," whenever it makes sense to, and then figure out ways to push the ideas into practice, whether by securing needed resources or taking the idea higher up the line.

ENCOURAGE A NEW STYLE OF LABOR-MANAGEMENT COMMUNICATION

Labor and management get to the point where the adversarial positions no longer serve either party effectively, and they have no choice but to sit down and work together to try to come to some better way. . . . I think that if labor and management leaders could both understand that they should—if they're sincere—share the same goal, which is to provide a quality service to the public, . . . then they would be able to sit down and come up with the kinds of solutions that are necessary.

Norma Goodling
Assistant to the Executive Director
American Federation of State, County and
  Municipal Employees
Council 13, Philadelphia
Philadelphia Hearing, May 1992

Much of what the Commission recommends earlier in this chapter would be the natural consequence of a closer working relationship between labor and management. For far too long an adversarial climate between the two has predominated. It is a climate that can stifle innovation and feed public cynicism about government's ability to get the job done. In governments in which labor and management work together the positive results are clear.

To achieve such a closer working relationship, the Commission believes that management and labor need to open up new and substantive channels of communication—whether or not workers are formally organized into unions, as 35 percent of the nation's state and local work force currently is. Management, for its part, must start including workers, including union leadership, in decision-making processes at the start, and not simply brief staff "from on high"at the end. Early engagement of a work force in change is a hallmark of the current quest for quality management, a factor too often ignored by those government executives who remain mired in a command and control mentality. Once labor and management have established a more positive relationship, unions should reciprocate by reconsidering protective devices inherited from the era of adversarial relations, such as the premium placed on seniority, overly elaborate "bumping" rules in the event of force reductions, and excessively constraining work rules.

Not only are there a host of promising examples of cooperative labor-management problem-solving across the country, but research indicates that unionized employees are more likely than non-unionized employees to make suggestions to management, given the opportunity. This approach certainly helped in Oregon, where members of a Service Employees International local worked with management to reduce a crushing social service work load. It led to positive change in Minnesota, where members of the American Federation of State, County and Municipal Employees helped restructure the state's mental retardation system. And it is an ongoing and very beneficial new style of operating in Madison, Wisconsin, where Labor International workers have been at the forefront of the quality movement, saving funds while increasing citizen satisfaction.

Few of us—perhaps none of us—know how to make government work better than those who do the front-line work. Continuing the old adversarial relationship in today's highly competitive world simply makes no sense and only drags government down. Cooperative action to make government more productive is in the interest of all government workers; the fruits of enhanced labor-management cooperation and labor-saving innovations should be shared by workers and the public.

6

REMOVING THE BARRIERS TO CITIZEN INVOLVEMENT

We believe that a fundamental priority of state and local governments must be to trust and work with citizens. Effective government requires that citizens be informed about policies, programs, and issues and be enlisted as active participants in the ongoing process of government. Government has to offer citizens the chance to be part of the solution, rather than merely a client for or object of its services. This paradigm requires a shift in how governments think of and treat citizens. It also requires that governments start opening the books in all areas, from the budget process to the campaign trail.

The ordinary citizen in approaching his or her government often encounters arrogance—"we know better," "we know best," and "we don't really want to hear your opinion"—and resistance to the ideas that citizens have to offer from their community experience. . . . Together with communities, government must begin to reaffirm a rhetoric of the public interest: that government is there to serve the people. It's there to be the steward of our shared common public resources and our shared public common life as a society and, with community, to work to find ways to become more responsive.

Jackie Leavy
Executive Director
Neighborhood Capital Budget Group
Chicago, Illinois
Chicago Hearing, June 1992

While it is true that the public tends to have more faith in some levels of government than in others, public suspicion of and cynicism about government are widespread. Asked in a 1989 survey to identify which officials—federal, state, or local—were the most honest, 13 percent of the public picked federal, 11 percent state, and 35 percent local, while one-quarter of the sample volunteered "none of the above." Although local governments fared better than the states and the federal government, the pattern is clear: People do not trust their governments. According to surveys, citizens still give high grades to localities for basic service delivery, and still want states to take the lead on key issues of public policy. But they have little faith that *any* government cares much about what they think, nor do they believe that government is run for them.

Government at all levels is failing to carry out one of its most critical responsibilities—to assist and enable citizens to participate meaningfully, beyond the voting booth and on a continuing basis, in the processes of government. Citizens feel estranged from government for many reasons, but among the most crucial is the reality that citizens are not adequately helped to understand what is happening in government, why it is happening, and what it means for them. As governmental structures and operations have grown larger and more complex, the need for keeping citizens fully and currently informed has intensified. After all, it is their government.

There are many good examples of government engaging citizens effectively in its processes. This includes such efforts as the Oregon Benchmark program begun in the late eighties. Citizens participate in an exhaustive process to set year-by-year achievement goals for the entire state on issues ranging from education to drug abuse. In some localities, "community policing" has offered a good vehicle for bringing citizens into the decision-making process. Still, government as a whole needs to be imbued with the critical importance of utilizing citizen input to help make better policy decisions and to improve the efficiency and effectiveness of governmental processes.

Not all the blame for the current situation can be laid at the feet of government, however. Clearly citizens need to reengage. Asking for increased and expanded services while fighting tax increases at every turn is a now-familiar and contradictory pattern in which citizens do not seem willing to acknowledge their role.

Although the Commission hopes that citizens recognize their part in the larger social compact of public service, there are steps that government can take now to reduce citizen suspicion and cynicism and also encourage public involvement in problem-solving and policy-setting.

RECOMMENDATION SEVEN: OPEN THE BOOKS ON GOVERNMENT

Open the books on government by providing detailed information on campaign financing and lobbying.

The view that government is run for the benefit of the few is clearly fueled by rapidly increasing campaign spending and lobbying activity. Of course, money has always been a part of the political process, and it is beyond the scope of the Commission's mission to judge the extent to which that is good or bad, although the increases in both campaign spending and lobbying activity raise serious questions about how untainted the process can really be. The most immediate problem, however, is money and lobbying activity *plus* secrecy. In combination, the Commission believes that they are detrimental to government's image and the public trust and thus recommends opening the books on government through the following actions.

MAKE CAMPAIGN SPENDING MORE VISIBLE

State and local elections have become big business, with total campaign spending by or on behalf of all candidates growing from $240 million in 1976 to $905 million in 1988. Concerns about the increase have led many states and localities—including ten states in 1991 alone—to establish new reporting practices or to limit campaign expenditures. The U.S. Supreme Court has clearly ruled that campaign spending of a candidate's own resources represents an exercise of free speech, although reasonable limits on contributions by others to political campaigns are acceptable. However, the lack of clear disclosure of who spends how much raised from whom and for what purposes can only heighten public suspicions of corruption. One way to address those perceptions, short of total public financing of campaigns, is to offer citizens access to clear information on campaign spending, on both who gives the money and how it is spent. Secrecy serves no purpose here.

Toward that end, the Commission believes that all states and localities ought to ensure that their current or planned reporting mechanisms include four key features:

➤ *Citizen access at reasonable cost to periodic reports* on campaign contributions during the election cycle, and within two weeks of each election.

➤ *Mandatory reporting by all candidates of significant information,* including the names, addresses, bank depositories, and treasurers of their campaign committees; the same information for any political action committees on which they hold leadership positions; and the name, address, occupation, and employer of anyone who gives more than $100 to their campaigns.

➤ *Mandatory disclosure by campaign committees of all expenditures within clear categories*—for example, media purchases, polling, and voter registration.

➤ *Provision by states and localities of some analysis of the statistics* to help citizens understand them more fully.

The Commission believes that states and localities should implement such sunshine laws for all campaigns. Cynicism is only natural in the absence of this kind of easily accessible information.

MAKE LOBBYING MORE VISIBLE

We are recommending that all expenditures by lobbyists and public officials be reported—no loopholes, all expenditures. This is not to encumber legitimate lobbyists, but to ensure that citizens have equal footing with special interests, and it is a way to bring people back into the process.

The Honorable Dick Molpus
Secretary of State, State of Mississippi
Jackson Hearing, January 1992

Lobbying activity at the state and local level is now a major industry. It also happens to be a major source of scandal. Legislatures in Arizona, South Carolina, and California have all been rocked by revelations of vote-buying. Many states and localities are trying to limit lobbying activities, including tightening controls on what lobbyists can give in the way of, for example, gifts and entertainment.

The Commission does not believe that lobbying is inherently bad. As with campaign spending, it is lobbying *plus* secrecy that hurts the image of politicians and government.

The Commission recommends that states and localities implement lobbying disclosure laws that meet five requirements:

➤ *Guarantee citizens access to periodic reports on lobbying expenditures* during key legislative and executive sessions in which decisions are made.

➤ *Register, by broadly defined categories, all lobbying organizations.*

➤ *Report by specific categories all expenditures on lobbying of any kind,* such as the number of full- and part-time lobbying personnel, and funds spent on mailing, phone banks, receptions, and so forth.

➤ *Identify public officials who receive gifts or services of any kind from lobbying organizations.*

➤ *Make information on lobbying activity and expenditures easily available at low cost to citizens.*

RECOMMENDATION EIGHT:
LIMIT THE POLITICAL FUNDRAISING SEASON

Limit the political fundraising season to the six months before an election and limit the use of carry-over campaign funds.

In the field of campaign finance, we are concerned that big monied interests are too dominant and ubiquitous in government. Individual citizens acting on their own initiative have less of a chance for access— and government less of a chance to listen to them—if elected officials spend too much of their time and energy raising large sums of money for future campaigns. This crowding out of their constituents by nearly constant fundraising not only denies state and local leaders the opportunity to interact with them, but also creates further misunderstandings of who "owns" government, especially when elected officials raise money during legislative sessions.

There is no simple solution to this problem. After all, the idea that all interests are special to someone and should be represented in the political process lies at the very core of the American ideal. As an issue of governmental process and fairness, however, the Commission recommends that states and localities place a moratorium on fundraising events until six months before elections and that campaign funds carried over from a preceding campaign not be used to fund a subsequent campaign or diverted for personal use. Fundraising events would no longer be held on a year-round, every-year basis. While some candidates would undoubtedly seek ways around such a moratorium, the Commission believes that a formal stated policy will set a tone and send a signal to citizens and elected officials alike that the first priority of office is making decisions, not raising campaign money.

RECOMMENDATION NINE: ENCOURAGE CITIZEN PROBLEM-SOLVING

Encourage citizen problem-solving by experimenting with citizen liaison offices and setting up a national service corps.

Even the best-led and most responsive government cannot possibly be the lone player in solving all of society's problems. Local governments, for example, cannot put a cop on every dangerous corner or a social worker in every fragile home. What government can do, however, is allow and encourage citizens to share the role of problem solver.

To encourage such a broadening of the role, states and localities ought to weigh each new program not just for cost, but also for its impact on this problem-solving capacity. The state of Colorado did so by working with local citizens on deciding where and how to spend child and family welfare funds.

Rebuilding civic capacity involves access to government. If public comment periods are scheduled at the tail end of the decision-making process, long after the key agreements have been hammered out, conflict and cynicism are an almost inevitable result. Denying citizens the basic information that might help them speak with greater clarity and authority on issues means that citizens will neither learn how to work with their government officials nor develop a basic level of trust in government. If citizens are to participate, they need to be included not merely early on in the decision-making process, but throughout it. If governments continue to offer citizens only last-second, shallow engagements, like public hearings or public comment periods, public cynicism will grow and public policy-making will suffer.

I would say—and it would be only a bit of an overstatement—that the public hearing is the most counterproductive instrument of government that we have today. It is counterproductive because it is neither public nor a hearing. That is to say, it has people there, but it is the showcase of those who would have a particular special interest. It is not hearing; nobody hears anything because nobody is listening.

David Mathews
President
The Kettering Foundation
Jackson Hearing, January 1992

Toward the overall goal of citizen reengagement, the Commission makes two proposals.

CREATE CITIZEN LIAISON OFFICES

The Commission urges that major agencies of large governments consider the creation of citizen liaison offices. These offices can serve as a mechanism for changing how agencies view their mission, helping assure that accurate and timely information about governmental policies, programs, and pending issues is provided to citizens, and enlisting citizens to serve on a volunteer basis and participate in governmental activities. We view this as an experimental approach for getting citizens plugged into government. The mission of these liaison offices should be fourfold:

➤ *Designing programs that engage citizens more creatively* in solving their own problems.

➤ *Providing advice to departments and agencies* on how existing and proposed legislation and regulations can be changed to assure better performance.

➤ *Seeking opportunities for greater involvement of citizens* within the decision-making process.

➤ *Supporting better outreach efforts to communities and citizens* within governmental departments and agencies.

With small amounts of funding for training and outreach, these offices could become instruments for community problem-solving. Our view is that the charter for these citizen liaison offices should be time-limited—that they should serve as catalysts and not necessarily become permanent fixtures.

CREATE A NATIONAL SERVICE CORPS

Every child should participate every year in activities appropriate to their grade-level. This should be a dynamic, participatory program that shows students how government is affecting them and how they can affect government.

Janet H. Clark and Carla Wall
Executive Directors
Mississippi First, Inc.
Jackson Hearing, January 1992

Political scientists have long understood that early exposure to public life leaves a lasting positive imprint on people. Those who participate early, whatever the activity, tend to be more involved in public service and activity throughout their lives. Therefore, the Commission endorses the concept of national public service. Models include Boston's City Year and the District of Columbia Service Corps, which work by giving people real public jobs in return for course credits, low-interest college loans, and scholarships.

Such public service programs generate at least three benefits for states and localities:

➤ *They introduce citizens to the demands and complexities of government work and public decision-making.* The "seasoning" of our citizenry through such real-world experience could help reduce the constant escalation of demands that puts such a burden on political and service-delivery systems government-wide; a taste of civic problem-solving helps constituents understand how difficult and complex a task it can be.

➤ *They create a larger pool of people interested in careers in public life.* As continuing surveys of college freshmen suggest, the pendulum of interest is swinging away from private interest back toward public engagement. What people need most now is the chance to experience the work that constitutes so much of what state and local government does.

➤ *They improve the very skills that permit citizens to address their own problems.* While such programs call for some financial outlay, national service will produce significant long-term savings, in part because every person who participates becomes a citizen problem solver.

Whatever shape a national service corps takes, the Commission urges that the final proposal provide for a strong partnership with state and local government—young people should be given the opportunity to work at all levels of government. The Commission also urges that the federal government pay its fair share of the costs.

7

REDUCING FISCAL UNCERTAINTY

Although this report is primarily concerned with the management and operation of state and local governments, the Commission would be remiss if it did not address the single most crippling fiscal issue that government budget offices face: the cost of Medicaid. Over the past decade, Medicaid has become the fastest growing line item in state budgets. As the federal government has dragged its feet over how to control health care costs and what to do about America's 37 million uninsured individuals, state budgets have absorbed huge cost increases and additional mandates for care. Those increases have eaten away at fiscal stability. They show no signs of abating; indeed, they seem to be accelerating.

Let me . . . tell you the kinds of services we provide in the city's public hospital systems. We provide half of the care for all New Yorkers who need ambulatory care; we take care of 30 percent of all the mothers, infants, and children in the city; we provide 30 percent of all the care to people with AIDS; half of all the city's psychiatric patients are treated in public hospitals in New York City. . . . We provide over 65 percent of all uninsured outpatient visits and a little less than that of all uninsured emergency room visits; we provide 27 percent of the uninsured inpatient care in the city.

Pamela S. Brier
Chief Executive Officer
Bellevue Hospital Center, New York City
Philadelphia Hearing, May 1992

States and localities have not been passive victims of the health care cost explosion, however. They have experimented with dozens of strategies for covering the uninsured and controlling costs, and in the process have come up with some methods for coping that the federal government ought to consider as it wrestles with the issue. The question now is whether the federal government can move quickly enough in its health care reform effort to prevent further serious fiscal damage to states and localities.

RECOMMENDATION TEN:
PROMPT THE FEDERAL GOVERNMENT TO LEAD, FOLLOW, OR GET OUT OF THE WAY ON HEALTH CARE

The federal rules on Medicaid are 694 pages long. The federal/state Medicaid manual encompasses six large texts. One chapter alone has been revised 12 times since last December. For every problem, government thinks there ought to be a new statute or regulation. The accumulation of 27 years' worth of rules is truly a bog.

Gary Clarke
Assistant Secretary for Medicaid
Department of Health and Rehabilitative Services
State of Florida
Tallahassee Hearing, May 1992

Recommendations on the specifics of health care reform, such as managed competition or caps on global costs, are beyond the scope of the Commission. However, in order to serve states and localities today, the federal government can take three actions:

➤ *Lead* by enacting a national health care package that will control costs and cover the uninsured, while possibly "federalizing" the Medicaid program as a consequence.

➤ *Follow* by backing states in their efforts at cost control through compacts, cost limits, insurance reform, and expanded federal funding of the Medicaid program.

➤ *Get out of the way* by reducing the obstacles that currently exist to further innovation in the states—for example, by reforming the Employee Retirement and Income Security Act (ERISA) to allow greater flexibility in coverage, and by allowing greater numbers of waivers on Medicaid rules so that states can experiment with ways to deliver the best health care to the maximum number of citizens possible.

The Commission is issuing a separate report on health policy that focuses on the state role and the financial crisis spurred by Medicaid. Medicaid is monopolizing state finances and crowding out public health services and prevention activities, stripping state governments of fiscal flexibility (see Figure 2). We are especially concerned that federalism, institutional, and managerial issues be taken into account in the debate on national health care reform. It will,

Figure 2: State and local spending for Medicaid per $100 of personal income, 1976 to 1992.

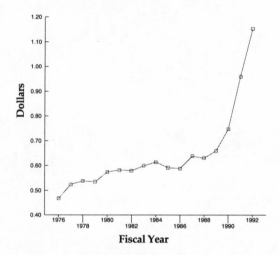

Notes: Spending paid for by federal aid is excluded. Medicaid spending for each fiscal year is divided by personal income in the calendar year that ended during it.

Sources: For Medicaid spending, U.S. Health Care Financing Administration, unpublished data provided March 18, 1993 (1992 spending is projected). For personal income, U.S. Department of Commerce, Bureau of Economic Analysis, unpublished data provided September 2, 1992.

for example, be critical to have highly qualified professional managers to run new systems. Whatever the federal government decides to do, the Commission hopes it will act quickly and decisively. The states cannot wait much longer for a resolution. With health care costs projected to rise by 30 percent again this year and next, the time has come for change.

8

CONCLUSION: A QUID PRO QUO APPROACH TO IMPLEMENTATION

A chieving higher performance will not be easy. Comprehensive reform never is. The temptation will always be toward tinkering and small-scale adjustment, toward turf protection and politics as usual. After all, the Commission is asking for all the stakeholders in state and local public service to give up something, and to take on more responsibility in return.

Yet the Commission firmly believes that whatever any one group gives up, it will receive much more in return. The Commission believes that if all the various interest groups view the report's proposals in terms of one broad quid pro quo, momentum for comprehensive action will be created.

Consider *chief executives*. The Commission asks them to engage in a new dialogue with the public, to set a clear vision of the future, and to put greater faith in citizens and front-line employees alike in helping shape and carry out what government does. In return it offers them more authority to shape their governments, their policies, and their staffs—in a phrase, to be change agents.

Consider *public employees*. The Commission asks America's more than 15 million state and local public workers—unionized and nonunionized alike—to take more risks and accept more responsibility. It asks them to make learning a lifelong ambition and quality work and better performance an ever-present goal. In return, the Commission asks government to give employees the challenging work they deserve along with a greater share in making decisions about how the job gets done. At the same time it asks government to make the necessary investment in the training and education that is the right of every hard-working public servant. It emphatically rejects "bureaucrat-bashing" by those seeking or holding elective office.

Consider *managers*. The Commission asks managers to get out of the supervising, disciplining, second-guessing, and double-checking role and to get into coaching, benchmarking, listening, mentoring, and championing—the essence of the *trust and lead* strategy. Managers must help sustain a climate that promotes innovation and accept some failure as the inevitable result of these creative efforts. In return, those managers who are ready to change will be freed from many of the mind-numbing regulations that occupy so much of their time, whether in hiring and firing personnel or in making purchasing decisions. This transformation will allow managers more time and greater freedom in shaping how their departments run. They, too, will have access to the educational opportunities they deserve, as well as the upward contact with executives they want and need.

Consider *citizens*. The Commission asks them to put government back into perspective—to recognize that, while government can do more, it does not have the capacity to solve every problem. Citizens must rediscover their role as community problem solvers. When citizens insist that government act, they need to recognize that government action costs money. They also need to realize that action requires giving leaders the authority to act. In return, the Commission recommends a much greater role for citizens in government, in part through citizen liaison offices, so that they can be involved at every step of the policy-making process. It also recommends that government end the secrecy that surrounds campaign financing and lobbying activity in too many states and localities.

The advantage to thinking in terms of such quid pro quos is that every party in the public service milieu can be invited to the table to share in a package of mutual give-and-take. Only by conceiving of change as such a shared effort can we move toward needed reform. As with any overhaul, merely replacing one or two parts here and there, or tuning one or two systems along the way, will not be as effective as changing the whole. The pressure is not on chief executives, public employees and their unions, managers, or citizens alone, but on all four groups to engage in building a public service that can look forward confidently to the task ahead.

True reform is impossible, however, without also changing the agencies and systems of government. Our chief executives, citizens, and public employees have been banging their heads against the bureaucracy for too long. Without the deregulation and reduction of government layers called for in this report, obsolete systems will continue to win out.

We end on a point worth remembering. The American governmental system operates under the oldest continuing democratic political charter in the world—our federal Constitution. Its basic values of pluralism and wide access are today the envy of many nations wrestling with the establishment of new democratic political institutions. In this world of instant communication, global competition, and rapid change, governments are challenged to be faster off the mark. We need stronger executive leadership to temper our pluralism—to get beyond the muddle of conflicting voices that often result in gridlock. We need to improve the capacity of governments at all levels to govern effectively. But we must never lose sight of the fundamentals. Our governmental system—though undoubtedly imperfect and often fractious—is a rich heritage. We can improve it. We must never weaken it.

BIOGRAPHIES

COMMISSION MEMBERS

William F. Winter, chairman of the Commission, served as governor of Mississippi from 1980 to 1984. His public career in Mississippi also included service as lieutenant governor, state treasurer, and state representative. Currently a senior partner in the Jackson, Mississippi law firm of Watkins Ludlam & Stennis, Governor Winter is chairman of the Kettering Foundation and is a past chairman of both the Commission on the Future of the South and the Foundation for the Mid South. He has been a Fellow of the Institute of Politics at the John F. Kennedy School of Government at Harvard University, the Jamie Whitten Professor of Law and Government at the University of Mississippi, and the Eudora Welty Professor of Southern Studies at Millsaps College. He was an infantry officer during World War II and the Korean War.

Meg Armstrong is the former executive vice president and chief operating officer of the Institute for East-West Securities Studies in New York City. Currently she is managing director of the Leadership Group, Inc., which provides consulting and training services for women leaders in the United States and around the world. Ms. Armstrong was the founding executive director and a board member of Women Executives in State Government. Her background includes designing management strategies for the presidential Grace Commission on federal government reorganization, directing the President's Reorganization Project on Economic Development from 1977 to 1978, and serving as director of Federal-State Relations for two governors.

Reubin O'D. Askew served as governor of Florida from 1971 to 1979 and as U.S. trade representative under President Jimmy Carter from 1979 to 1980. His career has included service in the 82nd Airborne Division and the Air Force. Currently Of Counsel to Akerman, Senterfitt & Eidson, P. A. in Orlando, Governor Askew is Distinguished Service Professor of Public Administration at Florida Atlantic University, Broward and a member of the board of the LeRoy Collins Center for Public Policy. A Fellow of the National Academy of Public Administration, he received his bachelor's degree in public administration from Florida State University and his law degree from the University of Florida law school.

Mary Jo Bane is currently assistant secretary-designate at the Administration for Children and Families at the U.S. Department of Health and Human Services. Prior to that she was commissioner of the New York State Department of Social Services, an agency where earlier in her career she had also served as executive deputy commissioner. For several years Ms. Bane was a Malcolm

Wiener Professor of Social Policy and director of the Malcolm Wiener Center for Social Policy at Harvard University's John F. Kennedy School of Government. She has authored many books and articles on human services and public policy.

Barbara B. Blum is currently president of the Foundation for Child Development. She was formerly president of the Manpower Demonstration Research Corporation when that organization began conducting work/welfare experiments in eight states. Mrs. Blum, an advocate and volunteer for disabled children for 15 years before working in state and local government, has served as commissioner of New York State's Department of Social Services and as head of the state unit responsible for closing Willowbrook. In New York City, she was deputy director for mental health and commissioner of special services for children.

Walter D. Broadnax, formerly president of the Center for Governmental Research Inc., is currently deputy secretary of the U.S. Department of Health and Human Services. His public sector career has included serving as both president of the New York State Civil Service Commission and commissioner of the state's civil service department; during his tenure he guided the creation of the Governor's Work Force Planning Initiative. Previously a faculty member at Harvard University's John F. Kennedy School of Government, Mr. Broadnax directed the Innovations in State and Local Government Awards Program of the Ford Foundation and Harvard. He is a Fellow of the National Academy of Public Administration.

Yvonne Brathwaite Burke, formerly a partner in the California law firm of Jones, Day, Reavis & Pogue, returned to the Los Angeles County Board of Supervisors in 1992, having previously served in 1979. Her tenure in elective office includes 12 years of combined service in the California State Assembly and U.S. House of Representatives. Ms. Burke served on numerous boards, including the University of California's Board of Regents. She was chair of the Los Angeles branch of the Federal Reserve Bank of San Francisco and is past chair of the Ford Foundation's advisory committee for the Innovations in State and Local Government Awards Program. Ms. Burke is a Fellow of the National Academy of Public Administration.

Karen S. Burstein, currently a New York State family court judge, has served in many government capacities. She has been New York City's auditor general, led the New York State Civil Service Commission and the state's civil service department, chaired and directed the state's Consumer Protection Board, and served as a New York State senator. Her career in New York State has also included serving on the state's Public Service Commission, chairing the Temporary State Commission on Workers' Compensation and Disability Benefits, and co-chairing from 1978 to 1989 the Governor's Task Force on Domestic Violence.

Henry G. Cisneros is the U.S. Secretary of Housing and Urban Development. Previously, he chaired Cisneros Asset Management Company, a national fixed-income asset management firm for tax-exempt institutions. Secretary Cisneros, who was a councilman for six years in the city of San Antonio, Texas, was elected mayor in 1981 and served four two-year terms. In 1985, he became president of the National League of Cities. Prior to being appointed as U.S. Secretary, he served on numerous boards; he was deputy chairman of the Federal Reserve Bank of Dallas, chairman of the National Civic League, and a member of the board of the Rockefeller Foundation.

John J. DiIulio, Jr. is Professor of Politics and Public Affairs at Princeton University and Senior Fellow in Governmental Studies at the Brookings Institution. He served as founding director of Princeton's Center of Domestic and Comparative Policy Studies and currently chairs the American Political Science Association's standing committee on professional ethics. Mr. DiIulio, who teaches both in the Woodrow Wilson School and the Department of Politics, concentrates on the areas of American politics, public management, criminal justice, and military affairs. His numerous publications include *Reconstituting the Public Service: Can Government Be Improved?*

R. Scott Fosler is president of the National Academy of Public Administration. The academy is chartered by Congress to help improve governance and public management at all levels—federal, state, local, and international. Previously, Mr. Fosler was vice president and director of government studies for the Committee for Economic Development, a national organization of corporate executives and university presidents. From 1978 to 1986, he was a member of the county council for Montgomery County, Maryland. Mr. Fosler is a Senior Fellow of the Institute for Policy Studies at Johns Hopkins University and serves on the boards of the Public Administration Service and the National Civic League.

Robert Fulton is a public policy analyst based in Patton, Missouri. He currently works on policy development as well as program delivery issues relating to children and families in the fields of health care, social services, training, child care, and employment. Mr. Fulton is senior advisor for the National Center for Children in Poverty at Columbia University. From 1983 to 1991 he served Oklahoma state government first as director of human services and then as cabinet secretary of social services. Prior to state service, Mr. Fulton was a senior staff member of the U.S. Senate Budget Committee and worked in a number of federal agencies, first as a careerist and then in senior policy and managerial positions.

John Herbers, a graduate of Emory University and a Nieman Fellow at Harvard, was a reporter and editor for *The New York Times* for 24 years. His assignments as a national correspondent included the civil rights movement in the South, Congress, the White House, state and local governments, politics, and social trends. He also served as assistant national editor in New York and as deputy bureau chief in Washington in the 1970s. After retiring from *The New York Times* in 1987, Mr. Herbers taught seminars on politics and the press at Princeton University and the University of Maryland and was a columnist and contributing editor for *Governing* magazine.

Elizabeth L. Hollander is the executive director of the Government Assistance Project of the Chicago Community Trust. From 1990 to 1991 she directed the Illinois Commission on the Future of Public Service. For six years she served as the commissioner of planning for the city of Chicago. Her prior positions include directing the Metropolitan Planning Council and serving as associate director of the Task Force on the Future of Illinois. Ms. Hollander is a graduate of Bryn Mawr College and attended the state and local program at Harvard University's John F. Kennedy School. She is an adjunct faculty member of the Illinois Institute of Technology's Master's in Public Administration program and a member of the institute's board of trustees.

Robert A. Kipp serves as group vice president of corporate communications and services for Hallmark Cards, Inc. as well as president of the Crown Center Redevelopment Corporation. Beginning his career as planning director of Newton, Kansas, Mr. Kipp later held city management positions in Lawrence, Kansas, Vandalia and Fairborn, Ohio, as well as Kansas City, Missouri, where he served from 1970 to 1983. A Fellow of the National Academy of Public Administration and a life member of the Missouri City Management Association, Mr. Kipp is a past president of the International City Management Association. He received a master's in public administration from the University of Kansas.

L. Bruce Laingen was executive director of the National Commission on Public Service from 1987 to 1990 and is president of the American Academy of Diplomacy in Washington, D.C. After serving in the U.S. Navy during World War II, he joined the foreign service, where his 38-year career included serving as ambassador to Malta, chargé d'affaires in Tehran, and vice president of the National Defense University. In 1984 he won a Presidential Meritorious Performance Award and in 1986 a Distinguished Public Service Award from the Department of Defense. A native of Minnesota, Ambassador Laingen is a graduate of St. Olaf College and the National War College and earned a master's degree from the University of Minnesota.

Ray Marshall was the U.S. Secretary of Labor under President Jimmy Carter. He currently holds the Audre and Bernard Rapoport Centennial Chair in Economics and Public Affairs at The University of Texas at Austin. He is a member of the new federal Commission on the Future of Worker/Management Relations. Mr. Marshall has a doctorate in economics from the University of California, Berkeley and is the author or coauthor of more than 200 books, monographs, and articles. Topics include such areas as the economics of the family, education and the economy, the competitiveness of the United States in an internationalized economy, and international workers' rights. His most recent publication, written with Marc Tucker, is *Thinking for a Living: Education and the Wealth of Nations*.

Ruth W. Massinga is chief executive of The Casey Family Program, a private operating foundation based in Seattle, Washington that provides foster care to more than 1,200 children in 13 states. From 1983 to 1989 she served as secretary of the Department of Human Resources in Maryland. Former president of the American Public Welfare Association in Washington, D.C., Ms. Massinga is a member of the National Commission on Children and is on the boards of the Family Resource Coalition and the American Humane Association. Ms. Massinga holds a master's degree in social services from Boston University.

William G. Milliken retired in 1983 as Michigan's longest serving governor; during his years in office he served a term as chairman of the National Governors' Association. Elected as chief executive in 1970, he moved into that office in 1969 after serving as lieutenant governor. He has also served in the Michigan State Senate where he became Majority Floor Leader. Governor Milliken chaired the Education Commission of the States and has been a president of the Council of State Governments. Prior to public service, he was president of J.W. Milliken, Inc., a chain of Michigan department stores. Governor Milliken currently serves as a director on a number of boards including both the Chrysler and Unisys corporations. He is a graduate of Yale University.

Richard P. Nathan is director of the Nelson A. Rockefeller Institute of Government and provost of the Rockefeller College of Public Affairs and Policy of the State University of New York in Albany. Previously, he was a professor of public and international affairs at Princeton University and a Senior Fellow at the Brookings Institution. Mr. Nathan served in government as associate director for the National Commission on Civil Disorders (Kerner) Commission, director of domestic policy research of the national campaigns of Nelson A. Rockefeller, assistant director for the U.S. Office of Management and Budget, and deputy undersecretary for welfare reform of the U.S. Department of Health, Education and Welfare. His books include *Turning Promises into Performance* and *The Administrative Presidency*.

Neal Peirce writes the country's first national column focused on state and local government themes, syndicated by The Washington Post Writers Group. He was a founder and remains a contributing editor of the *National Journal* and served in the 1960s as political editor of the *Congressional Quarterly*. His series on America's states and regions culminated in *The Book of America: Inside 50 States Today*. Among his numerous publications is the recently released book, *Citistates: How Urban America Can Prosper in a Competitive World*. Mr. Peirce is one of the founders of the Center for the Redesign of Government based at the National Academy of Public Administration.

Nelson W. Polsby, director of the Institute of Governmental Studies and professor of Political Science at the University of California, Berkeley, has taught American politics and government at the university for 25 years. He is currently president of the Yale University Council and is a member of the Academic Advisory Board of the American Enterprise Institute. Mr. Polsby has held Guggenheim fellowships twice and is a Fellow of the National Academy of Public Administration. A former managing editor of the *American Political Science Review,* Mr. Polsby currently serves on the editorial boards of four scholarly journals. His many books include *Congress and the Presidency, Political Innovation in America,* and *Consequences of Party Reform.*

Michael B. Preston is professor and chair of the Department of Political Science at the University of Southern California. Mr. Preston, who received his doctorate from the University of California, Berkeley, has also taught at the University of Illinois, Urbana and the University of Chicago. He has served as a vice president of the American Political Science Association and president of the National Conference of Black Political Scientists. A member of several editorial boards, he was associate editor of the *National Political Science Review.* His research focuses on urban and black politics and public administration. Publications include *The Politics of Bureaucratic Reform* and the recent *Racial & Ethnic Politics in California,* coauthored with Bryan Jackson.

Charles T. Royer directs the Institute of Politics at the John F. Kennedy School of Government at Harvard University and is a lecturer at the Kennedy School. In 1977 Mr. Royer was elected mayor of Seattle, Washington and served in that office for 12 years. He is a past president of the National League of Cities, served on the U.S. Conference of Mayors Advisory Board, and for seven years was the president of the American delegation to the Japan-American Conference of Mayors and Chambers of Commerce Presidents. He also chaired the National Advisory Committee to the Robert Wood Johnson Foundation's Health Care for the Homeless Project. Mr. Royer's service as mayor followed a career in newspaper and television journalism.

Lisbeth B. Schorr, a national authority on improving the future of disadvantaged children and their families, is a lecturer in social medicine at Harvard University, a member of the Harvard Working Group on Early Life, and director of the Harvard Project on Effective Services. Ms. Schorr holds leadership positions in many of the major national efforts on behalf of children, including the Carnegie Task Force on Young Children, the National Alliance on School Restructuring, and the boards of the National Center for Children in Poverty and the Public Education Fund Network. She co-chairs the National Academy of Sciences' Roundtable on Effective Services. Her book, *Within our*

Reach: Breaking the Cycle of Disadvantage, analyzes social programs that have improved the lives of disadvantaged children.

Max Sherman is professor and dean of the Lyndon B. Johnson School of Public Affairs, The University of Texas at Austin. He holds the J. J. "Jake" Pickle Regents Chair in Public Affairs and is a past president of the National Association of Schools of Public Affairs and Administration. He served in the Texas Senate from 1971 to 1977, was special counsel to the Governor of Texas, and was also the president of West Texas State University. Mr. Sherman is a Fellow of the National Academy of Public Administration and serves on numerous boards and committees including the National Advisory Committee for the Innovations in State and Local Government Awards Program of the Ford Foundation and Harvard University. He was recently named Distinguished Alumnus by his undergraduate institution, Baylor University.

Eddie N. Williams is president of the Joint Center for Political and Economic Studies, a national institution based in Washington, D.C. that researches and analyzes major national policy issues, particularly those affecting black Americans. He is a former vice president for public affairs and director of the Center for Policy Study at the University of Chicago. In 1988 Mr. Williams was awarded the MacArthur Foundation Prize Fellowship. He currently chairs the boards of the Pew Partnership for Civic Change and the National Coalition on Black Voter Participation. He serves on the boards of several organizations and corporations including the National Endowment for Democracy and the Grumman Corporation.

STAFF AND ADVISORS

Frank J. Thompson, executive director, is dean of the School of Public Affairs and associate provost of Rockefeller College at the State University of New York at Albany. He is immediate past president of the National Association of Schools of Public Affairs and Administration. Mr. Thompson has published extensively on topics of policy and administration and is editor of the Commission's companion volume, *Revitalizing State and Local Public Service.*

Paul C. Light, senior advisor, is a professor of planning and public affairs at the Hubert Humphrey Institute of Public Affairs at the University of Minnesota. He is currently a Senior Fellow at the Governance Institute and previously served as director of studies for the National Academy of Public Administration. Mr. Light is the author of six books including *Monitoring Government: Inspectors General and the Search for Accountability.*

Enid F. Beaumont, special advisor, is director of The Academy for State and Local Government. She is a past president of The American Society for Public Administration and a former vice president and director of the National Institute of Public Affairs at the National Academy of Public Administration.

Steven D. Gold, advisor, is director of the Center for the Study of the States at the Rockefeller Institute of Government, State University of New York. He previously served as the director of fiscal studies for the National Conference of State Legislatures.

Miriam Trementozzi, project manager, is a budget examiner on leave from the New York State Division of the Budget. She previously served as the executive director of a nonprofit organization.

Barbara C. Guinn, research assistant, recently received her master's degree from the School of Public Affairs, University at Albany and has been selected as a Public Management Intern with New York State's budget division.

REGIONAL HEARING WITNESSES

Identifying information is correct as of hearing date.

Jackson, Mississippi
January 16–17, 1992

Janet H. Clark and Carla Wall, Executive Directors, Mississippi First, Inc. Topic: *Connecting citizens and government.*

Alton Cobb, Mississippi State Health Officer. Topic: *Health delivery systems and health problems, particularly as they relate to the poor and minorities in rural areas.*

Steven D. Gold, Director, Center for the Study of the States, Rockefeller Institute of Government. Topic: *The outlook for state finances in the 1990s and the need for major reforms.*

David Mathews, President, The Kettering Foundation. Topic: *Public attitudes as identified through the Foundation's "Citizens and Politics" Project.*

The Honorable Dick Molpus, Secretary of State, State of Mississippi. Topic: *Reforms needed in state government.*

David Osborne, Coauthor with Ted Gaebler of *Reinventing Government*, and consultant to state and local governments. Topic: *On Reinventing Government.*

The Honorable Lynn Presley, Clerk of the Chancery Court of Jackson County and Clerk of the Jackson County Board of Supervisors. Topic: *Government performance issues.*

The Honorable Robert Walker, Mayor, Vicksburg, Mississippi. Topic: *Government performance and innovation at the local level* (addressed the Commission in Vicksburg).

Austin, Texas
March 25, 1992

Camille Barnett, Austin City Manager. Topic: *Total Quality Management and customer service in government.*

Ernesto Cortes, Jr., Southwest Regional Director, Industrial Areas Foundation. Topic: *Citizen action in government in Texas and other states.*

Fred Ellis, Director of Appointments, Office of Governor Ann Richards, State of Texas, and **Anne Wynne**, Board Chair, Texas General Services Commission. Topic: *Innovative approaches taken by Governor Richards to open up the agenda of state agencies through diversity in the appointment process* (addressed the Commission at March 24 dinner).

DeAnn Friedholm, Special Assistant for Health and Human Services, Office of the Lieutenant Governor, State of Texas. Topic: *State and local health issues and innovative programs addressing these issues.*

John Garth, County Judge, Bell County, Belton, Texas. Topic: *Innovations in county government.*

Billy Hamilton, Deputy Comptroller of Public Accounts, State of Texas. Topic: *Performance review of state government.*

Jan Hart, City Manager, Dallas, Texas. Topic: *Metropolitan governance and Dallas's recognition for top management practices* (addressed the Commission at March 24 dinner).

Kathy Whitmire, Institute of Policy Studies, Rice University, Houston, and former Mayor, Houston, Texas. Topic: *Executive leadership and federal mandates.*

Ric Williamson, State Representative and Vice Chairman of the Appropriations Committee, Texas State House of Representatives. Topic: *The performance budgeting process passed by the last Texas legislature requiring specific output and outcome measures of state agencies.*

Tallahassee, Florida
May 7, 1992

Robert Bryant, Superintendent, Gadsden County Schools. Topic: *Improving the climate for learning by addressing students' health and social services needs in schools.*

The Honorable Lawton Chiles, Governor, State of Florida. Topic: *Reshaping the public work force.*

Gary Clarke, Assistant Secretary for Medicaid, Department of Health and Rehabilitative Services, State of Florida. Topic: *Overcoming structural and fiscal restraints in Medicaid administration.*

Glenda Hood, Mayor Pro tem, City of Orlando and President, National League of Cities. Topic: *Government by the people.*

Mark Neimeiser, Legislative Political Director, American Federation of State, County and Municipal Employees, AFL-CIO, Council 79, Tallahassee. Topic: *The role of unions in improving public sector performance.*

Eugene Patterson, Pulitzer Prize-Winning Editor Emeritus, The *St. Petersburg Times.* Topic: *The Florida Voluntary Code of Fair Campaign Practices.*

Janet Reno, Florida State Attorney, Eleventh Judicial Circuit, Dade County. Topic: *Rethinking social services delivery on the state and local levels.*

Frank P. Sherwood, Jerry Collins Eminent Scholar in Public Administration, Florida State University. Topic: *On the need for a vision of the public service and recent reform efforts in Florida* (addressed the Commission at May 6 dinner).

Sacramento, California
May 21–22, 1992

Joan Braconi, Director of Research and Training, Service Employees International Union, Local 790, San Francisco. Topic: *The union role in improving public sector performance; employee involvement in decision-making.*

Jim R. Browder, Co-Chair, Ethnic Coalition of Southern California. Topic: *Building minority involvement in government leadership roles.*

Gerald H. Goldberg, Executive Officer, Franchise Tax Board, State of California. Topic: *Innovative strategies for human resources management.*

Mary E. Grogan, Director, Parks and Recreation Department, Modesto, California. Topic: *Quality circles in city government.*

Bonnie Guiton, Secretary, State and Consumer Services Agency, State of California. Topic: *Improving government efficiency and responsiveness.*

Gloria Harmon, Executive Officer, California State Personnel Board. Topic: *Achieving and maintaining diversity in the work force.*

The Honorable Barry Keene, Majority Leader, California State Senate. Topic: *Structural causes for policy gridlock and the argument for a constitutional convention.*

The Honorable Sunne Wright McPeak, Supervisor, District Four, Contra Costa County, California. Topic: *Innovation and leadership in* *improving performance; public/private partnerships in the delivery of public services.*

Richard Martinez, Executive Director, Southwest Voter Registration Project. Topic: *Consent of the governed and California's changing demographics; citizen disaffection from political participation.*

Linda Orrante, Assistant Director, Department of Social Services, Fresno County, California. Topic: *K-6 program: integrated social services.*

Mark A. Pisano, Executive Director, Southern California Association of Governments. Topic: *Forging solutions for improved public services through regional governance.*

Kevin Scott, Executive Director, Commission on State Finance, State of California. Topic: *The outlook for California's economic and fiscal well-being.*

David Werdegar, M.D., M.P.H., Director, Office of Statewide Health Planning and Development, State of California. Topic: *Overcoming the barriers to performance in the delivery of health care services.*

Chicago, Illinois
June 9, 1992

Michelle Carmichael, Caseworker, Illinois Department of Public Aid, and **Tanya Chapman**, Board Member, Women for Economic Security. Topic: *Women for Economic Security Project to create dialogue between Department of Public Aid caseworkers and clients to improve operations of the Illinois Department of Public Aid field offices.*

Jackie Leavy, Executive Director, Neighborhood Capital Budget Group, Chicago. Topic: *Keeping government open and accountable.*

Roberta Lynch, Director of Public Policy, American Federation of State, County and Municipal Employees, AFL-CIO, Council 31, Chicago. Topic: *Motivating front-line workers: a labor perspective.*

Howard A. Peters, III, Director, Illinois Department of Corrections. Topic: *Motivating government workers through participation.*

Jacqueline Reed, Executive Director, Westside Health Authority, Chicago. Topic: *Pushing past anger to organize both the community and government to improve the health care delivery system.*

Maria Whelan, Director, Chicago Department of Human Services, Children's Services Division. Topic: *Re-energizing a government work force.*

Philadelphia, Pennsylvania
June 22, 1992

Pamela S. Brier, Chief Executive Officer, Bellevue Hospital Center, New York City. Topic: *Strategic issues for public hospitals and their patients.*

Louis J. Gambaccini, Chief Operating Officer and General Manager, Southeastern Pennsylvania Transportation Authority. Topic: *Holding to a vision of the future while riding a fiscal rollercoaster.*

Norma Goodling, Assistant to the Executive Director, American Federation of State, County and Municipal Employees, AFL-CIO, Council 13, Harrisburg, Pennsylvania. Topic: *Council 13's role in upgrading state and local government performance.*

Theodore Hershberg, Professor of Public Policy and History and Director, Center for Greater Philadelphia, University of Pennsylvania. Topic: *On report* Reforming Philadelphia City Government.

The Honorable Stan Lundine, Lieutenant Governor, State of New York. Topic: *The challenges of managing state and local government in an era of sharp cutbacks in federal aid and increasingly complex problems in America's cities.*

Dianne E. Reed, Executive Director, Eastern Division, Pennsylvania Economy League. Topic: *Who's in charge?—rethinking human resources management in the public sector.*

Elizabeth C. Reveal, Director of Finance Designate, City of Seattle, Washington, and former Director of Finance, City of Philadelphia. Topic: *Making government work better.*

Alice M. Rivlin, Senior Fellow, The Brookings Institution, Washington, D.C. Topic: *On her book,* Reviving the American Dream: The Economy, the States, and the Federal Government (addressed the Commission at June 21 dinner).

RESEARCH IN SUPPORT OF THE COMMISSION

Many of the following papers will appear in the Commission's volume, *Revitalizing State and Local Public Service,* edited by Frank J. Thompson, to be published by Jossey-Bass, Inc. in the fall of 1993.

Bernard E. Anderson, The Anderson Group, Philadelphia. *Minority Employment in State and Local Public Health Agencies.*

Carolyn Ban and Norma Riccucci, Rockefeller College of Public Affairs and Policy, University at Albany, State University of New York. *Personnel Systems, Labor Relations, and Government Performance.*

Robert Behn, Institute of Policy Studies, Duke University. *Thinking About Executive Education in State and Local Government.*

Robert Behn, Institute of Policy Studies, Duke University. *Briefing memo on leadership colleges.*

Lawrence D. Brown and Michael S. Sparer, School of Public Health, Columbia University. *Between a Rock and a Hard Place: How Public Managers Manage Medicaid.*

Jorge Chapa, Lyndon B. Johnson School of Public Affairs, University of Texas at Austin. *Selected Data on Employment in State and Local Government.*

Jorge Chapa, Lyndon B. Johnson School of Public Affairs, University of Texas at Austin. *A Potential Role for Nonprofessionals in Rebuilding the Public Trust.*

Steven Cohen, School of International and Public Affairs, Columbia University. *Involving Front-Line Employees in State and Local Government Decision-Making.*

James K. Conant, Department of Political Science, University of Oklahoma, and Dennis Dresang, Department of Political Science, University of Wisconsin. *Career Professional Retention, Morale, and Recruitment in State Governments.*

Anthony J. Corrado, Jr., Department of Government, Colby College, Waterville, Maine. *Financing State and Local Elections: An Agenda for Reform.*

Anne R. Edwards, School of Public Policy Studies, University of Chicago. *Professional Internships in State and Local Public Service: Transcending the Traditional.*

Steven D. Gold and Sarah Ritchie, Center for the Study of the States, Rockefeller Institute of Government, State University of New York. *Compensation of State and Local Employees: Sorting Out the Issues.*

Patricia Ingraham, Maxwell School of Citizenship and Public Affairs, Syracuse University. *Pay for Performance in the States.*

Cristy Jensen, Public Policy Program, California State University at Sacramento. *Briefing Paper: California State Government.*

Rita Mae Kelly, School of Justice Studies, Arizona State University. *Diversity in the Public Service: New Needs, New Approaches.*

Donald F. Kettl, Department of Political Science, University of Wisconsin. *Privatization and the State and Local Public Service.*

John Mendeloff, School of Public Health, University at Albany, State University of New York. *The Requirements of an M.D. Degree for State and Local Health Directors—Prevalence, Impact and Desirability.*

Christopher Muste, Institute of Governmental Studies, University of California at Berkeley. *Public Opinion and Democratic Governance in the U.S. Federal System: The Dimensions of Public Attitudes Toward State and Local Government.*

John Parr, National Civic League. *The Role of Citizen Groups in Strengthening the Capacity and Performance of State and Local Governments.*

James L. Perry, School of Public and Environmental Affairs, Indiana University, and Kenneth L. Kraemer, Graduate School of Management, University of California at Irvine. *The Implications of Changing Technology for the State and Local Public Service.*

Deborah D. Roberts, Center for Public Service, University of Virginia. *The Challenge of Executive Leadership.*

Victoria Rodriguez, Lyndon B. Johnson School of Public Affairs, University of Texas at Austin. *Texas Government.*

Alice Sardell, Department of Urban Studies, Queens College, City University of New York. *Capacity Building for Medical Services: Recruiting and Retention of Physicians for Public Service.*

Lana Stein, Department of Political Science, University of Missouri at St. Louis. *Municipal Administrative Reforms: Hope or Reality?*

Frank J. Thompson, Rockefeller College of Public Affairs and Policy, University at Albany, State University of New York. *The Challenges.*

Bart Wechsler, School of Public Administration and Policy, Florida State University. *Restructuring Florida's Career Service System: The Chiles-MacKay Reform Initiative.*

THE STATE AND LOCAL PUBLIC SERVICE STRESS TEST

Score each question as accurately as possible, then add up your scores.

ON LEADERSHIP

1. How many cabinet-level officials of your state or local government does the chief executive select? (More applicable to large local governments.)

All	_____ 0 points
Most	_____ 3 points
Fewer than half	_____ 6 points

2. How many budget bills does your state or local government use for passing a final budget? (More applicable to large local governments.)

One and only one	_____ 0 points
Less than a dozen	_____ 3 points
Multiples of ten	_____ 6 points
Multiples of 100	_____ 9 points

3. How many programs are there in your state or local government for solving the problems of (pick one): (a) children, (b) families, (c) environmental protection, (d) crime, (e) homelessness, or (d) any problem you care about?

1 or 2	_____ 0 points
3 to 10	_____ 3 points
11 to 20	_____ 6 points
Too many to count	_____ 9 points

ON AGENCIES AND SYSTEMS

4. How many layers of management exist between the top of your state or local government and the employees who actually deliver services?

    Three or fewer   _____ 0 points

    Three to eight   _____ 3 points

    Eight or more   _____ 6 points

5. What is the ratio of managers/supervisors to front-line employees in your state or local government? (The ratio in the federal government is roughly one for eight employees.)

    One for every 20   _____ 0 points

    One for every 10   _____ 3 points

    One for every 5   _____ 6 points

6. How many of your state's best and brightest college students want to work in state or local government?

    A fair share   _____ 0 points

    Some   _____ 3 points

    None   _____ 6 points

7. How much time does it take for your state or local government to hire someone, from start to finish?

    Under 30 days   _____ 0 points

    31 to 60 days   _____ 3 points

    61 to 90 days   _____ 6 points

    More than 90 days   _____ 9 points

8. How many signatures does your state or local government require to approve a purchase of $100 or less?

    One   _____ 0 points

    Two or three   _____ 3 points

    More than three   _____ 6 points

9. How much unspent money are state or local agencies allowed
    to carry over from year to year (subject to executive approval)?

    As much as is left _____ 0 points

    Half of what is left _____ 3 points

    None of what is left _____ 6 points

ON WORK FORCE LEARNING

10. How much money (as a percent of total personnel spending)
    does your state or local government invest in training its work force?

    3 percent or more _____ 0 points

    About 2 percent _____ 3 points

    Less than 1 percent _____ 6 points

11. How many of the top jobs in your state or local government are
    occupied by women and minorities?

    About half _____ 0 points

    About a quarter _____ 3 points

    Almost none _____ 6 points

ON CITIZEN INVOLVEMENT

12. How hard is it for citizens to know how much candidates are getting
    and spending on campaigns, or how many people are lobbying
    government with how much money?

    Easy _____ 0 points

    About a day's work _____ 3 points

    Nearly impossible _____ 6 points

13. How much time each week do your elected officials spend raising
    money for their campaigns?

    Almost none _____ 0 points

    About an hour _____ 3 points

    About a half day _____ 6 points

14. When was the last time the media ran a positive story or editorial on something your state or local government does well?

Within the last week	_____ 0 points
Within the last year	_____ 3 points
Cannot remember when	_____ 6 points

ON FINANCIAL UNCERTAINTY

15. Looking back over the past five years, how often have your state or local government's revenue forecasts been wrong (off by more than 3 percent)?

Never	_____ 0 points
Once or twice	_____ 3 points
Every year	_____ 6 points

16. How fast are health costs rising in your state?

Under 10 percent a year	_____ 0 points
11 to 20 percent a year	_____ 3 points
21 percent a year or faster	_____ 6 points

THE CURRENT CLIMATE FOR REFORM
(MAXIMUM SCORE: 105)

0 to 35	Congratulations—but keep watch
36 to 65	A warning is due
66 to 95	Take action
96+	There is no time to spare

Name Index

Subject Index